Topics in Information Systems

Editors:

Michael L. Brodie
John Mylopoulos
Joachim W. Schmidt

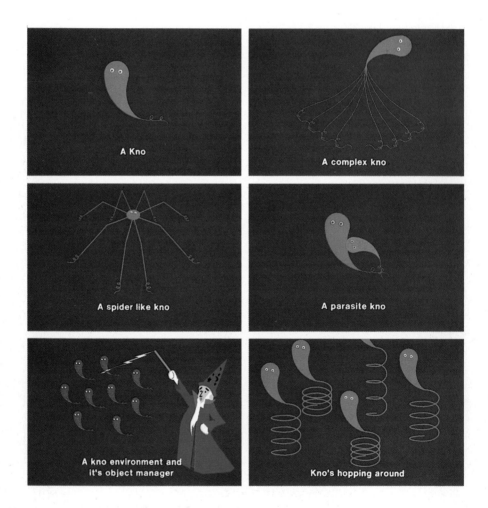

Office Automation

Concepts and Tools

Edited by
Dionysios C. Tsichritzis

With 86 Figures

Springer-Verlag
Berlin Heidelberg New York Tokyo

Series Editors

Dr. Michael L. Brodie
Computer Corporation of America, Four Cambridge Center
Cambridge, MA 02140/USA

Dr. John Mylopoulos
Department of Computer Science, University of Toronto
Toronto, Ontario M5S 1A4/Canada

Dr. Joachim W. Schmidt
Fachbereich Informatik, Johann Wolfgang Goethe-Universität
Dantestraße 9, D-6000 Frankfurt a. M. 11/FRG

Volume Editor

Prof. Dr. D. C. Tsichritzis
Computer Systems Research Institute.
10 King's College Road
University of Toronto
Toronto, Ontario, M5S 1A4/Canada

ISBN 3-540-15129-X Springer-Verlag Berlin Heidelberg New York Tokyo
ISBN 0-387-15129-X Springer-Verlag New York Heidelberg Berlin Tokyo

Printing: Beltz Offsetdruck, Hemsbach/Bergstr.
Bookbinding: J. Schäffer OHG, Grünstadt
2145/3140-543210

Topics in Information Systems

Series Description

Dramatic advances in hardware technology have opened the door to a new generation of computer sytems. At the same time, the growing demand for information systems of ever-increasing complexity and precision has stimulated the need in every area of Computer Science for more powerful higher-level concepts, techniques, and tools.

Future information systems will be expected to acquire, maintain, retrieve, manipulate, and present many different kinds of information. These systems will require user-friendly interfaces; powerful reasoning capabilities, and shared access to large information bases. Whereas the needed hardware technology appears to be within reach, the corresponding software technology for building these systems is not. The required dramatic improvements in software productivity will come from advanced application development environments based on powerful new techniques and languages.

The **concepts, techniques,** and **tools** necessary for the design, implementation, and use in future information systems are expected to result from the integration of those being developed and used in currently disjoint areas of Computer Science. Several areas bring their unique viewpoints and technologies to existing information processing practice. One key area is **Artificial Intelligence** (AI) which provides knowledge bases grounded on semantic theories of information for correct interpretation. An equally important area is **Databases** which provides means for building and maintaining large, shared databases based on computational theories of information for efficient processing. A third important area is **Programming Languages** which provides a powerful tool kit for the construction of large programs based on linguistic and methodological theories to ensure program correctness. To meet evolving information systems requirements, additional research viewpoints and technologies are or will be required from such areas as **Software Engineering, Computer Networks, Machine Architectures,** and **Office Automation.**

Although some integration of research results has already been achieved, a quantum leap in technological integration is needed to meet the demand for future information systems. This integration is one of the major challenges to Computer Science in the 1980s.

Topics in Information Systems is a series intended to report significant contributions on the integration of concepts, techniques, and tools that advance new technologies for information system construction. The series logo symbolizes the scope of topics to be covered and the basic theme of integration.

The logo will appear on each book to indicate the topics addressed.

	Artificial Intelligence	Databases	Programming Languages
concepts			
techniques			
tools			

The first book of the series, "On Conceptual Modelling: Perspectives from Artificial Intelligence, Databases and Programming Languages", Michael L. Brodie, John Mylopoulos, and Joachim W. Schmidt (Eds.), February 1984, which deals with concepts in the three areas, has the logo:

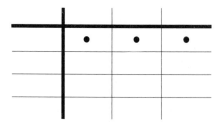

The second book, "Query Processing in Database Systems", Won Kim, David S. Reiner, and Donald S. Batory (Eds.), March 1985, which deals with Database and Programming Language Concepts, AI and Database techniques, and Database system tools, has the logo:

The third book, "Office Automation", Dionysios C. Tsichritzis (Ed.), March 1985, which deals with the design and implementation of Office Systems, has the logo:

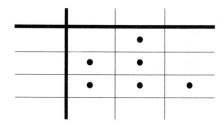

Future books in the series will provide timely accounts of ongoing research efforts to reshape technologies intended for information system development.

March, 1985

Michael L. Brodie
John Mylopoulos
Joachim W. Schmidt

Preface

The term "Office Automation" implies much and means little. The word "Office" is usually reserved for units in an organization that have a rather general function. They are supposed to support different activities, but it is notoriously difficult to determine what an office is supposed to do. Automation in this loose context may mean many different things. At one extreme, it is nothing more than giving people better tools than typewriters and telephones with which to do their work more efficiently and effectively. At the opposite extreme, it implies the replacement of people by machines which perform office procedures automatically. In this book we will take the approach that "Office Automation" is much more than just better tools, but falls significantly short of replacing every person in an office. It may reduce the need for clerks, it may take over some secretarial functions, and it may lessen the dependence of principals on support personnel. Office Automation will change the office environment. It will eliminate the more mundane and well understood functions and will highlight the decision-oriented activities in an office.

The goal of this book is to provide some understanding of office activities and to evaluate the potential of Office Information Systems for office procedure automation. To achieve this goal, we need to explore concepts, elaborate on techniques, and outline tools.

The main theme of the book is **the application of Data Base and Artificial Intelligence concepts and techniques to the implementation of Office Automation tools**. From Data Bases we take structure and property specification techniques. From Artificial Intelligence we take rule and event specification techniques. The book could be called "Data Bases and Artificial Intelligence techniques for Office Automation". We call it simply *Office Automation* to emphasize the importance of this area. Data Bases and Artificial Intelligence are important and, at this point, even fashionable for the general public. In the long run, however, Office Automation will affect more people, more institutions and our general way of life. Computers and Communications are the means for change. Data Bases and Artificial Intelligence provide the techniques for change. Office Automation is change: change that will affect more than half the working population of the world directly and the rest indirectly.

Word processing, electronic mail and advanced telephony are part of office mechanization. Office mechanization provides tools which enhance office workers' productivity. We represent the area of office mechanization in Part I of the book with its most critical aspect: **Integration**. The first integration problem is integrating users' views through appropriate user interfaces. User interfaces are probably the most important single factor in the adoption of an automated system. There are important directions and guidelines to be used for producing good user interfaces, and they are outlined in the first paper, "User Interface Design". The second integration problem is integrating the different system facilities. Products like Lotus 1-2-3 and Symphony are very successful in integrating word processing, graphics, data base and spreadsheet functions. Far more integration is needed among the office tools. In the second paper, "Document Management Systems", system integration of editing, retrieval, formatting, filing, and mailing is discussed, and an example system emphasizing integration is outlined.

Offices deal with information and knowledge. Filing and mailing happen to be two key areas in handling office information. Office scribing, e.g., word processing, is, in our opinion, only a secondary office activity. People want mainly to remember and to communicate (filing and mailing). They write things down only as a means to achieve these ends. If they had had another way of recording information, e.g., voice filing and mailing, they might not have written down anything in the first place. In Part II, we discuss **Filing**. The third paper, "A Multimedia Filing System", gives an example of an office filing system and discusses the relative merits of some of the design decisions. The fourth paper, "Office Filing", outlines a more general framework for multimedia document filing. In Part III, we discuss **Mailing**. The fifth paper, "Etiquette Specification in Message Systems", provides a framework for office communication. The sixth paper, "Intelligent Message Systems", describes a prototype system in which messages are active objects with their own rules of behaviour.

Office Automation implies the availability of tools for capturing and automating office procedures. In Part IV, we discuss **Procedure Specification**. Paper number seven, "Office Procedures", outlines a system with triggers for automatic handling of office forms. In the eighth paper, "An Object-Oriented System", a much more basic approach is taken. The paper introduces a generic object-oriented system which can be used as a basis for office procedure specification and automation.

To provide the proper system facilities and introduce office procedure design, we need models to clarify the concepts. In Part V **(Modelling)** we present two models. In paper number nine, "Conceptual Modelling and Office Information Systems", the general environment of the office and its associated objects is discussed. In the tenth paper, "A Model for Multimedia Documents", we look inside documents and exploit their structure.

Automation can cause havoc if it does not perform as anticipated. We should be able to analyze Office Information Systems and identify undesirable properties. Two examples are presented in Part VI **(Analysis)**. In paper number eleven, "Properties of Message Addressing Schemes", the routing of messages is carefully considered and related to a number of standard distributed-processing problems. In paper number twelve, "Message Flow Analysis", the flow of documents in offices is analyzed for loops, dead ends, etc.

Finally, performance considerations are important in office systems. We use office filing as a sample environment for the discussion of performance considerations. In Part VII **(Performance)**, we present two approaches relating respectively to performance analysis and special machines. In the thirteenth paper, "Access Methods for Documents", we analyze data and text retrieval mechanisms. In paper number fourteen, "Text Retrieval Machines", hardware proposals are evaluated for text retrieval.

This book has the format of the Alpha-Beta Reports which we have produced the past few years. As was customary with these reports, we end the book with a paper looking towards the future. The paper is called "Objectworld", and it outlines an imaginary world that could be very useful in the design of Office Information Systems.

The authors of this book are as closely connected with one another as their papers. All of them were members of a specific group on Data Bases and Office Automation at the Computer Systems Research Institute, University of Toronto. For about five years (1980-1985) we worked as a group on various topics chosen for importance, relevance, and our ability to contribute to them. This book summarizes our findings. We refer to many other contributions by other researchers. However, we concentrate on what we have done. We hope we have covered many interesting topics related to Office Automation. We did not exhaust the possible topics and we probably missed some important ones. This is not a book on "Everything You Wanted to Know about Office Automation". It is a book on "What We Can Tell You about Office Automation".

The ideas and terms appearing in the papers have some degree of inconsistency. The group always encouraged creative thinking, by allowing a certain degree of controlled anarchy. Individual projects had much flexibility and independence in their thinking. Only within the same project and system was consensus enforced. This state of affairs is apparent in the book. The book gives a snapshot of our thinking as it continuously evolved. At this stage of Office Automation development, it is important to highlight choices and not give recipes. Presenting an appearance of final, irrevocable truth would have been a disservice to the readers. The whole world of Office Automation is rapidly evolving. Dealing with it is like shooting at birds from a moving car (while the driver and the birds try to avoid each other). The office environment is changing as computer and communications technology evolves. One has to create tools capable of solving future problems on the basis of projected technology.

The material in this book was used many times in a graduate course on Office Automation given by the University of Toronto Computer Science Department. The prototype systems outlined in the papers are working, and most of them can be seen either as a demonstration or in videotape form. The programming was done by graduate students who also finished their degrees. The laboratory equipment consisted mainly of SUN workstations, and access to a VAX 11/780, all running UNIX^{TM}. We believe that interesting research on Office Automation can be carried out in such a basic experimental environment. We would have liked, however, to have had the capabilities of more advanced workstations, local area networks, and image and voice hardware.

The Data Base and Office Automation Group had many graduate students and visitors over the years, including: E. Bertino, C. Cheung, J. Chui, P. Economopoulos, K. Elles, C. Faloutsos, S. Gamvroulas, S. Gibbs, J. Hogg, R. Hudyma, J. Kornatowski, I. Ladd, A. Lee, D. Lee, P. Martin, M. Mazer, J. Mooney, O. Nierstrasz, D. Propp, M. Papa, F. Rabitti, K. Twaites, C. Thanos, M. Theodoridou, J. Vandenbroek, and C. Woo. We thank all of these people for their contributions. The research was a group effort, and it is hard to separate the individual contributions. The fact that all of these people were exposed to advanced office automation ideas is as important as the research results themselves. High quality professionals are the key element and critical resource for any effort in high technology. As a university, we are very proud to provide a challenging environment for these people, and we are sure that the systems they will produce in the future will be far superior to anything we did within our group.

March, 1985   D.C. Tsichritzis

Contents

Part I

Integration

1
User Interface Design

A. Lee
F.H. Lochovsky

ABSTRACT *User interface design is one of the most important and one of the most difficult aspects of designing a computer system. It is the contact point between the user and the system and determines to a large extent the usefulness and effectiveness of the system. In this paper, we examine the tools and techniques used for designing user interfaces. As user interface design is to a large extent an art, our goal is to highlight important issues in user interface design and not to prescribe a recipe for designing user interfaces.*

1. Introduction

The user interface of a system is unquestionably one of its most important components. It manifests itself at a number of levels of contact between the user and the system: physical, conceptual, and perceptual [Mora81]. Physically, it determines how the user interacts with the system. Conceptually, it determines how the user thinks about and explains the behaviour of the system. Perceptually, it determines whether the user accepts or rejects the system. As such, the user interface is a component that cannot be considered apart from the rest of the system. It cannot be designed haphazardly, added in hindsight, or just made to happen. Rather, it should be considered early in the design process and designed in conjunction with the rest of the system.

In this paper, we are concerned with the tools and techniques used for designing user interfaces. The tools and techniques of any trade evolve, but the tools and techniques of user interface design have had less than a decade to arrive at their present forms. As yet, there are no definitive experiences and no standard guidelines for building good user interfaces that we can draw from. However, there are some important principles emerging and several important design considerations which we will highlight.

One of the most important aspects of a user interface is its *conceptual model*. The conceptual model provides the mechanisms both for conveying knowledge to the user to perform his tasks and for assimilating this knowledge. Approaches to designing a conceptual model are discussed in section 2. In actually designing the properties and dynamics of the user interface, there are many design considerations. In section 3 we outline these considerations and some of the approaches used. To determine the suitability of the design of a user interface, we need to experiment with different techniques and see if they fit together well. Therefore, we need prototyping tools that will allow us to put such designs together quickly and cost effectively. Section 4 will discuss such a facility. Finally, our conclusions are presented in section 5.

2. Conceptual Model and User's Model

A *conceptual (system) model* is the system designer's abstract framework on which the *system* and the *world* in which it operates are based [Maye81]. It encapsulates the knowledge about the workings of the system and how this knowledge may be used to accomplish tasks [Mora81]. The underlying conceptual structures of the conceptual model are taught to the users to increase their understanding of the system, to provide them with an appropriate basis to reason about the system and its behavior, and to provide assimilative context to enable them to relate to new situations and tasks.

A *user's (mental) model*, on the other hand, is a personalized, somewhat high-level understanding of the conceptual model based on the user's knowledge and experiences. It is not only a personal description but also a prescription as well [MeVa82]. The user employs his mental model not only to perform tasks that were taught, but also to perform tasks not originally encompassed by the conceptual model (i.e., transfer performance).

Since a user bases his mental model on a system's conceptual model, it is very important that the conceptual model be properly conceived (i.e., that it be complete and consistent). A conceptual model that gives a cursory, incomplete notion of the system or is not cohesive or not thorough will make a system difficult to understand, and may result in conflicts between the conceptual and the user's models. A conceptual model that is inconsistent will frustrate the user and inhibit experimentation and learning. As a result, it may not provide the appropriate anchoring knowledge that is required for comprehension of the system and for assimilation of new situations and tasks.

There are two extremes in the formulation of conceptual models [GIIT83]:

Emulation   A conceptual model that emulates the familiar uses the user's knowledge, through analogies and metaphors of an existing system, to aid in the understanding of a new tool.

Innovation   A conceptual model that exploits the representational possibilities of a new tool, synthesizes and introduces new approaches of thinking and new methods of doing things.

There are many reasons to choose the emulation approach which happen to be reasons against choosing the innovation approach, and vice versa. The emulation approach may be intuitive, easier to learn, more likely to encourage user acceptance and able to minimize training required (although there is little experimental evidence to prove this). However, while analogies may be very effective for teaching novices about a system (i.e., as a literary metaphor), they can be dangerous when used for detailed reasoning about a system [HaMo82]. There may be many aspects of an analogical model that are irrelevant to the analogy, and some may in fact be in conflict with the system. Also, analogical models inhibit representation of new and innovative concepts (e.g., directories in a file system [HaMo82]). In some limited situations analogical models can be useful. However, they should not be adopted haphazardly or simply because they are easy to learn and use. Analogical models should be chosen because they are an appropriate representation of the conceptual model. Otherwise, the designers may in fact be postponing or ignoring teaching users new concepts and operations.

Superficially, the emulation/innovation approaches appear to represent a dichotomy. The premise in the innovation approach is that the system being modelled is very different from the concrete system and must be synthesized. However, on careful examination we may observe that it need not be a dichotomy at all. If the emulation approach is properly used (i.e., the analogical model does not inhibit the assimilation of new concepts), the dichotomy can in fact define a trajectory along which the user's model may be directed in a controlled way towards the conceptual model. As a consequence, the goal of the system growing with the user can be realized. The difficulty then is in finding a useful isomorphism between the analogical model and the conceptual model [GIIT83].

As we can see, analogical models can be exploited to advantage. By starting with a suitable analogical model, the user is not overwhelmed from the outset. Also, we can take advantage of the benefits associated with the emulation approach (i.e., easy to learn and easy to use). In office systems, such criteria are essential. Office workers, notably managers, have little interest in spending large amounts of time learning how to use a system to perform their desired tasks.

Whether one follows the emulation approach or the innovation approach, it is important to avoid haphazardly introducing restrictions or exceptions. They are not only difficult to understand, in the context of the rest of the system, but they also tax the user's ability to recall, and hamper his performance. Arbitrary, artificial restrictions clearly affect the complexity of not only the system but also the conceptual model. Just as it is important not to adopt poor analogical models, it is also true that designers should not introduce unjustifiable exceptions.

To illustrate some of the preceding issues, we draw attention to a text editing example. In the Xerox Star office system [SIKV82], the editing philosophy adopted is *edit original document with autosave*. Here, as the user edits a document, all changes that are made to the copy on the screen (i.e., memory copy) are reflected in the original copy (i.e., disc copy). This is unlike traditional text editing systems, which usually adopt the philosophy *edit copy with explicit save*. In this case, a distinction is made between the two copies of the document. This distinction is not only artificial, it is also inconsistent with a novice's mental model. The distinction is artificial because the user's intent in the first place was to modify the particular document. Otherwise, a backup copy would have been made explicitly, prior to the editing. It is inconsistent with a user's mental model because in a paper environment one edits the original version. As we can see, the Star's conceptual model for text editing is not only consistent, it is also self-consistent, with its overall emulation approach of mimicking a paper office.

3. Design Considerations

Formulating the conceptual model is the first, and perhaps the most important, step in designing a user interface. Once the basic philosophy of the system has been adopted, many other choices for the user interface follow naturally. However, it is difficult to formulate an appropriate conceptual model without some familiarity with user interface design considerations. In this section we will discuss these design considerations and highlight some of the more important approaches.

3.1. Input and Output Devices

The primary level of contact with an interactive system is the level of pragmatics [Buxt83]. This level has a strong effect on the user's perception of the system. A system's input and output devices greatly affect its pragmatics. An inappropriately chosen input or output device may make a task difficult to specify and hence difficult to do. For example, many systems use the keyboard for both text and operation entry. This results in a complicated interface and can cause the user to make silly mistakes due to a lack of awareness of his current context.

One objective in the design of a system is to choose an appropriate input device so as to minimize the number of input devices used. For example, the multi-touch, touch-sensitive tablet can represent many input devices, depending on the context in which it is used [BuHR84]. This can minimize the need to switch between input devices. Hence, if a single device can serve as several different devices (i.e., a virtual device) without overloading its semantics, it is generally preferable to using many single purpose input devices. For example, mice are general purpose input devices that allow pointing and selecting of objects (e.g., text, icons, graphics, etc.) displayed on the screen, as well as manipulation of control objects like cursors, menus, windows, and scrolling icons [NeSp79].

In choosing a suitable input device, reference to an input device equivalence tableau may be useful [GIIT83, Schi84]. The tableau imposes structure on a domain of input devices and serves as an aid in finding appropriate equivalences. As well, it makes it easy to metaphorically relate different devices. More importantly, the tableau is useful in quantifying the generality of various physical input devices. This allows us to match application needs to devices.

In terms of output devices, CRTs are the most commonly used device in interactive systems. The falling cost of sophisticated display technology now makes it viable to substitute graphics displays for standard CRTs. The graphics display is not only useful for displaying the final results of an operation, but can also be a mechanism by which the apparent complexity of the user interface can be reduced [Lodd83, Mill82]. It can greatly aid the presentation of operations, system information, and the intermediate progress of operations, through *visual representation*. This has the following benefits:

- It provides ease of learning and use because the display avoids forcing the users to remember conventions, since everything related to a task can be made visible.

- It improves user performance and reduces errors because objects and operations are visible to the user.

- It conveys an unspoken narration of all the user's actions and the system's responses, as well as ideas and information.

- It allows the user to utilize direct manipulation as opposed to descriptive manipulation (see section 3.4).

- It allows the designer to incorporate visibly meaningful feedback and help mechanisms which can develop mnemonics and other memory and learning aids.

Interactive text-editors and office systems like Bravo [Lamp78], Etude [HIAG81], Star [Seyb81], Lisa [Will83], and Macintosh [Will84] provide a bit-mapped display that can present a fairly faithful representation of the changes to the documents or resources available (i.e., an electronic desktop). They provide a "what you see is what you get" interface as opposed to an "embed-compile-print" interface. This, in effect, reduces the turnaround time, since one can perform an action and see the results immediately.

Great strides have also been made in other input and output devices. For example, voice hardware can be used for presenting information (e.g., speak out on-line help information) and for accepting input (e.g., operation recognition) [Andr84, Cann83, LeLo83]. Their falling costs and improving reliability and effectiveness make them candidates for improving the means of communicating with users.

3.2. Operation Set

The operations in a user interface are the set of actions (commands) that are provided for manipulating the objects and resources of the system. Two approaches are commonly used in designing the operation set. In one approach, a small set of *generic* operations that have few restrictions and exceptions, and minimal overlap in meaning or functionality is provided. Each operation embodies fundamental concepts with many of the *extraneous application-specific semantics* stripped away [SIKV82]. They can be used in a wide range of applications, always behaving the same way regardless of the type of object selected. In the other approach, a large set of application-specific operations is provided. Here, operations have limited range and are often customized to the specific application.

A small set of operations does not, however, necessarily imply less confusion or greater ease of use than a large application-specific set of operations. It might minimize the confusion normally associated with a large operation set. However, the generalizations may, in fact, obscure or eliminate certain necessary application-specific semantics. As a result, the user may misinterpret or misunderstand the effect of an operation in such situations. The net effect is that we have traded away one problem for another.

For example, when a Star document icon is MOVEd to a printer (i.e., to initiate the hardcopy operation), it is not clear what the system does with the moved icon, that is, which of the following occurs [SIKV82]:

- The system consumes (i.e., deletes) the icon.
- The system does not consume it but
    - puts the icon back where it came from.
    - places the icon in an arbitrary spot on the "desktop".
    - leaves the icon in the printer so that it must be explicitly moved out.

The first is acceptable because the printer icon would behave consistently with other function icons (e.g., when an icon is moved into an out-basket, the system mails it and deletes it from the desktop). In the latter cases, the printer icon would behave consistently with its physical counterparts (i.e., the behavior of an electronic analogue of a real printer should have no notion of deleting the piece of paper).

Large operation sets present a cognitive burden on the user in learning and using the system. As [Reis81] points out, the ease of use and likelihood of making errors in an interactive system can be measured by the complexity of the grammar of the language (i.e., number and length of the production rules). This of course does not take into account the binding of a number of actions into one chunk (i.e., *chunking*[1]) [Buxt83]. Nevertheless, it does not discount the fact that a large operation set can present a much larger cognitive burden then a smaller operation set.

3.3. Operation Syntax

The operation syntax determines the order in which and place in the specification of an operation at which the operands and the operation are specified. The operation syntax is generally in one of three forms - *prefix*, *postfix*, or *infix*. In *prefix* (verb/noun) syntax, the operation is specified first, followed by the operand for the operation. The operand of an operation in *postfix* (noun/verb) syntax is specified first and then the operation. An operation in *infix* (noun/verb/noun) notation is a cross of the prefix and postfix notations. This operation syntax

---

[1] *In psychology, chunking is the information processing ability of human beings to combine several small units into one large unit, which is just as easy to handle as its individual parts.*

is typically used when an operation contains more than one operand.

The postfix syntax is natural in graphics applications, where the operation serves double duty as a virtual *carriage return* delimiting the end of the operation specification. However, postfix is unnatural in alphanumeric mode. Here, the prefix syntax is the more natural form of operation syntax (i.e., carrying over natural language ways of doing things). Hence, there is an apparent inconsistency or perceived discrepancy in a mixed text-graphic system as to which syntax is more natural.

This problem may be resolved somewhat by making the object/scope of the operation the required operand, as in the Star [SIKV82, BFHL83]. This results in the user being able to deduce the syntax and semantics of unfamiliar operations. This is not meant to be the solution to the operation syntax problem; however, it does, from one point of view, resolve certain inconsistencies.

3.4. Manipulation Technique

The manipulation technique of a user interface is the way in which the objects of the system are manipulated. Two approaches are commonly used: *direct manipulation* and *descriptive manipulation* [HaKS83, Shne83]. Direct manipulation uses physical actions and selections on objects (i.e., recognize and point), whereas descriptive manipulation uses English-like syntax to describe objects and actions (i.e., remember and type). Descriptive manipulation is commonly associated with command language user interfaces.

Direct manipulation is commonly found in systems using a *what you see is what you get* philosophy (e.g., interactive editor-formatters). Unlike batch formatting, the user does not intersperse formatter commands between text. Rather, users cut, paste, and dress the documents, with the formatted result being immediately visible. Also, users do not need to contend with an edit-compile-execute work cycle. The annoyance and delay of debugging the format commands are alleviated because the results and errors are immediately visible.

It is easier in the direct manipulation approach to start using the system and to master its simple parts. A user need not remember as much. Each step of the user's actions is immediately visible. As such, it provides a visual narration of the actions and their results. Also, most operations are reversible. For nearly every operation there is an inverse operation; in certain cases, an operation has a natural inverse - applying the operation in the reverse direction.

Direct manipulation encourages the users to experiment with and capitalize on *transfer performance* - performance of a task for which they were not specifically trained. Features can be progressively assimilated and may therefore be amenable to skill acquisition. This is often referred to as the *onion* approach (i.e., layers of skin comprise increasingly advanced concepts), whereby the system's complexities are gradually unveiled as the user becomes comfortable and his understanding increases [Land83]. This is an invaluable aspect of the tool, not only because it allows the user to incrementally master the system but also for formulating the conceptual model. Unlike descriptive manipulation, direct manipulation, when used properly, can provide the means for evolving the user's mental model along the projected trajectory mentioned in section 2.

The direct manipulation approach works well with an object-oriented conceptual model in which a set of objects and orthogonal actions (i.e., any action can be applied to any object) are defined. If a message passing scheme similar to Smalltalk [GoRo83] is used to request actions, then new objects can be defined with a new combination of already-defined properties, while minimally upsetting the existing objects. The problems and complications associated with descriptive manipulation, when syntax structures are modified, are avoided.

However, there are some drawbacks to direct manipulation. The biggest drawback is that not all actions are simple, easy, or possible to demonstrate (e.g., finding all objects that satisfy a set of constraints). Descriptive manipulation may be better able to capture these actions concisely and clearly. For example, several discrete tasks may need to be performed, which involve a large number of keystrokes or button presses to perform a complicated action. Direct manipulation would benefit greatly if it could use short forms, abbreviations, and concise syntax like those used in descriptive manipulation to minimize the number of steps per task. This would also be desirable for expert users, who would want fast and less verbose user dialogues. In allowing both manipulation techniques to coexist, the benefits of each technique are realized.

An additional drawback of direct manipulation is that visual representation can be confusing, due to incorrect information, cluttered presentation, or misleading graphic representation [Shne83, Lodd83]. Pictorial representation can be somewhat deceiving, in that it may not necessarily be apparent what the cause of an error is (e.g., inheritance format attributes in interactive editor-formatters). The user may be misled by the appearance of the problem and may not actually identify its source.

3.5. Dialogue Technique

A dialogue technique is the method by which the user communicates his requests to the system. Dialogue techniques in current use include [FoWC81, FoVa82, NeSp79]:

- type-in
- function-key
- menu
- iconic
- gesture
- voice

A type-in approach requires the user to type operations in a well defined syntax, using the keyboard. It is a quick and efficient mode of input for expert users, but difficult for casual or novice users. In the absence of sophisticated input (e.g., mouse or tablet) and output (e.g., graphics display) devices, the prevalent dialogue technique is the type-in approach.

Function keys are special keyboard keys that represent an object or operation. They can either have a fixed meaning, or their meaning can change depending on the current context. Function keys provide easy operation and object specification, since it takes very little time to select a function key. They are appropriate for a small set of functions but are unsatisfactory when there are a large number of functions, because of the limited number of keys that can be set aside on a keyboard. They take up no screen real estate but are not as flexible as menus and gestures. By properly arranging the order and position of the function keys, operation specification is easily facilitated and *dangerous* keys are not accidentally selected[2].

Menus present all the possible choices in the current context to the user. Selections are made by number, by mnemonic letter, or by function keys. Menus are attractive because they require less cognitive effort on the part of the user, since all the options are listed. It is not possible to make a meaningless selection. However, menus are often annoying to the expert user. This is especially true when choices are hierarchically structured, and a number of menu selections are required to completely identify an object or operation. The user's input, when

---

[2] *In Etude, special keys for nouns* (e.g., word, sentence, paragraph, etc.), *verbs* (e.g., copy, move, delete, etc.), and *modifiers* are defined and arranged from left to right with *dangerous* keys placed in out-of-the-way positions. The keys are arranged in the order in which they are provided in command specification.

using menus, is paced by the system. There is thus a tradeoff between speed and accuracy.

Icons are graphic abstractions of operations or objects. They are usually selected by some form of pointing device (e.g., mouse or joystick). Icons are extremely useful for conveying ideas or information in a nonverbal manner, if the abstractions are appropriately represented[3] [Lodd83, Mill82]. Like fixed menus, icons can take up valuable screen real estate. However, iconic based interfaces require a user to "recognize and point" rather than to "remember and type", as in type-in based interfaces.

Gestures are simple graphical shorthand strokes (e.g., a check mark) [BFHL83]. They represent a natural form of dialogue technique, and are less complicated than on-line character recognition approaches [NeSp79], which require extensive user training and effective recognition algorithms. Gestures can reduce the number of subtasks when they are combined into appropriate tasks (i.e., by exploiting closure and composition — see section 3.7). Gestures also can reduce the syntactic complexity of dialogues and the number of modes occurring within a dialogue. Like the iconic dialogue, gestures can enhance the performance and learning of tasks that are difficult to verbalize [BFHL83]. They can decrease the number of input devices required, and may increase the utilization of specific input devices.

Finally, all the previous techniques have emphasized the written verbal-forms and visual-pictorial forms of communication. Very little consideration has been paid to the spoken verbal forms used in some spatial database management system applications [Bolt80]. Speaker dependent and independent voice recognition technology is currently available to complement situations where, previously, function keys and menus were used. This technique is relatively unexplored but seems to be just as suitable.

3.6. Use of Modes

A *mode* in an interactive system is a state of the user interface

that lasts for a period of time, is not associated with any particular object, and has no role other than to place an interpretation on operator input [SIKV82].

These special purpose context-sensitive states lock the user into a specialized and typically highly restricted functionality that severely limits flexibility [MeVa82]. Each additional mode, in which the user's input

---

[3] In fact, menus can be made up of non-textual icons.

is interpreted differently, adds to what the user needs to remember. As a result, the user is prone to making the mistake of trying to perform an action not permitted in the current mode. Such modal interaction forces the user to concentrate heavily on remembering *how* to do something instead of *what* is to be done. This can be counter-productive and should be avoided as much as possible [Tesl81].

Modes in the user interface often create what has been called the *dilemma of preemption* [Tesl81]. That is, when the facilities provided by the current mode do not include the one the user wants, he has to preempt what he is currently doing and move to a mode that does. This may result in a loss of information, because it has been erased from the screen. It may also cause the user to possibly forget the task at hand, as he is preoccupied with getting out of the current mode. It is unrealistic to anticipate and provide for all the possible alternatives that a user may require in solving a problem. Instead, the system should facilitate cognitive branching, so that the user can gracefully preempt the current subtask without loss of information or loss of context. Text editing and graphics editing are examples of tasks where the user may require a discontinuity in his problem solving strategy.

While modelessness may be desirable, it is difficult to achieve. Some modes are inherently part of the system and others appear through design. As such, it may not be possible to do away with them entirely. However, they should be minimized as much as possible, and they should be made as transparent as possible to the user. In designing a user interface, the important consideration is to identify when modes are appropriate and when they are not. To achieve the extreme - modelessness - much must be sacrificed, and the result may be a restricted scope in the applications that can be designed and the operations that can be performed.

3.7. Closure and Composition

Closure is the phenomenon in which operations in the user interface fuse together in such a way that the user views the set of operations as a single chunked operation [Buxt83, Schi84]. A user interface should be designed to exploit the phenomenon in which an operation, whether sequential or concurrent, triggers the next operation. In effect, one operation serves to reinforce another so that they logically connect to form a chunked operation. In fact, this technique is commonly applied in our everyday life (e.g., to change gears in a manual shift car). It is analogous to word associations commonly used to remember and recall definitions or a set of procedures. Like word associations, there are some benefits that can be reaped. The most obvious is that the cognitive burden of the resulting aggregate operation may be equivalent[4] to a single operation [Buxt83]. Hence, by properly incorporating chunking/closure into the design of the interaction, we can better utilize the rather limited but valuable cognitive resources that are available.

An example that clearly demonstrates the use of closure can be seen in the manner in which selections are made with pull-down or pop-up menus within Smalltalk [GoRo83], Apple Lisa [Will83], and Apple Macintosh [Will84]. With the use of one button press, positioning of the cursor over the selection, and then release of the button, the menu is made to appear, a selection is made, and the menu is made to disappear. With practice, selections of common menu items become single cognitive operations.

A discussion about closure is not complete without also discussing the importance of proper composition of operations. Whereas closure is concerned with the design of a chunked operation in which its parts are intrinsically related to the whole, composition deals with the smooth transition from one operation to another, wherein one operation does not necessarily imply the next operation. The objective is to combine tasks in such a way that they bind together strongly, to achieve better task performance and to render the performance of the task almost transparent to the user [Schi84]. In effect, the operations coalesce, to behave very much like a natural operation. Proper composition is not easy to achieve and is affected by a number of design factors (e.g., input devices, manipulation technique, etc.). The major emphasis is not on providing optimal tasks[5] but rather ensuring consistency throughout the domain of tasks.

3.8. Feedback

An important and invaluable element of the user interface is feedback [NeSp79]. There are two forms of feedback: user and system.

User status feedback provides feedback of all the user's actions. Examples of this type of feedback include echoing the character typed, highlighting the object or menu item selected, and displaying error messages for mistakes. In fact, error messages should always appear in the area currently being viewed or where the user is working (i.e., near the current tracker). However, this strategy may overwrite something that

---

[4]   Note, the amount of information in a chunk has no significant affect on the number of chunks that we can remember (e.g., no additional cognitive resources are required to remember words as opposed to letters.)

[5]   Two techniques, which are shown to be less than optimal for two tasks in isolation, may, when combined, yield a fairly optimal composite task [Schi84].

is already on the screen. In addition, if the user needs to refer to the message again, it might have disappeared. Therefore, an alternative strategy is to keep the error messages in the same area of the display, so that the user can always check to see if anything has gone wrong at any time.

System status feedback provides feedback of the progress of the system's actions. Time-consuming operations, or operations performed in a time-sharing environment, may result in a period of delay. Other than the initial echo to the user that the command has been accepted, he usually has no indication of what the system is doing until the operation has completed. In between the start and the end of the operation, a user who is not familiar with the operation, or is the anxious type, may interpret the delay to mean that the system is hung, is in an infinite loop, or has ceased operation. Hence, some form of intermittent feedback to indicate that the system is still alive and performing its task is important. For example, the Star has a number of cursors that indicate the state of the system whenever the user is in a mode, in addition to posting a message in the Message Area [SIKV82]. As well, it has an hourglass cursor that appears while the system is performing an operation. Percent-done progress indicators [Myer85] are another approach that actually allows the user to monitor the progress of a task. Instead of just a fixed hourglass cursor, "sand" can actually flow in the hourglass, to monitor not only the extent of the progress but also that progress is occurring.

3.9. User Aids

There are two forms of user aids that may be provided:

- Tools that alleviate anxiety and safeguard against detrimental changes.
- Tools that compensate for human limitations and limitations of screen real estate.

A major issue, typically associated with computer-based systems, is the so called *anxiety factor* [Good81a]. A system that does not attempt to alleviate the fear, apprehension, and uncertainty that users feel when they are using the system will merit very little consideration or interest from users. Even in the most straightforward of user interfaces, these feelings may arise because of the user's unfamiliarity with the system. The system should appear to be helpful and forgiving instead of instilling a feeling of "walking a tightrope" [Good81a].

A number of different kinds of aids provided by systems to alleviate anxiety can be cited. Some editors provide an *undo* operation to reverse the effects of the previous operation. In this way, the system appears to be more forgiving, as the user can correct mistakes. As well, the user is not afraid to experiment with operations. Many systems have a *help* operation that provides an on-line, condensed version of the system manual. Help might also be available as to the system's current state and the user's options at the current point. A *cancel* operation provides a means of terminating the current specification and gracefully returning to the operation level. In many systems, operations causing substantial changes require the user to *confirm* the operation.

Other forms of user aids include tools that make task performance easier for the user. Some tools compensate for human limitations. These are the tools that a computer system is ideally suited for. A *repeat* facility enables the user to repeat the last operation on a new selection [Good81b]. Some editors provide the user with the ability to perform *global searching and substitution* [Lamp78, Seyb81]. Other tools compensate for limitations on the size of the screen. For example, *scrolling* and *thumbing* facilities allow the user to travel freely through a document being edited or scanned in a window. Scrolling facilities permit the user to scroll a document. Thumbing facilities permit the user to jump around from section (i.e., page or other logical segment) to section of a document quickly.

3.10. Customizability

Designing a system targeted for a particular level of computer expertise (e.g., casual users) is rather short-sighted, not to mention discriminatory. The system should be usable by a range of user types. This can be achieved by including optional features. For example, a user should be able to choose the dialogue technique and the level of verbosity of the user-computer dialogue. As a result, expert users would not be encumbered by the facilities which are provided for the novice users, and vice versa. The system would thus allow a user to evolve a little further before outgrowing it, by elevating him to another level or choosing a faster way of doing things. The optional features result in a system that is more flexible.

4. User Interface Development Systems

It is clear from the previous sections that the process of user interface design is still very much in its infancy. Our knowledge and expertise is very limited. As a result, the question of whether the design of a user interface is suitable or effective cannot be answered until it has been prototyped and tested. Through testing, we can identify inconsistencies and problems with the design and correct for them.

In general, the first design and implementation of a user interface is far from being the desired end product. This is evidenced by the lack of good user interfaces. There is a need for an environment in which a user interface can be specified, designed, implemented, debugged, tested, evaluated, and then redesigned in an iterative fashion [MaCa83, SwBa82, BuSn80]. Since an iterative design methodology can be costly, the feasibility of such an approach hinges on the availability of a set of tools which facilitates each stage in the design process. A *user interface development system* within an appropriately structured operating environment is such a set of tools [TaBu83, RoYe82]. Its purpose is to aid in the design, implementation, and evaluation of interactive, graphical user interfaces. It supports structured forms of interaction, facilitates the graphical layout of an interface, controls input and output for the application, and aids in the evaluation of an interface. It gives the interface designer a high-level view of the system, leaving implementation dependent and low-level details to be managed by the system.

A user interface development system should contain the following components (see Figure 1) [Hill85, TaBu83]:

- manipulation and dialogue specification tools
- run-time support tools
- analysis tools

Virtually all existing user interface development systems have the first two components [TaBu83]. Respectively, they are known as the *specification* and *run-time support* components. The design and implementation is done by using the specification component. The run-time module provides the mechanism that actually executes the user interface. In addition, general system tools such as compilers, debuggers, editors, window managers, and graphics packages, as well as suitable hardware, support the user interface development system.

Ideally, the specification component is made up of a *dialogue builder* and *glue system*. Note that existing user interface development systems provide one or the other, but not both [TaBu83]. The dialogue builder provides a dialogue specification language for defining a library of interaction dialogues (i.e., customized dialogue modules). These are

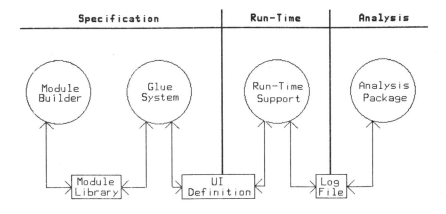

Figure 1: User Interface Development System Architecture.

usually designed and implemented by an individual with programming skills. The dialogue modules can then be *glued* together by the *glue system* into, hopefully, a coherent and unified dialogue language for the user interface. In most cases, this can be done by non-programmers [Hill85].

The run-time component communicates with the specification component via a shared file called the *user interface definition file.* This file contains the state transition information, which is kept in table form. The run-time component takes all the user interactions and interprets them according to the user interface definition. In addition, this component monitors usage, by recording information such as interaction errors, time between commands, etc., for analysis [Hill85].

Finally, to reap the benefits of a user interface development system, a component to analyze and evaluate the user interface on the basis of the data collected from testing (i.e., a run-time support component) is needed (see Figure 1). At present, there are no existing user interface development systems that support this component. However, its importance in the successful development of good user interface is unquestionable.

5. Conclusion

In this paper, we considered various aspects of user interface design. The first issue to address was the development of a good conceptual model of the system. Two approaches, *emulation* and *innovation*, were discussed. We discussed how the two, through careful design, can be combined to realize the concept of a system growing with the user as his expertise increases. Next, we examined various design considerations and their impact on the user interface. We discussed choice of input and output devices, size of the operation set and its syntax, choice of manipulation and selection technique, the use of modes, closure and composition of operations, feedback, user aids, and customizability of the user interface. Finally, we considered the need for tools to aid in the development of good user interfaces. We discussed the use of user interface development systems that allow a user interface to be designed, specified, tested, and evaluated iteratively.

Our understanding of how to build user interfaces and what makes a good user interface is still evolving. Today, user interface design is still largely an art. Hopefully, the exploration and evaluation of the techniques discussed in this paper will eventually make user interface design more of a science. At least, the techniques should help us build better user interfaces more cost effectively.

6. References

[Andr84] [BFHL83] [Bolt80] [BuHR84] [BuSn80] [Buxt83] [Cann83] [FoVa82] [FoWC81] [GIIT83] [Good81a] [Good81b] [GoRo83] [HaKS83] [HaMo82] [HIAG81] [Hill85] [Lamp78] [Land83] [LeLo83] [Lodd83] [MaCa83] [Maye81] [MeVa82] [Mill82] [Mora81] [Myer85] [NeSp79] [Reis81] [RoYe82] [Schi84] [Seyb81] [Shne83] [SIKV82] [SwBa82] [TaBu83] [Tesl81] [Will83] [Will84]

2
Document Management Systems

C.C. Woo
F.H. Lochovsky
A. Lee

ABSTRACT *Document management is a major activity in an office, and one that is readily amenable to computerization. A great deal of research and development has been done on facilities for editing, formatting, filing, retrieving and mailing documents in office systems. However, there has been a lack of attention to the integration of such facilities. In this paper, we discuss our view of what a document management system should be, and what facilities it should provide. An integrated document management system, Officeaid, is used as an example, throughout the paper, to illustrate our approach.*

1. Introduction

Office systems have matured in recent years from providing separate, primitive office functions to providing integrated capabilities. As well, the growth in interest in computers and electronic games has made non-computer-oriented people (e.g., office workers) more aware of the potential of computers in the office. The increasingly sophisticated demands in a computerized office require office systems with powerful and integrated facilities. Proper integration of these facilities is an important task requiring unifying concepts that can be used to tie together diverse physical capabilities.

In this paper, we focus on the document preparation, communication and management aspects of office systems. We will refer to such office systems as *document management systems.* As a means of integrating the different resources and facilities required, we take an object-oriented viewpoint. As the reader will see, this viewpoint is pervasive throughout this book (see for example the companion paper, "Conceptual Modelling and Office Information Systems", in this book). The objects in a document management system are the resources that people require to prepare, communicate, and manage documents. These include the documents themselves, document repositories, printing facilities, etc. These system resources are manipulated by office workers playing various office roles (e.g., manager, secretary, etc.), and using various system facilities.

We believe that an object-oriented viewpoint, when applied to document management systems, allows us to nicely integrate the resources and facilities required to prepare, communicate, and manage documents. We illustrate the integration that can be achieved using this approach by a specific example, Officeaid, a prototype document management system developed at the Computer Systems Research Institute at the University of Toronto. Section 2 discusses the use of office roles for structuring communication paths, and for controlling access to system resources and facilities. Section 3 outlines how an object-oriented approach can be used to provide an integrated model of the system resources available to users of a document management system. We focus particularly on documents and their properties. Section 4 discusses the facilities required in a document management system for manipulating the system resources and in particular for preparing, communicating and managing documents. Section 5 presents our conclusions.

2. Office Roles

To facilitate use of the system resources and facilities, and in particular the communication of, and access to, documents, it is helpful to structure the users in an office. In this section, a method for structuring users in an office is briefly outlined. The method is similar to the methods described in the companion papers, "Etiquette Specification in Message Systems" and "Properties of Message Addressing Schemes". It is based on roles and the ability of office workers to play roles.

The concept of a *role* is taken from the theatrical context, where a role is defined to be a part played by an actor on a stage. Roles can be used in document management systems to model office functions done by a user [RoSh82, Mart84, WoLo84]. An office role is the set of actions and responsibilities associated with a particular office function.

"Secretary", "Manager" and "Chief Programmer" are all examples of office roles. A user can be associated with more than one role. For example, an individual may play the role of a professor in the Computer Science Department, and also the role of director of the Computer Systems Research Institute. In addition, if there are five people that perform a particular office role **R**, then all five people are associated with **R**.

The notion of a user playing a role provides logical independence in specifying the capabilities of users with respect to system resources and facilities. In particular, it can be used to specify the access rights as well as the location (role) to which a document can be sent. For example, the role *director of CSRI* can be used in mailing and authorization without having to know which individual is currently the director. If the individual who plays the role changes, then only this fact needs to be changed: the access rights or mailing address of the role are not required to change.

In Officeaid, individual users are known as *agents*. Agents are assumed to be the basic entities within Officeaid, and are available for use in role definition. To define a role, the authorized document administrator fills out the system-supplied form shown in Figure 1.

In Officeaid, roles can be generalized (i.e., a subset of a role can be another role). For example, the role *graduate student in U of T* generalizes the roles *Computer Science graduate student in U of T*, *Business graduate student in U of T*, and so on. This mechanism can be used to refer to a set of roles without knowing the details of which users assume these roles. Furthermore, a role can be specialized (i.e., a role can be a subset of another role). Hence, a role like *Computer Science graduate student in U of T* specializes the role of *graduate student in U of T*. Specialized roles provide a mechanism to group agents into a smaller set, yet still preserve their required properties.

3. System Resources

In order to prepare, communicate and manage documents in a document management system, the users require various resources. We view these resources as the objects that the users manipulate to perform their various document management tasks. Taking an object-oriented view of these resources allows us to categorize system resources as to type, and to operate on the types as well as the specific instances. Viewing all the system's resources as objects also allows us to define generic operations that operate in a similar way on all objects regardless of their type (see section 4).

```
Define Role
```

```
       Role Name :
       Agents Included :   _____
                           _____
                           _____
       Roles Included :    _____
                           _____
                           _____
                           _____
       Agents Excluded :   _____
                           _____
                           _____
       Roles Excluded :    _____
                           _____
                           _____
                           _____
```

Figure 1: Role System-supplied Form

Officeaid defines a set of generic objects which represent the available system resources. These generic objects include *documents, file folders, envelopes, terminals, file cabinets, printers, mail trays,* and *garbage cans.* The objects are grouped by functionality and category. The functionality describes the functions of the objects: either they bear data (e.g. documents), provide a service such as acting as repositories for data objects (e.g., file cabinets store documents), or perform specific functions on data objects (e.g., printers produce hardcopy of documents). The data bearing objects in Officeaid are the document, file folder, and envelope objects. The server objects are the file cabinet, mail tray, garbage can, printer, and terminal objects.

There are three categories for each generic object in Officeaid. The *meta-type* category is used to group all the types of an object. The *type* category is used to group all the instances of a particular type. Finally, the *instance* category represents a particular instance of a particular type. For example, the document *meta-type* groups all the document types in Officeaid. A document type groups all the instances (documents) of a particular document type. Finally, a document instance is an instantiation of a particular document.

3.1. Documents

The basic information carrying entity in Officeaid is the document. The other Officeaid objects provide various facilities for communicating and managing documents. For example, file folders provide a way to aggregate documents while envelopes provide a mailing facility for documents. Because of the importance of the document object in a document management system, the rest of this section will discuss various aspects of document structure and contents. We first discuss the types of data that can constitute the contents of a document. We then discuss the structuring of documents. Finally, we consider the types of constraints that can be specified both on the document contents, and on the document structure.

3.1.1. Document contents

Documents are used to communicate information in the office. In a paper environment, anything that can be written on paper can be considered a document. Thus, a document management system must support at least text and attribute data types, where attribute data types are the traditional data types supported in programming languages and data base management systems. However, in the office there are other ways to communicate information, and these can also be regarded as potential constituents of documents. For example, documents such as letters, memos and reports may contain tables, graphics and images as well as text and attribute data. Voice data is also a very prevalent way to communicate in the office, and could form part of a document in an electronic environment.

It is thus very important to consider office documents as multimedia documents, and to provide support for the different data types [SIKV82, Zloo81, BAMT84, WEFS84]. To support multimedia documents, hardware facilities must be available for handling the different types of data. In addition, user level facilities such as editing must be provided for the different data types. Some approaches to dealing with multimedia documents are discussed in section 4.1 as well as in the companion paper, "A Model for Multimedia Documents".

Sometimes it is impossible to type a field of a document. That is, we don't know a priori that all the instances of that field are of a given type, or even for that matter that it is one data type. Take a letter as an example: if the body of the letter is a field, then any particular instance may have one or more data types as the content of that field. To handle such fields, a document management system should support the notion of an untyped field (i.e., a type which is as yet unknown).

Officeaid supports attribute and text data, and their associated editing facilities. However, as discussed in section 4.1, the architecture and user interface of Officeaid also facilitates the incorporation of other types of data. In particular, a facility for incorporating image data into Officeaid has been designed but not yet integrated into the system [EcLo83].

3.1.2. Document structure

To facilitate the communication and management of documents, a document management system should support the categorization of documents according to their type. That is, all documents with the same content structure belong to the same document type. Not only does this make management of documents easier, but it also facilitates the incorporation of more advanced office automation functions such as office procedures (see for example the companion paper, "Office Procedures").

The representation of document types and instances can be divided into two levels: the external representation and the internal representation. The external representation is concerned with what users see, how they see, and how they use what they see. The internal representation captures all the information of the external representation in an internal data structure. This data structure is transparent to the user, and stores the documents for future use. A sophisticated internal data structure (i.e., other than simple files) is required for a document to facilitate and improve the performance of operations such as querying and retrieval. Appropriate representations for the two levels facilitate the mapping between them.

The external representation of a document type is defined by one or more *document templates.* A document template specifies at least the following information:

1. The background information for the document template (e.g., headings, field names, etc.).

2. The layout (position) of the document fields on the document template.

3. The contents of the document fields (i.e., the data types of the fields).

For maximum flexibility, user level facilities should be provided for defining document templates [HePa79, Geha82, RoSh82, WoLo83, YHSL84].

Officeaid provides not only the ability to define document types via document templates, but also the ability to define *views* of document types. The Officeaid facilities for defining document templates and document views are discussed in section 4.2.

Internally, one could represent the document templates and document contents in any appropriate data structure. One common way to represent a document type, and that used in Officeaid, is as a relation (or table) in a relational data base management system [Gibb79, HePa79, Zloo81, RoSh82, LeWL84]. Then each document will be a tuple in one of the relations defined in the data base. The advantage of using a data base management system is that the filing and retrieving can be done more easily. However, currently, data types of the kind found in multimedia documents are not supported in commercial data base management systems. Additional facilities must be provided such as those described in Part II, "Filing", and Part VII, "Performance", of this book.

3.1.3. Document constraints

In a document management system, constraints are logical restrictions on document types and document field values. There are many constraints that can be specified on document types and document fields [Geha82, Woo83]. All of these constraints can be viewed as (pre-condition, action) or (post-condition, action) pairs. For example, associated with each document type can be pre-conditions and post-conditions, and their corresponding actions. The pre-conditions of a document must be satisfied before it can be used. For example, if a document is allowed to be accessed only by managers, any users other than a manager will not be permitted to access it. The post-conditions of a document must be satisfied before the document can be filed away. For example, all required fields are filled. Two sets of actions can be attached to each pre-condition and post-condition. One set of actions is performed if the associated conditions are satisfied. Otherwise, the other set of actions is performed. A useful action is to print messages to the user.

Similarly, pre-conditions and post-conditions can be associated with each document field. A pre-condition is a constraint that must be satisfied before filling a field. For example, some fields cannot be filled by the user. A post-condition is a constraint that must be satisfied after   a   field   is   filled.   For   example,   in   a   salary   field,

NEW salary > *OLD salary*. Again, two sets of actions can be attached to pre- and post-conditions. If the action part of the constraint is powerful enough, then it will act like an automatic procedure [Zloo81] (see also the companion paper, "Office Procedures"). For example, a document field can be calculated automatically after other document fields are filled in (e.g., tax and total from the subtotal).

Sometimes it is necessary to perform certain actions, depending on the state of the document data base at that time. This can be accomplished by extending the pre-condition or post-condition statement to include querying the document data base in a simple way [Astr76, Ferr82, Woo83].

The preceding view of constraints is very general, and can accommodate almost any kind of constraint. In addition, the constraints must be specified explicitly by the user. There are many constraints that are used very frequently, particularly constraints on document fields. Such constraints should be available as part of a document management system.

Besides type constraints on field values, OFS [Gibb79], Oz (see the companion paper, "An Object-Oriented System") and Gehani's work [Geha82] identify the following constraints which are applicable to document fields:

1. *key* - this field uniquely identifies a document; normally, the key is generated automatically by the document management system, and may not be modified by users.

2. *required* - this field must be filled when a document is created; once entered it cannot be modified.

3. *unchangeable* - this field may be filled at any time but once entered it may never be changed.

4. *signature* - associated with certain document fields may be a signature field which is automatically filled with the identification of the user or workstation whenever the document field is entered or modified; a signature field cannot be modified by the user.

5. *date created* - this field will be filled in automatically by the document management system with the current date when the document is created; this field may not be modified.

4. System Facilities

The facilities of a document management system are the operations available to the office roles for manipulating the system resources (objects). For true integration of facilities, operations should be designed in such a way that a user does not have many different protocols for using the system. Furthermore, for ease of use and learning, the way in which operations are specified should be uniform across objects as well as across operations.

In the same way that we structured the system resources, it is also useful to structure the system facilities. Not all users require all system facilities to perform their document management tasks. This consideration leads us to the notion of different environments in a document management system: a *default* environment which provides common or frequently used facilities that are accessible to all users, and one or more *application-specific* environments which provide facilities that are restricted to more knowledgeable users or are of less global interest.

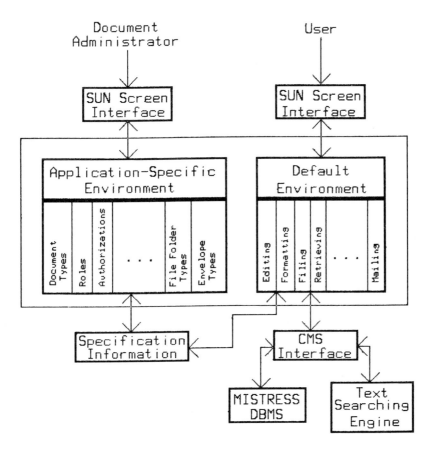

Figure 2: Officeaid System Architecture

In this section we will illustrate these two types of environments by referring to the Officeaid document management system.   The

Officeaid system architecture is shown in Figure 2.

4.1. Default Environment

Minimally, a user in this environment should have access to facilities that allow him to create and modify documents (i.e., edit), to define the appearance of documents (i.e., format), to organize documents (i.e., file), to find particular documents (i.e., retrieve), and to send documents to other users (i.e., mail). At the same time, this environment should provide a way to access the application-specific environments.

Like all the environments, the default environment must be concerned with providing a uniform and consistent interface to all the facilities available within the environment. One way to achieve this goal, and to achieve integration of facilities within an environment, is to provide a generic set of operations across all the objects. In this way, the semantics of an operation, when applied to an object, are the same regardless of the object to which they are applied. Integration of facilities is achieved by commonality of effect, as far as the user is concerned.

Officeaid provides the generic operations COPY, MARK, MOVE, QUERY, RETRIEVE, HELP, and UNDO to manipulate the objects in its default environment (i.e., the *documents, file folders, envelopes, terminals, file cabinets, printers, mail trays,* and *garbage cans* (see Figure 3)). The semantics (and applicability) of an operation depend on the functionality and category of the selected object. The applicability of an operation is apparent from its presence in the universal command window or in the pop-up menu that appears after an object is selected. The semantics of an operation are uniform across the categories of objects.

As an example, let us look at the semantics of the COPY operation. When applied to the meta-type category, the effect of the COPY operation is to switch to an application-specific environment for defining a new type of the selected object. For example, when applied at the meta-type level of a document object, the effect is to define a new document type. This simply allows the user to switch to the particular application-specific environment for defining document types (described in section 4.2). When applied to the type category, the effect of the COPY operation is to create a new instance of the selected object. For example, when applied to a specific document type object, the effect is to create a new instance of the document type. Finally, when applied to the instance category, the effect of the COPY operation is to create a replica of the selected object. For example, when applied to a specific document, a copy of that document is created.

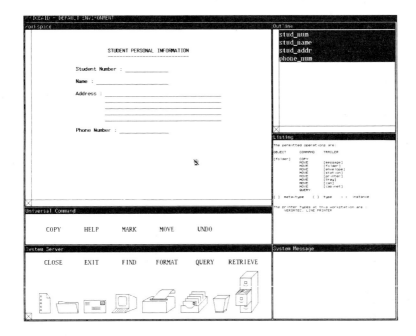

Figure 3: Screen Layout for Default Environment

Note that only the semantics at the last (instance) level are intuitive. The semantics at the other two levels are not intuitive, but they are consistent across objects. In this way, we maintain some familiarity for the user while at the same time introducing new concepts.

4.1.1. Editing

A document management system must provide an editing facility for preparing a document. The fact that a document may contain different data types requires that this facility allow the user to edit any of them. This means that the following tools are required:

- word processing for text editing like Bravo, ETUDE, and Scribe [FuSS82].

- geometric editor for structured graphics design (e.g., charts, figures, and diagrams) like PIC and IDEAL [FuSS82].

- paint/bitmap editor for free-hand drawing and editing of digitized images like MacPaint [Will84].

• voice editor like the one described in [Maxe80].

Currently, research is focused on finding a single set of operations that can be used in the editing of all data types [FuSS82]. The intent is to allow the data types to be nested in arbitrary combinations with a great deal of flexibility, and to reduce the amount of detail characteristic of existing multi-packaged document preparation systems. There has been some success with a limited set of data types (e.g., Star [SIKV82]). However, the lack of any major results may be due, in part, to the lack of appropriate hardware to support different data types, and also a lack of understanding of how to impose structure on images and voice.

In the absence of a uniform framework for handling different data types, a fully integrated editing facility is difficult to achieve. However, with clever use of the *boxes*-and-*glue* idea, first proposed by Knuth for format and page layouts [Knut79], along with information about the data type of the contents of a box and the application of certain user interface techniques (i.e., multiple windows), we can provide logical integration of separate physical facilities.

The boxes-and-glue approach uses two-dimensional objects, called boxes, that encase concrete entities such as characters, words, lines, paragraphs and pages. Boxes of varying sizes have reference points which are used to align them together horizontally and vertically. Glue is used to connect these boxes together. In this case, the content of a document can be constructed from a collection of boxes whose contents may contain only one type of data. To enter information into a box, the appropriate type of box (e.g., text, graphical, paint, speech, etc.) is selected, positioned and sized. The type of box defines the appropriate editor to be invoked. Note that, if similar actions in these editors are represented by one common protocol (i.e., same syntax, selection sequence, and manner of selection), it can greatly alleviate the complexity of using these various editors.

At present, Officeaid supports attribute and text data types. It provides the general text editing capabilities associated with normal editors as well as cut and paste operations. However, because of the nature of the user interface, it is very easy to apply the boxes-and-glue approach to support editing capabilities for other data types.

4.1.2. Formatting

A document template allows us to specify the position of the fields and background information for a document. In addition to this information, we also need to be able to specify the appearance (format) of the field contents and the background information when displayed or printed. Since we are able to categorize documents as to type, it seems natural to associate some formatting information with each document type. This formatting information is called the *document profile*, and it specifies the *default* appearance for the document fields and background information. In addition, we may want to change the appearance of specific fields of a document type. We therefore also need to be able to override the default format, and to associate a different format with parts or all of a document field. Similarly, for specific document instances, the override mechanism can be used to override the format for the document type (i.e., document profile or document field).

Most interactive formatters have a hierarchical structure and inheritance scheme for the format environment [FuSS82]. The format environment at any point in a document instance is the complete set of values (for all the format parameters) that are in force at that point. The root format environment of this hierarchy is the document profile. In a particular format environment, the value for a format attribute may be undefined. In this case, the format attribute inherits its value from a higher format environment; the particular format environment may extend all the way back to the document's document profile.

It should be noted that most existing interactive formatters are designed on the presumption that a high resolution display is available. However, there are also many less sophisticated ASCII-based displays in common use. To be flexible, we need to design a formatting facility that will display a readable document not only on graphical displays but also on non-graphical displays. Granted, this would be a less faithful representation, but at least some representation conveying the necessary information content. This is important, because not everyone may have access to a high-resolution graphics display, and many users perform non-graphical information processing.

Officeaid has a hierarchical structure and inheritance scheme for document formatting information. The format attributes are listed in the FORMAT system-supplied form shown in Figure 4. Associated with each Officeaid document type there is a document profile. To override an existing format attribute value, the user may issue the appropriate text processing command (see Table 1) or the general format command FORMAT. In the latter case, the FORMAT command displays the FORMAT system-supplied form shown in Figure 4. This allows the user to alter the values of format attributes not alterable by the commands provided in Table 1. Note that the FORMAT system-supplied form can be used to define specific paragraph formats or the format of a segment of text by filling in the appropriate format attribute values.

```
Format
    Font Size :          _____

    Font Type :          Bold    Italic  Roman

    Face Detail :        Box        Embolden  Italic    Reverse    Underline

    Base-Line Spacing :  _____

    Line Spacing :       _____

    Indent :             _____

    Left Margin Indent : _____

    Right Margin Indent : _____

    Header Indent :      _____

    Footer Indent :      _____

    Alignment :          Center    Flush Left  Flush Right  Justify

    Fill :               On

    Itemize :            Bullet Dash   Label   Number

    Itemize Indent :     _____

    Break Before :       _____

    Break After :        _____
```

Figure 4: FORMAT System-supplied Form

4.1.3. Filing

After documents have been created, some sort of file management facility is needed to allow the user to collect them into piles and
to put these piles away. In a paper office, there are typically two levels
of file organization: file folders and file cabinets. Having more levels
introduces management problems, and also becomes more complicated
for the user to deal with. A file folder can contain instances of documents either all of the same type or of different types. A file cabinet
contains various file folders. There are many different ways in which
the documents in a file folder and the file folders in a file cabinet may
be organized. A document management system must allow the user to
choose which way he wants to organize his documents.

Officeaid mimics the physical office by providing file folders and
file cabinets for collecting and storing documents. Two specific file
folder types are available (although others can be defined). Instances
of the first file folder type are immediately created for each new document type in Officeaid. Each of these file folders allows the user to collect the document instances of a particular document type, and put

COMMAND
Add
Delete
Replace
Alter Font
Alter Type Face
Alignment
Paragraph
No Paragraph
Move Right
Move Left
Add Space
Delete Space
Delete Blank Lines
Add Blank Lines

Table 1: Text Processing Commands

them in one place, the file folder. Unless otherwise specified, document instances are filed in their corresponding file folders. The other file folder type is a dossier, which is analogous to a dossier in OFS [Gibb79]. Here, instances of the file folder type may contain document instances of different document types. File cabinets can also be defined by the user, and can contain file folders of any type.

4.1.4. Retrieving

When a document is filed away in a document management system, it is necessary to be able to retrieve it at some later point in time. Typically, two types of retrieval patterns are observed. In one case, the user is not quite sure of what he (or she) is looking for, in which case, he needs to scan or browse a number of documents. On the other hand, he may have an idea of what he is looking for, but tends to be vague when he formulates his request (i.e., a fuzzy query). Both of these must be supported in a document management system. The former is fairly straightforward: the user simply flips through the batch of documents. The latter is somewhat more difficult, and the technique must allow the user to formulate his fuzzy request, and also find all documents that are relevant. Query by example is generally recognized as being one of the best techniques to handle such query formulations [Zloo81]. It is an extremely flexible and powerful technique, because very few restrictions are imposed on what the user can say (i.e., patterns may be used), and it allows the user to formulate a request fairly naturally and quickly.

Officeaid uses the query-by-example technique to locate documents for retrieval. Aside from retrieving documents from particular file folders, users may also request documents which may be in one of the file folders in the file cabinet (s). This is, of course, not very fast or efficient, but it is a natural request. As well, the retrieval facility allows the user to retrieve file folders from file cabinets, envelopes, and mail trays, and documents from envelopes and garbage cans.

4.1.5. Mailing

Documents are used to in an office to communicate information as well as used to record it. Communication facilities are therefore a fundamental part of a document management system. However, offices require more sophisticated communication facilities than those provided by electronic mail alone. Electronic mail is inadequate because it has a very flat communication structure, and also does not enforce an etiquette of communication (see the companion paper, "Etiquette Specification in Message Systems"). In addition, electronic mail does not provide facilities for using, to advantage, the document structure information. For example, one might want to screen mail based on its content.

A mailing facility in a document management system therefore should provide the capabilities for managing as well as transmitting documents. By using the document structure and communication paths inherent in an office, the document mailing facility can provide the following additional features which are not available in traditional electronic mail systems:

1.   Specification of the recipient using office roles.

2.   Grouping together of documents in a structured manner for mailing (e.g., a user can mail a dossier to another user [Fong83]).

3.   Filing and retrieval facilities for mail similar to those for documents.

In Officeaid, mailing is done by creating or selecting the appropriate document, placing it inside an envelope, and putting it in the out mail tray to be sent away. The complete document retrieval facilities can be used to select the appropriate documents, but operations for placing them in envelopes have to be issued individually for each document. However, Officeaid can group documents into objects such as dossiers and mail these. When selecting mail from mail trays, the user can browse through the mail trays or he can selectively pick mail from a mail tray using the document retrieval facilities. When mailing is coupled with automatic procedures and/or a document routing capability, the user can be relieved from much of the routing specification required for mailing documents [MaLo84, Tsic84].

4.2. Application-Specific Environments

For the application-specific environments, we can assume that the users are more sophisticated than users of the default environment. This implies that we can provide more powerful operations to deal with application-specific requirements. As a result, these environments have to be restricted to certain users (i.e., document administrators). Officeaid provides several application-specific environments, among them template design, routing specification, and procedure specification [WoLo83, MaLo84, Prop83]. In this section, we will discuss one of the application-specific environments available in Officeaid, namely template design.

4.2.1. Template Design

All users (including the document administrators) by default log into the default environment. To switch to the environment for defining a new document type, the user selects the COPY operation, the document object, and the meta-type category. To define a document template for a document type, the following actions are required:

1.   Enter background information.

2.   Define document fields.

3.   Layout document fields.

4.   Specify repeating groups or tables if any.

When defining a document type, the user may have to manipulate a number of system-supplied forms at the same time. To allow this, Officeaid provides two working areas in the user interface: the workspace area and the miniatures area (see figure 5). The workspace area displays the system-supplied form for the user to fill in. The miniatures area displays the miniaturizations of the system-supplied forms that the user is working on. It acts as a reminder to the user of what the unfinished tasks are, and also provides a visual abstraction of the state or extent of the incomplete work. As well, it provides the mechanism for switching from one task to another easily by simply selecting the miniature, in the miniature area, corresponding to the desired task.

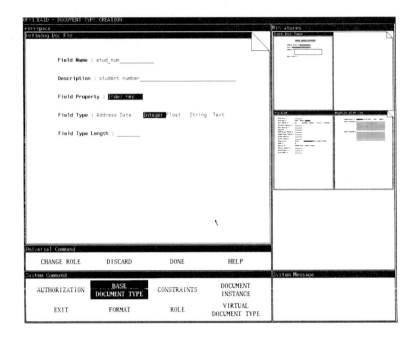

Figure 5: Screen Layout for Document Type Creation

A benefit of using a data base management system to store documents internally is that data can be shared, using views. Officeaid incorporates this facility by introducing two kinds of document types, namely *base* and *virtual*. In data base terms, a base document type corresponds to the stored data base representation, while a virtual document type corresponds to views of the stored representation. That is, a virtual document type is supported by providing transformations on base document types.

A base document type is defined by specifying the layout for the document type using document fields and background information. The position of a document field in a document template is indicated by pointing to the desired position, entering the desired background text, and then pointing at and dragging the desired field name to the appropriate location [WoLo83].

A virtual document type is defined by specifying transformations on base document types. The following three basic transformations are supported:

1. Projection.

2. Selection.

3. Cross Product.

When constructing the layout of a virtual document template, projection is implicit in the selection of the document fields. However, if a base document type name is selected, then the transformation is a cross product. Selection is specified by filling the condition field in the virtual document type system-supplied form. Using the above method, the order of performing or selecting the transformations is not significant. Furthermore, from these basic transformations, it is possible to synthesize more complicated transformations such as joins.

As in a data base environment, updates to virtual documents introduce some data integrity problems. However, in Officeaid, the document administrator is forced to specify the virtual document types in such a way that the system can detect and intercept transformations on a base document type that would lead to data integrity violations [FuSS79].

In addition to specifying the document template, the user can also specify constraints on the document type and document fields, authorization for using and changing the document type, and formatting information for the document template and document fields (see Figure 5).

5. Conclusion

In this paper we discussed what a document management system is and what facilities it should provide. We took an object-oriented viewpoint of the resources and facilities of such a system. The system resources corresponded to the various objects that the user had available to prepare, communicate, and manage documents. The system facilities corresponded to the operations available for manipulating the objects. Office roles were used as a means of controlling access to the system resources and facilities and for structuring the communication paths in an office.

A specific example of an integrated document management system, Officeaid, was used throughout the paper to illustrate our ideas. Officeaid provides integration of resources and facilities by treating all system resources as objects. This allows us to structure the system resources in a uniform way (i.e., meta-type, type, and instance levels). Integration of facilities is achieved by uniformity of effect of operations on objects.

Officeaid is implemented on a SUN workstation [Sun82] in the C programming language [KeRi78] under the UNIX operating system

[ThRi78]. The MISTRESS relational data base management system [Rhod81] is used as the underlying storage and access mechanism for the system.

6. References

[Astr76] [BAMT84] [EcLo83] [Ferr82] [Fong83] [FuSS79] [FuSS82]
[Geha82] [Gibb79] [HePa79] [KeRi78] [Knut79] [LeWL84] [MaLo84]
[Mart84] [Maxe80] [Prop83] [Rhod81] [RoSh82] [SIKV82] [Sun82]
[ThRi78] [Tsic84] [WEFS84] [Will84] [WoLo83] [WoLo84] [Woo83]
[YHSL84] [Zloo81]

Part II
Filing

3
A Multimedia Filing System

D. Tsichritzis
S. Christodoulakis
A. Lee
J. Vandenbroek

ABSTRACT *This paper outlines an Office Filing System for multimedia documents. The system uses signature techniques for fast filtering. It uses miniatures, voice excerpts and a game environment for effective browsing and selection of the desired documents. Some implementation issues, user reactions and future directions are discussed.*

1. Introduction

In this paper we discuss the design and implementation of a facility for filing office objects. With the advent of the widespread use of office information systems, such a facility is much needed. As people exchange text documents, voice documents, records and facsimile, they will need to file them and retrieve them in a flexible manner. Such filing activity serves two purposes. First, it enables the users to store and retrieve the information relevant to their own work. Second, it enables the system to retain information from which it can feed corporate data bases to augment the "corporate memory" [MoRo79].

We will refer loosely to *documents* as the office objects related to filing. A document can be a *data base record*, a *text document*, a *voice document*, or an *image*. It can also be any combination of the above. For instance, a document may consist of:

a)   attribute values, e.g., date, sender

b)   text part, e.g., letter contents

c)   voice part, e.g., voice annotation

d)   image part, e.g., digitized photographs

A *document* in our context consists of a *header* that has a unique identifier. The *contents* consist of various sections of attribute values, text, image, and voice. (For more details on the structure of multimedia documents see the companion paper by F. Rabitti.) We want to provide a facility for filing and retrieving such multimedia documents.

A simple way of filing and retrieving documents utilizes labels. Each document is labeled with a name and stored in a separate file. It is retrieved through a search of the file directories, e.g., UNIX^{TM} hierarchical file directories. The approach is effective, irrespective of the nature of the document's contents. It is equally applicable to data, text, voice, and image, or any combination of these. The management of names, however, becomes difficult for the user and does not work well in the presence of many documents.

Another simple approach is to file all documents sequentially and to search them sequentially to select the needed documents. It is the method applied when doing a library search, using a microfiche reader. The ordering of the documents can facilitate the search, e.g., alphabetic, chronological, etc. The method works well when we do not have many documents and/or the documents have an order which is very meaningful to the user. However, it is time-consuming to sequentially scan all documents, when we have many documents and want to access them in many different ways.

A third approach is to abstract certain properties of the documents and encapsulate them in attribute values. The approach is used in information retrieval when doing keyword searches. The search is effected in terms of a selection of attribute values. The selection filter is specified through a query involving a Boolean expression of simple, *attribute* $<op>$ *value*, conditions. The method is effective when the attribute values adequately represent the properties of the document and when the environment is static. It implies a priori knowledge of the properties which are important for searching purposes.

A fourth approach is to retrieve documents according to a pattern present in them [Salt80, FlUl80, Hask81, AhKW78]. This approach works well for text. The text part of a document can be qualified according to a regular expression of strings (words, combinations of words) present in it. For voice and pictures, however, patterns are not easy to define, and they often require complicated and time-consuming pattern recognition techniques [Redd76, BaBr82, EHLR80]. Note that what can be a natural pattern for the human eye/ear is not as easy to pin down in terms of computer-oriented documents. (For more on content addressibility of multimedia documents, see the companion paper by S. Christodoulakis.)

Finally, a fifth approach to retrieving documents is to encapsulate their properties in abstractions which are easy for the users to recognize. The users proceed to search for the documents with the aid of these abstractions. An abstraction can be closely related to a document; e.g., it can be a *miniature* image of the document. Abstractions can also be unrelated to the exact contents of the document; e.g., a particular tune may identify a person, or an icon an idea. An association easily recognized by the user relates the seemingly independent abstraction of the document to the document itself.

In this paper we will deal with multimedia documents. We will use, therefore, a combination of the above techniques for flexible document retrieval. In this way, the facility will be effective for each medium of communication and will be especially suitable for combinations of data, text, voice and pictures.

Information retrieval facilities consist usually of two parts; a *filtering* capability and a *browsing* capability. Filtering enables the user to specify what he (or she) would like to see or, equivalently, the documents which he does not wish to see. The browsing capability enables the user to pinpoint in the filtered documents the ones which he actually wants. In many systems the browsing capability is only an afterthought (especially true for Data Base Systems). It deals only with the presentation of the selected documents to the user. It is not considered an integral part of the selection. In addition, the filtering and browsing are considered as two independent and consecutive steps without any relation to each other. In the case of office filing, the browsing capability is very important. We will consider it as important as the filtering capability for selection purposes. This approach is necessary because the user filters are rather vague. The user does not adequately remember what he is looking for. Filtering alone cannot pinpoint the desired documents. In addition, voice and image filtering according to contents is difficult to implement because it may imply pattern recognition. In this case it is advantageous to emphasize browsing rather than filtering.

We believe that the browsing aspect is a dual method to the filtering for selection purposes. We provide, therefore, "play" methods supporting browsing in the same way that we provide access methods supporting filtering. We also allow filtering and browsing to be interleaved. That is, while browsing, we can modify the filter for selection of the documents we are currently browsing. In this way, filtering and browsing proceed concurrently, enabling the user to pinpoint the appropriate documents. The additional advantage of this approach is that the dynamics of the interaction between the user and the system are greatly improved. The user does not get bored waiting for the filtering, nor swamped with its results when they come in bursts. Instead, the user is provided with a continuous stream of filtered documents from which he can select, by advanced browsing methods, the documents he wants. The browsing is also implemented as an interesting game to further appeal to and retain the interest of the user.

2. General Design

Documents in our Office Filing System are structured, consisting of a unique identifier and a number of *fields*. Each document has a *date* field, a *sender* field and a *subject* field which are attribute fields. Attribute fields have a maximum length and take single values from a domain of values. In addition, a document has fields which are unstructured and of variable length. These fields consist of text, images, and voice annotations. Images include graphs, tables, captions, bar charts, pie charts, diagrams, and pictures. Images may appear anywhere in the document. Voice annotations are parts of the document that are used to clarify and enhance it. For instance, they can be verbal comments about the document or an utterance to attract the attention of the reader.

All incoming documents are filed in a general document file. The user searches for the required documents, guided by a vague recollection of the contents of the documents and a vague image of what the documents look like. The user initially provides a partial specification of the document contents [Zloo75]. This partial specification of the desired documents acts as a filter. The filter restricts the attention of the documents in the document file to a manageable subset. The filter can be changed dynamically by tightening its specification.

The filtering capability is by no means an exact one. The user seldom specifies an accurate filter. His specification will allow more documents to qualify than the ones he absolutely wants. These additional documents are eliminated in the browsing mode by the user. To assist the user in identifying the appropriate documents, *miniatures* and *fasttalk* are provided. Miniatures are realistic visual abstractions of the documents which are displayed for the user during browsing, as in [FeND81]. At the same time as the miniature appears in view, the fasttalk can be heard. The fasttalk is a voice excerpt associated with the document, which highlights the document's meaning. On the basis of what the user sees and hears, he can decide if the document is one of the ones he wants retrieved. If so, the document corresponding to the miniature is displayed to the user along with a playback of the voice annotations for the document.

To select the miniature to be viewed in full, the user identifies it by shooting it down with a toy cannon. Using miniatures and fasttalk rather than the documents themselves, the user can skim over many more filtered documents. In this way his browsing capability is enhanced. In addition, the presence of many more document abstractions enables the user to spend more time on the more interesting choices. The user should also be able to control the speed at which the abstractions are displayed.

3. User Interface

The screen layout of our system appears in Figure 1. Our implementation environment consists of a SUN computer which provides a page and a half of bit-map display. On the left is a whole page of document, while the right is half a page of screen real estate used for menus and miniatures.

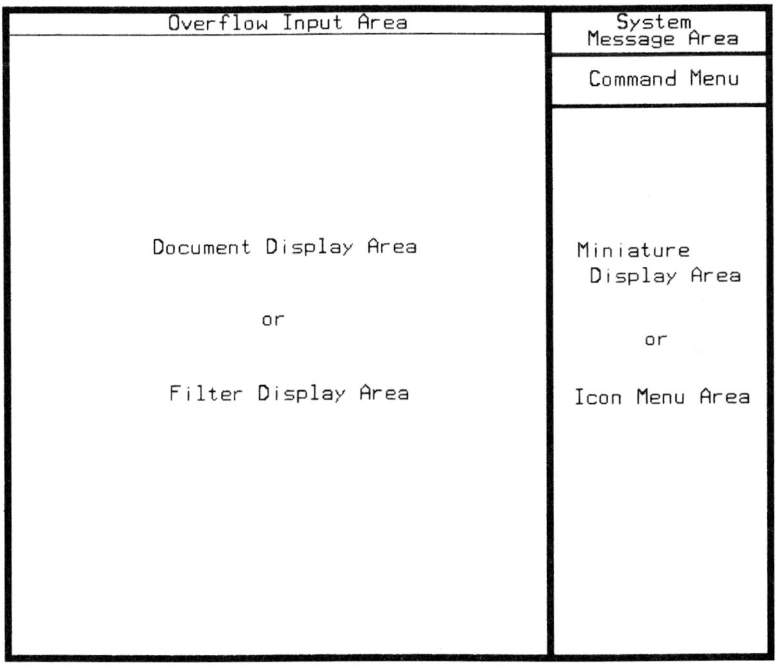

Overflow Input Area	System Message Area
	Command Menu
Document Display Area or Filter Display Area	Miniature Display Area or Icon Menu Area

Figure 1: Screen Layout

The status of the display depends on the current mode. There are three modes:

1. Create/append - the user creates or appends to the filter. This state can be recognized by the appearance of the filter template and the contents of the filter (in the case of append mode) on the left of the screen and the icon menu area on the right (refer to Figure 2a). An icon is a graphical representation of an object [Lodd83]. These icons are similar to those found in the Star [SIKH82] and the Apple Lisa [Will83].

2. Browse - the user is playing the abstractions (miniatures and fast-talk) for the documents that are filtered by the system. Miniatures are scrolled on the right side of the display while the filter remains on the left side.

3. View - the user has just frozen the browsing of the miniatures, to view one of the documents in more detail. The expanded document appears on the left while the right side of the screen remains frozen (refer to Figure 2b).

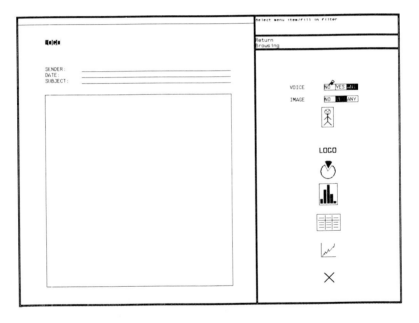

Figure 2a: Screen Layout of Create/Append Mode

The *filter* used by the searching process is the conjunction of all the restrictions on the data, text, voice, and image values of a document. The template of the filter and its icon menu appear in the Filter Display and Icon Menu areas shown in Figure 2a.

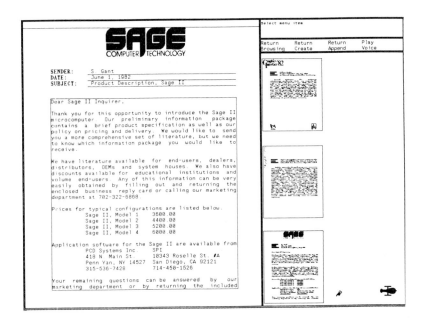

Figure 2b: Layout of View Mode

Restrictions on attribute and text values are provided as values and patterns. For each of the attribute and text fields, a field restriction may be defined. Each field restriction is a conjunction of conditions. The syntax of the field restriction is given by the following pseudo grammar:

$$
\begin{aligned}
\text{field\_restriction} &= \text{element} \mid \text{field\_restriction "\&"} \\
&\quad \text{element} \\
\text{element} &= \text{string} \mid \text{element} \mid \text{string} \\
\text{string} &= \text{word} \mid \text{wordpart} \mid \text{string word} \mid \\
&\quad \text{string wordpart} \\
\text{word} &= \text{letters} \\
\text{wordpart} &= \text{"*" letters} \mid \text{letters "*"} , \text{"*"} \\
&\quad \text{letters "*"} \\
\text{letters} &= \text{digit} \mid \text{char} \mid \text{symbol} \mid \text{letters} \\
&\quad \text{digit} \mid \text{letters char} \mid \text{letters sym-} \\
&\quad \text{bol}
\end{aligned}
$$

A field restriction need not be provided for each of the data and text fields. In such cases, a null field restriction is assumed for the particular field. The field restriction is entered in the appropriate field entry on the filter, using a by-example approach [Zloo75].

The following types of restrictions may be placed on images:

1.   There are images present in the documents being sought. The user specifies approximately where these images reside in the documents and the type of image.

2.   There are no images present in the documents being sought.

3.   The documents being sought may or may not contain images (a null restriction).

The selection of the appropriate condition is facilitated by selecting the light button beside the appropriate image entry in the filter.

If the user specifies that there are images in the desired documents, then the positions and image types are identified by dragging the "x" icons or object icons (e.g., graph, pie chart, etc.) and positioning them in the appropriate place on the filter template. The "x" icons (representing any type of image) and the object icons are picked up from the icon menu. Selecting an object icon implies that the desired image is represented by this object icon. In our implementation, an image is a single indivisible object (e.g., a pie chart). Within a filter create or append session, the user may drag any of the positioned icons (those placed in the same session) into the menu area to remove the image from the filter. The icons appearing in Figure 2a represent the image types recognized in the Office Filing System. They are, from top to bottom:

1.   picture (i.e., any other image type)

2.   logo or letterhead

3.   pie chart

4.   bar chart

5.   table

6.   line graph

7.   any of the above image types

The user specifies the voice restriction by selecting the light button (for voice) corresponding to whether voice annotation is present or absent, or by selecting ANY for don't care (refer to Figure 2a).

Commands for the Office Filing System are located in a command line area near the top of the screen. The appropriate command is selected, using the appropriate light button. The command menus that appear depend on what mode the user is in. The command menus for the various modes are:

Create/append Mode

Return to
Browsing

Browse Mode

Exit OFP	Create Filter	Append Filter	Scroll Down	Fasttalk Off

View Mode

Return to Browsing	Create Filter	Append Filter	Play Voice

To exit the Office Filing System, the "Exit OFP" button is selected while the user is in the View mode. When the Create Filter light button is selected, it indicates that the user is to provide a new filter. A blank filter template appears on the left part of the screen, and the user is in the Create mode. After all the restrictions are added, the Return to Browsing button is selected. When the Append Filter light button is selected, it indicates that the user wants to augment the existing filter with more restrictions. The user can now edit in the restrictions and select Return to Browsing when finished. When the Scroll Down light button is off, the miniatures are displayed from bottom to top; when the button is on, the miniatures are displayed from top to bottom. The speed of the scrolling is determined by the length of the fasttalk and the Rasterop operation. The user can turn the fasttalk on and off by turning the Fasttalk Off light button off and on, respectively. As long as this light button is on, no fasttalk is spoken. In the View mode, the user can play the voice annotations by turning the Play Voice light button on. In our current implementation, voice annotations and fasttalk are played back at normal speeds. To return to the other two modes, the user selects the appropriate return light button.

4. Abstraction from Documents

Information abstracted from the documents consists of:

1. Signatures.
2. Miniatures.
3. Image Description.

4.   Fasttalk.

In our system, we use a signature technique as an access method for attribute and text values [TsCh83]. The method is based on super-imposed coding [ChFa84]. A fixed length signature, which is a bit string, is created for the attributes. A separate signature is created for each block of the body. These signatures within the block signature are determined by taking each non-trivial word in the body or in the attributes, splitting it into successive, overlapping triplets of letters, and hashing each triplet into a bit position. If the word is too short, additional bit positions are created by using a random number generator, which is initialized with a numeric encoding of the word. Thus, a constant number of bits corresponds to each non-trivial word. These bits are set to one. The size of the signatures and the number of bits per word can be determined in such a way that the performance of the system is optimized. (For more on this technique, refer to the companion papers by S. Christodoulakis and C. Faloutsos.)

To see whether a given word appears within a logical block of the document, the signature of this block is examined. The same transformation is performed on the word, and the bits determined by the transformation are examined. If they are all one, the word is assumed to appear in the document. Otherwise, the document is skipped. This access method retrieves supersets of the qualifying documents. Parts of words can also be specified in queries. More complicated query patterns (including conjunctions and disjunctions of words) can also be examined.

The miniatures for the document are formed by first taking each word within the document and representing it with a variable line thickness, to account for the ascenders and descenders in the letters of the word. Then the bit-maps of the images are extracted, and an "n" factor reduction is performed (i.e., every "n" bits are reduced into one bit). This reduction is sensitive to bits that are on. That is, if a majority of the "n" bits are off then the one bit is turned off. Otherwise, the bit is turned on. To complete the miniature, the reduced bit-maps are merged with the corresponding textual portions of the document.

Simple image descriptions can be abstracted from the document, such as the image types present in it (e.g., graph, table, bar chart etc.) and their positions. This information will be automatically gathered, since it is reasonable to assume that the image creation will be conducted with the aid of specialized image editing tools that are aware of the image type being created.

In our current system, the fasttalk is created manually by the user. It contains a short (one to two seconds of talk) description of the document's contents, or an excerpt of the document. It is important to use automatic techniques to obtain a fasttalk which highlights the voice annotation of a document.

5. Implementation

The Office Filing System outlined in this paper has been implemented using UNIX™, and runs on a SUN computer [ThRi78]. The SUN [Sun82] is an MC68010 based system that combines graphics, processing, and networking capabilities in a desk-top workstation. It has a high resolution (1024 by 800 points) bit-map display that can show two pages of text, and graphics of a reasonable resolution. A mouse (a hand-operated device) facilitates input of graphical information. The SUN UNIX™ operating system is based on the Berkeley 4.2 BSD version of UNIX™ and the ARPA IP/TCP protocols [Sun82]. The Ethernet local area network connection allows SUN workstations to share resources and to access such services as electronic mail, file storage, and printing.

We used the Instavox RA-12 Rapid Access Audio Unit [Inst82] for storing voice documents. Voice documents are stored on 15-inch diskettes, each of which can contain about 27 minutes of speech. Unfortunately, voice documents are stored in analog form, which does not allow changes in playback.

The implementation of the Office Filing System is divided into three processes.

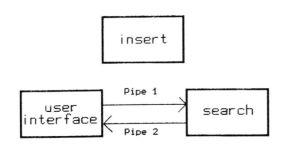

Figure 3: The Office Filing System Implementation

The insertion process is used to add new documents to the document file. In addition, this process generates the information with which the filter will be compared when the user is searching for documents. The search process will search for documents satisfying a given search filter. The user interface process, as we described earlier, is concerned with the specification of a tighter filter. It allows the user to browse the miniatures through a game playing environment and view a document in more detail.

Communication between the user interface and the search processes is limited to two uni-directional pipes. The user interface process passes the filter information, the directory indicating where the files are, and the commands to change the search direction to the search process along pipe 1. The search process, in turn, passes to the user interface process pointers to the documents that meet the restrictions of the filter, along pipe 2. In the remainder of this paper we will elaborate on the insertion and searching capabilities of the system.

The user provides four files to the insert process. These four files contain various pieces of the document (i.e., text and attributes, images, voice annotations, and the document's fasttalk). We assume that a text editor has created the text and images portion of the document and a simple voice editor has created the voice files. The insert routine processes the information contained in the four input files and appends them to the appropriate files making up the document data base.

The document data base consists of several files. The four input files are appended to the corresponding four files of the document data base. The remaining files of the document data base are created by the insertion process. These are described as follows:

-    An ASCII file which contains the text and attribute components of the document is provided as input. The insert routine generates the signature entries for the text and attributes components of the document and places them into the *signature file* of the document data base.

-    A file containing the position and size information for the images present in the document is provided as input. It also contains the bit maps for these images and information about the image types. Using the contents of the ASCII input file and this file, the miniature is created and placed into the *miniatures file* of the document file.

-    Two more files contain the *voice annotation* and *fasttalk* portions of the document. In this implementation, the files contain analog signals of the corresponding voice annotation and fasttalk, and are stored on a separate, direct-addressable audio storage device [Inst 82].

-    The last file of the document file is a pointer file. It contains information about the other six files of the document data base. Each entry in this file gives the location and size of each portion of the document in the other files.

The "insert" routine consists of the three subprocedures that update the files of the document data base based on the input files (refer to Figure 4). The insert routine also updates the pointer file according to the information returned by the subroutines.

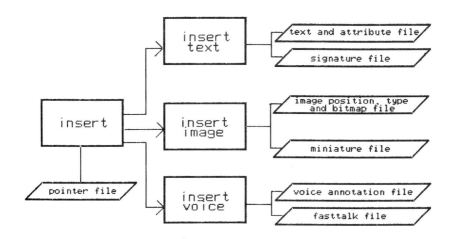

Figure 4: Insert Procedure Outline

The "search" routine calls three search procedures to progressively isolate the documents that satisfy the filter conditions. The sequence of calls and inputs is shown in Figure 5.

Each document is passed through the three search procedures sequentially and the respective medium restrictions specified in the filter are checked. The documents that finally pass "search text" are those that qualify under all the medium restrictions contained in the filter, including the one for the text and attributes.

The "search image" routine first checks the entry in the pointer file to see if the document contains the minimal number of images required. If so, the routine verifies that the positioning of the images is indeed within the minimum rectangle for the images and the types of the images match those specified in the filter. The check is accomplished by looking up the corresponding image file. If the absence restriction is specified, the search process merely checks to see that there are no images in the document.

The "search voice" routine requires only a search for the presence or absence of voice annotations in the document.

The "search text" routine retrieves the signatures for the incoming document and examines whether or not the document satisfies the restrictions on the text and attribute values.

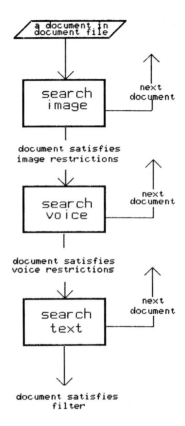

Figure 5: Search Procedure Outline

The result of the searches is a filtered subset which is passed to the user interface for browsing. The miniatures for these documents are displayed and the fasttalk portions are played. When the fasttalk of a given document is played, the corresponding miniature of the document is highlighted by a box on the screen.

6. Architecture

Our prototype system's architecture is unsuited to the particular task of filing large numbers of electronic office documents. If the documents are filed directly at the users' workstations, e.g., in a SUN, the storage space is likely to be exceeded, particularly if electronic documents contain images and digitized voice. Moreover, the shared access of these documents can be a problem. Locating the document filing functions on a host computer, e.g., a VAX 11/780, which supports the user workstations as terminals, has the advantage of exploiting a powerful operating environment. The available operating systems can support a variety of software for Data Base and information retrieval systems. However, these "traditional" tools may be not adequate in handling electronic documents containing different types of data (as text, image, graphics and voice), and the performance obtained for large volumes of documents compared to the cost would probably be unacceptable. This is because a general purpose environment cannot be streamlined for a specific application. For example, since searching through a large volume of documents is a I/O intensive activity, going through a general purpose operating system can impede and slow key I/O functions. Moreover the eventual use of special hardware can be difficult to exploit. We should, therefore, look at other architectures that provide office filing.

It seems best to build the office filing function on a special office file server, accessible over a Local Area Network. The use of a file server over a network allows the workstations to share the filing services. The file server can be built to achieve an optimum cost/performance ratio. Most file servers available today are general purpose, oriented to files handling. Electronic documents can be seen only as ordinary files, the only type of document retrieval by address or name. The advantages of a network file server can be enhanced if the server is specialized for the filing and retrieval of multimedia documents. With this approach, the document search by content can be effectively implemented. In fact, by locating the filing and retrieval functions on a dedicated server, it is possible to target the hardware and software choices towards the specific task of document storage and retrieval. Better cost/performance results can be attained, since the decisions about the hardware/software architecture of the server can be focused on the specific problem, and subsequent hardware and software changes will not reflect on the rest of the system.

For example, instead of using a file management system as part of a general purpose operating system, the document server could use specialized software that implemented suitable access methods for best performance in document retrieval. Specialized hardware could also be used for certain critical operations (i.e. for a text scanning filter), if found necessary for real-time performance (see the companion paper on "Text Retrieval Machines"). Special storage devices for high data volumes (i.e. optical disks, improved technology magnetic disks) could be employed in the server for more efficient storage of the different document components (attributes, text, images, audio). However, the main advantage of the document server approach is that all these decisions are in large measure independent from the rest of the system and can be reversed, as technological improvements become available.

It should be noted that a shared multimedia document file server will generate a considerable bandwidth requirement for the communication network connecting it to the user workstations. The multimedia documents accessed on the server will have to be transmitted for viewing in the workstations. If many voice/image parts are present, the bit rates may be considerable. Suppose that the access methods of the server are very fast. The performance of the total system may be limited by the ability of the network to move the documents and the workstations to obtain and display them fast enough.

A separate file server introduces the need for a separate workstation to server interface. The query language as it was outlined in this paper is user oriented. This obviously is not the proper interface language between the workstation and the server. A compact form of the query, which will not need extensive parsing by the server, should be produced at the workstation. In this way different workstations having different user interfaces could be interfaced to the same server. The document structure that the server uses and sends out should also conform to certain standards for structuring and formatting documents. In this way, documents can be viewed by different kinds of workstations.

In considering the problem of filing and retrieving documents, one can observe that the majority of documents filed in the office environment are either never or only seldom retrieved. Only a small minority are accessed regularly to be consulted, reviewed, annotated upon, or modified. In this latter category we can include all the documents corresponding to form blanks, letter templates, and document types in general, which are frequently used to create document instances. In fact, the typical life cycle of a document will involve a period of frequent access during creation and perhaps for a short time (in the order of a few months) following. After this initial activity, the document is rarely accessed. Thus we can define two functional requirements for the file server: the dynamic function and the archival function. The former function is more concerned with handling those documents which require a fast access time and which may require modifications and annotations. This function also includes the handling of fast growing files (intensive insertion of documents). The latter function is more concerned with the handling of very large volumes of documents. These documents are stable; that is, they are not likely to be modified. Insertions are infrequent and generally in batches. Longer access times (even in the order of one or more minutes) can be allowed for searching these large volumes of archived documents. The main constraint for the archival function is its cost-effectiveness. Strict requirements on storage cost per document are imposed in order to make feasible the goal of archiving a large quantity of data. The order of magnitude for archival filing should be in the tens of gigabytes, while for the dynamic filing can be in the hundreds of megabytes. This creates a need for large capacity storage devices which do not need an update capability, e.g., optical disks. It is interesting to ponder whether the dynamic and archival functions should be in a common server, or on separate servers.

Office filing cannot be discussed in isolation. It has to take into account the general office system architecture. As developed in our discussion, the type of architecture that appears most suitable is a collection of modular functional components that are connected via a communications facility. Such systems adapt to changing needs in the office by adding and removing components - a process which is assumed to be quite simple (e.g., that requires no software modification). The kinds of components needed for an office information system include:

communications facility

This is the link that binds together the entire system. The communications facility, in whatever form it appears, must allow the flexible addition of components, and support the transfer of data at the rates needed for audio and image.

file server

The file server performs the storage and retrieval of documents used within the office. Considerations here are short retrieval time and flexible query specifications. An important observation of the information found in offices is that a large proportion of it is not retrieved and most of it is not modified after it is created. We envisage the file server as providing extremely fast retrieval for those documents that are frequently accessed and undergoing change. For the large proportion of office information that is seldom accessed or modified, there are less stringent response time requirements. The main consideration in this case is the storage capacity, which should be as large as current technology can provide (for example, the optical disk would be an appropriate medium).

user workstation

Each user is equipped with a workstation from which he can access the facilities provided by the office information system. There are a number of issues relating to the workstation, such as processing capability, the need for local secondary storage, and the type of peripherals needed for a good user interface.

special purpose devices

A number of devices such as OCR (optical character recognition), digital image scanners, optical disk writers, network gateways, and laser printers may be too expensive to be located at the workstation and should be provided in globally accessible servers.

7. Experience and Future Directions

The following are the highlights of our prototype system.

1.   It stores and retrieves multimedia documents.

2.   It interleaves filtering and browsing for flexible document selection.

3.   It uses signatures as an access method for text selection.

4.   It uses miniatures and fasttalk as abstractions to aid the user in faster pinpointing of the desired documents.

5.   It uses information about images in terms of their type and their positioning.

6.   It uses a game to improve user interaction and retain user interest.

It should be noted that the selection in terms of attribute values and text patterns is based mainly on filtering and appropriate access methods. The selection in terms of voice and images is based mainly on playing fast abstractions in a game environment. In this way, the user's ability for fast and effective browsing is enhanced.

We have had many critical comments from the users of our system, mainly about the user interface and some of our design choices. We discuss them because they provide important feedback on our design. We should point out that certain techniques were severely handicapped by our implementation environment, with the result that their benefits were left unexplored or unrealized.

The SUN was not a powerful enough workstation to implement scrolling of images effectively. The lack of graphics processing power ultimately eliminated the possibility of having variable scroll rates. Note that the MC68010 is not only responsible for the graphics, display, and input but also much of the operations of the workstation. The competition for the processor cycles severely limited the attention required to move bit-maps rapidly around the screen. As a result, we were not able to exploit variable scroll speeds to aid the browsing of the documents (i.e., miniatures). In fact, the mediocre scroll rate obtained was unbearable for browsing large numbers of miniatures. In this situation, the idea of shooting the miniatures as they scrolled by was rather cute but added very little to the effectiveness of the browsing. A fairly powerful workstation with dedicated graphics processor was clearly required. If the accessing had been effected by a separate file server then the workstation may have been adequate for providing a proper user interface.

If variable scroll rates were possible, the mouse would not be a suitable input device for controlling them. To have supported this in the current implementation would have required pressing the buttons repeatedly to incrementally step the scroll rate up or down. Although this would have achieved the result, it would not have been as effective. An isometric joystick or 2 axis joystick would be more natural. Pressure or tilt along one axis would provide the information for speeding up or slowing down the presentation of the miniatures. Positioning of the cannon would be facilitated by moving along the alternate axis (for 2D joystick). Squeezing the trigger would fire the cannon.

The speed at which the Instavox unit played back the fasttalk and voice annotation was also less than adequate. In some sense, this should also have limited the rate at which the next miniature could be made available (although we did not notice this much because of the slow scroll rate). As a result, the short annotations that were used in place of real fasttalk were restricted to a few tidbits of preselected information. If many documents which contained fasttalk were retrieved, it would sound as if someone was very quickly turning the volume of a radio up and down. Our system had only one talker for these messages. If the fasttalk originated from a variety of voices it would be even more disruptive.

One possible solution would be to play the fasttalk in a different fashion. At the start of the fasttalk, the volume should be low, and it should increase reasonably quickly (how fast we do not know) before the distinctive phrase or tone is over. It should also decrease in volume at the end. This would add some continuity to the sounds, avoiding the abrupt silence-to-sound changes we have experienced. Hopefully, this will not confuse the listener so that he cannot distinguish between successive fasttalk messages.

The consensus opinion of users was that our fasttalk was not very useful for identifying the documents and was more of an annoyance than an aid. However, it was not clear that a different method of fasttalk would have been more useful. The lack of suitable voice hardware for digitizing the speech left the applicability of the actual fasttalk concept unresolved.

The way in which the system currently presents the documents (i.e., miniatures) to the user only works effectively if those displayed contain images and the images are quite different from one another. However, if the displayed document is mainly textual, the miniatures are not very useful. This requires that the user recall details such as structure of text blocks. It also presumes that the user has seen the document and knows what it looks like (quite an assumption). Many documents with the same type and without distinguishing images will appear the same, especially if they are all greater than a page in size (currently we display only the first page). This situation is not that disconcerting, however, since the selectivity technique for text is

powerful. The selectivity of image documents is weak; however, miniatures supplement it to add to the performance and usability of the system.

It may be appropriate to have alternatives to our miniatures, for
presenting the abstractions to the user. Some possible schemes include:

1.   less faithful miniatures (i.e., the data fields could be displayed in
      full while the text portion is miniaturized)

2.   display of certain fields only

3.   a stack of faithful/less faithful miniatures representing the entire
      document if it is more than one page long

4.   some indication of whether the document contains voice annota-
      tions

Clearly, there should be a number of alternate presentations from
which the user can choose. This would be like allowing the user
different ways of viewing numerical data (e.g., bar charts, pie charts,
line charts, mixed charts, etc.), as in spreadsheet applications.

Our miniaturization technique is inadequate. It overemphasizes
the "dark" regions of the document. Text and images whose bit patterns are predominantly ones (a bit on in the bit-map corresponds to a
dark pixel) tend to be the only distinguishing features of the miniatures. Line graphs and other light "grey" areas show up very little, if at
all. We should use an algorithm whose threshold for dark regions is
higher than its threshold for light regions. In this way, the system will
try to maintain a higher ratio of "on" versus "off" bits for the light
regions of the miniatures, when compared with the original region in
the document, than for the dark regions. It might also preserve the
lines for the line graphs in the miniatures. In this way, the distinguishing features of the light regions will be preserved. The features of the
dark regions are expected to remain in the transformation even with
the higher threshold.

The interface of our system is based on the by-example approach,
combined with menus. The by-example approach [Zloo75, Zloo81] has
the advantage of being a non-procedural, two-dimensional language,
and so can mimic the physical objects of business and office environments (e.g. forms, reports, papers). The user constructs his requests
by giving the system an example of a reply to a request. The menu
approach allows display on the screen of the full choice of options available. Hence it prevents the user from making selections outside this
range. We found query formulation to be easy in this framework.
Furthermore, usage of the mouse allows the user to quickly point at
items in the menu area and to move them on the screen, as well as to
select the appropriate commands. However, the interface described
provides the user with few means to tailor the browsing process to his

own needs. In fact, while query formulation is not a long process, the browsing phase can take a considerable amount of time.

We have also received suggestions concerning the inclusion of several useful ideas to the system. For instance, the system does not give any indication of how many more documents are to come. This information is not available when the display and selection work in parallel, as in our case. However, we can solve this in part by using progress indicators to show how many documents out of the total number have been searched. The progress indicator may be updated after each document is examined, or only when the current match relates to the entire set of documents. This progress information, i.e., how far the search has proceeded and approximately how much longer it will take, would be a valuable aid during the browsing phase.

The system does not allow the user to mark or set aside particular documents for further perusal at a later time. One might wish to set the documents aside for later reference as they are found. It is not hard to incorporate a collection and naming capability for this purpose, e.g., dossiers.

Another issue concerns query reformulation. The only way to change the current query in our system is to add conditions to those already expressed in the query, that is, to restrict the query. When the user restricts the query, the search continues forward. However, it would be desirable to broaden the query or change it dynamically by deleting or modifying conditions. In this case the search would start again from the beginning, but the documents already seen by the user would not be displayed again. In the current implementation, the only way of broadening the query is to exit from the browsing process and specify again the filter with the modified conditions. This can be very annoying, since the user has to see documents for a second time.

The game-playing environment was not found to be very appropriate for an office environment. Games offer a challenge, the possibility that the player might lose. A situation in which the user would lose in our system would be missing a miniature and being forced to interrupt the browsing to back up. This was found to be counter-productive. If the challenge is not there in a game, the user quickly becomes tired of it. The game loses its mystique and the user may feel silly or simply hampered.

Our system has general shortcomings in content addressibility of voice and images. The system in essence puts labels on voice and images and associates them with specific locations on the documents. It does not deal directly with their contents. There is no notion of content addressibility in terms of voice and images. It is important to use a small degree of voice and image recognition to provide rudimentary content addressibility.

General voice recognition is not necessary. As a matter of fact, it may be an overdesign for filtering. First the person will have to use the exact word(s) mentioned, then, for most existing systems, a similar pronunciation. We doubt that a user will find such an environment useful. On the other hand, certain keywords may be adequate for filtering voice messages. The system can concentrate on these while dropping all other words. To help the system concentrate, the tone, the volume, or any other indication can be used to emphasize the keywords in the voice message. We feel that a limited voice recognition device with appropriate software indexing tools may provide an adequate degree of content addressibility. However, it should be pointed out that the recognition is on-line.

Images present other problems and challenges. As with voice, we do not need to solve the general image recognition problem to provide image filtering. Images in an office environment are not random. They are stylized; e.g., logos, graphs, etc. In addition, their representation may be in graphical form rather than as a set of bit-maps. The input devices may produce representations which are structured, and they are amenable to searching and filtering. Even general images have colour, background, and other characteristics which can be used for filtering without the system fully recognizing the image's contents. However, integrating stylized image filtering in a nice way will not be easy. There may be many ideas which have to be tested to arrive at some compromise between flexibility to the user and implementation difficulties. There is much danger of overdesign. That is, we can incorporate many clever filtering methods which in practice may prove useless. Experimentation is necessary.

In all our efforts regarding image and voice, we are hoping to find compact representations of them which will be adequate for searching purposes, in the same way that text signatures do not capture the meaning of the text but are adequate for filtering purposes. Can we find successful representations (signatures) for voice and images and find out how they are best used? In the companion paper, "Office Filing", many techniques relevant to this point are discussed. We feel that limited recognition combined with compact representations for searching will be adequate for the degree of content addressibility we need in an office environment. In addition, most images have associated captions and many voice segments are annotations on documents. This means that the content addressibility in terms of data and text will always be the primary aid in locating the images and voice segments.

8. References

[AhKW78] [BaBr82] [ChFa84] [EHLR80] [FeND81] [FlUl80] [Hask81] [Inst82] [Lodd83] [MoRo79] [Redd76] [Salt80] [SIKH82] [Sun82] [ThRi78] [TsCh83] [Will83] [Zloo75] [Zloo81]

4
Office Filing

S. Christodoulakis

ABSTRACT *We discuss issues related to the development of a multimedia information system for an office environment. Multimedia documents are composed of text, image, voice, and attribute information. We describe the multimedia document structure and its internal representation. Information may be extracted from digitized documents for the purpose of enhancing content addressibility and achieving better compression. Content addressibility in this environment is achieved by specifying conditions on attributes, text, images, and document presentation format. An access method based on signatures is outlined for attributes, text, and image objects. Query reformulation, multimedia document formation, and communication are also discussed in this environment.*

1. Introduction

There is a growing interest among computer science researchers about office information systems that handle complex data such as text, attributes, graphics, images, and voice ([VLDB83a, VLDB83b, VLDB84]). We will call the unit of multimedia information a *multimedia document*. Multimedia documents are composed of attribute, text, image, and voice information. Some of the functions that these systems may provide are creation and filing of multimedia information, content addressibility of multimedia documents, automatic insertion of documents in a paper form, and multimedia document transmission and reconstruction in a different site.

There are several important problems associated with the development of such systems. Some of these problems are identified next.

1.1. Query environment

Queries in this environment may be different than queries in traditional Data Base Management System (DBMS) environments. Information required in offices is diverse in nature, may be coming from diverse sources (letters, ads, publications, government statistics), and has diverse formats [McLe83]. It is desirable that the insertion process be completely automatic or at least semi-automatic. Thus it is important that a powerful query capability be used for content addressibility. Otherwise the information may not be found by the users.

Users may only have a vague idea of what they are looking for. Their understanding of what they want and how to specify it may increase as they look at other documents. Their queries may prove to be inaccurate. In that case they may want to reformulate them. Other users may want to enhance their retrieval capability by specifying characteristics of the documents that have to do with the presentation form of the documents rather than the content. Queries on the image and text parts of documents are not often handled by traditional DBMSs.

The users in this environment may vary considerably. Most of them will be occasional inexperienced users. However, the system may also be used by experts in certain fields, for filing specialized multimedia documents.

1.2. Content addressibility in various data types

Content addressibility in multimedia documents presents serious problems.

Content addressibility in documents containing attribute value and text information can be achieved by allowing the user to specify expressions involving the attribute values of the document as well as regular expressions of words appearing within the text document ([AhKW78, TsCh83]). Structures for efficient retrieval of formatted data from single and multi-file environments have been studied extensively for various retrieval request types and frequencies ([TeFr82, Wied83, Chri84a]). Content retrieval from text files has also been studied for various environments, and efficient methods have been described ([SaMc83, Rijs79, TsCh83, Lars83, ChFa84]).

Content addressibility of the image document and voice document parts is much harder. One reason is noise. Significant information (content) is hidden among irrelevant information, and has to be extracted. Second, there is no clear distinction among patterns. Image patterns may present a degree of similarity with other image patterns. In contrast, text patterns belong to categories. Given a text test pattern and a document the test pattern either exists in the document or it does not. Finally, structural relationships of objects and parts of objects in images may be very complicated. To recognize an object, recognition of the parts of the object as well as of the structural relationships may be required.

Picture recognition involves very expensive pattern recognition routines ([ToGo74, DuHa73]). In addition, picture recognition of general pictures is still difficult ([BaBr82, Pavl77]). Existing experimental and commercial systems based on high-power machines (array processors) can be successful only when much knowledge about the scene presented in a picture is available.

Speech recognition presents similar problems ([Redd75, Redd76, EHLR80, Elec83]). Currently, only speaker dependent, discrete speech, voice recognition devices with a limited vocabulary of words are widely available. The speaker has to train the voice recognition system to recognize the limited vocabulary. Typically, this involves repeating several times each word to be stored in the vocabulary. Discrete speech (words are separated by a pause) is divided into words, and each word is compared with the words in the vocabulary. If it matches closely one of the words in the vocabulary the word is "recognized". Some systems allow more than one vocabulary to be stored, but the size of each vocabulary is further reduced. The storage requirements of a vocabulary for speech recognition are very large, and the algorithms for finding approximate matches are expensive.

1.3. Information Organization and Access

In an office information system environment good naming, structuring, consistency, and quality of information is not easily maintained. Files in this environment are seldom static. The information is usually diverse, and people do not like to spend time on organization and reorganization of information. In addition, errors may be inserted along with information. Methods like automatic insertion, using an optical character recognition capability, or a speech recognition device, or typing secretaries, are error prone. The query capability and the access methods used should be able to cope with these problems. Dealing with these problems may have a significant effect on system performance. Performance may suffer because of the large volume of data, its diversity and unstructured nature, and the requirements of the query environment.

1.4. Query Interfaces

Users of office information systems may have very diverse backgrounds. The precise syntax required by many DBMSs may not be appropriate for this environment. The high-quality screens, voice input-output, and other sophisticated devices now available have the potential for providing very effective interfaces. It is desirable that the query interface facilitate the specification of user queries.

1.5. Information extraction and internal representation

In a multimedia document environment, several possible methods of document creation exist. Multimedia documents may be interactively generated in a given station and sent to another station via communication lines. In the receiving station, additional editing of the document may take place. Alternatively, documents may be in paper form. A powerful image segmentation and OCR capability may be used for extracting the information from the digitized documents. Content addressibility in images may require additional information extraction. Moreover, the information in various images may contain much redundancy. For example if an image of a document contains a simple graph, this graph may be encoded in an internal representation form, with much reduced storage requirements. Thus an internal representation may be used to reduce storage requirements as well as communication costs.

1.6. Multimedia document external representation

In a multimedia information system, capabilities should be provided for presentation of multimedia documents. A multimedia formatter should combine attributes, text, images, and graphics in an easy-to-use capability. The formatter may use existing information in the system. Thus, information extraction from documents stored in the system is needed. Moreover, since several editor formatters may exist in the organization, there is a need for a mapping from the internal representation of these formatters to the internal representation of the office filing system.

In this paper, we present an approach to multimedia office filing. We first describe the structure of multimedia documents. We discuss internal representation and presentation. We then describe the information that is extracted from documents that come in the system in a digitized form. Then we describe capabilities provided for content addressibility of multimedia documents. We describe issues related to user interface and query reformulation. Then we describe the access method used. Finally we discuss multimedia document formation.

2. Structure of Multimedia Documents

In this section, we present the logical and the physical structures of multimedia documents [Chri84b] (see also the companion paper by F. Rabitti).

The proposed logical components of a multimedia document are shown in figures 1a and 1b. Multimedia documents have a *type* associated with them, and they are composed of one or more of the following: a set of attributes, a voice part, a text part, and a set of images. In addition, multimedia documents may have an annotation part. The document type contains a minimal common information (a set of common attributes) in a large number of documents.

Attributes have an attribute name, a type, and a value. The value may be a repeating group of values.

The *text part* is composed of *text sections*. Each text section is composed of *text paragraphs*. Each text paragraph is composed of *text words*. Each text word is composed of overlapping *parts of words*. This structuring of the text document allows queries to restrict retrieval, on the basis of the proximity of words within the text document, as well as to associate annotation with each of the text components.

An *image* is composed of an *image type*, a *vector form*, a *raster form*, a *statistical part*, and a *text part*.

The image type can be:

graph   if it contains at least one graph
pie chart   if it contains at least one pie chart
histogram   if it contains at least one histogram
table   if it contains at least one table
statistical any of the previous
picture   anything else

The vector form represents the image as a set of *image objects*. Image objects may be *regions*, *polylines*, or *text*. They are represented as a set of *ordered points* and a set of *parameter values*. Points are pairs of

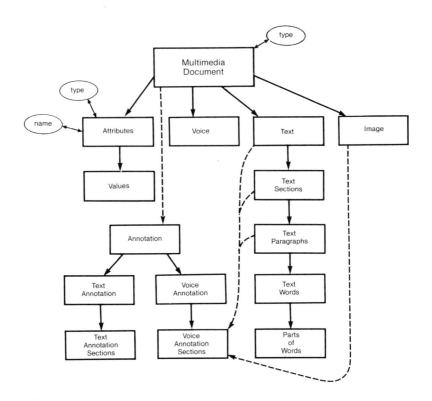

Figure 1a: Multimedia document structure

values indicating the position of a point within an image. Points may be connected to form lines, polygons, polylines, etc. The parameter values indicate important characteristics of regions, polylines , or text, and can be used for content addressibility. Image objects may be *hierarchically structured.* Regions may contain other regions, polylines, or text. Hierarchical relationships can also be used for content addressibility. Image objects are described in more detail in the section on information extraction.

The object caption is composed of object *caption words.* Object caption words are of the type text, and are composed of parts of words.

The raster form represents the image as an ordered set of pixels in two dimensions. The raster form of an image may contain overlapping *raster objects,* which are sets of adjacent pixels. Each raster object corresponds to a distinct vector object of the same picture, which is a closed polygon. The implication is that the set of pixels composing the

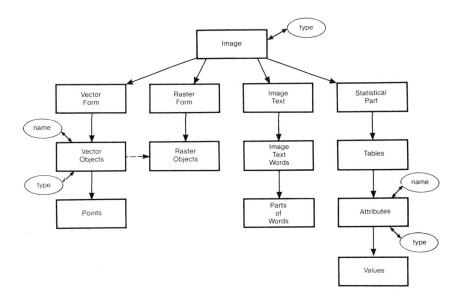

Figure 1b: Multimedia document structure (image part)

raster object is defined by the boundaries of the vector object when it is superimposed on the raster form of the image.

The statistical part of the image is composed of a set of *tables*. Each table has a set of *attributes*. Attributes have a *name*, a *type*, and a set of *values*. Tables within an image are independent of each other. We do not allow joins among tables. Tables are used internally to store the statistical information contained in images of the type graph, pie chart, histogram, or table.

The *image text part* is composed of *image text words*. Image text words are composed of *parts of words*. The image text part is text-related to a given image. The text part is formed by the following:

- The image caption of a given image,
- Text paragraphs related to the image,
- Text annotation,
- Object caption words of objects within the image,
- Attribute names of attributes in the statistical part of the image,
- Attribute values of attributes of the type text in the statistical part of the image.

The voice document is composed of *voice words*.

Annotation is composed of *text annotation* and *voice annotation*. Text annotation is composed of *text annotation sections* and voice annotation is composed of *voice annotation sections*.

Annotation may be associated with a text document, text section, text paragraph, text word, and an image. Annotation is a further informal explanation about the contents of a document, paragraph, word, or image.

3. Internal Representation and Presentation Form of Multimedia Documents

The presentation form of the constituents of a document may be different from the internal representation of the document, to allow for better secondary storage and communication bandwidth utilization. A typical typed page of text, if stored in an ASCII form, may require up to four kilobytes of memory, while if stored as a compressed bit-string, it may require in the order of sixty kilobytes of memory. Thus it is important that documents use a compact *internal representation*. On the other hand, we would like to maintain the *presentation form* of the documents so that they are always shown to the users the same way. The *document descriptor* provides the mapping of the internal representation to presentation. The storage overhead required for the descriptor is small.

The internal representation of an image does not need both an object form and a raster form. It may have only one of the two. An example of an image in which both forms exist in the internal representation is a photograph where objects have been identified and stored in the object form, for enhancing content retrieval. An example of an image having only a raster internal representation is an uninterpreted photograph. An image having only an object form as internal representation can be an engineering design. At the presentation level, however, the object form may be used to display the design in a raster display.

The internal representation of the object form of an image is a collection of objects. With each object, it is stored information related to its type (polygon, circle, etc.), its name, name display specifications (font, size, position of display), shading information, and the coordinates of a set of points. Other information specific to the object type, which enables the reconstruction of the set of points which compose an object, is also stored.

The internal representation of statistical type images (graphs, pie charts, histograms, tables) is a collection of tables. This information is not displayed and , in fact, a duplication of information. The information about the objects composing the presentation of these images in a specific device is also maintained. The duplication is not very large, and the approach facilitates both answering queries on the image contents and presenting the image in a different form; or in the same form but with different parameters, e.g., a different coordinate system. In addition, it can be used to display the contents of the image in devices which do not have graphics or bit-map display capability.

The presentation form of a multimedia document in an output device will be called a *physical document*. With a physical document we associate some default information (such as font, size, line spacing, etc.), which is used for displaying the document in an output device.

The structure of a physical document is shown in figure 2. A physical document is divided into *physical pages*. Each physical page is composed of *rectangles*. A rectangle can be a *text rectangle* or an *image rectangle*. Rectangles are identified by their *location* within a physical page and their *size*.

Image rectangles correspond one-on-one to images of a multimedia document.

Text rectangles may contain information that is used for displaying documents in an output device (alternative font, alternative size,etc.). Since sequences of words may be displayed in a different way, we also use *word sequence rectangles*, which are contained within text rectangles.

Finally, the voice document and annotation document parts of a multimedia document are not displayed in the physical document. However, the voice part of the document, voice annotation sections, and text annotation sections are mapped one-on-one to image rectangles and paragraph rectangles of the physical document. An *indication* of their existence is a special symbol associated with the relevant rectangle, which may be optionally displayed in the output device. The indication symbol can denote *voice indication*, *voice annotation section indication*, or *text annotation section indication*.

A *descriptor* is associated with each created multimedia document. The descriptor indicates the parts of the document, the internal form for each part, and its mapping to a physical document. We have implemented a descriptor that makes the mapping from the internal representation to a physical document, as described before [CVLL84].

Compression information may also be encoded in the document descriptor. The compression method to be used in such an environment depends also on the system workload and the devices used. In addition, since there may be a variety of techniques that can be used [GoWi77], the particular method used and its parameters may be encoded within the descriptor. This may be more important for the

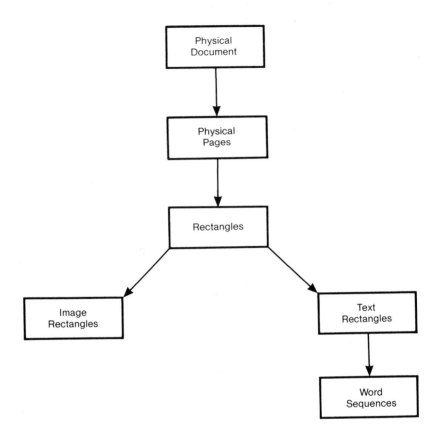

Figure 2: Physical document structure

image part than for the text or attribute parts of multimedia documents, due to the large number of bits in images. The simplest case is the encoding of an image as a set of objects (and regions of uniform shade). The image is expanded to a complete bit-map at presentation time. A variety of other encoding techniques may also be considered to achieve a good compression ratio.

4. Information Extraction

The purpose of information extraction is twofold: to achieve better storage utilization and to enhance content addressibility. Some multimedia documents will come to the system in bit-map form. Algorithms to separate documents in bit-map form into text sections and image sections are presented in [WoCW82], and the experimental results are satisfactory. Moreover, automatic recognition of text can be successful for a variety of fonts. Thus the above techniques can be applied to documents to extract the document parts and the information that is necessary for reconstructing them. This information will be stored in the document descriptor. For graphics information coming in the form of a bit-map further information may be extracted to achieve more compact internal representation.

We will treat bit-maps and graphics in a similar manner. Information is extracted from the bit-maps at document insertion time, using an information extraction subsystem, and is stored with the document. Thus, pattern recognition takes place once per document and not for every query. This is essential for a large repository of information. General purpose algorithms are applied to the bit-map in order to extract information about the dominant *regions* of the bit-map. Region expansion techniques provide such algorithms. The histogram of the bit-map of an incoming picture is examined to evaluate the dominant bit-map levels, on the basis of the peaks and valleys of the histogram. This information is used to establish thresholding values that will give an original segmentation of the picture into regions [BaBr82]. Split and merge techniques can then be applied to decide the final set of regions [HoPa74]. The technique is most successful in defining dominant regions, not details. Further segmentation of the picture will probably require knowledge on the content of the picture, and cannot be done easily with general purpose techniques. Moreover, it may not be as profitable (or desirable) for our environment.

Each region in a picture is defined by its surrounding boundary. We recognize *special types of regions* that are often encountered in office environments. Such regions are *square* regions, *parallelogram* regions, *circle* regions, and *ellipsoidal* regions, depending on the shape of the surrounding boundary. There are two reasons for recognizing these special types of regions. The first is better compression, as in the case of the circle, where only its centre and radius have to be stored. The second reason is faster content addressibility, since not all regions have to be examined to see if they satisfy special properties. In the case of a graphics editor being used to create images, the information about special types of regions can be very easily extracted without the need for pattern recognition. In the case of images containing bit-maps, recognition of special types of regions is necessary.

We also recognize *user defined regions*. These regions are defined by users and stored in a *defined image dictionary*. For each of these regions, a special *code name* and *anchor point* are defined in the dictionary. These user-defined regions from the graphics editor can be used to place a copy of the region in question within an image using the anchor point (after adjusting the size of the region). The user can insert new user defined regions into the dictionary at any point in time. The search of the dictionary can be done by name (text words attached to the definition of the region) or by browsing. Browsing is useful when the user does not remember the name, or when the differences between defined regions are very small (qualitative). In the latter case, content addressibility in images becomes more important, because the user cannot use appropriate words to define the properties of the image that he is looking for. The search for the images that contain a user-defined region can be done by the code name of the region for images created within the system. Information describing the region (parameters) is also extracted and stored with the definition of the region. The purpose is to facilitate the search for images that have not been created with the local graphics editor.

We associate *region parameters* with each region. In the case of bit-maps, parameter values for these parameters are extracted after the segmentation of the bit-map into regions. The purpose of the parameter values is to enhance content addressibility. The user can specify certain images, using the defined-image dictionary, or extracting a region from an image that he has seen while browsing through images of the system, or by drawing the image that he wants (or a very loose approximation of it) in his screen. The system will extract parameters describing the specified image (or it will retrieve these parameters from the defined-image dictionary). The user can specify the values of additional parameters about the region by using a menu. The system will try to match the parameters of the defined region with the parameters of the images in the system.

Some region parameters are described below.

1. *Elongation Descriptor*

The elongation descriptor describes the axis of maximum length of the object, its orientation, size, and position within the image, as well as the maximum distance of a point in the perimeter of the region from this axis (width). When there are two or more candidates of approximately the same length for an elongation axis, the one that separates the object most symmetrically is chosen for reasons of robustness. The elongation parameters are useful when the user cannot recall precisely the description of the object. They also provide better selectivity in case the user does not want to allow rotation, translation, or scaling of the object specified in his query.

2. *Perimeter Descriptor*

The perimeter descriptor describes the perimeter of a region in an approximate way. This description is independent of rotation, translation, and scaling of the object. We assume that the perimeter of the region is first approximated to retain global characteristics and avoid noise. Polygonal approximations can be used for this purpose [Pavl77]. Then a set of parameter values which describe the perimeter can be extracted. This set of parameter values can be used to achieve good selectivity in the retrieval of qualifying images, provided the user has adequately drawn the shape of the object. The user can also use the defined-image dictionary, or the parameters of a region from another retrieved image. The nature of these parameters and their use are described in the section on the access method.

3. *Texture Code*

This code represents one of the texture patterns that are stored in a library of textures known to the system. The graphics editor uses this library to generate images in which certain regions are filled with a particular texture. Texture codes are used for fast content addressibility and for compression.

4. *Shade and Colour Descriptor*

If there is a unique shade or colour within a region (e.g., when the image has been created with an image editor), the *shade code* and *colour code* are stored within the shade and colour descriptor. For images containing bit-maps, where every pixel may potentially have a different level of intensity or colour, shade and colour codes do not make sense. However, there are regions with approximately uniform shade or colour. For example, sky in an outdoor picture or the background of an artist's drawing. This type of picture may appear frequently in advertisements or expository material. There may also be a clearly dominant but non-uniform shade or colour (for example sea with white waves). Thus, within the shade and colour descriptor we store information about the *dominant shade range* and *dominant colour range* (and the percentage of pixels involved).

In addition to regions within an image, we may have *polylines* and *image text.* Polylines are collections of connected line segments. *User-defined polylines* are named polylines stored in the defined-image dictionary for reasons of compression and content addressibility, as was the case with user-defined regions. Such polylines may represent, for example, resistors, capacitors, or more complicated circuits. Polylines and text may be inserted in images by using the image editor. When images composed of polylines and text are created outside the system, and inserted in the system in the form of bit-maps, extraction of the text and polyline information may be simple. A *polyline descriptor* can be defined in the same manner as the region descriptor, to abstract the global characteristics of the polyline and allow retrieval based on the similarity of two polylines.

Several regions, polylines, and text may be within an image. In addition, regions, polylines, and text may be *hierarchically structured.* Regions may contain other regions or polylines or text. The hierarchical structure may be used in user queries to restrict the number of qualifying images.

5. Content Addressibility

In our approach, multimedia documents are retrieved by specifying document content information instead of a unique document identifier. The user will have some idea of the content of documents that he wants to see (or not see), and will specify this information in his query. The system will try to return all relevant documents to him.

The user may specify a document type. He can then specify conditions on attribute values of the attributes for this document type. Conditions on the text part of multimedia documents involve Boolean conditions of text words or parts of words.

We would like to avoid the general pattern recognition problem associated with images in our system, and still provide as much content addressibility as possible. In some cases converting image recognition problems to attribute and text recognition problems provides us with a powerful alternative. Image content addressibility can be achieved by specifying conditions on the image text part and the image statistical part, as well as similarity conditions on image objects. Similarity conditions are matched with the parameters of the image objects. These parameters have been extracted and stored at document insertion time. Thus, pattern recognition does not take place at query time (with the possible exception of the extraction of information from a picture drawn by the user).

Retrieving documents based on conditions on an image's text part is different than specifying conditions on the text part of the document [CVLL84]. The former specifies a document that has an image related to the condition specified. The latter specifies a document related to the condition specified.

An image may contain a number of statistical objects (graphs, pie charts, histograms, tables). Each one of these has an internal representation in the form of a table. The user can focus his attention on only one of the statistical objects at a time [CVLL84]. We do not allow relationships among tables. Conditions on tables may be very selective, so that the size of the response is limited. The presentation of a document allows more than one statistical object (graphs, tables, etc.) to appear in the same image.

Examples of possible queries on statistical images and the way in which they can be formulated follow:

1.   Give me any documents with images that have to do with IBM

.IBM exists in the text part of the image

2.   Give me any documents that have statistics on IBM

.image type statistical
.IBM in the text part

3. Give me any documents that have a graph related to IBM

.image type graph
.IBM on text part

4. Give me any documents with statistical figures relating IBM sales and year

.image type statistical
.IBM sales and year are attribute names
(the user may specify partial match on the
attribute names if he is not sure about the
exact name of the attribute)

5. Give me all documents that have graphs in which all IBM sales are greater than CDC sales

.image type graph
.attribute values of IBM sales greater than
attribute values of CDC sales

For images that are not of a statistical type and do not contain image text, the user is still able to query directly on the image objects. The user specifies his queries on images with the help of the graphics editor, the special type images dictionary, the defined-images dictionary, the texture dictionary, and the shade and colour dictionary.

The specification of the query can be done interactively by using the image editor to draw objects and their structural relationships. Alternatively, the user may extract and further edit images that will be used as filters. The extraction may be from one of the dictionaries as well as from a retrieved image during browsing.

The user can specify a texture directly, by using the texture dictionary. He can use the image editor and the menu to specify a basic repetition pattern and the way in which this pattern is repeated. He can also specify a shade or colour for a region, or a range of shades and colours and the percentage of pixels of the region that should be within this range.

The user may also want to allow flexibility about the objects that he draws. He may indicate that rotation, translation, scaling, and mirror reversal is allowed. He may also indicate uncertainty about the exact shape of certain corners or the relative length of an edge. Finally, he may want to indicate the level of confidence in his specification. If the user is not very confident about the shape of the object, only general measures are examined for matching.

The system tries to match the user description of the object with the descriptions of the stored objects. A similarity measure is computed, and images with similar objects are returned to the user. The user may redefine the value of the similarity measure if he wishes. The system also indicates to the user which object was qualifying from a given image, so that the user is able to see a possible error or omission in the specification of his query. If one or the other occurs, he may want to further edit the image of his query or he may want to redefine the image.

Region expansion techniques can be used to find the dominant objects of an image. Structural relationships of objects are hierarchical, so detection of relationships is easy. In the case of a more specialized environment for a particular application, we can use application-related techniques.

1.   The general purpose region extraction techniques can be substituted for or complemented by environment specific or semi-automatic region extraction techniques. The system will allow the user to specify which algorithms are applied. The algorithms will return to the system the points of boundary of each region in the image. The system will then proceed to extract the parameters for each region.

2.   More application-specific information can be extracted and stored with the image. The system still uses the general purpose routines to access a superset of qualifying images. It then performs certain procedures (from a set of user-defined procedures) on the retrieved images, using the additional application-oriented parameter values stored with the image, in order to further restrict the size of the response to the query. A set of user-defined procedures is known to the system, and the user can specify one or more by name. The results of applying these procedures on the stored images are compared with the results of applying the same procedures on the query images.

3.   Both the extraction method and the internal representation of the system can be replaced by user defined methods. The system only provides general support to the user: user interface support, content addressibility on the text and attribute parts of the multimedia documents, and directory management.

In summary, the user is able to specify the following for content addressibility:

1. Conjunctions of attribute values and attribute ranges.

2. Conjunctions of disjunctions of words or parts of words appearing within the text document, text section or text paragraph.

3. Existence of voice.

4. Existence of images.

5. Approximate location of an image.

6. Conjunctions of words or parts of words (related to the image) appearing within the text.

7. For statistical images (piecharts, graphs tables etc.), existence of attributes, attribute values, relationships of attribute values.

8. Similarity relationships of image objects for non-statistical images.

9. Conjunctions of the above.

6. Query Reformulation

The user interface should provide a browsing-through-qualifying-documents capability for the user. Miniatures of qualifying documents can be displayed on the screen in a way that simulates sequential scan through qualifying documents. The user can interrupt the sequential scan and look more closely at particular qualifying documents (see the companion paper, "A Multimedia Office Filing System" [TCEF83, CVLL84]).

In a multimedia information system environment, a user may not exactly describe the information that he wants. For example, in text retrieval synonyms, words with similar meaning, are allowed for content addressibility. This is not typical of a Data Base environment, where the information is well-structured and named, and attributes take values from a fixed set of attribute values.

Dynamic query reformulation in image documents is very important. The information extraction process may fail to name all the existing objects within an image. There may be several reasons for this:

1. The extraction algorithms did not identify the object.

2. In the case of semi-automatic extraction, the person extracting the information was too impatient to be careful.

3. Certain objects may not be very clear within a given picture. This will affect both manual and automatic extraction of information.

4. Certain objects were not known or considered important at the time that the images were inserted in the multimedia document repository.

It is possible that the user will feel the need for query reformulation at some point, as he browses through the documents. Something in these documents may prompt him to better specify his query. He may be receiving too many documents back. The query reformulation may restrict the number of qualifying documents; also, it may expand the query with a disjunctive term, or it may completely change the query. We allow options for query expansion, using an environment dependent thesaurus and query modification (more restrictions). The search can continue forwards or backwards, or can restart without displaying the documents seen so far.

For images, the query reformulation capability should allow the user to extract a part of an image and use it for expanding his filter. This will be useful when a user, as he browses through documents, sees an object that he wants. It will be easier for him to extract this information from the image itself rather than redraw the image. It will also likely result in a more accurate specification of the query.

A user may not be able to draw or specify his image objects very well. Therefore, he starts by using text words to select documents that possibly contain an image similar to the one he wants to use in his filter. When he finds such a document, he extracts the information that he wants and uses it as a new filter.

Thesaurus mechanisms have been used traditionally in information retrieval for replacing one word in a query with its synonyms. An expansion of the thesaurus idea would be to use thesaurus mechanisms that associate words with their pictorial representation in the defined image dictionary.

7. Access Method

Multimedia documents coming into a station are stored in general files. An access method based on *signatures* is used to achieve fast response time to user queries. A signature of the multimedia document is much smaller than the multimedia document itself, and restricts the attention to a small number of qualifying documents (see the companion paper, "Access Methods for Documents").

Information stored in the signature file contains signatures of text image and voice data. The text signature scheme is based on superimposed coding (again, see the companion paper, "Access Methods for Documents"). A fixed-length-block signature is created for each block of text data. Initially, all the bits of the block signature are set to zero. The signature is constructed by taking each non-trivial word in the text document, splitting it into successive overlapping triplets of letters, and hashing each triplet into a bit position within the block signature.

These bits are set to one. If the word is too short, additional bit positions are created by using a random number generator, which is initialized with a numeric encoding of the word. Thus a constant number of bits corresponds to each non-trivial word. The size of the signature and the number of bits per word can be determined in such a way that the performance of the system is optimized (see the companion paper, "Access Methods for Documents").

To see if a given word appears within a logical block of the document, the signature of the block is examined. The same transformation is performed on the word, and the bits determined by the transformation are examined. If they are all one, the word is assumed to appear in the text document. This access method retrieves supersets of the qualifying documents. Parts of words can also be specified in queries. More complicated query patterns (including conjunctions and disjunctions of words) can be examined by reference to the signature. Information related to attribute values is also abstracted by means of a signature technique. The only difference is that order-preserving transformations are used to answer inequality queries. Further evaluation shows that the approach is more appropriate for an information system environment than word signatures [TsCh83, Lars83] or indexing techniques.

Important information regarding images, such as image type and approximate location, is also inserted in the abstraction file, together with an indication of the existence of a voice section in the document.

As we mentioned before, the user may ask similarity queries on image objects. Similarity functions for image objects may be produced in a variety of ways. Similarity functions for polygons and shape numbers have been used in the past [Lee72, BaBr82]. However, these techniques are not robust in our environment. The number of polygon edges that the user draws may differ from the number of edges that the object has. Polygonal approximations do not control the number of edges of the resulting polygon. Thus, for polygons with different numbers of edges, it is difficult to define meaningful similarity measures. Shape numbers pose a similar problem: the procedure that tries to approximate the perimeter of the polygon with a given number, n, of line segments (order of the approximation) is not guaranteed to succeed. In addition, neither similarity measure is applicable for polylines. Fourier descriptors of the perimeter [GoWi77] seem more appropriate for objects that are very similar.

We propose an access method that is based on signatures (projections). Signatures for image objects share a common property with signatures for text words: the more signatures kept, the less information lost about the image object or text word. In the limiting case of an infinite number of signatures, the image object or the text word can be perfectly reconstructed.

We have used a signature-based approach in the past to identify locations of objects, for classification in a particular application environment (chest X-rays) [KCBC75]. The office environment, however, is much more general, and we need to define more general signature extraction techniques and similarity measures.

Signatures of the perimeter of a region (or polyline) can be obtained in four different axes, each of which coincides with one of the edges of the rectangle that surrounds the image. This rectangle is formed from the elongation axis and the width, and is normalized so that the elongation axis is a unit. The signature in one of the axes is formed from the histogram of the distances of the farthest points of the object's perimeter from the axis. Information about the peaks of this histogram is maintained.

The similarity measure takes into account the relative heights of the peaks of the histogram, as well as their distance, in the histogram line. The distance is important when objects have been drawn by users, because the peaks of the two objects (the one in the document and the one that the user draws) may not coincide. The similarity measure should also take into account the relative area occupied by the object, as well as the other options specified in user queries, e.g., elongation parameters and shade. We are performing experimentation to tune all this information into a meaningful measure.

The blocks of the access file are accessed sequentially. The sequentiality of access, the use of large blocking factors, and the small size of the access file result in a low cost for the access method.

8. Presentation and Communication of Multimedia Documents

Documents may be interactively created, using the bit-map display capability of a workstation. The text formatting software may provide the same basic features seen in traditional formatters [FuSS82]. Alternatively, the formatting software may be integrated with the filing capability, so that new documents are synthesized from old ones. The *page browsing interface*, the *extraction interface*, the *comparative interface*, the *voice editor*, the *graphics editor*, and the *annotation editor* are the primary tools for interactive information extraction, multimedia document formation, and interactive document annotation.

A possible method of formatting multimedia documents, using the office filing system, is the following: An office worker sits in front of his terminal, specifies a query, then browses through miniatures of qualifying documents to locate documents that seem relevant. When a miniature seems relevant, he stops the document browsing interface and uses the page browsing interface to look through the pages of the document for relevant information. If he finds relevant information, he uses the extraction interface to extract this information (text, images, etc.). Finally, when he is satisfied with the amount of information extracted, he selects the most appropriate pieces to synthesize a new report, by means of the comparative interface.

The comparative interface differs from the sequential browsing interface in that it subdivides the screen into several windows, so that different pieces of documents are displayed at the same time. Thus the user can compare the information for as long as he wants. He can select, and replace the information that is least appropriate, until he is satisfied. The comparative interface is well-suited for selecting the best images for a report. A graphics editor can be used for further editing or to change the presentation of these images (e.g., from a graph to a histogram). Finally, the formatter can be used to put together the pieces of the new document. A voice editor is used to add the voice message and an annotation editor to add the annotation (text and voice) at various places in the document. We are currently implementing a multimedia formatter, such as described above, that will be capable of extracting information from existing documents, comparing it, and using it to synthesize new documents.

The multimedia document formatter directly creates the document descriptor which makes the mapping of the internal representation to presentation. However, it may not always be desirable or possible to use this formatter to create new multimedia documents. Users often have strong preferences, and they resent having to learn a new formatter. There may also be particular applications within the organization that are best served by specialized packages (e.g., a special statistics package that automatically creates graphs in a given format). Finally, documents may be prepared on workstations that do not have a bit-map display capability.

In all of these cases, different formatters may be used. If these formatters are not known to the system, the only way that documents can be reconstructed is if a bit-map of the document is transmitted to the system, and information extraction and recognition take place. Since these functions are expensive, we allow the possibility that the system has some knowledge of other frequently used formatters. The *transformation software* is a set of routines that maps documents derived using these formatters to documents in the system, and vice versa. We are implementing a transformation software package that supports documents that have been formatted with a popular formatter like the UNIX™ -ms *troff* macro package and with the *Pic* package for graphics, which are described with the document structure presented earlier in this paper, using the transformation software. The presentation form is stored within the document descriptor, as was the case with the documents derived with the system formatter. We also provide the reverse mappings.

The interactive image editor formatter assists the user in creating images interactively, extracting information from other images already in the system. It also manually edits digitized images, extracting the information in them and possibly discarding the raster form of the image, which is expensive to store.

The image editor is also useful for specifying or reformulating queries that refer to non-statistical images. Thus the image editor becomes an important part of the management system for multimedia documents. It is useful for document formation, change of presentation form, query specification, query reformulation, information extraction for achieving content addressibility, and information compression. The image editor should be powerful enough to support these functions. In addition it should provide a pleasing interface to the user.

The general objects that may be created are circles, ellipses, polygons, arrows, points, B-splines, rectangles, and collections of line segments. These are used as primitives for creating or editing more complicated forms of images. Additional information is kept for statistical objects. Examples are location of axis, minimum and maximum values in axis, graph points, histogram heights, pie chart sectors, and table columns. The display coordinates may be automatically created from the attribute values of certain attributes in tables. The user may change these parameters while he is editing the image, in order to obtain a different presentation.

9. Concluding Remarks

In this paper we have discussed issues related to the development of a multimedia information system for an office environment. Documents in this environment are retrieved on the basis of content. The user can specify attribute value relationships as well as words or parts of words that appear in the text part of multimedia documents. Image content retrieval is achieved by allowing queries on the image text part, statistical queries on images of the statistical type, and queries on similarity and spatial relationships among image objects. Some aspects of the presentation of documents may also be specified in queries. We presented issues related to information extraction, user interface, query reformulation, access method, image creation, and multimedia document presentation and transformation. We described the internal representation and the presentation form of multimedia documents and the mapping between them.

We are implementing a multimedia information system for an office environment based on the framework described in this paper (see the companion paper, "A Multimedia Filing System", and [TCEF83, CVLL84]). This is an on-going project, with many parts under implementation or design. Our purpose is to examine in depth and experiment with many different ideas. It is possible that not all the ideas will be incorporated in the final system. However, in order to decide on a good set of options, we have to know the details of their implementation, the advantages and disadvantages of the final result, and the additional complexity that they will give to the system. In addition, we should know how well these techniques can be used in an integrated system. Finally, we will have to balance these factors with the requirements and satisfaction of the users.

10. References

[AhKW78]   [BaBr82]   [ChFa84]   [Chri84a]   [Chri84b]   [CVLL84]
[DuHa73]   [EHLR80]   [Elec83]   [FuSS82]   [GoWi77]   [HoPa74]
[KCBC75] [Lars83] [Lee72] [McLe83] [Pavl77] [Redd75] [Redd76]
[Rijs79] [SaMc83] [TCEF83] [TeFr82] [ToGo74] [TsCh83] [VLDB83a]
[VLDB83b] [VLDB84] [Wied83] [WoCW82]

Part III

Mailing

5
Etiquette Specification in Message Systems

D. Tsichritzis
S.J. Gibbs

ABSTRACT *We outline an environment in which communication roles between persons, and the associated rules, can be specified. Such an environment can serve for the specification of an etiquette of communication which is enforced by the electronic message system. The rules of communication are important in providing a management approach for an organization.*

1. Introduction

As electronic message systems become more widespread, and communication networks interconnect, a new set of problems is emerging [Brot83]. We expect these problems to become worse in the years ahead. We should, therefore, understand them and provide the necessary mechanisms for solving them.

The first problem is junk mail. It is extremely easy and quite cheap to send a message to a long list of persons. In doing this, the sender gets maximum visibility and has the feeling of not having missed anybody. Unfortunately, the majority of persons receiving the message have to "pay the overhead" of reading it. Junk mail can be reduced only if the sender can pinpoint the appropriate recipients. At the same time, the receivers should have an easy way of classifying their messages that ensures protection against certain kinds. In current systems, the receivers have to write their own sorting programs in order to isolate the important messages. The rules which they use to sort their messages are one-sided and unknown to other users.

In most systems, messages are presented in the order in which they are received. Each new message deals with something new. The recipient has to switch mental processes continuously, to bring in the appropriate context for each message. The situation may be the reason persons get upset and reply rudely. The user should be able to structure and read the messages according to subject. In addition, within each subject the previously exchanged messages should be readily available to provide the necessary context.

A related problem is that the addressing space of message systems is quite flat. There is a set of known addresses and the subsets provided by distribution lists. Organizations on the other hand are not flat. There are only certain allowed paths of communication in an organization. Electronic mail, the way it is used today, bypasses this hierarchy. Top managers get unwanted details, and lower personnel embarrass themselves by inappropriate use of electronic mail paths. The answer is to account for the roles of people in an organization, and provide message paths only along carefully laid out management lines. This implies that communication paths have well defined rules governing the messages which can pass through them.

Messages in current electronic mail systems are exchanged between mailboxes that represent individual persons. A person may have several mailboxes, but they are related to physical locations of machines and connectivity of networks, and not organized according to the kinds of messages he receives. A user may easily end up having three or more mailboxes which he has to manage continuously. If he changes his physical address or logs in on different machines, he has to write his own rerouting programs, or notify his colleagues about the new method of accessing him. All these difficulties arise because mail is exchanged and deposited according to physical and not logical properties. There is a strict dependence between the message addresses and the communication paths and eventual machines and mailboxes in which the messages are deposited. The situation will improve only if there is a clean separation between logical addressing properties and the physical characteristics of the transport system that delivers the messages.

It is the position of this paper that such problems appear because there is no way to enforce an etiquette of communication. To whom you can talk, what you can say, and in what way you can say it are governed by important rules in human communication. In electronic message systems there are no restrictions; the system transports the wrong messages to the wrong persons. There need to be ways to enforce certain formats of communication between parties. The rules of proper message protocol will not be voluntarily followed in a broad community of impersonal users. There should be ways that the system enforces certain rules of proper behaviour once everybody agrees on them.

In the following sections, we will investigate the problem of formally specifying etiquette within message systems. Our goal is to develop a specification language which can be used to describe the customs of a particular user community. The message system will be governed by these specifications and will automatically enforce the rules described therein.

2. Etiquette in Electronic Message Systems

One definition of etiquette is "an item of behaviour prescribed by rule or custom"[1]. Within many of the larger electronic message systems are guidelines that are accepted and followed by most of the user community. For example, on USENET [Hort81], members of newsgroups (special interest groups that post messages to "bulletin boards") are advised to:

-    avoid being rude or abusive
-    avoid sarcasm and facetious remarks
-    take precautions with possibly offensive jokes

These, and other such admonitions (see [Schw83] for a complete list) define what is acceptable behaviour on USENET, and so are clearly examples of etiquette.

The above rules are concerned with the style and meaning of messages appearing in the system. Without full natural language understanding, there is little the system can do to enforce these rules. It is not even certain that one would want a machine to automatically flag such things as offensive jokes and sarcastic comments; such action is a form of censorship and contrary to the idea of an electronic bulletin board as an open forum.

Rules that are more amenable to automation are those that suggest the proper actions for particular, well-defined circumstances. For example, suppose the sender of a message has incorrectly specified the message destination, and the system has not detected this error but delivered the message to an unsuspecting user. For users of the Laurel electronic message system [Brot83], the recommended procedure is:

---

[1] *Webster's Third New International Dictionary*

> When you realize a message is not for you, use the Forward command to send it back to the sender along with a polite comment that the message has reached the "wrong number"... Once you have determined that you have received a "wrong number" message, *stop reading it.*

A second example from Laurel concerns the proper "publication" (i.e., broadcast) of the responses gathered by an initial query for information made to some public or semi-public forum (a bulletin board, newsgroup, distribution list, etc).

> Messages should be considered "private" unless otherwise indicated. If your intention is to publish the responses, then by all means make that intention clear in the same message that poses the original question. If your message did not make the intention clear, and you decide you would like to publish the responses, then follow up each response, asking whether you may do so.
>
> If the intention to publish is clearly indicated in the original message, then publication of any response is fine, as long as the response does not explicitly mention that it should be considered private.

What we would like is to be able to describe such rules to the system so that it can aid users in following the proper procedures.

Our description of message system etiquette will rely on four concepts: the *messages* themselves, *roles*, *paths* between roles, and *rules*. We assume that messages consist of a *body* containing the part of the message visible to the user and a *header* containing system information. Both the header and the body consist of named *message attributes*. A *message type* is a particular structure of message attributes. Roles are the sources and destinations of messages in the system. When a person is associated with a particular role, he is said to be *playing* the role. This allows the user to examine all messages sent to the role, and to send messages originating from the role. A path is a connection between two roles. There may be many paths between roles, so a path name is necessary. Examples of paths could be a "first class" path and a "general delivery" path. The actions of the system will depend on the path over which a message is sent. Rules govern the communication between roles and therefore the behaviour of the message system. The information embodied in rules includes such things as which roles a user may play, what paths are available to a role, and what messages can go through a path.

At this point, the reader may wonder about the difference between authorization roles that persons have for security purposes, and our roles for communication purposes. In both cases roles can be structured, and in both cases they govern access to information, e.g., records and messages. Authorization roles give potential access, while communication roles provide alarms to perform access on the information. The real difference has to do with the purpose that is eventually encoded in the rules associated with roles. The purpose of authorization roles is to guard the objects carrying information (records, messages) against the agents accessing them. The purpose of communication roles is to guard the agents (persons) against unwanted objects (junk mail). A person's authorization may vastly exceed his real need for information. It is a philosophical point. Up to now we had an image of persons starving for information. We may now be in a situation where persons have to guard themselves against too much information.

Roles are not fully exploited in present message systems. For instance, in current message systems, mail addressing is via physical locations, person names, or sets of users. People, on the other hand, communicate between roles they play and not simply as persons. The use of roles, rather than the names of people, as message destinations raises a number of issues. For example, a person may feel that he has only one role (to be himself), or may want to assume many roles and behave differently for each one. The system should not force users to have a single role, but should make it easy for them to manage their roles. Also, a message should be treated in accordance with whether it comes from a person as a professor, teacher, advisor, consultant, hobbyist, athlete, etc. The fact that a particular person can play all these roles is not important. First, he does not play them all at the same time. Second, there are times that a role is generic and can be played by more than one person. Finally, some roles are played by organizational units, e.g., departments and companies, and not by persons. In addition, a person may want to be accessible only in certain roles. Being able to address him in one role does not necessarily mean one can address him in another.

Similarly, rules are used only on an informal, ad hoc basis in current message systems. For example, one user might follow a rule that says, in effect, "messages with no subject line will be ignored". However, other users are under no compulsion to follow this rule when sending mail to the user in question, and may not even be aware of the rule. As with roles, the presence of rules introduces many issues. For example, certain rules may be specified within each role as part of the role definition, and so be local to that role. A more interesting case, though, is when a rule is shared among many roles. The system may impose "meta-rules" on the sharing, such as a priority scheme among the roles or an exclusion property between the roles. Rules can also be defined for the communication between more than two roles. Finally, the most difficult problem is to enforce properties of global behaviour among many roles communicating indirectly. For instance, in a strictly managed organization there may be a rule that a role cannot bypass a lower level of management and communicate with its superiors. The problem of specifying and enforcing global rules is very difficult. A more realistic approach is to define loosely global rules. We then specify sufficient local rules to obtain the desired overall effect. This may overburden the local communications, but it is probably the simplest way to enforce global properties.

3. Role and Path Specifications

A role represents anything that can act as the destination (or source) of a message. Thus, roles generalize the notions of mailboxes, bulletin boards, newsgroups, and distribution or mailing lists found in present electronic message systems. Typically the number of roles present in a system will be larger than the number of users (users often play more than one role). Since this can be a considerable number (on the order of thousands) it is necessary to impose some structure and organization on the roles. Our approach to role organization makes use of *role types* and *role instances.*

Many roles with similar properties can be represented by a role type. For instance, all teachers, all basketball players, all singers can be role types. A type has properties which are characterized by attribute values. For example, PROFESSOR could be a role type used by university professors. For each type there is a different attribute value for name and title, which identify a role instance of the type. More formally we say that a role type consists of

$$N(A_1, \cdots, A_n)$$

with N, the role type name and $A_1, \cdots, A_n$ its attributes. A role instance is obtained by giving values for $A_1, \cdots, A_n$.

Roles are interrelated by the "precedence" or CANPLAY relationship. For instance, a professor role CANPLAY a teacher role. This means that a person associated with the system in his professor role can potentially have access to all messages addressed to his teacher role. His own rules as professor may only affect his access. One can depict this relationship in graph form by placing an arc from role r_1 to role r_2 if r_1 can assume r_2. By convention we will say that r_1 is a *higher* role than r_2.

The precedence relationship can be 1:1 between roles. For instance a dean can also have a role as a professor. While he is a dean he can also play the role of the professor and receive mail in either role. However, no dean is two professors and no two deans are the same professor (usually)!

The relationship can be 1:N, as from a professor role to a teacher role. A professor can have more teacher roles, one for each course he teaches. However, each teacher role relates to a particular professor role.

The relationship can be N:1 as from a set of athletes to a generic team player for each team. Each individual athlete role is higher than his role as a team player. However, no athlete can be a team player for more than one team.

Finally, there may be an N:M relationship between roles, as is usually the case with interest groups. Many person roles participate in each interest group which plays a role of "any person interested in a specific subject". However, each person can participate in many roles of "interested party". Notice that in the two last cases a generic common role groups a number of individual roles into one. When a message arrives, any or all of the agents associated with the role can obtain it, depending on the role's rules. In addition, when a person sends out mail from a generic role his identity can be omitted. He is one of the persons sharing the interest of the group.

The relationship CANPLAY usually establishes a directed acyclic graph (dag) of roles. The graph is directed because the relationship is not reflexive. It is acyclic because a cycle would indicate that a lower role can indirectly assume a higher role. In many cases this dag will represent a hierarchy. There are *high* roles and *low* roles in the dag. A *high role* is a role that no other role can assume. A *low role* is a role from which no other role can be assumed. It is interesting to point out the semantics of these two extreme cases. High roles usually correspond to persons as private individuals. From that role they can access any mail that is received in any other role they play. Low roles usually correspond to either *public persons*, or *generic roles*. A person publicly receives mail which can be accessed from other roles he plays. A generic role is a role shared by many individuals that gives them a way to exchange impersonal messages on a subject as a group.

One way to view a CANPLAY hierarchy is as a collection of *role trees* corresponding to the roles played by different users. Roles that are shared by many users lead to connections between the trees. Role sharing is very important between roles in different role trees. In this way we can create common interest groups among persons, or assume the responsibilities of someone else.

A link is a connection between two roles, and indicates that one role may send messages to the other. Communication links between roles on the same path of a role tree may not be needed. A superior role can always communicate freely with its inferior roles. Communication links between roles in the same hierarchy may be needed, although the roles may be able to communicate through a common ancestor. Links are represented by HASPATH, an N:M relationship between role instances. In graph form, HASPATH identifies all possible communication paths in the system. The HASPATH relationships are defined independently of the CANPLAY relationships. In the simplest case, all edges in the HASPATH graph are the same. More generally the edges are coloured, and correspond to the different transfer protocols. For example, one type of path may be used for high-priority messages, a second type of path for messages that must be acknowledged. The behaviour associated with a path type is specified in the same manner as message type and role behaviour. In general each path type will have a set of rules that describe communication over path instances. Distinguishing path types allows a richer semantics. For example, specification of paths over which messages must be acknowledged will require referring to such things as original messages, acknowledgements, failed deliveries, and waiting periods. Thus, application level concepts are introduced into the message system.

An interesting notion is the set of roles which can potentially be reached from an existing role. We can take two approaches, a formal approach and an informal approach. A role, a, can reach informally all persons (and all roles they play) which are connected directly or indirectly with it. We can obtain all these by taking the transitive closure of all the role trees connected to the tree of the particular role a, through communication paths. Any role in these trees can potentially become aware of any information sent from the role a. We call this set of roles the *informal communication scope*, because it assumes that individual persons play their roles rather loosely and transmit information freely from one role to another. This situation should not happen in a well-managed organization. We should look at a much more formal approach to role playing. For instance, we can assume that sensitive information received in a role is available only to its superior roles. Under this assumption we should take the transitive closure of roles not in terms of trees connected, but by going only upward in each tree and taking connections. We obtain in this way a set of roles called the *formal communication scope* of role a. These roles can potentially learn information coming from a. They do so through communication paths and role superiority.

Suppose a role, a, is related indirectly with a role, b, through a chain of CANPLAY and HASPATH relationships. This does not guarantee that anything role a sends through that chain will reach role b. Role b can potentially get a message from role a. If all the relationships are exercised, role b will receive the message. Here, very important sets of roles are *cut sets*. If all cut set members choose not to transmit along communication paths, the information will not reach a particular role or person. For example, in a corporate organization administrative secretaries might preview messages, either of certain message types, or sent from certain roles, or coming over certain paths. Such messages would be forwarded to the president or executive at the secretaries' discretion. Thus these secretaries could effectively block certain messages and so form a cut set.

Now let us consider the mechanics of message transfer within a system based on roles. In general, the system requires the following information:

1.   the sender role
2.   the receiver role
3.   the message type and attribute values
4.   the path type

When a user inserts a new message, he does not need to specify everything. His sender role is implicit unless he changes it. The receiver role is explicitly specified, unless the system is able to deduce the receiver from message attributes (such as the subject) [Tsic84]. Once both sender and receiver roles are known, the system determines whether transfer is possible, by examining the HASPATH relationship. The transfer is allowed to take place if there is a path (of the required type) from the sender role, or any roles inferior to it, to the receiver role. (If there is a path, but not of the type requested by the user, the system informs the user of the alternative path.)

We will now present an example that illustrates many of the above concepts.

Example 3.1 Business Roles

Suppose we have the following role types:

> *PrivatePerson*
> *PublicPerson*
> *UnionMember*
> *UnionBulletinBoard*
> *Consultant*
> *CompanyEmployee*
> *CompanyBulletinBoard*

PrivatePerson roles receive mail only from a small set of known acquaintances, while PublicPerson roles have no such restrictions. There is one instance of each of these role types for each user of the system. Instances of the UnionMember, Consultant, and CompanyEmployee role types are in a 1:1 correspondence with union members, consultants and employees. The UnionBulletinBoard role type encompasses roles shared by all union members; analogously, CompanyBulletinBoard roles are shared by company employees. Instances of a bulletin board role type can be used to organize the broadcast messages. For example, within CompanyBulletinBoard there may be instances dealing with memos from the company, personal announcements from employees, local entertainment, and so on. In general, these instances will be created and deleted as interest in the corresponding topic changes. The CANPLAY relationship is represented schematically in figure 1.

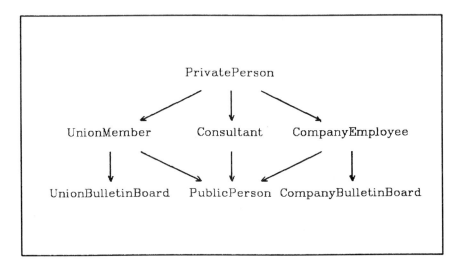

Figure 1: A CANPLAY relationship

We will use a single path type. The HASPATH relationships are:

PrivatePerson	→	PrivatePerson
PublicPerson	→	UnionMember
PublicPerson	→	Consultant
CompanyEmployee	→	CompanyEmployee
UnionMember	→	UnionBulletinBoard
CompanyEmployee	→	CompanyBulletinBoard
PublicPerson	→	PublicPerson

Here we have specified that only PrivatePerson roles can send to PrivatePerson, while UnionMember and Consultant roles will receive from PublicPerson or superior roles. The CompanyEmployee roles can only communicate between themselves, and the HASPATH relationships here would follow the corporate structure. The two BulletinBoard role types will only receive messages from their associated members. It is important to note that a relationship at the type level induces relationships at the instance level. In many cases, such as the HASPATH relationship between PublicPersons, the relationship holds for all pairs of instances, so it is not necessary to store the relationship on a per instance basis.

4. Rule Specifications

The semantics of roles, messages, and paths is expressed by rules contained within role, message, or path type specifications. Rules are intended to identify the suggested or proper course of action in a particular situation. We require that the rules be represented in a form that can be interpreted by a machine. We will restrict rules to the following somewhat artificial structure:

> rulename:
> > $<$context$>$
> > $<$action$>$

The $<$context$>$ describes a prototypical situation that precedes invocation of the rule. The information specified here includes the operations that lead up to invocation, the performers of the operations, and a description of the objects (messages, roles, paths, etc.) involved. An operation may be performed by a user (either directly or through some procedure acting on his behalf) or by the system itself. The $<$action$>$ lists operations to be performed if $<$context$>$ occurs. We are not interested in forming a general office procedure specification language, and so will consider only those operations dealing with messages. Specifically, these are:

> Play (r)
> Display (r)
> Send (m, r, r', p)
> GrantPlay (r, r')
> RevokePlay (r, r')
> GrantAccess (r, r', p)
> RevokeAccess (r, r', p)

where m is a message, r and r' are role instances, and p is a path. The Play operation is called when a user begins to play a role: it merely establishes the user as the player of the role. The Display operation is used to view the messages sent to a role. The operation of Display will depend upon the user interface desired. It would, in general, allow the user to browse through the set of messages that have been received by the role.

The Send operation introduces a message to the system. Here the parameters are the message itself, m, the source and destination roles, and the path p.

The four operations — GrantPlay, RevokePlay, GrantAccess, and RevokeAccess — are used to change the privileges of a role by modifying the CANPLAY and HASPATH relationships. GrantPlay allows a player of role r to also play role r'; RevokePlay denies this privilege. GrantAccess creates a path p, from role r to role r'. RevokeAccess removes the path. Note the similarity of these operations and analogous operations for authorization access.

Notice the similarity of role rule specification, and rule specification in an object environment (see the companion paper, "An Object-Oriented System"). A role can actually be viewed as an object in such a system.

We will now look at some examples of the rules appearing in role and path specifications.

Example 4.1 Public Person Roles

A PublicPerson role has no restrictions on who may send to the role, but can only be played by the person whose name is the same as the name of the role.

```
role type name:    PublicPerson
rules:
    WhoCanPlay:
    context      Play(r); performed by u
                 r a PublicPerson
                 u a User
    action       continue if r.Name = u.Name
                 error otherwise
```

Example 4.2 Private Person Roles

As with a public person role, there must be agreement between the name of a private person role and the name of the person playing the role. A private person role differs in that it only receives messages from an explicit set of roles (the acquaintances of the role). Needless to say, the person who plays the role specifies its acquaintances.

role type name: PrivatePerson
attributes: acquaintances
rules:
    WhoCanPlay:
    context   Play(r); performed by u
                    r a PrivatePerson
                    u a User
    action   continue if r.Name $=$ u.Name
                    error otherwise
    WhoCanChangeAccess:
    context   GrantAccess(r, r', p); performed by u
                    r' a PrivatePerson
                    u a User
    action   continue if r'.Name $=$ u.Name
                    error otherwise
    WhoCanSendTo:
    context   Send(m, r, r', p)
                    r' a PrivatePerson
    action   continue if r $\in$ r'.acquaintances
                    error otherwise

Example 4.3 Public Bulletin Board Roles

Messages sent to public bulletin board roles can be read (displayed) by any person. A public bulletin board also places no restrictions on who may send to it. The only restriction is that bulletin boards may not originate messages.

role type name: PublicBulletinBoard
rules:
    WhoCanSendTo:
    context   Send(m, r, r', p)
                    r a PublicBulletinBoard
    action   error

Example 4.4 Moderated Bulletin Board Roles

A moderated bulletin board will only receive messages from a specific role — the moderator.

role type name: ModeratedBulletinBoard
attributes: moderator
rules:

WhoCanChangeAccess:
context   GrantAccess(r, r', p); performed by r''
              r' a ModeratedBulletinBoard
              r'' a Role
action   continue if r'' = r'.moderator
              error otherwise
WhoCanBeSentToBy:
context   Send(m, r, r', p)
              r' a ModeratedBulletinBoard
action   continue if r = r'.moderator
              error otherwise
WhoCanSendTo:
context   Send(m, r, r', p)
              r a ModeratedBulletinBoard
action   error

Example 4.5 Mailing List Roles

A mailing list role can be played by any person on the mailing list. The role can only send to itself and will only receive from itself. The actual mailing list is represented by an attribute of the role.

role type name: MailingList
attributes: thelist
rules:
    WhoCanPlay:
    context   Play(r); performed by u
                  r a MailingList
                  u a User
    action   continue if u CANPLAY some r'
                  ∈ r.thelist
    WhoCanChangePlay:
    context   GrantPlay(r, r'); performed by r''
                  r' a MailingList
                  r'' a Role
    action   continue if r'' ∈ r'.thelist
                  error otherwise
    WhoCanBeSentToBy:
    context   Send(m, r, r', p)
                  r' a MailingList
    action   continue if r = r'
                  error otherwise
    WhoCanSendTo:
    context   Send(m, r, r', p)

r a MailingList
action   continue if r = r'
              error otherwise

Example 4.6 Acknowledgement Paths

As a final example we will look at a path type specification. Here the path is used for messages which must be acknowledged. However we do not wish to generate an infinite stream of responses to responses. We will use a special message type called Acknowledgement, instances of which are not, in fact, acknowledged.

path type name: AcknowledgementPath
rules:
        SendAcknowledgement:
        context   Send(m, r, r', p)
                       p an AcknowledgementPath
                       m not an Acknowledgement
        action

                       Send(m', r', r, p)
                       m' an Acknowledgement

5. Implementation Considerations

The implementation of an environment providing roles, paths, messages, and rules takes different directions, depending on the tools available in a particular system. This also depends on the degree of structure that we want to impose on roles and their communication.

Consider an environment where Data Base facilities are available, including a capability for specification of office procedures. Such environments were outlined in the papers, "Office Procedures" and "An Office Filing System". In addition, they have been implemented in many other projects, e.g., OBE [Zloo80]. We will assume the existence of a network and a set of addresses capturing the physical communication between machines and mailboxes. The addresses correspond to the electronic mail addresses as they are used in most existing systems. For example, decvax!mcvax!ariadne!dt is a USENET address. The communication path may be inherent in the specification of addresses, or it can be given by a mapping relating address names to paths [Tsic84].

Suppose we want to have a very strict structure of roles and their communication. In that case, we will assume that all roles correspond to role types, e.g., merchants, professors, companies, etc. Each role type is an entity type and can be represented by a relation in the Data Base system. Each CANPLAY relationship between a pair of role types will be represented by a Data Base relationship, and will be provided either as a separate relation, or as a join of appropriate attributes of the relations representing types. For instance, according to the example in section 3, the role *PrivatePerson* will be represented by a relation PERSON (ID, NAME, ...), the role *Company employee* will be represented by EMPLOYEE (PERSONNEL NO, CO, NAME, ...). Their CANPLAY relationship is either a separate relation, PERSON-CAN-PLAY-EMPLOYEE or it is a join according to a common attribute, e.g., PERSON.ID. The HASPATH relationship can be represented in the same way. In a strict structuring approach, each pair of role types will have their HASPATH relationship represented by a different relation. The rules associated with role types and their paths are encoded in procedures which are associated with relation types. They are automatically invoked by certain relational operations, e.g., "insert a message" will invoke the procedure which obtains the address of the appropriate role name and the path to that address.

We assume the existence of mapping relations, mapping roles to addresses, and mechanisms that map addresses to communication paths. All of these mechanisms are transparent to the user, who sees only roles, messages, logical paths and rules. It should be noted that some of the role and path procedures are also invoked automatically by the arrival of messages and not by a user operation. For that reason we need triggers as in OBE, or any facility for office procedures that can be automatically invoked.

A second approach using the same implementation tools, will not distinguish very much between role types. We will have very few role types, perhaps just one, and the different roles will be denoted by attributes of the particular role type. The CANPLAY and HASPATH relationships can be encoded in one relationship each. All the rules regarding communication etiquette are captured by the procedures associated with the single role relation and the relations representing CANPLAY and HASPATH relationships. In such an approach we have to have fewer communication rules, or the procedures associated with the relations will become very involved. To retain flexibility, we may need to allow persons or groups of persons to associate rules with their own hierarchy of role instances. In such an environment the roles and their communication rules are more freely specified, but the users have to encode their own rules.

The two approaches described so far correspond to the tradeoff present in the design of Data Base applications. We may separate the information space into many entity types, in which case names of entities imply properties. In our environment, the communication rules are predefined and automatically associated with role type names and path names. Alternatively, we may have very few generic entities, with the interpretation of their properties explicitly stated. In our environment, there is no role separation in types, and the communication rules are explicitly stated.

Consider an environment in which an object-oriented system is available such as Smalltalk-80, or the one that appears in the paper, "An Object Oriented System", in this book. The roles can correspond to objects and the role types to object classes. The CANPLAY relationships are represented by the class-superclass hierarchy. The HASPATH relationships are represented by the acquaintances of the object class. In this case the rules are directly associated with the roles as objects. For example, the rules of a role type will be associated as rules of the corresponding object class. There is no need to associate automatic procedures capturing the rules, since they can be captured by the objects themselves.

As in our previous discussion, we may choose to separate roles into different object classes, or we may choose to have "one" object class. It depends on whether or not we want to prepackage properties and rules, and associate them with role names. The message-passing capability between objects provides the notification of the arrival of a mail message in a particular role. The mail message itself can also be considered an object.

Such an environment gives us a very interesting choice. If we view mail messages as objects, they may or may not have their own rules. In the first case, messages are completely passive, are manipulated directly by the roles, and obey the rules associated with the roles. In the second case, messages may inherit rules from the originating roles. From then on they are objects obeying their own rules. When they arrive, for example, at a receiver role they do not obey the rules of the role as an object. Instead, they obey their own rules. The paper, "Intelligent Message Systems", by J. Hogg, outlines a system outlined in which mail messages are active objects.

Our discussion points out that the implementation of a role model depends on the underlying system capabilities. We can take a procedural, or an object-oriented approach. Independently, we can insist on a strict separation of role types and path types; or we may view roles and their communication paths as generic and encode the differences in complicated rules. It is difficult to argue the advantages and disadvantages of each approach, since it depends very much on the environment we want to create. In addition, there are no strict boundaries, but a continuum between the extreme cases. Future message systems should give the choice to the application developer. In the same way that we do Data Base design, we should be able to do role and communication path design for a particular application.

6. Concluding Remarks

The use of roles outlined in this paper should help deal with emerging problems like junk mail. A user can broadcast a message to interested roles and not to groups of persons. In addition, a person can give priority to his important roles and their associated messages, and overlook his non-exclusive roles that receive much unsolicited mail.

It is interesting to note that roles can be set up without reference to persons. A role can exist without an existing person, but only through its connection to a hypothetical person. In addition, a role can be set up very low in an organization, belonging to somebody having a position high in an organization. In this way, an executive vice-president can also be a fictitious office worker, in order to check how well his instructions filter from middle management down to the rank and file. He can communicate freely in that role with other workers, and exchange opinions about the company.

We should comment briefly on directories and files. At first glance, structuring roles resembles structuring names of files in directories, or structuring names of mailboxes. However, the intent and semantics are different. We structure role names for communication purposes, not for filing purposes. The way one files things has to do with the way one wants to structure his information. The way one structures roles is the way one wants to be perceived by others for communication purposes. The former is inward-looking and the latter outward-looking, in an organization.

Finally, in none of our discussion did we emphasize geographic separation and physical transport of messages. In terms of implementation it should be. obvious that the specifications outlined will be partitioned into many sites, and copies should be kept consistent. We chose to ignore for the time being the physical distribution problems of communication, and concentrate instead on the logical properties.

It should be pointed out, however, that the information relating to roles, paths, and their rules does not change very fast. Hence, we can distribute the data base containing this information more easily than a transaction-oriented data base. The problem of transporting mail messages geographically is not novel. Communication networks and name servers are solving many of the problems of physical communication and routing.

The most important aspect of rules of etiquette is the ability to provide a management approach. Modern management deals more with issues of communication than with issues of control. It is not important whom you can order around, but to whom you can talk and under what constraints. For example, the power of a vice-president stems from the fact that he can talk to other vice-presidents, the president, and certain other powerful persons in an organization. If we accept that position, specifying the rules of etiquette and role structure in an organization is very important. It defines the management structure of the organization. Strictly managed organizations will have a very strict, hierarchical role structuring. At the same time, they may allow informal communication connections and groups to move information up, down and sideways in the organization. Free role structuring is very important for communication between persons belonging to different organizations. It hides many of their important roles, and they present only a substructure of roles to the world. It is interesting to ponder the difficulties that might arise when different role structures have to be merged. It may take some time for persons in one structure to become familiar with the roles of persons in another. The situation is illustrated in the merging of companies: people have to learn to get along with each other.

We feel that organizations are essentially run by transmitting information along their role structure. They have established rules of behaviour within their role structure. A management structure is defined indirectly by the communication structure. It is rather interesting that organizations that pay a great deal of attention to management introduce electronic mail, which can change their methods of management so dramatically, without any study of its effect. Finally, it is easy to explain why current electronic mail systems do not impose rules or etiquette. They have been designed with an emphasis on free exchange of ideas, mainly between researchers who abhor any notion of control. Etiquette, however, does not imply control, but simply good manners.

7. References

[Brot83] [Hort81] [Schw83] [Tsic84] [Zloo80]

6
Intelligent Message Systems

John Hogg

ABSTRACT *An* intelligent message *is an active object that interacts with its recipients and, on the basis of the responses that it collects, decides whether to route itself to further recipients or terminate. A prototype system has been developed in a single-machine environment. When intelligent messages are implemented in a distributed environment using multiple copies, problems arise in coordinating the actions of these copies and in communicating between them. Solutions to these problems are proposed.*

1. Introduction

An office has been defined as "a mechanism that maintains the state of the business" [ElNu80]. An essential component of this state maintenance is communication: communication between people, communication between systems, and communication between people and systems. Traditionally, inter-personal communication has relied on a wide variety of media: personal contact, the telephone, memos and papers. In the comparatively new field of office automation, several new media have appeared, such as electronic mail and voice messaging.

Personal contact and the telephone are "real-time" or "two-way" methods of communication, while the other media listed allow communication from the initiator to the recipient only; any reply must be a separate message. The distinction is important. Messages are sent for two reasons: to deliver information and to request it. Those in the first category are complete in themselves. Messages which collect information, however, must be followed up by an explicit action on the part of the recipient. This is not difficult to obtain in face-to-face or voice communication, but other message types are more likely to be ignored or filed away for "future action". The more complicated the response required, the more likely this is to happen. As an illustration, the University of Toronto database group circulates lists of technical report abstracts under a cover sheet instructing recipients to mark those reports that they wish to acquire, and to pass the list on to any colleague who has not yet checked his or her name off. These lists take weeks to make the rounds of the department!

Like all message systems in use today, the database abstract lists are *passive* messages. They are strictly data and perform no actions themselves. This is also true of current electronic mail (email) systems, the only difference being that in the latter case delivery can be faster, cheaper, and more widespread. However, with the increasing interest in object-based systems, it is not difficult to envisage an *active* message, which would collect responses from recipients and then forward itself to other recipients as required. The basic idea is simple yet potentially very exciting, and is the subject of this paper.

Section 2 of this paper explains the central concepts of an intelligent mail (*imail*) system. Section 3 describes a prototype system that was constructed to demonstrate the feasibility of these concepts and test out ideas. Section 4 explains the problems that are encountered when the imail concept is extended to large networks, and builds a framework for solving these problems. Finally, Section 5 describes ongoing and future work in the area of intelligent messages.

1.1. Previous Work

The concept of an intelligent message, or object-based, communication system is not a new one. Vittal [Vitt81] has described a system called R2D2 (for Research-to-Development-Tool for Message Processing) in which messages are capable of performing certain actions on their own. In particular, messages can tailor their interactions with a user, depending upon the responses they receive from that user. Conceptually, Vittal considers an active message to be a single self-modifying entity. He does not discuss the problems and power associated with multiple copies or dynamic routing.

Byrd, Smith and deJong [BSdJ82] describe an actor-based programming system within the context of SBA [Zloo80]. Using a modified version of PL/I, actors can be programmed to perform tasks such as calendar scheduling. These actors interact with SBA boxes and are not primarily intended to increase the power of person-to-person communication.

2. Imessage Concepts and Terms

An imessage is basically a special type of object [Robs81]. This means that we can propose imessage systems that have all of the capabilities of object-based systems. While this would mean that the power of an imessage is tremendous, it would also make our problem area so large that useful statements would be difficult to make. We have therefore adopted a more restricted view of what an imessage is and what it can do.

An imessage is a *script*, made up of a list of *questions*. It is *run* in turn by various *recipients*. The running of a script by a single recipient is called an *interaction*. In the example given above, of an imessage for inquiring about the procurement of technical reports, an interaction might involve a list of questions of the form, "Do you wish a copy of this report?", followed by the question, "Can you suggest any additions to the recipient list?" After each interaction the imessage may be *shipped* to additional recipients. The entire lifespan of the imessage is called its *execution* and may involve a number of interactions and moves before the imessage is *terminated*. At termination, the imessage returns to its *sender* with the information that it has collected.

An interaction is composed of a series of questions. Each question begins with the printing of a *query* on the user's terminal after which a *response* from the user is collected. This is followed by a list of *commands* from a small but fairly powerful language. The commands may process responses, cause questions to be skipped over, repeated or slightly altered, or cause the imessage to be shipped to additional recipients or terminated. This format of query-response-processing may seem overly restrictive. Before building our prototype system we built a tiny (less that 100 lines of C Shell [Joy80]) proto-prototype system in which imessages were arbitrary shell scripts. We found, however, that this additional power was not necessary. The question interface was sufficient for almost all useful imessages.

It would clearly be possible, and potentially useful, to allow interactions with not just users but also their databases, and with other imessages. The concept of such a general-purpose object is a very exciting one with a bewildering number of possibilities and ramifications. Some of these are discussed in the companion paper by D. Tsichritzis, "Objectworld". In this paper, however, we only consider objects that interact with human users.

Imessages are intelligent in that their actions may vary according to their *state*, or memory. This memory is initially set by the sender, and may thereafter be altered according to the responses received from recipients. Both phases of an imessage's execution, interaction and shipping, may depend upon the state. During an interaction, questions may be skipped or repeated, depending upon answers given by the current or an earlier recipient, and, at the end, the message may be forwarded to various users that the recipient directly or indirectly suggested.

This dynamic routing [Maze83, Tsic84] is in contrast to the static routing associated with conventional email systems. Most systems provide for static, single-hop routing only, in which the sender specifies one or more recipients to whom the message should be transmitted. The recipients may in turn send further messages to other users, but this is a separate action on their part; the original message covers only the one hop. The next stage up from this is multi-hop static routing, where the path that a message will take is predefined by its initial sender. When the path is defined by the message itself as it visits its recipients, as in imail, the routing is dynamic.

This routing may be in parallel (as in our example) or in series, with new *destinations* being added to the end of the list. More complicated combinations of these two routings are of course possible in theory, but were not considered worth investigating.

Up to this point we have been treating an imessage as a single entity. In a centralized environment, this is a simple and feasible approach, and was the one used in our single-machine prototype system. Clearly, however, if an imessage is to run on a loosely-coupled network, it will require multiple *copies* to achieve reasonable concurrency in parallel interactions. These copies must work together and can communicate through the use of *meta-messages* (*MMs*). It should be stressed that these communicating copies together make up one imessage. Different imessages do *not* interact with each other.

A side effect of the dynamic nature of imessages is that we must rethink our concepts of ownership. Conventional email belongs to its sender as it is being composed, the system it is on while it is in transit, and its recipient after it has arrived at its destination. Once sent, a message cannot be recalled or redirected. (This has on numerous occasions been cause for grief after sober second thought.) This ownership policy is inappropriate to imail. After an interaction, the imessage must forward itself to further recipients; it cannot remain in the possession of the previous recipient. More strikingly, an imessage which has completed its task (e.g., the finding of a volunteer for a task) should terminate and return to its sender. Even if other recipients have noted the presence of the imessage in their mailboxes, it is not theirs; although they do not know it, they do not want to see its contents. Therefore, it must be pulled out "from underneath them". This difference is in itself neither good nor bad.

At each interaction, zero or more recipients are added to the imessage's list of destinations. Instead of thinking of these as being additional destinations for a particular copy, it is convenient to think of a number of new copies being created, each with a single destination. This gives us a "family tree" of copies, with each interaction resulting in the spawning of a (possibly empty) set of children. The advantage of this is that a copy has a very limited lifespan and set of tasks to perform.

3. An Imail Prototype System

In order to assure ourselves that the concept of imail was feasible and useful, we constructed a prototype system [HMGT83, HoGa84]. Since we were working in a UNIX^{TM} environment we made the interface as similar as possible to UNIX^{TM} mail [Shoe79].

There are four stages in an imessage's life: composition, sending, the execution phases of repeated interactions and shippings, and the final return to the sender. Execution is the simplest from the user's point of view. Little knowledge is required to receive imail, so we will cover this aspect first.

3.1. Receiving Imail

On typing the command *imail*, the recipient is given a list of headers giving, for each imessage, its number, the sender, the sending date and a subject. At this point he or she can specify an imessage number and one of the commands r(un), q(uit), or d(elete). A simple carriage return will cause the next remaining imessage to be run. Thus, any user who knows the command name can receive imail.

The "d", or delete, command is a way of getting rid of junk imail. (Junk mail of one form or another seems to be a hazard of any cheap form of communication.) A deleted imessage will never be seen again. The command "q" will drop the user out of imail but will leave the mailbox as it was at that point. The default is "r", which causes the script to interact with the user. The interaction may be aborted in standard UNIX^{TM} fashion with the RUBOUT key, which will cause all responses received up to that point to be deleted. The imessage remains in the mailbox and may be started again.

All responses given by users are stored in an imessage's *history*. We also chose to store the times and dates that each user was sent the imessage, saw its header, ran it but quit part way through, and ran it to completion or deleted it. At any point during an imessage's execution, its owner can check out its status and history. We do not claim that this is a good feature in an office, as opposed to a research environment. Historically this information has not been available to message senders, and it may be considered to be "snooping". This is purely a matter of custom, which does not mean that it may be ignored.

Clearly, problems could arise if two recipients simultaneously try to run an imessage which is offering an item to the first taker, and both request it. The obvious answer is to lock the imessage in some way so that such an incident cannot occur. Ideally, we wish to maximize concurrency, and allow two users to run an imessage simultaneously if the script is such that they cannot adversely affect each other. However, that requires some knowledge by the system of what the imessage actually does. For our simple system we chose the simple expedient of locking the entire imessage. Users' mailboxes do not actually contain the imessage itself; they contain a *notification* of the imessage, of which only one post-office copy actually exists. Possession of the lock for this copy guarantees that no other user can simultaneously run it. A request for an imessage that is being run results in a polite request to try again later. As part of the discussion of imail distribution, we will discuss the problems of concurrency more deeply.

3.2. Sending and Receiving Back Imail

An imessage is sent off by its creator by being given as input to *imail*, together with an optional subject (which appears in the recipient's header line), a *timeout*, or time at which to terminate if it has not done so already, and a list of initial recipients. The script language is described in the next section. It is translated into C Shell, and this C Shell script is what the recipient actually executes. Other options would have been to build an interpreter for the script language, translate directly into executable code, or design some other intermediate language and build an interpreter for it. Using C Shell as a target language, however, considerably simplified our task. The translator itself was built using the Lex lexical analyzer [LeSc75] and the Yacc compiler-compiler [John75].

An imessage may terminate for three reasons: it may time out, it may run out of destinations to ship itself to, or it may explicitly terminate itself after accomplishing some task. When any of these situations occurs, UNIX™ mail is used to return the results of the execution to the sender.

It is possible to process responses in two places: "on the fly" during interactions, or "after the fact" when the imessage has terminated. The latter approach is more suitable for complicated statistical queries, but the former may be essential just to allow the imessage to be "intelligent". We therefore support both. Commands for simple processing exist, but all responses and the values of *variables* (explained below) are returned to the sender, who may process or discard them as required.

3.3. Creating an Imessage

Imessage scripts are written in a special imail language. A script, as mentioned earlier, is a series of questions. Each question starts with a line beginning with ">" and optionally containing a one-word label. The text of the query follows. On all except possibly the last question, this is followed by a response collection. The text making up the query starts in the leftmost column, but the response collection and all further commands are indented one or more tab stops. *If* commands may be used to conditionally perform certain commands; their scope is denoted by a further one-stop indentation, and *ifs* may be nested in a similar manner.

The response collection is of the form "*get <number> <type>*" where *<number>* is an optional upper and/or lower bound on the number of items in the reply and *<type>* may be *numbers, words, logins* (UNIX[TM] user ids), or *text*. Examples are "get words", "get 2- numbers" and "get 1-2 logins". Along with other languages purporting to be easy to use, the *get* will automatically reprompt for incorrect numbers or type of responses.

A list of commands to process the replies may also be present. Apart from the previously-mentioned *if*, *print* will print a message. *Ship* will add a login to the list of imessage destinations if the imessage has not already been there, and *reship* will send the imessage back in any case. *terminate* will terminate a message immediately. *Next* takes as an argument the number or label of a question and causes it to be performed next.

The remaining command is *set*, used to set *variables*, of which there are three kinds: *response, local* and *global*. Any of these may appear on the right side of a *set*, which is an assignment supporting simple arithmetic and concatenating operations. A response variable cannot appear on the left side. One response variable exists for each question and is given the value of the reply to that question. It is indicated by a "#", followed by the number of the question, its relative number, or its label. For instance, "#2" refers to the response to the second question, "#-2" to the response to the question before the previous one, and "#who" to the response to the question labelled "who".

Local and global variables are indicated by words prefixed by "!" and "?", respectively. Both may be assigned initial values at the beginning of the script. A local variable is reset to this value at the beginning of each interaction, while global variables retain their values between interactions. Besides appearing in *set* commands, variables may appear in the text of queries or in *if*,ship,reship, or *print* commands.

3.4. Examples of Imessages

To show what this looks like in practice, the following is an imessage to perform the technical report questionnaire we have been using as an example.

```
login ?mailingList = dt fred oscar mazoo hogg
>
Which of the following technical reports
would you like CSRI to acquire?
(Answer yes or no for each.)

Ellis & Nutt, "Computer Science and
Office Information Systems",
Xerox PARC SSL-79-6.
                get 1 boolean
>
Johnson, "Yacc: Yet Another Compiler Compiler",
Bell Labs TR-32.
                get 1 boolean
>
Smith, "Function of the Orgasm in Higher Molluscs",
CSRI-999.
                get 1 boolean
>
The present mailing list is: ?mailingList.
Can you suggest any other names? (y/n)
                get 1 boolean
                if #4 = no
                        next end
>getnames
Who would you suggest? (logins, please)
                get 1- logins
                ship #getnames
                set ?mailingList = ?mailingList + #getnames
>end
Thanks!
```

For the purpose of illustrating the *next* command only, the last two questions were separate. However, in the next example, to find three volunteers, we can just as well accept a null reply and ship the imessage to no new recipients.

```
number ?vols = 3
>
CSRI needs ?vols more volunteers to
assist in testing a prototype system.
Would you be willing to do this?
        get 1 boolean
        if #1 = yes
                ?vols = ?vols - 1
                print Thanks!
I'll get in touch with you.
                if ?vols = 0
                        terminate
>others
Do you know anybody else who might be interested?
        get logins
        ship #others
>
Thanks.
```

Earlier it was stated that processing could be done at two times: "on the fly", or after the imessage had terminated. By processing the responses during an interaction, we can decide whether an imessage has found a solution to a problem. Our last example is an imessage which performs some statistical calculations to determine whether it has collected an acceptable set of responses.

In a *Delphi experiment* [Brun75], a number of recipients are presented with a question and some sort of previous consensus on the answer to it, and are asked to give their opinions. The consensus is modified by these answers, and the question is repeated to the same or perhaps other subjects. This continues until a termination condition occurs. Given current trends in polling, it could be claimed that a modern election is a type of Delphi experiment, with the termination condition being election day. However, a more interesting variety from the point of view of message behaviour is one in which a question is asked repeatedly, until the expert opinion offered converges to a narrow range. More precisely, we can repeatedly ask recipients a question until the standard deviation of their answers falls below some threshold level.

The following imessage does just this. It is sent out to a number of recipients. Whenever forty of them have replied, it recalculates the average and variance of their opinions. If the variance is less than 0.1, the imessage terminates. Otherwise, it reships itself to its entire recipient list. (Those recipients who did not answer the previous iteration will not receive two copies of the imessage; the later one will replace the earlier.)

```
number ?n = 0
number ?sum = 0
number ?sqsum = 0
number ?maxvar = 0.1
number ?itresps = 40
number ?avg = 4.0
number !var = 0
>
What do you think the inflation rate for next year will be?
The last average prediction was ?avg.
        get 1 number
        set ?sum = ?sum + #1
        set ?sqsum = ?sqsum + #1 x #1
        set ?n = ?n + 1
        if ?n = ?itresps
                set ?avg = ?sum / ?n
                set !var = ?sqsum / ?n - ?avg x ?avg
                set ?n = 0
                set ?sum = 0
                set ?sqsum
= 0
                if !var > ?maxvar
                        reship
                        next last
                print Thanks. Goodbye!
                terminate
    >last
    Thanks!
```

3.5. Experience with the Imail Prototype

The imail prototype was an interesting exercise and yielded many useful insights into the concept of an active message system, but it was certainly not suitable for use in a real office environment. Regardless of the value of the underlying ideas, a successful office tool must have an interface that office users (as opposed to computer users) can easily manipulate. This was realized at the time that imail was designed, and an attempt was made to keep the set of commands reasonably simple; however, the result is basically a programming language. While all programming languages from about FORTRAN on have been described as "English-like" and "easy to use", they all require training and a certain approach to understanding problems, and algorithms which may not be intuitive to non-computer specialists.

This has not worried us overly, since the object of the exercise was not to investigate interfaces but rather to test out the underlying concept and gain insight into what an active message system can do. A procedural interface is sufficient for a programmer's test-bed, and might in fact be the best way to build complicated imessages. Most imessages, however, fall into a small set of simple categories (surveys, searches, etc.). This suggests that a menu-based system could be used to modify one of a small set of templates, to make it perform the desired task, without requiring a naive user to do more than make simple selections and provide text. These templates, and any complicated imessages, would then be written in the underlying imail language. This is analogous to many database systems in which casual users use packages written by database specialists. If we are to have specialists, then the underlying language need not be simple, so long as it is powerful. It would actually be possible to have a number of different languages, ranging from our script language to one or more conventional programming languages. The only restriction would be that they must all compile to a single target language.

A "by-example" interface [Zloo80] is another option which may hold promise, but it is not clear precisely how this approach would be used. While this may in the end be the best approach to take, we are not pursuing it at this time.

Imail did suffer from a small number of users. For an email system to be a success, it is essential that it be used regularly by a large number of users [Tuck82]. If a certain "critical mass" is not reached, users will not check for mail. Our site does in fact have well over this critical mass of email users, and if imail had been integrated into that system there would have been no problem. However, as a small test system, we were reluctant to modify the operating system to check for imail in the same way that it checked for email when a user signed on, so users had to make a conscious decision to put such a checking routine into their startup file. This automatically limited the circle of people who were aware that they had been sent an imessage.

Imail is not a replacement for conventional mail. Many if not most messages need no reply. Of the remainder, most will not need the full power of imail; they will be messages sent from one user to another to collect a single reply. This means that in order to use it most effectively, imail must be integrated into a conventional mail system, so that a user has a full spectrum of message types that are accessible in a coherent, uniform manner.

4. Distributing Imail

4.1. The Motivation for Distribution

As computing power becomes cheaper and computers physically smaller, there has been a trend to distribute this power throughout an organization. "Office of the Future" scenarios invariably envisage a personal workstation on every desk, connected by a local area network (LAN) or private branch exchange (PBX). This architecture can represent a challenge to application designers, since applications involving cooperation or sharing must be distributed.

Shoch and Hupp [ShHu82] have described an experiment in distribution in which a "worm" program moves itself around in an Ethernet [MeBo76] environment, begging time on idle machines. While their results are not directly applicable to distributing imail, they do indicate the potential of mobile "intelligent" objects.

While imail has not yet been extended to a LAN or PBX environment, there is no reason why this should be difficult. The bandwidth of these systems is more than sufficient to allow one central machine to function as the "post office". As in our centralized version, notifications of mail can be put in the users' mailboxes, and a locking scheme of whatever desired complexity can be used to ensure that two conflicting interactions do not occur. The key point is that the network communication time is so small as to be totally invisible to the human user.

A far more difficult situation arises when we attempt to spread imail, not across an office or building but across one or more corporations that may have many sites spread across a continent or a planet. While each site may have a high-speed local network, if the internetwork communication is slow, it will no longer be possible to rely on a central, unreplicated imessage copy. A good current example of such a network is USENET. It contains upwards of a thousand different machines, mostly running UNIX^{TM}, connected over dial-up lines in a fairly arbitrary topology that is centred in the United States but reaches out to Australia, Korea, and Japan in one direction, and Crete in the other. The end-to-end transmission time is measured in days. Real-time coordination is clearly impossible.

Another growing trend is the use of single-user machines connected to no network, but able to dial up any other machine at will. Here we have, within a local dialing area, a population of machines which can for some purposes be assumed to be infinite and which are all able to talk to each other.

4.2. The Problems of Distribution

In attempting to distribute an imessage across either of the networks above, we find that we are lacking information both about the imessage and about the network on which it is executing.

The imessage itself will be made up of multiple copies. These copies may in turn spawn other copies. While knowing the location of a brother is not a difficult problem, knowing where cousins are is another matter entirely. As we move down the generations, the problem gets worse. If we allow an arbitrary number of generations, then synchronizing in the obvious way through ancestors may require arbitrarily long meta-message paths, and thus be arbitrarily difficult. The other obvious method is to use a central coordinator, some site which all the copies will agree to send MMs to whenever they spawn off children. This ceases to be cost effective when the net reaches a certain size; coordinating copies in Korea and Crete by passing messages to Saskatoon is not only expensive, but also so slow that when MMs arrive they will no longer reflect the state of their copies. Eventually we must face the fact that copies cannot have complete information about other copies, i.e., we cannot know the exact number or locations of all the copies at one time.

Not only can we not know the locations of all the copies, but, in some cases, the network itself may be only vaguely understood. USENET is an amazing example of totally decentralized administration: nobody is running the show. A new site connects to it by finding a neighbor willing to pass mail and news on. It announces itself to the net as and when it pleases, and as a result, there is *no* accurate map of the net *anywhere*; some sites haven't bothered to proclaim their existence. A limiting case of this is the non-net formed by a number of personal computers. The topology is in one way simple: the net may be represented by a complete graph of size N. The problem is that N is very large, and we do not know more than a small subset of the nodes' addresses when we initiate a new imessage. So again, we have an indeterminate number and location of sites.

Ideally we would like to hide the existence of the net entirely from its users, barring the additional delay required to pass messages along. As we will see, this is not, in general, possible, except at the cost of losing all concurrency entirely and making the total execution time the sum of the individual interaction and shipping times. We are therefore interested in coming as close to this ideal as possible, while minimizing the costs of coordination in imessage execution time and MMs.

An issue which we will not concern ourselves with here is the routing of copies during shipping, and MMs during coordination. That is, we will assume that if a copy knows of the existence of its destination, it will also know an effective way of getting itself there. This can be a major problem in itself [Tsic84], but it is treated elsewhere.

The correctness of the underlying centralized imessage is another issue that will be assumed in this section. While it is a very important problem, it is more of a programming-language one. We assure ourselves that a program does what we think it does by proving that certain properties hold in the formal language description of the program. As we do not feel that our language is the best model for future systems, there is little point in trying to suggest how scripts written in it could be shown to be correct.

4.3. Coordination in Distributed Databases

Much work has been done in the past on ensuring correctness in database systems that are operated on by multiple processes, in both the centralized and distributed states [EGLT76, KuRo81, BeGo82]. It is natural to ask whether the lessons and techniques of databases apply to imessages; after all, a copy can be thought of as a small part of a database that happens to move across the network.

The most useful concept from distributed database theory is probably that of *serialization*. A database is presumed to be altered by a series of *transactions*. Before a transaction, the database is assumed to be in a consistent state. A transaction will alter the database and may temporarily make it inconsistent, a simple example being the temporary "disappearance" of money when it has been removed from one account but not yet deposited in another. When a transaction finishes, however, the database will once again be consistent. Thus, if a number of transactions are run serially, the database will be consistent when they have all finished.

To maximize throughput and minimize response time, we wish to overlap transactions as much as possible, while still maintaining the consistency property. A number of techniques to do this exist; a good tutorial is [BeGo82]. In essence, they all delay or roll back operations on the database to ensure that the order of operations will generate a final database state equivalent to that for some schedule of operations in which the individual transactions were performed serially.

This is also a key property for imessage executions. We wish to hold up the various interactions as little as possible, yet at the end have a result equivalent to running the interactions serially, and stopping to coordinate the copies completely between each interaction.

Unfortunately, techniques such as two-phase locking [EGLT76] and transaction certification [KuRo81] are not directly applicable. Imessages are not databases, and the "transactions" involve humans interacting with them in real time. Two-phase locking involves delaying a transaction until enough locks have been obtained to guarantee that no other transaction can interleave its operations in any way that will cause an inconsistency. A human will not wait several hours for this. Certification takes another approach: it assumes that transactions will seldom affect each other and lets them start at any time. When they are ready to write, it checks whether this writing will cause an inconsistency. If so, the transaction is declared invalid and restarted. This checking may also involve the passing of MMs over great distances and has the additional disadvantage that humans do not like being told that the interaction they have just completed is invalid and must be repeated.

4.4. Imessage States

We must now try to decide exactly when two copies may undergo interactions in such a manner as to cause an inconsistency in the state of the imessage. First, let us consider a case in which no inconsistency can ever result. Suppose that we wish to find a number of people willing to sign a petition. Our approach will be the typical imail one of starting with a small set of likely signatories, and asking them all to add their names and suggest other people who would be willing to do the same.

In this situation, each copy can act independently. Ignoring the problem of multiple copies being sent to one individual (which is easy to solve), we find that any number of copies can simultaneously be interacting with different users. No problems will occur.

Now, let us consider a very similar problem: that of obtaining *exactly* N signatures, for any N. Suppose that N-1 have already been obtained. Then if any copy finds a willing recipient, all copies should simultaneously terminate. Furthermore, if any copy is interacting with a recipient, all other copies should wait until it is finished, since it may be successful. In other words, the only way that we can guarantee serializability is by coordination of our copies so that serialization actually occurs! Why is there such a difference between these two situations?

It was earlier claimed that in the simple case of a single, centralized imessage, the actions taken during or after an interaction would depend only upon the *state* of the imessage and the responses it receives. This state is composed of a memory, or set of variables.

In the distributed case, the imessage is composed of a number of copies, which may have difficulty communicating with each other. As the copies spawn different children at each interaction, they will develop *local* states which differ from each other. What we were referring to earlier as the state of the imessage now becomes the *global* state; it is the sum of all the local states.

Our goal is to conceal the existence of the distributed nature of the imessage from its users, insofar as is possible; to do this, the various copies must work together. That is, their actions should depend upon the global, and not the local, imessage state. There are two basic ways of solving this sort of problem in distributed database situations: either all processes read all database copies and write to their own (the database itself is distributed) or, alternatively processes write to all copies and read from their own (the, database is replicated). Maintaining correctness is then a matter of ensuring that reads and writes are scheduled in such a manner as to result in a consistent database state after all transactions have finished.

We can initially adopt either approach in handling imessages as well. A copy can read from its local state and write to all other copies' local states, or write to its own local state only and read all copies' states. The first alternative of read-local, write-global has certain advantages, as we will see. Initially, assume that there exists some sort of global communication technique that has a non-trivial but affordable cost. We will later describe where this will actually be necessary and how to accomplish it.

Assuming that the cost of each read or write to or from a local state is similar, global reads and writes will cost about the same. However, a local read can be completed much more quickly (i.e., in real time) than a global read. A global *write*, on the other hand, will take longer than a local write to complete, but may be initiated very quickly. This makes an interaction with an imessage a self-contained and therefore real-time proposition.

4.5. Variable Categorization

Up to this point we have been assuming that a copy's local state is a single monolithic entity. This, however, will not, in general, be the case. A copy's state contains a number of variables, some of which may be used only by the copy itself. Examples are responses to particular questions, or a variable containing the number of hops that the copy and its direct ancestors have traversed (this can be used as a measure of the distance of a particular recipient). These *private* variables do not need to be propagated from one local state to another, and thus no coordination is required.

The other end of the scale is the *monolithic shared* variable, of which the "done" flag in the single volunteer search above is an example. When this flag is set, all copies must immediately stop interacting. This type of variable obviously requires coordination between copies, if correctness is to be maintained. In between these two types of variables, however, there is a third type: the *decomposable shared* variable. Consider the imail script to find three volunteers that was given in the previous section. If a copy knows that only one volunteer has been found to date, it can safely go ahead and interact with a user, provided only that two other copies do not first find willing recipients.

We can assign one *token* for each of the volunteers to the imessage as a whole, then require that a copy obtain a token before it interacts with a recipient. There are many useful imessages which can use this token approach; any imessage which is searching for a number of entities can have them represented by tokens. (The same is true for an imessage attempting to give things away — this is equivalent to searching for a recipient.) If the number of tokens relative to the number of imessages is large, each copy can "carry" one or more. If there are few tokens, then the imessages must be split into groups which can share a token. This may still be a great improvement over the case in which all tokens are represented by one global variable, because we may be able to use the locality of sets of recipients (e.g., at the same site), to allow communication between the copies sharing the token to be done at interaction time. That is, all the copies can offer themselves to recipients, and lock themselves only when another copy in the group is actually interacting.

Using tokens means that, provided our shared variables are decomposable, we can use our slow or expensive communication paths for relatively few and time-insensitive messages, i.e., only those MMs concerned with the distribution and management of tokens. This management is of course a problem in itself.

4.6. Copy Coordination

Earlier we stated that it was convenient to view an imessage as a family tree, with each copy having only one destination and spawning off children as the last step of its interaction. This has the advantage of keeping the operations performed by a copy simple. However, it also means that a considerable amount of coordination between copies may be required. As mentioned earlier, each copy's actions are determined by its local state, which must represent the global state. This state is comprised of the copy's destination, its results, and any tokens that the script requires. Results must be returned, and destinations and tokens may have to be matched between different copies. We will examine the latter problem first.

4.7. Token-Destination Matching

Consider first an imessage with only one type of token. (We can generalize this to several types of token if we wish.) When the imessage is created, it will have n initial destinations and m tokens. As time goes on, the number of tokens will decrease, while the number of destinations may decrease, remain steady, or increase. Our problem is to find a way to assign tokens and destinations to copies.

In the absence of tokens, the obvious approach is to merely create one copy per destination, as mentioned above. However, if tokens are present, the problem becomes more difficult. A copy cannot interact without a token, just as it cannot interact without a destination. A certain symmetry is present; if tokens are plentiful and destinations are rare, it makes sense to "carry" several tokens in a copy and divide them amongst child copies. However, if tokens are rare but there are numerous destinations, it will be simpler to carry the destinations as a variable and create one child for each token.

We cannot, in general, rely on either situation being the case. An imessage with a set number of tokens to give out to willing recipients may initially be token-rich (i.e., have more tokens than recipients), but later become token-poor as they are gradually accepted. The ratio can thus vary over time. A greater problem is that it may also vary over space. One branch of an imessage family tree may find many token acceptors but few additional destinations; another branch may find the opposite to be the case. Clearly, the destinations and tokens must be brought together through some coordination process.

If the underlying network has very strong connectivity, (i.e., passing a message from any node to another node is a cheap and fast process) then we can set up a central "matchmaker", or central coordination station, to accept surplus tokens and destinations and pair them up.

(A "surplus" destination is one given to a copy with no tokens, while a surplus token belonged to a copy which was provided not with new destinations.) However, if our network has slow links (e.g., USENET) this will not be feasible. We must still use some sort of matchmaking process, but it must have greater locality.

The next step is to set up several local coordination stations that can easily be reached by copies with tokens or destinations to be matched. The limiting case of this occurs when every site at which a copy has interacted becomes a coordination station for the copy's children. At this point, however, we find that the coordination stations are no better: they too can run dry of either commodity. We must start passing tokens and destinations up the tree.

The use of tokens is reminiscent of the use of semaphores in operating systems [HGLS78]. In order to obtain access to a resource (one of a number of imessage-dependent items) we must first "stake our claim", and avoid conflict between two or more copies (independent processes) by obtaining a token. In designing an operating system, it is crucial that if two processes simultaneously request a token, exactly one of them receives it. If we can produce code or hardware to coordinate the process of obtaining or releasing a token that is safe from race conditions, then we need not worry about race conditions occurring elsewhere in critical parts of processes.

This is a well-understood problem in operating systems design. At least one indivisible "test-and-set" instruction is provided in the basic hardware, and from this it is simple to construct a semaphore which will always be in some consistent, legal state. In moving from a single machine to a local network, the problem is complicated somewhat, but the same general solution may be adopted.

Applying these techniques to imessage copy coordination, however, is not so straightforward. In operating systems work, the time required to send a message from a process to a semaphore is comparatively small. The semaphore itself can therefore be put in some single, stable location. Increasing the speed of token distribution by carrying tokens along with copies, and distributing them without going back to a single central location, means that just finding the location of the tokens is a non-trivial matter.

The simplest way of having copies know where to go to coordinate with other copies is, in fact, to use the imessage "family tree" to specify the coordination locations. In this case, when a copy dies it does not disappear completely, but rather it becomes dormant, so that it can perform coordination actions for its children. It will only truly die when all these children (and their descendants in turn) have died.

Now, a copy interacts with a recipient and produces zero or more children, with one or more tokens to divide between them. If either no new destinations are supplied by the interaction or no tokens are left over afterwards, the remaining commodity should clearly be passed up the family tree to some ancestor which can receive them, and the copy can die. However, if children are spawned and given tokens which they can in turn give to their descendants, the copy must go dormant, so that it will be available to coordinate tokens or destinations that its descendants cannot use. The problem arises when these tokens or destinations are returned. Should the dormant copy pass them, in turn, to its parent, or should it hold onto them in the hope of receiving the other commodity from some other descendant?

Models and strategies for making this tradeoff are currently being investigated. The length of time one has to wait for commodities to be passed up from descendents depends upon the speed of connecting links, the expected response times of recipients, and the probabilities of tokens being consumed and new destinations being generated.

5. Conclusions

Communication by intelligent messages which perform their own response collection and routing is feasible and valuable. Our prototype system points out the need for a friendly interface, for such a system to be successful in a working environment. The use of various layers of interfaces, with a simple menu-driven one at the top level, seems desirable. This environment could be built today for a centralized or LAN system.

Distribution of imail over loosely-coupled networks is a much more difficult problem, upon which we are currently working. As communication between office workers tends to have considerable locality (those we wish to speak to tend to be those closest to us), problems in distribution do not preclude a practical and valuable production system from being built.

Imail is interesting not only as a problem in itself, but also as a very restricted part of the Objectworld described in the paper by Tsichritzis. Techniques for coordinating widely-separated processes, in a network whose nodes are controlled by a large number of owners with attitudes varying from friendly to indifferent, are needed in Objectworld. The imail project thus involves a spectrum of work, from the short-term and practical to the long-term and conceptually exciting.

6. References

[BeGo82]   [Brun75]   [BSdJ82]   [EGLT76]   [ElNu80]   [HGLS78]
[HMGT83] [HoGa84] [John75] [Joy80] [KuRo81] [LeSc75] [Maze83]
[MeBo76] [Robs81] [ShHu82] [Shoe79] [Tsic84] [Tuck82] [Vitt81]
[Zloo80]

Part IV

Procedure Specification

7
Office Procedures

J. Hogg
O.M. Nierstrasz
D. Tsichritzis

ABSTRACT *This paper outlines an effort to introduce automation into forms-oriented office procedures. The system allows its users to specify a set of operations on electronic forms. Actions are triggered automatically when certain events occur, for example, when forms or combinations of forms arrive at particular nodes in the network of stations. The actions deal with operations on forms. The paper discusses the facilities provided for the specification of form-oriented automatic procedures and sketches their implementation.*

1. Introduction

Office *automation* implies that procedures followed in the office are understood, specified, translated into programs, and performed automatically by computers and communication devices. There are many problems, however, in accomplishing any degree of automation in the office.

The first difficulty is that most offices follow many procedures at the same time. Studies have indicated that thousands of different procedures are inherent in the operation of each office, and they are different among offices. In addition, the procedures are not always well understood and leave much flexibility for human intervention. It is a very difficult task to capture the procedures in any meaningful model which can later be used to guide the procedure specification.

The second difficulty is related to the nature of office procedures. Unlike regular data processing, office procedures have many exceptions. In fact, the whole office function seems like an exception-handling activity. Usual programming environments are very good at specifying repetitive procedures on vast amounts of data. They are not appropriate for specifying exceptions, especially when the exceptions are not well tabulated.

The third difficulty relates to the decision-oriented aspects of offices. There are many decisions in an office, even mundane ones, which involve vast amounts of knowledge and experience that are beyond the capabilities of any computer system. When office procedures are dependent on such decisions, they require human intervention. When human intervention is predominant, the automation aspects vanish. User interfaces and database access tools are more helpful than the specification of the procedures themselves. Only a very small part of the decision-oriented procedures can be fully automated.

Finally, office procedures are better understood at the local level. Individuals or offices know more about what they are doing than outsiders. The specification of their procedures may be feasible. When procedures specified at the local level are combined they may have difficulty achieving overall goals, or satisfying well-accepted constraints. Manual procedures are linked by humans who have much versatility in ironing out problems and incompatibilities. Automated office procedures do not show the same flexibility.

There are basically two design choices for a facility for office procedure specification. First, we need to decide what capabilities to provide in the specification. Second, we need to decide on the way of presenting this facility to the user. The generality of the specification is closely related to its goal. If it is mainly a requirements specification facility, without plans for implementation; it can be very general and powerful, for example, OSL [HaKu80]. If an implementation is desirable, then some of the generality needs to be sacrificed. For example, the specification language used in SCOOP is less general, but it has been implemented [Zism77].

There is also a choice of implementation environment. If the facility is implemented in LISP or some other powerful artificial intelligence tool, then a powerful specification environment can be put together with a reasonable effort. The problem of such an approach, however, is to achieve an acceptable level of performance on a small workstation. If the facility is implemented in a regular software environment, then the implementation effort is considerable. As a result, the facility is rather limited, but the performance is acceptable.

The second design choice relates to the user environment. If the specification facility is used by programmers, then it can resemble a programming language. If the specification facility is mainly geared to office workers with minimum programming expertise, then it should incorporate a very simple user interface. In the end, the size of the manual is as important as the functionality of the system.

In the rest of the paper, we outline an office procedure specification facility related to forms. Forms are used to specify procedures relating to form processing. Two kinds of procedures can be specified. Queries can be stated in relation to information on forms which are present in many different workstations. The query procedures are automatically executed in a distributed fashion and they return the cumulative results. The second kind of procedure deals with coordination of forms arriving at a single workstation. Depending on the specification, actions related to forms are automatically triggered and performed.

The specification and automation of forms-oriented procedures is realistic for two reasons. First, forms structure information in a manner which is easily amenable to computerization. Second, forms-oriented procedures are well understood, and carefully designed in an office environment. This design includes not only operations on forms at the local level but flow of forms among different office sites.

The specification facility is provided on top of OFS, a passive form-processing system. OFS is an electronic forms management system [Cheu79, Gibb79, Tsic82, TRGN82]. It provides an interface to MRS, a small, relational database system [Hudy78, Korn79, Ladd79]. OFS and MRS were written in C, within the UNIX^{TM} operating system [KeRi78]. They have both been distributed widely to organizations.

An OFS system consists of a set of stations distributed over a number of machines in a network. Each user has a private set of forms residing in his station. A user may only manipulate those forms which he temporarily "owns", in the sense that they are part of his database. Communication and interaction between stations is achieved by allowing users to mail forms to one another.

A distinction is made in OFS between form types, form blanks, and form instances. A *form blank* is simply the form template used to display a form instance. A *form instance* corresponds to an actual filled form, represented as a tuple in the database of forms. Its fields may have values assigned to it, and it always has a unique key assigned at creation time by the system. A *form type* is the specification of a form blank and a set of field types. A *form file* is a relation used to store all forms of the same type, belonging to a station. The collection of form files for a station is a *form database.* Figures 1 and 2 show a form blank and form instance, respectively, for the form *type* called *order.* Note that some fields of the form instance need not have values associated with them. The key field must have a value which is automatically assigned by the system.

```
┌─────────────────────────────────────────────────────┐
│                                                       │
│   ORDER FORM    Key : _____                     │
│                                                       │
│   Customer number : _____                     │
│       Customer name : _____                 │
│                                                       │
│         Description : _____                 │
│               Item : _____                      │
│               Price : _____                     │
│           Quantity : _____                      │
│               Total : _____                     │
│                                                       │
└─────────────────────────────────────────────────────┘
```

Figure 1: An order form blank

Form fields may be of six different types. Manual fields of type 1 may be inserted or modified at any time, type 2 fields may be inserted at any time but not modified, and type 3 fields must be inserted at form creation and never modified. Automatic fields of type 1 are key fields, always the first of a form; type 2 are date fields, and type 3 are signature fields, bearing the station's name if the preceding field is filled in.

```
┌─────────────────────────────────────────────────────┐
│                                                       │
│   ORDER FORM      Key : 00001.00000___                │
│                                                       │
│   Customer number : 354_____                    │
│       Customer name : CSRL_____               │
│                                                       │
│         Description : Office Forms System___           │
│               Item : 254_____                   │
│               Price : 200.00_____              │
│           Quantity : 2_____                     │
│               Total : _____                     │
│                                                       │
└─────────────────────────────────────────────────────┘
```

Figure 2: An order form instance

Form operations are creation, selection, and modification. Forms may also be attached to *dossiers*. Dossiers are lists of forms which are not necessarily of the same form type, but which have something in common that the user wishes to capture.

Forms may not be destroyed, although they may be mailed to a "wastebasket station", which conceptually shreds the electronic form. The wastebasket station may in fact archive rather than erase a form, depending upon the needs of a particular application. Form instances are unique, and must always exist at exactly one location in the system. They are either in a form file or waiting in a mail tray. Forms may be mailed from one station to another. They must wait in a mail tray, and be explicitly retrieved in order to be placed in the receiving station's form file. Copies may be made of forms, but they are assigned a unique key, consisting of the key of the original form together with a system-generated copy number distinguishing the copy from the original.

Form files may be accessed as a whole, using a relational MRS interface. However, in this case, no protection is provided against illegal operations such as destroying a form or creating a form with a key that is already in use. Therefore, the MRS interface is not meant to be used except by privileged users.

OFS is basically a passive system, that is, the user has to initiate every action. The only automatic form processing that OFS will do occurs if a form is mailed to a special automatic station. Such a station periodically reads its mail and submits the forms as input to an application program. These programs must be written so as to preserve the integrity of forms files. Consequently, the specification of an OFS automatic procedure requires a great deal of knowledge of the inner workings of OFS, and is therefore not intended for naive users. In the rest of the paper, we will discuss automatic procedures which have been implemented on top of OFS.

2. Distributed Queries

Some office activities may require information which is spread over more than one station. We will discuss how a station user specifies a query which is automatically performed on different stations, and how the result of a query is presented to the user.

As the first step in query specification the user selects the form type on which the query is to be performed. The form template is then displayed on the screen. A *query sketch* is next created by partially filling the template. This serves as an example, and informs the system of the kinds of forms qualifying for the query. This approach has been used in QBE, SBA, and OBE [deJo80, Zloo80]. The user may fill in zero or more fields of the template; values entered into the fields are interpreted as selection conditions. For example, if the user enters

">10" into a field, then all forms which satisfy the query will have values greater than 10 in this field. In addition to ">", one can also specify "<", or "=", etc., as well as a pattern match. Such a condition is known as a simple condition. For each field, it is possible to specify a field condition which is a disjunction of simple conditions. The forms that satisfy the query will satisfy the conjunction of all field conditions.

Once a query sketch has been created, the user next specifies the scope of the query. The allowable choices are as follows:

Local: In this case the query is performed on the station database of the issuing station.

Group: In this case the query is performed on all station databases on the same node as the issuing station.

Global: In this case the query is performed on all databases in the network (this includes the mailboxes at the control node).

Explicit: In this case the user lists the station names of the station databases that are to be searched.

After specifying the scope, the query can be processed automatically. The results are stored in a temporary database belonging to the issuing station. This database contains *images* rather than objects; the objects themselves still reside in their respective station databases. A form image differs from a form, in that it is temporary and read-only. It is also invisible to other automated procedures that process forms. The tuples from this temporary database may be displayed by the station. When this occurs, the identification of the station database in which the form was found is also indicated.

Each query involves a single form type. It is not possible to directly specify operations involving more than one form type. However, arbitrarily complex multiple-type joins may be performed by first individually constructing complete temporary databases. The station user can then invoke a relational database system, and express his query (now over the local temporary database), using a high-level set-oriented relational query language.

An example of a query sketch is shown in figure 3. This query will search for meeting announcements from "Vassos", on the subject "office automation" or "database". If this query is performed with a local scope, then the meeting announcements sent to the station user (or at least residing at his station) will be searched. If this query is performed with a global scope, then all meeting announcements in the system will be searched. By using the "Response" field of this message type, it is also possible to determine who has replied to the meeting announcement.

The strategy for processing a query automatically is determined by the scope of the query. Again we distinguish the following cases:

```
┌──────────────────────────────────────────────────────────┐
│                  MEETING ANNOUNCEMENT                      │
│                                                            │
│            To : _____   Key : _____        │
│          From : Vassos_____  Date : _____       │
│                                                            │
│        Subject : *office automation*|*database*_____    │
│        Remarks : _____    │
│                                                            │
│   Meeting Date : _____    │
│   Meeting Time : _____    │
│      Location : _____    │
│                                                            │
│      Response : _____    │
│                                                            │
└──────────────────────────────────────────────────────────┘
```

Figure 3: A query sketch

Local: In this case the query manager is not used, and the station process itself performs the query on its station database.

Group:

In this case the station process sends the query to the query manager for the node. It then waits for an answer from the query manager.

Global/Explicit:

In this case the station process sends the query to a control node manager. The control node manager then passes the query to all query managers within the scope of the query. This may include the query manager on the control node. The various query managers perform the query on their nodes, and send the answer back to the control node manager. The control node manager assembles the answers in a temporary database, and may also perform the query on the mailbox if it is included in the query's scope. Finally, the control node manager sends the temporary database to the station process which issued the query.

Two problems arise in the automatic processing of queries: concurrency control of interfering global or local operations, and control of data movement due to mailing operations. Two algorithms, the centralized concurrency control algorithm and the centralized movement control algorithm [TRGN82], are used to circumvent these problems.

The concurrency control problem refers to the scheduling of operations which may conflict with queries. There are two such sources of interference, local updates and other queries. The system gives precedence to local updates. Stations are allowed to modify, create, or copy forms, even while queries are in progress. In addition, separate queries can operate concurrently. However, in this case, scheduling of the queries is required. For example, suppose data item X on station i initially has value a_1, and then is changed, by a local update operation, to value a_2. Similarly, on station j, the data item Y is changed from b_1 to b_2. If we have two queries q_1 and q_2, it is possible that q_1 will see X as a_1 and Y as b_2, while q_2 will see X as a_2 and Y as b_1. Whether we consider q_1 as occurring before or after q_2, this result is inconsistent with the history of X and Y.

The source of this problem is that two distinct queries with overlapping scopes may be performed in different order on different nodes. This problem can be solved by having the control node manager serialize query requests. Each query, when accepted by the control node manager, is given a progressive sequence number: Seq (query). This is similar to the use of timestamps. However, since the Seq numbers are generated from a single node, any sequential ordering can be used. Queries are sent by the control node manager to the satellite nodes in this order. The network protocol ensures that the order of queries sent from one node to another is equal to the order received. Since there is a single query manager at each node, the queries are performed in this order, i.e., of their Seq numbers.

The movement of messages from one station database to another also introduces difficulties with query processing. In particular, the following pathological situations must be avoided.

The message M is missed by a query:

1. The query is performed on node i while the message M is on node j.
2. Message M is transferred to node i.
3. The query is performed on node j.

The message M is counted twice:

1. The query is performed on node i where it sees the message M.
2. Message M is transferred to node j.
3. The query is performed on node j where it again sees the message M.

We handle these problems by carefully orchestrating the order in which queries are performed. We also pay attention to the movements of forms in the mailboxes. A query is first performed on the station databases by the query managers, and then on the mailboxes by the control node manager. For messages that are transferred, it is necessary to keep track of the sequence number of the last query that has seen the message.

3. Form Procedures

The main automation facility deals with procedures that handle forms arriving at a station, and it is provided by the TLA system [Hogg81, Nier81]. (TLA stands for "Three Letter Acronym", and, unlike most acronyms, requires no apologies.) The user interface is presented in terms of objects with which the OFS user is already familiar. Specifying operations within a procedure corresponds closely to performing those operations within a manual system. A user who is editing an automatic forms procedure manipulates *sketches* of forms. *Sketches* are form-like objects representing the forms that the procedure will eventually manipulate. The same form template that OFS uses to display form instances is used quite differently in TLA, to describe preconditions and actions in office procedures. The specifications are non-procedural and have a simple syntax.

TLA does not assume any knowledge of the system state other than what is available to the user in his (or her) form file or mail tray. This corresponds to the notion in OFS that users can only manipulate the forms that they "own". Anything happening outside a user's own workstation does not concern him. The domain of automation is that of the individual workstation. The complexity of determining when to trigger a procedure is thereby considerably reduced.

An automatic procedure is meant to capture the notion of an office worker collecting forms at his desk until a "complete set" is compiled. He can then process the forms and file them or send them on their way. Processing of the collection of forms may cause forms to be modified or new forms to be added to the set. Reference tables and calculating tools are made available through an interface to a local library of application programs.

The other aspect of automation supplied by TLA is that of "smart forms", which automatically fill certain fields using previously filled-in fields as arguments. The domain here is that of the form alone, so triggering takes place whenever a form is created or modified.

There are two types of automatic fields. The first type is filled in only if all its arguments fields have values. The other type accepts null values, and is filled in even if some arguments fields are missing. Fields are initially filled in sequence. When an automatic field is reached, an application program written in a conventional programming language (usually C or the UNIX™ Shell) is executed. The output from this program is assigned to that field. If any of the argument fields is subsequently modified, the automatic fields which use it are also updated. Typical applications are arithmetic operations, such as sales tax calculations, or database queries, such as filling in a customer's address.

"Smarter forms" with fields that change value depending upon time conditions, the state of the system, or any other variable, were not implemented. Some "smarter form" problems can be solved with TLA's automatic procedures.

Automatic procedures have preconditions and actions, but no postconditions in the usual sense. Satisfying all preconditions guarantees the successful completion of all actions. There is only a very limited sense in which a procedure may "fail". For example, it may never be triggered, because missing forms do not arrive. Postconditions may be interpreted in terms of the preconditions of another procedure to which control of the forms is passed.

Automatic procedures run concurrently with the manual functions of the users. Conflicts can arise over the form manipulations. Forms being collected by an automatic procedure can be modified or shipped away manually. They can even be "stolen" by a competing automatic procedure. This implies that when a complete set of forms is gathered for a procedure, it has to be temporarily "removed" from the system. This operation safeguards the forms until they are processed.

4. Interface

The specification of an automatic procedure in TLA bears some resemblance to SBA and OBE [deJo80, Zloo80]. The precondition segment of a procedure bears a resemblance to a QBE query, with forms instead of tables as the data objects. In the simplest form of a TLA precondition, putting a value in a field of a precondition indicates that a form is to be found with a field matching that value. The action segment of the procedure is similar. The simplest operation is to assign to a field the value specified in an action.

The order in which forms needed by a procedure arrive is not important. The order in which actions are performed is not specified in detail. TLA merely ensures that the procedure be logically consistent. The specification is non-procedural. The user indicates what forms are to be collected, and what is to be done with them. He does not specify how they are to be collected or how the actions are to be performed.

Preconditions in TLA describe what, when and where. For each procedure there is a *working set* of forms. The working set may include forms that come only from certain workstations, forms local to the station specifying the procedure, or forms that have just been processed by another automatic procedure. One may also specify a procedure to run only at certain times or ranges of times.

A TLA procedure is a collection of "sketches". A *sketch* resembles a form, but is to be distinguished from form blanks, form types or form instances. A *precondition sketch* indicates a request to the system to find "a form that looks like this". An *action sketch* indicates a request to modify a form that has already been obtained. In either case, a sketch describes a form instance before or after processing by the procedure. The medium of specification of a sketch is the same form blank that is the template for the form instance being described. Actions and preconditions which do not refer to information found on a form are specified by *pseudo-sketches* of "pseudo-forms". For example, the condition that a procedure process only forms coming from user "john" must be indicated on a special *source pseudo-sketch.*

Sketches are used to capture the restrictions referring to values that appear on the face of the forms in the working set. *Local restrictions* are constant field values, sets or ranges of values, and relations between values of the fields on a given form. The local restrictions refer only to the values appearing on a single form in the working set. TLA tries to determine whether a given form satisfies the local restrictions (including the source condition) for a sketch in some automatic procedure. If it does, TLA notes the information and attempts to match that form with other forms to obtain a complete working set for that procedure.

Figure 4 is an example of a precondition sketch instructing TLA to watch for order forms requesting "Veeblefetzers". Since this information can be found right on the order form, it is a *local* precondition. A sample procedure including such a sketch might perform the single action of returning a form that says "We stopped making those things years ago!"

```
┌─────────────────────────────────────────────────┐
│                                                   │
│   ORDER FORM      Key : ─────────────             │
│                                                   │
│   Customer number : ───────────────               │
│      Customer name : ─────────────────────        │
│                                                   │
│      Description : Veeblefetzers─────────          │
│             Item : ─────────────                  │
│            Price : ─────────────                  │
│         Quantity : ─────────────                  │
│            Total : ─────────────                  │
│                                                   │
└─────────────────────────────────────────────────┘
```

Figure 4: A precondition sketch

Global restrictions on the working set of an automatic procedure are the join conditions between values of fields appearing on different forms. One expects all the forms in a procedure's working set to be linked by certain common field values. Matching field values are therefore probably adequate to model many applications of automatic procedures. However, simple inequality restrictions may also be specified.

Figure 5 shows how a link is made to find an *inv* form for the item requested on an *order* form. Each sketch in a procedure has a name assigned by the user. This name is a prefix to the field name. In this way a field of a different sketch can be referenced within a sketch. Note that one could alternatively have placed the restriction "=inv.item" in the item number field of the *order* precondition sketch.

```
┌─────────────────────────────────────────────────┐
│                                                   │
│   INVENTORY RECORD  Key : ───────────────         │
│                                                   │
│              Item :  =ord.item_____              │
│             Price : ─────────────────             │
│   Quantity in stock : ─────────────────           │
│                                                   │
│   Description : ─────────────────────────         │
│                                                   │
└─────────────────────────────────────────────────┘
```

Figure 5: A global (join) precondition

We can also restrict the source of mail being processed by an automatic procedure. Suppose, for example, that the accounting department receives an order form from the order department. This may be interpreted as a request to forward a customer's address to the warehouse so that the order may be filled. If, however, the order form arrives from the warehouse, this may indicate that the order has gone through, and that an invoice should be mailed out. Figure 6 shows an origin pseudo-form sketch for such an application. Forms may thus be processed differently depending upon their point of origin. Alternatively, the special field *not* may be filled in to indicate that only forms coming from stations not listed in the pseudo-sketch should be processed by the procedure. The pseudo-station *me* is also available to indicate that forms must (or must not) come from within the station's own files.

All form modification actions are indicated on action sketches. Every form manipulated by a forms procedure has a precondition sketch and an action sketch. Actions which do not concern themselves with field values must be expressed via pseudo-forms.

The action sketch indicates all insertions and updates to the form. The values to be inserted may be constant values, e.g., an authorization, copied field values, or possibly function calls to application

```
ORIGIN PSEUDO-SKETCH                              NOT: ___
Stations:
ordering________________________  ________________________
________________________________  ________________________
________________________________  ________________________
________________________________  ________________________
________________________________  ________________________
________________________________  ________________________
________________________________  ________________________
________________________________  ________________________
```

Figure 6: An origin pseudo-sketch

programs. We distinguish, therefore, between the original and the updated values of any field. A field that must be copied to another form may itself be modified, and the wrong value must not be used. Furthermore, the function calls may access both the original and updated values of fields. In fact, the original value of a field will often be one of the arguments to a function call update to that field.

The action sketch in figure 7 illustrates several features. The *price* of an item is filled in by copying it from an *inv* form. A program called "mult" is called to calculate the total. Finally, the original value of *quantity* is accessed, whereas the updated value of *price* is used. Note that the symbols "#", "?" and "!" are used to respectively access functions, original field values, and updated field values. If none of these symbols is used, a constant string value is inserted.

```
ORDER FORM      Key : ____________________

Customer number : _____________
  Customer name : ____________________

    Description : ____________________
           Item : _____________
          Price : ?inv.price_____
       Quantity : _____________
          Total : #mult !price ?quantity
```

Figure 7: An action sketch

Some analysis is needed to ensure that every updated file ultimately depends only upon values originally available on the working set of forms. It is clearly incorrect to update each of two fields by copying over the updated value of the other. Suppose that the *price* field of the order form were updated to "!inv.price" *and* the *price* field of the inventory form were updated to "!order.price". No order of execution could make sense of the request.

Field constraints must be obeyed. Procedures that create forms must fill in certain fields. Procedures that modify forms must only modify fields of an appropriate type. Implied actions must also be evaluated, if a procedure modifies or inserts a field which is an argument to an automatic field.

After all form modifications are completed, zero or more copies of each form are made. Each form or copy may then be left in the user's files, inserted into a dossier or shipped to another station. The mechanism used to specify these operations is the *destination* pseudo-sketch; an example is shown as figure 8. Copy 0 is the form manipulated by a procedure, and one additional destination pseudo-sketch is filled in for each copy of that form. The operations available are *leave, ship* and *dossier*. The first of these requires no *where* argument, but the others require the name of a station or a dossier, respectively. This may be given as a simple constant or a field function value, just as in action sketches.

```
┌─────────────────────────────────────────────────────────────┐
│                                                               │
│   DESTINATION PSEUDO-SKETCH          COPY: 0___               │
│   Operation: ship_____                      │
│       Where: accounting_____                      │
│                                                               │
└─────────────────────────────────────────────────────────────┘
```

Figure 8: Destination pseudo-sketch

A weak sort of postcondition is available by employing a function call to decide the operation, dossier name or shipping destination. General postconditions can only be achieved by cooperating form procedures that accept different cases of the working set of forms. Suppose, for example, that the processing of an order causes the quantity of an item in stock to dip below a certain acceptable level. We may wish, at this point, to send a memo to the manager, initiating an increase in the production of the item. The procedure which processes the order is incapable of *conditionally* producing this memo as a postcondition to inventory update. It could unconditionally produce such a memo and then functionally decide to mail it either to the manager or to a garbage collection station. A cleaner approach, though, is to have a separate procedure that searches for low inventory items, and then sends the memo.

With this approach, individual tasks are clearly identified. Automatic procedures are simple and completely devoid of control flow. Furthermore, the implementation is simpler, because postconditions correspond to separate procedures. The low inventory checker, for example, is only invoked when an inventory form is updated.

5. Implementation

An automatic forms procedure in TLA is specified by a collection of sketches, and consequently describes *what* is to be done rather than how to do it. The sketch representation is very convenient for the user. This format, however, is wholly unsuitable for implementation. The specification must be analyzed and translated for greater run-time efficiency.

We cannot predict when the forms required to trigger a forms procedure may arrive. The processing must, therefore, be broken into distinct parts. The specification, in terms of sketches, contains information of four basic kinds: local (form) constraints, global (working set) constraints, duplicate form types (so that one form is not used to match two sketches within a single working dossier), and actions. The execution of a forms procedure makes use of these four specifications at different stages. It is convenient to process these specifications at procedure definition time, and translate them into formats that require no further run-time analysis.

Suppose that TLA is notified of the availability of a form for automatic processing. It first checks whether the form matches the local conditions of any precondition sketch for that form type. The local conditions are comprised of the source restriction and the field constraints. If a form does not match the local constraints of any precondition sketch, then TLA assumes that no procedure is prepared to handle it. Suppose that a form does match the local constraints of one or more precondition sketches. That form is then a candidate for a working set for a number of procedures. It is immaterial whether or not a working set including that form is complete. There is always the possibility that at some time the missing forms of the working set could arrive.

The form instance in figure 10 matches the local condition of the precondition sketch in figure 9, i.e., *quantity*>0. There may not necessarily be a global match if there is no order form with the same item number. Even if there is an order form with the same item number, it may not satisfy the other constraints of its precondition sketch.

Nevertheless, TLA notes that a local match has been made, and waits for the rest of the working set to arrive.

INVENTORY RECORD Key : ————————

Item : =ord.item———
Price : ————————
Quantity in stock : >0————————

Description : ————————————

Figure 9: Precondition sketch

INVENTORY RECORD Key : 00001.00000——

Item : 465————————
Price : 16000.00————
Quantity in stock : 12————————

Description : Workstation————————

Figure 10: Form instance matching local preconditions

TLA checks the local constraints of a form, records its findings, usually determines that the form does not complete a working set, and then waits for more forms to arrive. Further processing may not occur for some time. All local constraints for forms of the same type are extracted from all procedures and stored in a common file. This file is opened to check the local constraints of a given form for all procedures.

After the local constraints have been matched for a form, TLA checks link conditions between the corresponding sketches of the procedure. The link conditions are stored in files by procedures. Suppose that, in the previous example, TLA found an order for item 0002. It would note that the link between the inventory and order form precondition sketches was satisfied by these two form instances. If the working set consisted of only these two forms, then the procedure actions would be performed. Otherwise, TLA would wait until forms were found to match the remaining links of the procedure.

Even if forms arrive together, the processing of the forms is sequential. TLA treats each form individually. A locking algorithm guarantees that two forms cannot be processed at once at a given workstation. Generally, forms will not arrive simultaneously. One can expect a considerable delay between the establishment of local constraints and the evaluation of links between forms.

Actions are performed only when a working set of forms has been compiled. Actions are stored in a separate file. TLA preprocesses procedures, to check the legality of actions and to determine a legal order of execution if one exists. No further run-time analysis is performed. Actions run to completion.

The example in figure 11 *implicitly* requires that *price* must first be copied from the inventory form before its value may be multiplied by the *quantity*. This establishes a legal order of actions for that sketch.

```
ORDER FORM      Key : _____

Customer number : _____
   Customer name : _____

      Description : _____
             Item : _____
            Price : ?inv.price_____
         Quantity : _____
            Total : #mult !price ?quantity
```

Figure 11: Ordering of actions

An admittedly unlikely case is captured in figure 12, which is triggered if TLA detects two inventory forms for a single item. Since there are two precondition sketches in the procedure, TLA assumes that they refer to two *different* forms in the working set. Otherwise, any inventory form would trivially satisfy both precondition sketches, and thus trigger the procedure. When the procedure is written, TLA notes immediately that two precondition sketches describe forms of the same type. It performs a key comparison of those forms in any working set identified to guarantee that they are not one and the same.

The TLA automatic procedure interpreter is triggered upon receipt of mail, form creation and form modification. Since the last two are the responsibility of the user, triggering in these cases involves only the spawning of a new interpreting process. In the first case, however, the interpreting process is initiated by the user who sent the mail.

```
┌─────────────────────────────────────────────────────┐
│                                                       │
│   INVENTORY RECORD  Key : ──────────                  │
│                                                       │
│                     Item : ──────────                 │
│                    Price : ──────────                 │
│         Quantity in stock : ──────────                │
│                                                       │
│              Description : ───────────────            │
│                                                       │
└─────────────────────────────────────────────────────┘
```

Precondition sketch *inv1*

```
┌─────────────────────────────────────────────────────┐
│                                                       │
│   INVENTORY RECORD  Key : ──────────                  │
│                                                       │
│                     Item :  =inv1.item───             │
│                    Price : ──────────                 │
│         Quantity in stock : ──────────                │
│                                                       │
│              Description : ───────────────            │
│                                                       │
└─────────────────────────────────────────────────────┘
```

Precondition sketch *inv2*

Figure 12: Duplicate form types in a procedure

Automatic procedures are meant to run regardless of whether the user to whom the corresponding station belongs ever signs on after the procedure is written. Mail in the system is routed through a host control node. The sending station sends a message to the host consisting of the contents of the form tuple and the name of the station which is to receive the mail. The host then stores the form, updates the receiving station's mail tray and sends a message to the recipient's station. At the recipient's station machine, the interpreting process is started. It communicates with the host, asking for images of each new form in the recipient's mailtray. The interpreter maintains files of form images for each form available for automatic processing. It deletes the images when the forms have been processed either automatically or by the user. The images are copies of the contents of each form for use by the interpreter alone, and are stored just as forms are stored. The user, however, has no access to the images as forms. They may not be modified, shipped away, or otherwise manipulated. They are not properly forms or copies of forms, but merely *images* of forms.

Mail may arrive while the interpreter is running. It, therefore, continues to process all mail until it discovers an empty tray, in a manner similar to that of the line printer deamon in UNIX^{TM}. Only one interpreter may run at any time for a given station. In this way we eliminate interference problems between interpreters. A lock is placed on the running of the interpreter for a given station.

6. Sketch and Instance Graphs

The working set of a form procedure is abstracted in terms of a *sketch graph*, with the sketches as coloured vertices, and the matching conditions as edges in the graph. The form-gathering algorithm must find corresponding forms, and satisfy matching conditions of the sketch graph. An *instance graph* is associated with the forms retrieved. The interpreter tries to match the sketch graph in the instance graph.

Consider the precondition sketches in figure 13. A link between the account and order forms is established across the customer number. A link between the order and inventory forms is captured by *two* global conditions, one by item number and the other by quantity.

The corresponding sketch graph is shown in figure 14. Each sketch is represented by a labelled/coloured node. Each collection of global conditions between a pair of sketches is represented by a single edge.

When a form is passed to the interpreter, it first reads the file of local constraints for the forms of that type. Whenever a match is found, the interpreter notes which sketch of which procedure is matched by the form, and it enters a tuple consisting of the form type, the form key, the procedure and the sketch matched into a relation (called "NODE").

The file of global constraints for the matched procedure is then read. For every link concerning the matched sketch, the system establishes whether the current form satisfies the join conditions with any of the forms previously recorded in the NODE relation. For every new link found, the system inserts a tuple into another relation called EDGE. EDGE records the form keys, types, sketch names, and the procedure name of every link established.

The NODE and EDGE relations describe an instance graph, with forms as vertices or nodes and links between them as edges. The vertices are coloured according to which sketch the form matches. If a form matches two or more distinct sketches in one or more procedures, it is multiply represented, once for each sketch. Procedure names partition the instance graph, since there can be no links between sketches of different procedures. For each partition, we wish to match the

```
┌─────────────────────────────────────────────┐
│                                               │
│   CUSTOMER ACCOUNT                            │
│                Key: _____          │
│                                               │
│   Customer number:  =order.number_____      │
│         Credit rating: _____      │
│             Balance: _____       │
│                                               │
└─────────────────────────────────────────────┘
```

```
┌─────────────────────────────────────────────┐
│                                               │
│   ORDER FORM      Key :  _____      │
│                                               │
│   Customer number : _____           │
│       Customer name : _____       │
│                                               │
│       Description : _____         │
│              Item : _____             │
│             Price : _____             │
│          Quantity : ≤inv.quantity__           │
│             Total : _____             │
│                                               │
└─────────────────────────────────────────────┘
```

```
┌─────────────────────────────────────────────┐
│                                               │
│   INVENTORY RECORD Key : _____      │
│                                               │
│              Item :  =order.item__            │
│             Price : _____             │
│      Quantity in stock : _____        │
│                                               │
│       Description : _____         │
│                                               │
└─────────────────────────────────────────────┘
```

Figure 13: Precondition sketches of a procedure

sketch graph that describes the working set of forms for that procedure. Nodes are assigned a unique colour for each sketch, and the corresponding colours are used in the instance graph. An instance of the sketch graph, then, must be found within the instance graph.

Figure 15 shows the instance graph for the procedures of figure 13. Forms have been found to match each of the precondition sketches of the procedure, but there is no complete working set. When a

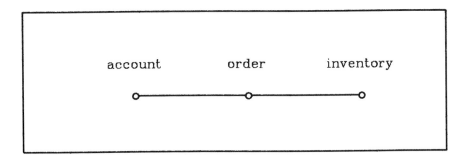

Figure 14: A sketch graph for a single procedure

working set is found, it is processed and disappears from the instance graph. Note that most of the disconnected subgraphs of the instance graph are in fact subgraphs of the sketch graph. In the last case, however, there are two orders for a single item, and the relationship is not that simple. The first account form to complete either working set will complete the "copy" of the sketch graph to be found in the instance graph.

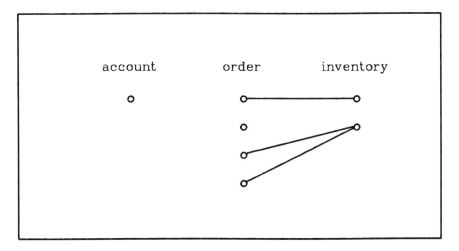

Figure 15: The instance graph for a procedure

The relationships between the forms in the working set of a form procedure are usually best expressed in terms of the join conditions. The sketch graph will generally be connected. The instance graph, however, will more often consist of several partially complete working sets of forms, and so will usually be disconnected.

If the join conditions imposed on the working set of forms are "nice", then each connected subgraph of the instance graph will also be a subgraph of the sketch graph. It is conceivable, however, that two forms satisfying a precondition sketch may each satisfy a join condition with a third form satisfying a second sketch in the same procedure. This anomaly will occur if the imposed join conditions are "not nice enough". In this case, the connected subgraphs of the instance graph are not as simply related to the sketch graph. Thus, establishing when a complete working set of forms has been compiled requires careful analysis.

When the system has finished processing a form, we know that the instance graph contains no copies of the sketch graph. If a copy of the sketch graph is identified, then a working set has been found, the procedure is executed, and the corresponding nodes and edges are purged from the instance graph. No more working sets remain. When a new form arrives, a working set of forms may be completed only if that new form is included. The analysis of the instance graph, then, need only concern the connected subgraphs that include nodes representing the new form.

Join conditions giving rise to sketch *trees* seem natural, since the "cheapest" description of the relationships between sketches would contain no cycles. If A is related to B and B is related to C, then one would hope not to find any other relationship holding between A and C. In practice, however, things may not be that simple. Join conditions might give rise to cycles, or even disconnected sketch graphs. Suppose that the warehouse, for example, has a single *value* form at its workstation, keeping track of the total dollar value of its stock. The procedures which update it would include a blank precondition sketch for a *value* form. Since there is no confusion about *which value* form is needed, there are no local or global conditions to be specified for it. The corresponding sketch graph in figure 16 is therefore disconnected.

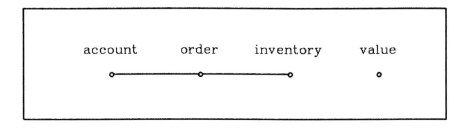

Figure 16: A disconnected sketch graph

7. Graph-Chasing

The algorithm which searches the instance graph for a copy of the sketch graph employs a list of *potential working sets*. Initially there exists a single such set, containing only the key of the newly added form. Edges are traversed in the instance graph and keys are added to each set until all edges and nodes in the sketch graph have been checked.

We start at the node of the sketch graph corresponding to the new form. We traverse edges leading out from that node, and check off any new nodes that we reach. We may follow any previously untraversed edges leading from any node we have thus far reached. Edges will lead back to old nodes wherever cycles occur. If the sketch graph is discon-nected, then the subgraph containing the first node will be traversed first. Edges not in that subgraph cannot lead from old nodes until an edge is traversed which checks off two new nodes.

The sketch and instance graphs in figure 17 will be used to illus-trate the graph-chasing algorithm. The example contains both cycles and disjoint subgraphs.

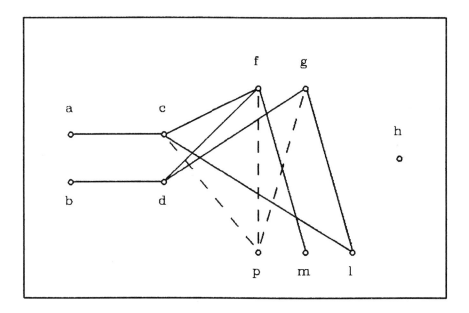

Figure 17: Sample sketch and instance graphs

Sketches 3 and 5 are sketches for the same form type, but represent distinct forms in the procedure. The terms $\{a,b,c, \cdots p\}$ are keys belonging to forms that match the local conditions of the sketch graph. Form a, for example, matches sketch 1. Edges in the instance graph represent joins. Forms c and f, for example, satisfy the global conditions between sketches 2 and 3.

The addition of form p results in the completion of the working set (a,c,f,h,p) where previously no complete working set existed. The algorithm presented here will identify this set of forms.

As we trace a path through the sketch graph, we try to mimic our actions nondeterministically in the instance graph. If we follow an edge in the sketch graph, we attempt to follow that edge in the instance graph for each set in our list. For each success, we add a new key to some set, and for each failure, we delete a set. Suppose that several edges may be traversed in the instance graph for a given edge of the sketch graph. We then split the current set and add a new node for each copy. The closing of a cycle in the sketch corresponds conceptually to a select on the set list. In this way we ensure that links actually exist in the instance graph for the two relevant forms represented in each set.

Figure 18 describes the steps followed in locating the working set in our example. If at any point all working sets are eliminated, the algorithm halts, with no working set of forms identified.

The sketch and instance graphs are described as follows: The sketch graph is $G'(N',E')$, where $N'=\{1, \cdots n\}$ is the set of colours and E' is a subset of $N' \times N'$ containing no (i,j) such that $i=j$. F is the set of form keys. The instance graph is $G(N,E)$, where N is a subset of $N \times F$ and E is a subset of $N \times N$. Furthermore, we adopt the convention that if $x=(i,k)$ belongs to N, then $x'=i$ and $x''=k$, and if $e=(x,y)$ belongs to E, then $e'=(x',y')$.

In the example,

$$N' = \{1,2,3,4,5\}$$
$$E' = \{(1,2),(2,3),(3,5),(2,5)\},$$
$$F = \{a,b,c,d,f,g,h,l,m,p\},$$
$$N = \{(1,a),(1,b),...(5,p)\}, \text{ and}$$
$$E = \{((1,a),(2,c)),((1,b),(2,d)),...((2,c),(5,p))\}.$$

We note, then, that for each x in N, x' must belong to N', and for each e in E, e' must belong to E' — i.e., nodes and edges in the instance graph correspond to nodes and edges of the sketch graph.

Suppose that finding a complete set of forms is equivalent to locating an instance of the sketch graph within the instance graph. We can express this as follows: We seek all subsets N'' of N such that

1. $\{x' | x \in N''\} = N'$

potential working sets					
1	2	3	4	5	
				p	p is a new form matching sketch 5.
		f		p	From node 5 in the sketch graph we can reach node 3 along edge $(3,5)$. The edges $((3,f),(5,p))$ and $((3,g),(5,p))$ in the instance graph are followed, and the potential working set is "split".
		g		p	
	c	f		p	The edge $(2,3)$ is now followed, splitting the first set of the previous step.
	d	f		p	
	d	g		p	
a	c	f		p	Follow edge $(1,2)$.
b	d	f		p	
b	d	g		p	
a	c	f		p	Edge $(2,5)$ completes a cycle. Perform a select on the sets resulting from the last step. Since $((2,d),(5,p))$ is not in the instance graph, two potential working sets are lost.
a	c	f	h	p	All the edges in the sketch graph have been traversed. A form that matches sketch 4 must be added.
a	c	f	h	p	Check that form f differs from form p.

Figure 18: Finding a working set of forms

and

2.   for each (i,j) in E', there exist x and y in N'' such that $x'=i$, $y'=j$ and $(x;y)$ belongs to E — i.e., for each node and edge of the sketch graph, there exist unique corresponding nodes and edges in the spanning graph $G[N']$.

In the example,

$$N''=\{(1,a),(2,c),(3,f),(4,h),(5,p)\}.$$

The algorithm for finding all such subsets N'' makes use of the knowledge that any working set of forms must include the most recently added node, say x. Furthermore, there are two checklists, *node* and *edge*, with slots for each element of N' and E', respectively. These record whether or not the edges and nodes have been inspected. All are initially set to false, and a set list, D, is initially set to empty. Each set has n slots to hold all the keys of any working set of forms found by the algorithm in figure 19.

Let x in n represent the newly added form.
Add a set to D, with slot x' set to x''. x must belong to the working set.
Set *node*$[x]$ to true: check off *node*$[x]$ of the sketch graph.
for each $e = (i,j)$ in E' such that *edge*$[e]$ is false **do**
    if both *node*$[i]$ and *node*$[j]$ are false **then**
        for each set in D **do**
            for each (y,z) **in** E **where** $y' = i$ **and** $z' = j$ **do**
                copy the set
                set slot i to y'', slot j to z''
            end for
            delete the original set
        end for
    else if exactly one of *node*$[i]$ and *node*$[j]$ is false **then**
        /* without loss of generality, *node*$[i]$ */
        for each set in D **do**
            for each (y,z) **in** E **where** $y' = i$ **and** $z' = j$ **and** y'' **is already in slot** i **of the set do**
                copy the set
                set slot j to z''
            end for
            delete the original set
        end for
    else if *node*$[i]$ and *node*$[j]$ are true **then**
        for each set in D **where** (y,z) **is not in** E **and** $y'' = 1$, $z'' = j$ **do**
            delete the set
        end for
    end if
    set *edge*$[e]$ to true
    set *node*$[i]$ to true
    set *node*$[j]$ to true
end for
Check that forms of the same type are different.

Figure 19: The graph-chasing algorithm

If D is empty when the algorithm is finished, then no working sets were found. If D is not empty, then the "first" set containing no duplicate keys is chosen as the working set.

The station's owner may attempt to move some of the forms in the working set while the interpreter is running. Each of the forms must therefore be set aside. Each form in the working set is deleted from the system so that the only copy is the interpreter's image of the form. If any of the forms cannot be found, then the interpreter restores all the forms retained thus far, and aborts the forms procedure.

If all the forms are successfully obtained, then the interpreter performs the set of actions. In the translation phase, the legality of actions, implied actions, and a legal order of actions have already been determined.

Actions may "fail" if a string is too long to be inserted in a given field, or if a form is mailed to a non-existent station. In the former case, TLA chooses to insert the null string by default, with the understanding that both humans and procedures are intelligent enough to interpret this, not as a value, but as a non-value. In the latter case, OFS (and consequently TLA) returns the mail to the sending workstation. Since TLA procedures are capable of recognizing the source of mail, it is presumed that this anomaly could be appropriately dealt with if a user felt it necessary.

8. Concluding Remarks

Our form-processing facility captures, in some sense, what is meant by an "automatic forms procedure". The context of OFS limits the range of possible actions upon forms. There are also many things that persons can do with OFS which have not been modelled in TLA. Automatic procedures, for example, are not smart enough to expect the timely return of a form which has been shipped away.

Form flow is determined by the particular configuration of procedures across the system. It is the responsibility of the users and an office administrator to model and analyze so that there are no undesirable side effects resulting from a particular combination of automatic procedures. Such analysis should be performed within a reasonable complexity bound, and it should be performed mechanically if at all possible (see the companion paper, "Message Flow Analysis").

The complexity of interpreting automatic procedures and form-gathering clearly depends on:

1. the size of the working set for a procedure,
2. the number of automatic procedures running at workstations, and
3. the number of form images "waiting" in the instance graphs of a workstation.

The complexity of identifying a sketch graph within the graph grows if the sketch graph is not merely a subgraph of the instance graph. Obviously, whatever factors contribute to this complexity must be considered in any "good office design". However, exactly what constitutes "good design", and to what extent it is feasible, is not easily established.

Partly completed working sets of forms may or may not have a particular meaning in terms of exceptions and errors. If forms are "missing" from a working set, the present forms may also be part of another working set. The missing forms would determine which procedure is to be activated. There is no way of telling which procedure forms are missing until they arrive. Missing forms may never arrive. There is no way of interpreting their absence as an error, except by placing some arbitrary time limit upon form-gathering.

Forms may satisfy partly completed working sets for a number of procedures. There is a need for some convenient way of displaying these sets. Users could interpret what is "missing", and possibly act on this information. Instance graphs could be quite complicated. Several partly completed sets may overlap in a single instance graph. A graphic display would present this information in a much better fashion than lists of form keys.

A simple feature that would increase user interaction with automatic procedures would be a function whose value is determined by the user. When the interpreter sees this function assigned to a field in an action sketch, it holds all the forms in the working set. It then notifies the user when he next signs on, and waits until the user makes a request to inspect the working set. At that point the user is allowed to assign a value to the field (or possibly abort the procedure), and then execution will resume.

Form flow between stations in TLA is determined by the interplay of automatic procedures. Flow of execution could be made more explicit by passing control between procedures in different stations. One should then also pass working sets of forms between procedures. In this way one could explicitly determine the order of operations. Procedures could then be called from other procedures without the need for form-gathering. Decision points could be modelled by branching rather than by a variety of similar working sets of forms. Which procedure is to be called could be decided by evaluating a function whose arguments are field values from the working set.

Many office automation systems have been strongly influenced by the SBA [deJo80] and OBE [Zloo80] systems and Officetalk [ElNu80]. The most noticeable exceptions are SCOOP [Zism77] and BDL [HHKW77], which are, however, more office-systems programming languages than office workers' languages. TLA uses forms that are manipulated at workstations, like Officetalk; the non-procedural interface for defining procedures was in large part inspired by the work of deJong and Zloof. However, TLA takes a somewhat different approach from either.

A goal of the TLA project was to provide a facility for automating office procedures, which could be used by office workers, as opposed to computer professionals, with a minimum of training. As a result, there was an emphasis on providing familiar concepts and a highly uniform interface.

The form is a very familiar concept to all office workers. Therefore, the idea of a sketch is an easy one to teach. By contrast, the SBA notion of boxes is both useful and powerful. However, it has no analog in the office of today, and therefore requires a more expert office worker in its use.

In TLA, "conditions" (constraints) appear within a form itself. This reflects an underlying philosophy in the TLA project that the user interface should be as uniform as possible. There are no separate condition boxes attached to forms within the underlying manual system, and therefore there are no separate conditions attached to sketches. Information that absolutely cannot be obtained from the form fields (such as the source of the form) is specified using pseudo-sketches that resemble forms as closely as possible.

Our form specification facility, like its base systems, OFS and MRS, runs on very small computers. Most of the development was done for an LSI-11/23. It will essentially run on any UNIX^{TM}-oriented workstation. This means that the hardware required for TLA is affordable by any office large enough to benefit from automation. At the same time, incremental growth can be easily achieved by adding additional machines, of a wide range of sizes, to a local net.

OFS, MRS, and TLA have been implemented on machines running under UNIX^{TM}. Compatibility with OFS was maintained in TLA. Changes to code, and the internal representation of an OFS system were mostly additions to modules and UNIX^{TM} file directories. Where existing files and code were modified, compatibility was maintained, so that OFS would simply ignore the added TLA features. Conversion costs from an OFS system to one that supports TLA are negligible, and any TLA system can be run with the OFS subset. In essence, OFS, MRS and TLA are completely integrated.

9. References

[Cheu79] [deJo80] [ElNu80] [Gibb79] [HaKu80] [HHKW77] [Hogg81] [Hudy78] [KeRi78] [Korn79] [Ladd79] [Nier81] [TRGN82] [Tsic82] [Zism77] [Zloo80]

8
An Object-Oriented System

O.M. Nierstrasz

ABSTRACT *Applications in Office Information Systems are often very difficult to implement and prototype, largely because of the lack of appropriate programming tools. We argue here that "objects" have many of the primitives that we need for building OIS systems, and we describe an object-oriented programming system that we have developed.*

1. Introduction

One of the great difficulties in implementing office information systems and prototypes for testing new OIS concepts is the unavailability of appropriate programming languages. A great deal of effort is therefore spent "re-inventing the wheel" whenever a new prototype is developed. In this paper, we discuss our efforts to address this problem by developing a simple, object-oriented programming environment. We argue that "objects" are a natural primitive for programming many OIS applications (see the companion paper, "Objectworld"). They are far more appropriate (if they can be implemented efficiently) than a high-level language such as C or Pascal.

In papers such as [HaSi80, ElNu80, HaKu80, Morg80, SSKH82], office behaviour is described as being event-driven and semi-structured. Office activities exhibit a great degree of parallelism and "bursty" behaviour, meaning that activities alternate between running and suspended states. Activities may have to coordinate several documents, or even synchronize themselves with other activities. Messages and documents are sometimes highly structured, especially in the case of forms. Typically these documents also have certain constraints and functional capabilities not generally associated with databases. Many of these issues are addressed directly by object-oriented programming [ABBH84].

Objects bear comparison to abstract data types [Gutt77], actors [Hewi77], and SBA/OBE boxes [deZl77]. Many of the properties of our object model are also exhibited by Xerox' Smalltalk system [GoRo83, Gold84]. Objects combine data and program by allowing the programmer to specify the nature of the data that the object may hold, that is, its *contents*, and also the allowable set of operations valid for those data, that is, the object's *behaviour*. The object construct therefore exhibits several "nice" properties, among them modularity, encapsulation (of data and operation), strong typing, and duration. The last is important, since objects typically have a longer lifetime than the execution of most programs. In addition, our object model allows for specialization of objects, and automatic triggering of the object's *rules* (operations) wherever appropriate. Finally, because the operations are explicitly bound to the data, an extra measure of security is achieved, without any loss of generality. The object model appears to be as powerful as more traditional machine models that separate data and program.

In the following section we shall discuss our abstract object model, and we will demonstrate some of the power of objects. The remaining sections deal with the implementation of our prototype object-oriented programming system, called *Oz*. Specifically, we discuss the user interface, the internal system design, and the details of object management.

2. The object model

In this section we shall describe in some detail what we mean by the term "object", and how it can be used as a programming tool. Specifically, we discuss the relationship between the data and the program elements of objects (called *rules*), and we explain under what circumstances the rules may be executed.

2.1. Object classes

Perhaps the key distinguishing characteristic of objects is encapsulation. An object, like an abstract data type, forces us to describe our data, and the operations that manipulate them, together. Once we have completed our specification of an object class, we can be certain that instances of that class will not be abused by anyone's attempt to perform invalid or inappropriate operations on them.

An object is responsible for anything that happens to it. Furthermore, in our object model, we give objects the responsibility of executing that part of their behaviour that is to be automatically triggered whenever pre-defined conditions are met. Any object can therefore become active at any time, if the right conditions arise to cause it to spring into action.

Objects are divided into *object classes*, which are comparable to the notion of types. Any object is an *instance* of some given object class. The classes are characterized by their specifications, and the instances are characterized by their values. As an analogy, we may compare object classes to database schemata, and object instances to values in the database (such as relational tuples).

Objects have both data and "program" components. We refer to these as *contents* and *behaviour*. The contents of an object can be described by a set of *instance variables*. The values of these variables will characterize any given object instance. The behaviour of an object is given by a collection of *rules*. These "rules" resemble the procedures or subroutines of a program, with the exception that there is no "main" program to call them. The rules are invoked by other objects, or *acquaintances*, that the object agrees to deal with.

Rules may contain local (temporary) variables, and executable statements that modify the instance variables, just as a subroutine might, but they may also contain a set of *triggers* or preconditions on the execution of the rule. If any one trigger condition fails, then the rule may not be executed. A common trigger condition is to restrict the allowable object classes of the object invoking the rule, as in the following example.

In the simple example in figure 1, we define part of a *customer* object. It is defined to be a specialization of an *office* object. *name* and *owner* are instance variables, and *set_name* is a rule. The invoking object (indicated by the special symbol "~") must be an *office* object whose owner is also the owner of the *customer* object. The *name* variable may be manipulated by other rules as well, specifically, it may be initialized at the time of creation.

2.2. Events

If a rule b of object B is invoked, then there must be an invoking rule a of an acquaintance A. Rule b can fire if and only if both it and rule a are completely satisfied, that is, all their trigger conditions are met. For example, the *ch_name* rule in figure 2 invokes the *set_name*

```
customer : office {
      /* instance variables */
      name, owner : string,

      /* rules */
      set_name (n) {
            /* invoking acquaintance */
            ˜ : office,
            n : string,

            /* a trigger condition */
            ˜.owner = owner;
            name := n;
            }
      }
```

Figure 1: A simple object specification

rule of figure 1. Both rules must be satisfied for an event to fire.

```
ch_name {
      c : customer,
      m : memo,

      m.creator = "legal";
      m.oldname = c.name;
      c.set_name (m.newname);
      m.omega;
      }
```

Figure 2: an invoking rule

Furthermore, rules *a* and *b* may invoke other rules in yet other objects. All of these rules must be satisfied before any of them may execute. This is what we call an *event*. If any rule participating in an event has a trigger condition that fails, then the event fails. If all the rules are satisfied, then the event may *fire*, and all rules participating in the event are executed.

A rule is allowed to invoke itself. The trigger conditions within such a rule then monitor instance variables or an acquaintance. The *ch_name* rule in figure 2 is self-triggering, and monitors the arrival (creation) of a *memo* object from the *legal* department, indicating a change-of-name. In this example, the *memo* object could not invoke the *set_name* rule directly, since it is not an *office* object. When an event occurs that alters the instance variables or those of the acquaintance, the trigger conditions must be checked to see if a new event must be fired. The firing of one event may therefore "cascade", and cause other events to (eventually) be fired.

Trigger conditions may dictate the allowable message classes of acquaintances invoking a rule, the type of value passed by a communicating acquaintance, predicates over those values, and predicates over the instance variables of the object itself.

There are two special rules included in the behaviour of any object. The *alpha* rule is used to create new object instances, and the *omega* rule is used to destroy an existing object instance. The *alpha* rule may thus be used to specify the conditions under which objects may be created, whom they may be created by, and what instance variables should be initialized to when they are created. Of course, any side effects of object creation can also be included by causing the *alpha* rule to invoke other rules in acquaintances. The *alpha* rule for the *customer* object might be used to initialize the *name* variable. Once an object is created, other rules in its behaviour may be triggered.

omega {
    ~ : *user,*

    ~.owner = owner;
  .}

Figure 3: an omega rule

The *omega* rule, given in figure 3, ensures that only the *owner* may destroy the object, and the act must be performed directly by the *user*, not any subordinate *office* object. Another possible use of the *omega* rule is to keep a log of the circumstances under which an object was destroyed.

2.3. Specialization

New object classes may be created from old ones by the process of specialization. A specialized object class is a *subclass* of some parent *superclass*. The subclass may have:

1.   more instance variables: the existing instance variables are inherited from the superclass, and new variables are made available to instances of the subclass

2.   more rules: the existing rules are inherited from the superclass and new rules are available to instances of the subclass

3.   restricted domains: instance variables are inherited from the superclass, but they may assume values only from subdomains

4.   restricted rules: rules are inherited from the superclass, but they may have additional trigger conditions to further restrict the cases under which they may fire

The definition of specialization given here is very similar to that used in the Taxis system [GrMy83].

Specialization is important, in that it ensures that new classes derived from some superclass have at least the properties of the super-class. All *office* objects might thus, for example, be defined to have *owner* variables set at creation, and rules that prohibit destruction by anyone other than the current owner. An important open issue is how much alteration of existing behaviour should be allowed in subclasses. If a specialized *office* object has altered behaviour or additional behaviour that completely undermines the behaviour of the unadorned *office* object class, then the fact that it is a "specialization" is virtually meaningless.

2.4. Expressive power

As described in [NiMT83, Moon84, Twai84], Oz objects can easily be used to capture the behaviour exhibited by event-oriented models such as finite automata and Petri nets. The state of an automaton can be easily described using the instance variables of an object, and the rules for changing states can be captured in the general language of the object's rules. In addition, one may associate additional side effects with the state transitions given by the underlying model. A typical application would be to implement *augmented Petri nets*, as described by Zisman in his dissertation [Zism77, Zism78]. In this formalism for specifying procedures, Petri nets are augmented by additional preconditions and actions that refer to the world outside the model.

Office procedures, as described in a companion paper in this book, can also be implemented using objects. Trigger conditions in the office procedures translate directly into trigger conditions of a procedure object, and actions similarly translate into object rule actions.

Objects can also be used to easily capture electronic forms. An electronic form would be represented by a single object class. Form instances would correspond to object instances, with each field of the form being represented by a single instance variable. Additional, "hidden", instance variables might also be used to maintain internal information about a form, such as who created it, or when it was last modified. All form types could therefore be implemented as specializations of a standard *form* object class, with a few minimal properties. Since a form's behaviour is entirely determined by the rules of its object class, there is no danger of corrupting existing forms by adding new applications to a system. These new applications would still be forced to make use of the form interface defined by the object's behaviour.

A wide variety of important field types [Geha82] can be implemented with comparative ease. Some of the possibilities are fields that must be supplied when a form is created, and then may never be changed, fields that must be filled in a particular order, fields that function as locks on other fields, and signature fields that are automatically filled when a particular action is performed. Restricted views can also be implemented, since the identity of an acquaintance must be made available before an object will release any information. Since the language for specifying actions is general-purpose, there is virtually no limit to the kinds of fields that can be implemented.

Intelligent messages, as described in the companion paper, "Intelligent Message Systems", are implementable using objects. In this scenario, messages are objects that not only store information, but carry procedures with them for dynamically altering the content of the message, and for altering or refining their destination. Since arbitrarily complicated procedures can be encoded in the behaviour of an object, intelligent as well as passive messages can be designed using the object formalism. For a discussion of various "flavours" of interesting objects, see the concluding paper of this book.

Finally, objects provide an elegant mechanism for ensuring data security and integrity. *Roles*, as described in the companion paper, "Etiquette Specification in Message Systems", can be implemented with objects. A trivial example of this is the use of the *owner* variable in *office* objects. In the hierarchical object world described in the concluding section of this paper, objects could be equipped with instance variables that are themselves *role* objects. The *role* objects may be arbitrarily complex (or as simple as the *owner* variable), and they may be thought of as authorization currency in object transactions. Since objects cannot be forged in an object world, the possession of a particular kind of *role* object may be used to guarantee certain powers or capabilities.

3. User Interface

Our prototype object-oriented programming system makes use of an explicit *user* object class to represent users. Whenever a user interacts with the universe of objects in any way, he does so under the guise of a *user* object. The system was designed in a highly modular fashion, so that one would not necessarily be forced to use one particular user interface. One interface might be appropriate for system developers and another, more appropriate for naive users who do not do their own programming. We describe here a simple, but general, interface that is adequate for illustrating the power of our system. The material discussed in this section is covered in greater detail in chapter 4 of the M.Sc. thesis by Twaites [Twai84].

3.1. The *user* object class

The user interface is a "back door" into the system that allows us to make instances of the *user* object class appear to spontaneously initiate events. The *user* object class has its own predefined behaviour just as all other object classes do. In addition, there is a special *io* rule to enable us to exchange information with other objects, and a facility to allow users to temporarily create new rules. This latter capability is necessary if we do not wish to limit our actions to what is set out in the *user* specification. Of course, any given implementation of a user interface may choose whether or not to allow arbitrary interactions between *users* and other objects. Programmers might require a general, unrestricted interface such as is provided by Oz, whereas applications might present highly specialized interfaces. The kinds of objects that a user may create and interact with can be explicitly governed by his *user* specification. Furthermore, it is possible to provide a variety of *user* specifications corresponding to a variety of roles to be played by the users of a system. System administrators could thereby control the valid interactions between roles. (See the companion paper, "Etiquette Specifications in Message Systems", for a discussion of roles.)

The predefined *user* behaviour would normally include an *alpha* rule, restricting authorized users to creating new users, as well as rules for keeping track of login passwords, and so on. This predefined behaviour may naturally be specialized to restrict or extend the power of certain users.

The *io* rule is used by objects that require human intervention for the completion of events. As an example, consider the *ok_user* rule in figure 4 that checks whether a password is valid before allowing an object to change state and continue communicating with a *user*.

The *io* rule is used to print a message and retrieve a value. Only if the value returned is acceptable will the rule and the event fire. Since a response must be received before the condition may be tested, *io* rules are handled in a slightly different manner from other rules. Events including *io* rules must be suspended, pending the user's

ok_user {
    /* acquaintance must be a *user* */
    ~ : *user*,

    /* print message and test response */
    passwd = ~.io ("password: ");

    U := ~; /* remember the user */
    ok := TRUE; /* change state */
    }

Figure 4: using the io rule

response. If, in the meantime, anything happens to disable the event (such as the object being destroyed), then the event simply dies.

Temporary rules are used to expand the automatic behaviour that is predefined for *user* objects. This facility is provided because it is not possible to predict everything that a user may wish to do. Users can therefore "tailor" their *user* objects by temporarily adding new rules. Temporary rules may be used, for example, to create new object instances, to query existing objects (through their rules), or to modify objects.

3.2. System commands

The current user interface presents the system through a screen, as shown in figure 5. Commands are entered in the first area. The second area is used to indicate the current mode. The interface message area is used to display messages pertaining to the user interface. The object manager message area is used to display messages from objects using an *io* rule. These messages may or may not require a response. A message that is purely informative requires no response, and is not blocking any waiting event.

Whenever an object class or a temporary rule is being edited, the user interface screen is replaced by that of the editor, until the editing function is completed.

There are five top-level commands in the system, each with a one-letter name. The commands are all in prefix order, with the operator preceding the operands. The commands are:

h :   Help facility.

l :   Logout.

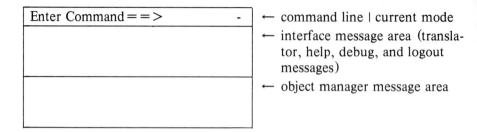

Figure 5: Screen layout

m [*message number*] :
> The specified message in the object manager message area is displayed, and a response to the *io* rule may be made.

t [[<] *temporary-rule-name*] :
> The specified temporary rule is executed. If preceded by a "<", the user is placed in the editor, and the new or existing rule may be edited.

c [*object class*] :
> The user may edit the new or existing object class definition. Upon exit from the editor, the definition may be translated and (upon error-free translation) added to the universe of object classes.

A BNF grammar for object classes and rules is presented in the appendix of this paper.

4. System Design

The Oz system is written in the C programming language [KeRi78], and runs on a VAX 11/780 under the UNIX™ operating system. The current implementation consists of under 4000 lines of C code. The VAX was chosen for the UNIX™ program development environment and for its availability rather than its size. The Oz system could easily have been developed on a smaller, stand-alone system such as a Sun workstation (which also runs UNIX™). One of the goals of the project was to allow users to share the same object universe. We decided, therefore, to have one process per user, plus a single process dedicated to object management. The system interface is via the user processes. Requests and commands that affect the object universe are then passed on to the object manager, which updates the database of objects. Conversely, when events take place that affect users, the object manager notifies the appropriate user processes. The division of labour between system interface and object manager is intended to be transparent to users.

One of the difficulties in using UNIX™ as an environment for implementing Oz is that processes cannot share memory. The communicating processes would be forced either to pass information through temporary files, or to make use of UNIX™ "pipes", which are buffers for passing streams of data. For the sake of speed, the latter approach was chosen.

A related difficulty was that processes may not communicate via pipes unless they are "related", that is, they have some common ancestor. This problem was solved by introducing a special "host" process that babysits the pipes and spawns new user processes. Whenever a user wishes to enter the system, the host process is signaled, and a new user process is created. (Signals may be sent between arbitrary processes, provided they have the same "group id", and the process identification of the receiver is known.) The new process inherits the pipe from the host, and communication with the object manager is enabled. The host is only retired when there are no more user processes connected to the object manager *and* the object manager has exhausted its current list of work to do. The next person entering the system will (transparently) create a new host and a new object manager.

Finally, we had to decide whether to make use of pipes in either direction, between the object manager and each of the user processes, or have just two pipes (one for data traveling in either direction) shared by all the user processes, or use some further variation. For simplicity's sake we decided to use just two pipes. There appeared to be no realizable efficiency gains by having multiple pipes, since the object manager could read messages from ten pipes no faster than from one. Whenever a process places a message on one of the pipes, it notifies the receiving process by sending it a signal. Reads and writes are guaranteed by UNIX™ to be atomic actions, thus ensuring the integrity of the messages. Signals, however, are not queued, so a reading process must always check the pipe after reading a message, to be certain that the pipe is empty.

Since processes are blocked if they attempt to write to a full pipe, write-request, write-ok, and receipt-acknowledgement signals are used to inform processes about the status of a pipe. The object manager makes sures its messages are received before attempting to send new messages to other user processes, and user processes must request a free pipe before they attempt to send a message to the object manager.

Although these considerations may be of interest to someone implementing an object-oriented programming environment, they do not have a direct bearing on the object model as described in the previous section. They do, however, illustrate the gymnastics one must go through in order to implement objects in an environment with an architecture that is better suited to supporting processes, files and stream i/o.

The messages that are sent between the user and object manager processes are all of a standard format. Each message consists of four pieces of data: the message type (represented by a short integer), the process identification of the sender (for acknowledgement purposes), the length of the message (in bytes), and the message body (generally a character string). User processes currently may send the following messages:

login request:
   sent if a user wishes to log into the system

change class definition:
   sent if a user wishes to add, change or delete an object class

temp rule:
   a temporary rule is being sent for immediate execution (and subsequent disposal)

instance manipulation:
   the user wishes to manipulate an object instance (currently handled through temporary rules)

reply to message:
   the message body is the response to an outstanding *io* rule message

logout request:
   sent if a user wishes to exit the system.

There is a corresponding set of messages that may be sent by the object manager

logout:
   acknowledges a logout request; the user process may exit, die, and return control to the calling program (usually the UNIX™ shell)

changing user contents:
   a change has occurred in the *user* object corresponding to the logged-in user; the user process maintains a consistent version

io rule message:
   a message from another object is sent to the *user* object via the *io* rule; a response may be in order

response to previous user message:
   a response is given to a previous temporary rule, an object class definition change or a logout

login successful:
   used to inform the user process that an attempt to log in has been

successful

5. Object Management

The object manager is responsible for storing and retrieving objects, and it must find and execute events. Object storage is divided into two components. Since all objects of the same class share the same behaviour, it is only necessary to store that behaviour once. Object instances of the same class are distinguished only by their contents. Thus only the instance variables are actually stored for each object instance. Object rules and the variable declarations are stored separately, in a structure that supports the notion of object specialization.

5.1. Storing and retrieving objects

In the compilation and translation of object definition, the instance variable names are converted to integers which serve as indices into a table of information about the variables. The correspondence between the variable names and the indices is stored in a symbol table. The information about the variables includes:

1. whether the variable is an instance variable or a temporary variable

2. the type of the variable

3. if the type is *object*, then the object class

4. the location of the value held by the variable

Of course, only the permanent (instance) variables are stored. Temporary variables exist only when events are being fired, and storage for them is provided at that time.

Similarly, a certain amount of processing takes place when rules are translated. Rule statements accomplish four things:

1. they may establish conditions which, if false, cause an event to fail

2. they may assign values to temporary variables

3. they may pass information to an acquaintance

4. they may update the value of an instance variable

The first three of these functions are done while events are being assembled. The last may only be performed if the event does not fail. It is, of course, possible to update an instance variable to some value sent by an acquaintance in a single statement. Statements are therefore decomposed into simpler statements that fall into just one of the above categories, and assignments to instance variables may be translated into two statements: an assignment to a new temporary variable, and reassignment to the instance variable only if the event succeeds. The simplified rule statements are then stored in a list structure and interpreted at run-time.

Specialization of object classes is implemented by storing rules and variable declarations in an *m-way* tree [HoSa76]. Nodes in the tree correspond directly to nodes in the specialization hierarchy. To determine which rules and variables, or which versions of rules and variables apply to a given specialization, one simply searches *up* the tree to the root. One therefore inherits the closest version of a rule or a variable. If the rule or variable does not apply to the given specialization, then the search ends with failure at the root of the tree.

5.2. Event-searching

Rules may either be explicitly invoked, or they may be self-triggering. The self-triggering rules wait for some condition to become true, and the triggered rules wait to be invoked by another rule belonging to some acquaintance (possibly another rule in the same object).

Event execution begins with self-triggering rules. A depth-first search algorithm is used to build the event. Whenever a call to a rule in an acquaintance is made, a branch is made in the tree, and execution continues at that level. If execution successfully completes at a certain level, control returns to the level above, and eventually to the self-triggering rule. If it does, an event will have been constructed, and the tree will be traversed to update the instance variables.

If at any point a rule fails, the backtracking of the depth-first search algorithm takes effect, and an alternative acquaintance is sought. This process continues until an event is constructed, or all possible acquaintances at some level are exhausted.

In addition, if an *io* rule is encountered, the event is suspended and the event-tree is saved, pending a user response. In this implementation, the objects in the tree are marked, and not used in other events until a response is received.

Since the event construction always starts with a self-triggering rule, a queue is kept of all such rules. The object manager repeatedly attempts to construct events starting with these rules until it succeeds. Although far more efficient schemes were initially considered, the simplicity of this approach made it quite adequate for the purposes of the Oz prototype. An alternative is outlined in the following section.

Note that no synchronization problems ever arose, since the object manager would never attempt to execute more than one event at a time.

6. Observations and Conclusions

The Oz system served primarily to demonstrate that certain ideas about programming with objects were workable. Not only is the object model powerful enough to capture interesting behaviour, but it appears to be quite workable as an implementation language. Our experience with Oz leads us to several conclusions about what is required to produce a useable object-oriented programming language. In addition, there are a number of open questions and philosophical puzzles concerning the proper way to implement such a language (see also the companion paper, "Objectworld").

6.1. Basic requirements

First of all, one would need to get rid of processes and files. They are not only conceptually incompatible with object-oriented programming, but the overhead they introduce could only serve to slow down an implementation by an order of magnitude (say). Instead, one would need a large, permanent, virtual memory. The address space required would certainly be larger than the host computer's primary storage, and would have to include at least all of available secondary storage. Since files will not exist, all of secondary storage will be available for the storage of objects (although "files" could be made available through the object interface). The virtual memory provided could be very simple. There would be no notion of objects associated with pages of memory at this level, although the pages themselves could be viewed as objects.

An object manager would use the virtual memory to permanently store objects. It would have to be able to bring any object into main memory quickly, given a unique object identification (*id*), and it would have to "swap out" inactive objects intact. An important requirement would be always to keep the object versions on disk at least coherent, and as up-to-date as possible. The object manager would also include (or work in tandem with) an event manager that would decide what objects were currently of interest. Requirements for the event manager are discussed the next section.

Certain objects would function as interfaces to device drivers. These objects would include the disk drive, the terminal, a communications network, and so on. A uniform object interface to everything would be desirable, so that even the operating system kernel, and pages of memory, could be dealt with as objects, by privileged programs. This is important if the language is to have any credibility as a systems implementation language.

6.2. The event manager

Events trigger other events. An event that has failed once will always fail, unless something happens to change the state of one of the objects involved in the event. It follows, as a consequence, that it is only necessary to check whether or not events are fireable, when variables mentioned explicitly in trigger conditions are altered by other events.

It suffices, therefore, to keep track of a queue of recently altered (and created) objects. For each object in the queue, one must determine what new events may be triggered as a consequence of the state change, and then attempt to construct an event. If no new event is found, the object is removed from the queue. Otherwise an event is found, and all altered participants are added to the queue. Of course, the queue need not be handled in a strictly sequential fashion. It is only necessary to ensure that all objects in the queue are handled eventually, and preferably before any objects that are added later. True concurrency may be achieved if several events are searched for at once.

To construct events, one would need to keep track of who is acquainted with whom, and determine which objects may initiate an event involving the one in the queue. It is open at this point to what extent one may intelligently choose possible events. To a large extent, this depends on how carefully the language is designed. The event manager should be presented with a clear list of possible acquaintances, to eliminate random searching. The event mechanism should be presented to the object programmer in such a way that it is clear how costly it will be to search for events, depending on how objects are designed.

Obviously, one would save time by checking only events that have a reasonable expectation of succeeding. A good language design can eliminate a great deal of fruitless event-checking, by making it possible at compile-time to note which events might trigger other events.

6.3. Object domains

A more sophisticated way of organizing objects is needed. A flat object universe makes event-searching a horror if there are many objects. One may easily organize objects hierarchically into *domains*. Each object is then an instance variable of some parent object, which is its domain. Conversely, all objects are the domains for their instance variables.

Parents are automatically acquainted with their children, and vice versa. It immediately follows that children can (ultimately) only become acquainted with anything in the outside world — and even with other siblings — through their parents. A parent may access its children through the instance variable names, but all other objects must do so through the children's *ids*. An *id* may thus be thought of as an indirect reference to an object. Once an object becomes acquainted with other objects, however, it becomes a free agent. A parent may choose, of course, to be protective, and always act as a middleman for certain of its children. The only other object that would necessarily be acquainted with *all* objects in the system would be the object manager. System objects or other privileged objects could then learn the identity of any object through the object manager, even when the parent is reluctant to reveal it.

Instance variables save space for objects. This is consistent with our intention that everything be an object. In *Oz*, only primitive objects (strings, etc.) were instance variables, but, in general, instance variables can hold any object. A parent may create a child object by saying to the system, "create an object for me, and put it *here*". If the object is destroyed, the space may be reused. Note that an object may only create another object if it has a place to put it. Otherwise it must find an acquaintance who is willing to be a parent.

Since one does not necessarily know the classes of all objects that one will become acquainted with, there should be some facility for discovering the class of an acquaintance. Similarly, an object would need to be able to discover what rules are valid for that acquaintance, and be able to *dynamically* address an arbitrary rule. Both of these problems may be addressed by supplying default rules to all objects in the language for revealing class and behaviour information, and for accessing rules dynamically using, say, strings composed of rule names. This is comparable to facilities in languages such as APL, LISP, and Snobol, that allow one to compose strings of commands and execute them through an interpreter.

6.4. Rules and instance variables

A wider variety of instance variables is needed. Instance variables could be primitive objects, such as integers, characters and object *ids*, or they could be complex objects. One would naturally want to have arrays of objects, but it also appears highly desirable to allow for *lists* of objects. A list would be similar to an array, but of unbounded length. Furthermore, whereas an array could contain gaps for nonexistent objects, lists might consist of existing objects only. Lists are important to have if certain objects and domains are to grow without bound. In particular, a *text* object would likely have an instance variable which is a list of characters (a string).

Rules similarly require some re-thinking. Explicit *assert* and *fail* statements appear to be more natural than the present scheme of simply stating conditions. (A *fail* statement is equivalent to *assert*(FALSE), and an *assert*(<cond>) is equivalent to *if*(not <cond>) *then fail.*) The ability to spawn asynchronous events may also be necessary for certain applications, though it is not clear what would happen to an event spawned by another event that fails.

A cleaner notion of event-searching results, if we force objects to provide a list of acquaintances with which they may be interested in communicating within some event. Clearly, the longer these lists get, the more work that must be done to search for events. The cost of event-searching is more directly in control of the object programmer. Ideally, the programmer should be able to tightly specify precisely the circumstances under which event-searching should take place. A carefully designed object would then cause a minimum of unsuccessful event searches. Again, a good language design will make the cost of triggering for alternative object specifications very apparent to the programmer.

6.5. Open issues

There are a number of questions for which it is more difficult to provide adequate answers. Some of these may be religious issues that can be argued a variety of ways. Others may quite significantly affect the function and semantics of the language and the system, but in ways that are not yet obvious. Still others do not seem to yield any appropriate solutions. We shall briefly discuss a few of the more interesting questions.

Are rules objects? Certainly object specifications are themselves objects (possibly *text* objects), and the executable code must be stored as an object, but there appears to be no conceptual justification for viewing rules as objects. Alternatively, it would be very convenient to be able to dynamically create rules, store them as instance variables, and execute them. Temporary rules could be handled in this fashion. Certain objects could then modify their own behaviour, or deal with arbitrary acquaintances in interesting ways. A good example would be a debugging object used to develop new object specifications.

Should objects be allowed to change their own specification by adding variables or rules? If an object has a list of rules, and rules are objects, then an object could just create a new rule and add it to the list. Somehow this seems to run contrary to the principle of an object as a sort of abstract data type. Instead, perhaps one should have to create a new object class and convert old objects to new objects. This would avoid horrendous problems in managing objects that are always changing their own representation. Furthermore, if it is possible to dynamically create and store temporary rules as instance variables, then it is no longer necessary to alter the default behaviour of an object.

Since one does not necessarily know the classes of all objects one may become acquainted with (since objects of new classes will likely become acquainted with old ones), there must be a way to get at the rules of these new objects. The suggestion made earlier was to allow for dynamic invocation of rules. This might be sufficient justification for a *rule* primitive object class which would be used just to store rule identifiers (as opposed to strings containing their names).

Temporary variables present some philosophical problems. Are they objects too? They can hold the same information that permanent objects can, but they come and go with apparent abandon. This may be a religious issue, since one can take the view that events are atomic, and, as a consequence, temporary variables never really exist.

More seriously, one should consider what is meant by assigning a value to an instance variable. Since instance variables are objects, one should never be able to simply "assign" a value to them. Rather, one should have to invoke a rule in the object, and pass the value to be assigned. Of course, this must eventually stop with primitive objects, so one could consider the notation ":=" as shorthand for invoking an implicit *assign-value* rule. Complex objects must be treated with more respect, however. It follows then that the only "values" appropriate for passing between acquaintances are primitive objects such as integers, characters and object *ids*.

An exception to this rule would be if an object is to change domains. It might be necessary, for example, to send an object from one machine to another. The alternative would be to destroy the original of an object, and to create a "copy" in the new domain. For many object types, however, it might be undesirable to allow the creation of copies in this fashion. Far simpler and much more elegant would be to permit objects to change domains. In the case of primitive objects such as integers, *ids* and strings, it is simpler to make a copy of the object, and pass that when communicating with an acquaintance. If a large object is to be passed (rather than simply its *id*), duplication of the object is likely to be undesirable, for efficiency reasons. In environments where objects represent documents or private communications, it is important to be clear that the actual owner of the object may change, rather than just its apparent owner.

If several object systems are to be connected via a network, and these systems are allowed to exchange objects, then it is important to ensure that all objects have *ids* unique in the entire object universe. All objects on a given machine should therefore be provided with identifiers that somehow indicate the host machine on which they were created (or the object manager should at least be able to handle identifiers for objects originating from a different machine, if they may superficially coincide with local identifiers).

A thorny question is how to handle events taking place between two (or more) machines. A reasonable approach is to appoint *overseer* objects that act as go-betweens for all the objects on a given machine, and those on other machines. The *overseers* would then be the only objects to partake in very simple events limited to exchanging objects between systems. Once an object has moved to a different system, it can take part in more complicated events.

As a final comment, we should point out some of the dangers of muddying the atomicity of events. If an event is allowed to "partially fail", or to fail but spawn another event before failing, then there is a potential for unauthorized information to leak from an object. Atomic events have the desirable property that none of the participants in an event give up any information unless all of them agree to a mutually acceptable contract (consisting of all the trigger conditions). An event, by definition, has no side effects unless it fires. If this definition is relaxed even slightly, then the security of all objects is threatened. Any attempts to do so would therefore have to take this into account by preventing pending events from communicating with external objects or with other events.

7. Appendix: BNF Grammar for the Oz Language

The BNF grammar presented below uses the following meta-symbols and meanings:

::=	shall be defined as
|	alternatively
[x]	zero or one instance of x
{ x }	zero or more instances of x

"xyz"   the terminal symbol xyz
< x >   the non-terminal symbol x where x is a sequence
           of letters and hyphens beginning with a letter.

```
<object> ::= <object-class> ":" <super-class> "{"
       { <declaration> ";" }
       { <rule> }
       "}"

<object-class> ::= user
       | <identifier>

<super-class> ::= object
       | <object-class>

<declaration> ::= <variable> { "," <variable> } ":" <type>

<rule> ::= <rule-name>
       [ "(" [ <variable> { "," <variable> } ] ")" ]
       "{" { <statement> ";" } "}"
       [ "(" [ <variable-value> ] ")" ]

<statement> ::= <declaration>
       | <condition>
       | <send>
       | <assignment>
       | <function>
       | <sub-rule>

<condition> ::= <variable-value> <comparator> <expression>

<comparator> ::= "="
       | "!="
       | "<"
       | "<="
       | ">"
       | ">="

<send> ::= <send-name> "." <rule-name>
       "(" [ <variable-value> { "," <variable-value> } ] ")"

<assignment> ::= <identifier> ":=" <expression>
```

```
<function> ::= <identifier>
      "(" [ <variable-value> { "," <variable-value> } ] ")"

<sub-rule> ::= "{"
      <statement> ";"
      { <statement> ";" }
      { "|" <statement> ";" { <statement> ";" } }
      "}"

<expression> ::= <variable-value>
      | <function>
      | <send>
      | <arithmetic-expression>
      | "(" <expression> ")"

<arithmetic-expression> ::= "-" <expression>
      | <expression> <arith-op> <expression>

<arith-op> ::= "*"
      | "/"
      | "+"
      | "-"

<rule-name> ::= alpha
      | omega
      | io
      | <identifier>

<send-name> ::= <identifier>
      | "~"
      | "*"

<type> ::= integer
      | string
      | <super-class>

<variable-value> ::= <variable>
      | <value>

<variable> ::= "~"
      | <identifier>

<value> ::= <integer-value>
      | <string-value>
      | "*"
```

| *nul*

<identifier> ::= <alpha> { <alphanumeric> }

<integer-value> ::= <numeral> { <numeral> }

<string-value> ::= <double-quote> <character> <double-quote>

<alphanumeric> ::= <alpha>
  | <numeral>

<alpha> ::= "a" | "b" | "c" | "d" | "e" | "f" | "g" | "h"
  | "i" | "j" | "k" | "l" | "m" | "n" | "o" | "p" | "q"
  | "r" | "s" | "t" | "u" | "v" | "w" | "x" | "y" | "z"
  | "A" | "B" | "C" | "D" | "E" | "F" | "G" | "H" | "I"
  | "J" | "K" | "L" | "M" | "N" | "O" | "P" | "Q" | "R"
  | "S" | "T" | "U" | "V" | "W" | "X" | "Y" | "Z" | "_"

<numeral> ::= "0" | "1" | "2" | "3" | "4"
  | "5" | "6" | "7" | "8" | "9"

<double-quote> ::= the double quote character (").

<character> ::= any character - the conventions for non-
  printing characters, single quote and "\" are the
  same as in the C programming language [KeRi78].

8. References

[ABBH84] [ElNu80] [Geha82] [Gold84] [GoRo83] [GrMy83] [Gutt77]
[HaKu80] [HaSi80] [Hewi77] [HoSa76] [KeRi78] [Moon84] [Morg80]
[NiMT83] [SSKH82] [Twai84] [Zism77] [Zism78]

Part V

Modelling

9
Conceptual Modelling and Office Information Systems

S.J. Gibbs

ABSTRACT *In this paper we explore the relevance of an area of computer science known as conceptual modelling to the design of office information systems. It is our position that office information systems and data modelling share a number of problems in common and should mutually benefit from any exchange of ideas. We begin by first reviewing conceptual modelling. In the second section we then look at three office information systems from a conceptual modelling perspective. Finally we describe the rationale behind a conceptual model intended specifically for office information systems.*

1. Conceptual Modelling

A data model can be viewed as a specification language for representations of the real world. That is, given a problem in an application domain, one uses a data model to specify a representation of that portion of the real world relevant to the problem. The representation may contain both a static, or structural aspect and a dynamic, operational, aspect. It is the task of a database management system to provide a physical implementation of a particular data model by translating the structures of the model to physical storage structures and the operations to physical operations.

There are three data models prevalent in current applications: the network, hierarchical, and relational models. With traditional network models, a specific example being CODASYL [TaFr76], data is organized by using *record types* and *set types*. Record types specify the structure of record instances, set types specify (functional) relationships between record instances. The hierarchical data model [TsLo76] is a restricted form of the network model in which relationships are arranged in a tree. The relational data model [Codd70] organizes data into n-ary *relations*. The structure of a relation consists of a number of *attributes* over underlying *domains*.

The increasing complexity of database applications has raised questions concerning the three traditional data models [Kent79]. For example, Hammer and McLeod [HaMc81] claim that these models force the user to think in terms of computer-related concepts rather than the natural structure of the data. This is most evident in the network and hierarchical models where logical relationships are associated with physical access paths. Langefors [Lang80] argues that concepts of relational database theory, such as joins and normalization, have arisen from processing considerations, and that even the relational model is more concerned with organizing data for processing purposes than with using natural structure.

A second criticism is made regarding the semantics of the structural primitives within these models. Schmid and Swenson [ScSw75] illustrate the ambiguity of semantic relationships among relational attributes. This is shown to result from the inability of the relational model to distinguish properties of objects from relationships between objects; both are modelled by the same structure. Other forms of "semantic overloading" also occur in the relational model [McLe78].

The area of data modelling that deals with problems such as the above is known as *conceptual data modelling* [ACM80, Brod80]. Conceptual modelling refers to the use of representations that capture the natural structure of data. Consequently, the emphasis is away from machine or processing-oriented representations and more towards an information-oriented perspective. A number of alternative data models, collectively known as *semantic data models*, have been developed for conceptual modelling. Some of the more well-known semantic data models and related languages are:

- the semantic binary data model [Abri74],
- the basic semantic data model [ScSw75],
- the entity-relationship model (ER model) [Chen76],
- the semantic hierarchy model [SmSm77a, SmSm77b, SmSm79],
- the modelling and programming language TAXIS [MyBW78, MyBW80, Wong83],
- the semantic data model (SDM) [HaMc78, HaMc81, McLe78],
- the extended relational model (RM/T) [Codd79],

- the functional data model and the data language DAPLEX [Ship81], and the conceptual language Galileo [AlCO83, AlOr83].

Additional information on these and other semantic data models, e.g., [Senk75, RoMy75, Rous76, Lang77, Lang80, SuLo79], may be obtained from data modelling surveys [KeKT76, WoMy77, McKi81, TsLo82].

As mentioned previously, the main goal of semantic data models and conceptual modelling in general is to capture the natural structure inherent in an application. The advantages of models based on natural structure are that they: simplify the design of complex systems by providing a modelling methodology; give a high degree of logical independence, as is required by evolving applications; document the structure of a system at varying levels of detail; and aid the user in interpretation of data. We now examine the constructs used by many semantic data models in their attempt to represent natural structure.

1.1. Object Orientation

One of the origins for the claimed use of natural structure is the ability of semantic data models to specify constructs that correspond directly to real-world entities. We will refer to this as the *object-oriented approach*, and the associated construct as an *object*. (Many models do not use the term "object" but choose instead "token" or "entity".) With the object-oriented approach, the designer determines the real-world entities to be modelled and *then* specifies their object representations. The procedure is more one of adapting the model to the world than the world to the model.

A number of refinements or varieties of objects are possible. Abrial, for example, distinguishes between *concrete* and *abstract* objects [Abri74]. A concrete object represents a physically existing entity such as a person or thing. An abstract object resembles a concept, for instance a number or a colour; something which has not come into existence at a particular time. A second division is between *independent* and *characteristic* objects [ScSw75]. An independent object is one that may exist in isolation, unrelated to other objects. A characteristic object is a secondary object used to describe an independent object. Independent objects are natural units for insertion and deletion, while characteristic objects form natural modification units. Similar to characteristic objects are *dependent* objects, an example of which are the "weak entities" of the ER model. The existence of a dependent object is subject to the existence of some related independent object. If the independent object is removed, so are all its dependent objects. This is often referred to as a *dependency constraint* [WoMy77] or as an *existence dependency* [Chen 76].

Generally, objects may possess some structure. A *property* of an object is a named relationship between the object and a value (alternate terms are "characteristic" and "attribute"). Most semantic data models allow the value of a property to be a set, i.e., a multivalued property. Where a significant difference arises is in whether or not concrete objects may become property values. Three examples of models that do not allow concrete objects as property values are the basic semantic data model, the ER model, and RM/T. When properties cannot take concrete objects as values, an additional mechanism is needed to represent relationships between concrete objects. In the basic semantic model and RM/T, this additional modelling construct is known as an "association"; in the ER model it is simply referred to as a relationship.

The introduction of an explicit construct for relationships leads to a number of design alternatives. First, the relationships themselves may be allowed to participate in other relationships. This is not possible in either the ER model or the basic semantic model. RM/T, however, has both relationships that are treated as objects ("associative entities") and those that are not ("nonentity associations"). Since associative entities are in fact objects, they are free to participate in object relationships. A second design alternative is whether or not relationships may take properties. Here again different models make different choices. In the basic semantic model, a relationship cannot be described by properties (this is sometimes described as a non-information-bearing relationship), while the ER model does allow relationships to take properties.

1.2. Abstraction Mechanisms

An abstraction mechanism is something that allows us to hide or ignore unwanted detail. Within data models, abstraction mechanisms are used to construct higher-level constructs from a number of lower-level constructs or primitives. There are three abstraction mechanisms that are commonly identified: *classification*, *generalization* and *aggregation*.

● Classification

Many objects in a large data space will have similar structures, that is, they will share a common set of properties. Classification allows one to ignore the details of particular objects by using a construct which represents a set of objects with similar structure. In this section we shall use the term *class* to refer to the construct resulting from classification; other similar terms include "object type", "entity set", and "entity type". Members of a class are referred to as *instances* of the class; the opposite of classification is referred to as *instantiation*.

Classes have the dual aspects of a *type*, i.e., a structural specification, and a set. For example, the class PERSON may refer to both a collection of people and a particular property structure. Some models develop the notion of types prior to introducing classes. For example, in Galileo one can define a type which is not associated with a class. However, the converse, a typeless class, is not possible since by definition every class has a type aspect.

In some models, for example TAXIS and the semantic hierarchy model, classification can be applied more than once. This results in a class whose extension is a set of classes (referred to as a *metaclass* in TAXIS). Furthermore, instances of a metaclass may be treated as objects, i.e., classes themselves may have properties (not to be confused with the properties of instances of the class). An interesting observation concerning multiple levels of classification is that for most applications two levels appear to be sufficient [MyBW80]. (Note that typed programming languages, such as Pascal, provide only one level of classification.)

• Generalization/Specialization

Generalization refers to the formation of a single class by combining two or more distinct classes. The extension of the resulting class contains the extensions of the initial classes. In practice it is *specialization*, the inverse of generalization, which is used to generate new classes.

Consider the directed graph whose nodes correspond to classes, where an arc from one node to a second indicates that the second is a specialization of the first. Since a class cannot be both the specialization and the generalization of another class, there can be no closed paths within the graph. In some models, TAXIS for example, the graph is connected, and there is always a most general class. Other models, such as SDM and Galileo, define "base classes", from which specializations are derived. However, this is not an important distinction, since one can easily introduce a most general class, such as THINGS, for which each base class is a specialization [HaMc81].

A number of methods are used to specify how the derived class (the specialization) results from the parent class (the generalization). One method, found in RM/T and an early version of the semantic hierarchy model [SmSm77b], is to partition the parent by using the values of a particular property (sometimes called a "category attribute"). More generally, a predicate involving the properties of the parent type may be specified, and the derived class consists of those instances of the parent class satisfying the predicate. TAXIS, SDM, and Galileo support this form of specialization. One may also introduce a specialization indirectly by adding additional properties to the type of the parent class; this is common in TAXIS. Other methods include explicit construction of the derived class by selecting instances of the parent class or by the application of the intersection operator to two parent classes. Depending upon the method used, it may be necessary to enforce strict hierarchical specialization [HaMc81], in which case a class is the specialization of at most one other class.

The section on classification described how the class notion is composed of two aspects: an intensional, type aspect and an extensional, set aspect. Specialization is essentially a relationship between classes and, as one expects, this duality is again evident. The extensional aspect of specialization is that the derived class forms a subclass of the parent class, i.e., the extension of the derived class is a subset of the extension of the parent class. The intensional aspect of specialization is that the type of a derived class is a subtype of the type of the parent class. This behavior is clearly illustrated by Galileo, where, as mentioned previously, the set and type aspects of a class are separated.

Since the type of a derived class must be a subtype of the parent's type, it is only necessary, when specifying the structure of a derived class, to indicate that part which differs from its parent's structure. The remaining part of the derived class' structure is obtained from the parent, hence; the derived class *inherits* the structure of the parent. *Multiple inheritance* refers to the case in which the derived class has more than one parent, and so inherits two or more structures. Multiple inheritance can introduce name-clash problems [GoBo80b], so either the user must be cautious or the model must enforce a naming convention.

- Aggregation

Aggregation refers to how certain model constructs may be viewed as collections or *aggregates* of other model constructs. Two forms of aggregation are used by semantic data models. The first, which has been called *Cartesian aggregation* [Codd79], views a class as an aggregate of properties. Cartesian aggregation can be applied successively in most semantic data models, that is, objects do not have a flat structure. For example the class PERSON may be viewed as an aggregate of the properties NAME and ADDRESS, while ADDRESS may in turn be viewed as an aggregate of STREET, CITY, and COUNTRY.

The second form of aggregation, known as *cover aggregation* [Codd79] (an alternative term is "user-controllable grouping" [HaMc78]), views an object as an aggregate of other objects. The example given in the literature concerns ships and convoys [HaMc78, Codd79]; here a particular convoy can be viewed as an aggregate of ship instances. Cover aggregation bears a close resemblance to classification; the difference seems to be related to the notion of membership. The membership of an object in a (base) class is statically determined by the object's structure; membership in a cover aggregate, however, is dynamic, and likely to change as events occur in the real world.

1.3. Semantic Integrity Constraints

Consider a particular representation of some application domain as specified by a data model. A *constraint* is any condition present in the application that must be satisfied in order to achieve a complete and consistent representation [ACM80]. The constraints expressed by data models have been described as being inherent or explicit [Brod78]. *Inherent constraints* derive from the constructs of the data model itself; they may be considered as restrictions of the model. An *explicit constraint* is one expressed by using a constraint specification facility; frequently such constraints are called *semantic integrity constraints*.

A number of commonly occurring constraints have been identified and will now be described. Inherent constraints vary from model to model, and, furthermore, a constraint inherent in one model may require explicit specification in another. Consequently, the inherent/explicit categorization is model dependent and will not be used in the following.

A *type constraint* restricts the values of a property or relationship to the instances of a particular class. The domains of the relational model also serve this purpose, so type constraints are sometimes referred to as "domain constraints". Type constraints are also used in models with procedural constructs, such as TAXIS and Galileo, to restrict the values used as arguments of procedures. A *uniqueness constraint* occurs when the value of a property or group of properties must take unique values over a class. The traditional example occurs in the relational model, where the properties (attributes) which must take a unique value are called a "key". We mentioned the *dependency constraint* when introducing dependent objects; the *existence constraint* [WoMy77] is of a similar nature. This constraint requires the removal of all relationships with which an object is involved, should the object itself be removed (this is also referred to as "referential integrity" [Codd79]). A *cardinality constraint* imposes a restriction on the cardinality of relationships between classes. Both the binary semantic data model and the entity-relationship model make frequent use of these constraints. A further constraint is one in which a property value is calculated or derived from other information. SDM and Galileo provide a number of mechanisms for deriving property values. For example, in SDM a property value may be calculated by using an arithmetic expression involving other property values, or by applying operators such as "minimum" or "average" to a class. Finally, a common constraint is to forbid the modification of certain properties. This is illustrated by TAXIS, where unmodifiable properties are known as "characteristics".

There are two methods commonly used for the specification of semantic integrity constraints [HaMc75]. The "state snapshot approach" or *static specification* involves identifying possible states of the representation. The second, the "state transition approach" or *dynamic specification* focuses on the allowable state-altering operations. These two methods may be characterized as declarative versus procedural, since the first is descriptive in nature while the second is obviously procedural. Certain constraints are more suited to one method than the other, and so, for full generality, both methods are often necessary [TsLo82]. As examples: In the binary semantic data model, type and cardinality constraints are declarative, other constraints are embodied in procedures. In TAXIS, uniqueness and type constraints, and unmodifiable properties are declared in class definitions; further constraints are specified using procedural means. In DAPLEX, explicit constraints can be specified either declaratively using a logical assertion or procedurally by using an operation sequence.

2. Office Information Systems

The implementation of an office information system is a major programming effort requiring database, communications, and graphics software. (Design requirements of office information systems are discussed in [BrPe84].) As a result, few systems have been developed that contain all the functions needed by an OIS. Instead we find a number of systems which have concentrated on different aspects of the OIS. A brief description of a number of these systems follows.

Two of the earlier endeavours in office automation were the Business Definition Language (BDL) [HHKW77] and the report of the CODASYL end users facilities committee (EUFC) [Lefk79]. BDL is a very high-level programming language which arranges business applications in terms of three components: form definition, document flow, and document transformation. The EUFC describes an object-oriented interface for CODASYL databases; many of the ideas proposed by the EUFC are now found in commercial systems [SIKV82, Will83].

PIE (Personal Information Environment) [GoBo80a, GoBo80b], NUDGE [GoRo77], and Odyssey [Fike81] use techniques from artificial intelligence to provide user support in specialized areas. PIE extends the Smalltalk programming language [Inga78, BYTE81] with multiple inheritance and a context mechanism. As an example, a user may view a document in different contexts, such as prior to and after revision, or a group of users may use contexts to organize the contributions of different members. NUDGE is a scheduling program that uses general knowledge about people, their activities, and meeting places to resolve scheduling conflicts. Odyssey assists the user in completing travel arrangements by keeping a record of the trip plan as it is developed and by supplying information as it is required. The knowledge representation language KRL [BoWi77] is used to construct electronic forms on which the planning activity is centred.

Scoop [Zism77] and OfficeTalk-D [ElBe82] are concerned with the specification and automation of office (or business) procedures. Scoop uses an augmented Petri-net (APN) formalism to specify the actions and timing conditions of office procedures. An APN interpreter monitors the state of procedure instances and determines when actions are to be performed. OfficeTalk-D is an extension of OfficeTalk-Zero [ElNu80], an early prototype office information system from Xerox. In OfficeTalk-D office procedures are modelled by information control nets (ICNs) [ElNu80], a formalism whose primitives are activities and repositories of information. An ICN is translated into an internal representation stored in an entity-relationship database. The entity types include *activity*, *task*, *actor*, and *role*. The relationship types include *status* between activities and tasks, *precedence* between activities, *player* between actors and roles, and *performer* between roles and activities. OfficeTalk-D is implemented in a highly distributed environment; the activities of a single procedure instance may be performed on different nodes in the network. Additionally, a graphic-based user interface realistically depicts the forms used by the office procedures.

A number of systems have investigated various problems associated with forms handling. FOBE (Form Operation By Example) [LuYa81] and OPAS (an Office Procedure Automation System) [LSTC81, LuCS82, SLTC82] extend database languages (for data definition and processing) to encompass hierarchically structured forms. The MIT office workstation [AtBS79] uses a knowledge-embedding language to define form constraints (derived fields and type constraints). OFS [Cheu79, Gibb79, Tsic80] translates form operations (form filling, filing, mailing, etc.) into operations on an underlying relational database management system. TLA [Hogg81, HoNT81, Nier81], is an extension of OFS with provisions for forms procedure specification and automation. Further extensions to OFS have included a global query facility to evaluate form queries over a network of stations [RaGi82, TRGN82] and a voice-response system using a text-to-speech synthesizer [Lee81, Lee82].

The three systems we will examine in detail, the Star Information System from Xerox, the Kayak project at INRIA, and the System for

Business Automation from IBM, are more general in their scope than the systems mentioned above. These three systems deal with information other than forms and have addressed communications and user interface problems.

2.1. The Star Information System

The Xerox Star [SIKV82, SIKH82, PuFK83] is the first commercially available system to provide a uniform graphic-based interface for a multitude of office functions (Apple's Lisa computer [Will83] now offers many of the features available on the Star). Naturally, considerable time was spent on the design of the user interface, and, in the words of the Star's designers [SIKV82;246]:

> We have learned from Star the importance of formulating the fundamental concepts (the user's conceptual model[1]) *before* software is written, rather than tacking on a user interface *afterwards.*

The "user's conceptual model" chosen by Star is that of the office as a collection of physical objects obeying certain laws. In order to see how this model has been incorporated within Star it is first necessary to look at Star's architecture.

The Star system runs on Ethernet [MeBo76], a 10M bps local area network developed by Xerox for office applications. Attached to the Ethernet are specialized *servers* and a number of user workstations. The available servers include a file server for shared files, a printer server, and a network gateway server which allows access to public data networks. Each user workstation contains a processor with 512K bytes of main memory, up to 29M bytes of disk memory, a 1024 × 808 bit-mapped display, and a pointing device known as a *mouse*.

The graphic display is used for a visual simulation of an office desktop. Objects placed on the desktop are represented by small graphic symbols known as *icons.* There are various classes, or types, of icons defined within the system and these correspond to common office objects. Examples of icon classes include folders, documents, mailtrays and printers. The user may "move" an object by pointing to its icon with the mouse and then pointing to a new location on the desktop. For instance, to print an object, the object is simply moved to the

---

[1] *This quotation illustrates a potential source of confusion in the application of data modelling to office information systems. While data modelling and software systems design in general share much terminology, a number of terms are used with quite different connotations. For example, "conceptual model" as used in this quotation refers to a set of guidelines or principles to be followed during implementation; not to a high-level formal representation of the real world as in data modelling.*

printer icon.

The Smalltalk programming language was used during the early development of Star and there is a correspondence between Smalltalk classes and icon classes. Just as Smalltalk classes are arranged in a superclass/subclass hierarchy, so we find icon classes similarly arranged. Every icon is either a *function icon* or a *data icon*. A function icon performs some action such as printing an object or transferring an object to another location. Examples are printer icons and mailtray icons. Data icons are passive and resemble traditional files. Examples of data icons are documents and folders.

In general, one may view a physical object at varying levels of detail. For example, if we see a closed book on our desk, the only information we gain includes such things as the name of the book and its physical location. It is this type of information that is represented by an icon. However, we may choose to open the book and inspect a page or two, in which case we are provided with much more information. Analogously, Star allows icons to be "opened"; this operation creates a *window* in which the object is displayed in more detail. Once an icon has been opened the user may inspect the object or modify the object by performing editing operations within the window. Upon completion the window is closed and the icon reappears.

When an object is viewed in a window, a transformation takes place during which properties of the object are used to determine the format in which the object is displayed. For example, objects such as documents contain a property for specifying the font. The value of this property is implicit in the display image when the document is viewed through a window. *Property sheets* allow the user to view these properties explicitly by using a representation which is closer to the object's underlying structure. (Property sheets are only associated with data icons; function icons have *option sheets* which allow the selection of certain function options.)

In Star a small number of "generic" commands are used to perform many different office functions. The most important of these commands are MOVE, OPEN, CLOSE and SHOW PROPERTIES/OPTIONS. As previously mentioned, MOVE can be used to mail an object by moving it to a mailtray. Similarly, an object to be filed is moved to a file cabinet. SHOW PROPERTIES and SHOW OPTIONS display property sheets and option sheets, respectively. To retrieve an object one could perform SHOW OPTIONS on the file cabinet; this allows a search condition to be specified which is then evaluated by the file cabinet. To reformat an object one would use SHOW PROPERTIES. To edit one uses OPEN and CLOSE. Many of these commands are performed by simple pointing actions using the mouse; typing is kept to a minimum.

The streamlined quality of Star as well as the successful integration of a number of functions make it an attractive system. There are, however, some disadvantages. Perhaps the most serious from a modelling point of view is that the data management facility [PuFK83] is in essence a simple file system. Although data can be modified, queried, and formatted by using the Star's graphic interface, there is no attempt to describe the logical inter-relationships of the data. Consequently constraint specification and querying are not as sophisticated as in database management systems, nor is the controlled sharing of data by multiple users possible. Furthermore, the data management facility uses structuring notions ("records", "fields", and "tables") that differ from those used by the remainder of the Star system ("objects/icons", "properties", and "types/classes").

2.2. The Kayak Project

Kayak [Naff81a, Naff81b, Quin81, Sche81] is a French government sponsored research project (now completed) concerned with a broad range of office automation problems. The project has developed both hardware and software components for office information systems. Examples of Kayak hardware include a multimedia office workstation (called the "Buroviseur") [Naff81a, Sche81] and two local area networks: DANUBE [Naff81a], a bus network similar to Ethernet, and TARO (the TAble ROnde) [Naff81a], a token-passing ring network. Software components include PLUME [Naff81b, Quin81], a general purpose editor for the Buroviseur, and AGORA [Naff81a], a computer-based message system. The Buroviseur and PLUME exemplify the variety of information occurring in office information systems and so will be discussed in more detail.

The architecture of the Buroviseur is similar to the Star workstation mentioned above. As with the Star, the Buroviseur contains local disk storage, a local processor, a bit-mapped display and pointing device, and a network interface. The most notable difference is in the area of audio capabilities. The Buroviseur contains additional hardware for performing a variety of speech-oriented functions. Specifically, the Buroviseur can perform speech synthesis (both from encoded speech and text-to-speech synthesis), speaker-dependent word recognition (with a 100 word vocabulary), and telephone dialing and answering (the telephone itself, though, is not integrated with the Buroviseur, i.e., voice messages cannot be stored or processed).

The PLUME editor was designed to take advantage of the hardware capabilities of the Buroviseur by allowing the user to create *multipletype documents*, that is, documents that contain more than one data type. PLUME presently supports text information, raster graphics, and vector graphics; planned additions include arbitrary bit-maps and voice annotation.

A PLUME document has a hierarchical structure with three node categories: atoms, units, and segments. An atom is a primitive data value. For example, a text atom is a single character, a raster graphics or bit-map atom is a pixel, a vector graphics atom is a line. Units are sequences of atoms. A unit forms a word in the case of text, a region in raster graphics, and a polygon in vector graphics. Finally a segment is a collection of either units or other segments (so the hierarchical structure can be more than three levels deep). A number of attributes (such as font, justification, etc.) can be specified at various levels of the hierarchy; they control the presentation of the document in a window on the Buroviseur's display.

Besides the creation of documents with PLUME, the Buroviseur allows the user to perform other operations such as document mailing and retrieval; a description of the remainder of the user interface is, however, rather hard to obtain. Perhaps what this brief description of the Buroviseur best illustrates is that the introduction of multimedia data is not without cost, and that much of this cost is born by the editor which must provide greater functionality than traditional text-only editors.

2.3. The System for Business Automation

The System for Business Automation project at IBM has developed a number of software systems. The earliest was Query-by-Example (QBE) [Zloo77], a popular two-dimensional language for specifying relational queries and general database operations. More recently the project has developed Office-by-Example and the System for Business Automation itself. These two systems have a number of common features but are based on slightly different underlying philosophies. Office-by-Example (OBE) [Zloo80, Zloo82] is an extension of QBE, the main additions being: a greater variety of data objects (QBE simply supports relations), including forms, hierarchical database structures, documents, reports, and menus; two-dimensional program objects; a facility for specifying operations to be performed when certain events occur; and a mechanism for transferring data objects between users. The System for Business Automation (SBA) [deZl77, deJo80, deBy80, BySD82] is based on the actor programming methodology [HeBS73, Hewi77] in which objects ("actors") execute a procedure ("follow a script") in response to invocation ("receipt of a message"). Recall that the Star also derives from an object-oriented message-passing language (Smalltalk) and, as one expects, SBA bears a close resemblance to the Star. There is, howver, a major difference in emphasis between the Star and SBA. Star aims to create an environment in which the user performs an electronic analogue of his or her traditional information processing activities. SBA's goal is a language in which the user can completely automate certain office activities. In essence SBA allows the user to specify a greater range of procedural information than does the Star.

Of the three systems, QBE, OBE, and SBA, only the first is commercially available; however, there are prototype implementations of both OBE [Zloo82] and SBA [BySD82]. We will look more closely at SBA since it is in this system that data modelling techniques and abstraction mechanisms are more easily discerned. SBA is still under development, so it is difficult to find a consistent description of the system. The following is based on [deJo80] and [deBy80].

An SBA system is a collection of objects. There are various categories of objects. Tables and forms are the most extensively described; other categories include graphic objects and "semantic" objects. In general, objects are instances of types. When a type is defined, the properties ("fields" in SBA terminology) of its instances are specified, as are certain operations and constraints. Subtypes are allowed and there is an inheritance mechanism for properties, operations and constraints.

SBA objects are constructed from two-dimensional abstract objects known as *boxes*. Boxes may be nested, i.e., one box may contain another. Boxes collect together the information used in defining an object type or specifying an object instance. There are four sections to an SBA box: IDENTIFIER, INPUT, OUTPUT and CONTENTS. The IDENTIFIER section has two parts, TYPE and NAME. TYPE simply refers to the type of the object associated with the box; NAME is a value which is unique for each instance of the type (a key).

A box may be activated by certain events, or by certain conditions holding true within the system. The INPUT section describes the events which cause activation. An event is either the receiving of an object, a specific time occurring, or an update taking place.

During activation of the box, new objects may be created. The OUTPUT section identifies what, if any, objects are created and where they are to be sent.

The CONTENTS section describes the operations performed when the box is activated. Operations are built from a small number of operators. These include the PRINT, UPDATE, INSERT and DELETE operators found in QBE, and the operators COPY and TO. The first four operators are used to display, update, insert or delete an instance of a type. COPY creates a copy of an object and TO "sends" an object to a second object.

In addition, the CONTENTS section contains a PICTURE box and a MAPPING box. The PICTURE box specifies the layout of the object associated with the main box by identifying the fields to be displayed and their relative positioning. The MAPPING box specifies constraints upon the field values of the object associated with the main box. There are two types of constraints: field values which are derived from fields internal to the box, and field values which either may be derived from other objects or must bear some relationship to these objects. The first type of constraint is specified by using a subbox whose INPUT section identifies the field values needed to calculate the derived field and whose OUTPUT section identifies the derived field. The CONTENTS section of this box contains an expression which performs the calculation. When the main box needs a value for the derived field this subbox will be activated. The second type of constraint is specified in a manner similar to a QBE query. The constraint makes use of example elements that are bound to values when the constraint is evaluated. These bound values are then used as field values.

After an object has been created, constraints of the second kind are *decoupled*. This means that changes in the objects which were used during constraint evaluation will no longer have an affect. This is very important when defining constraints upon forms. For example, the PRICE field of an ORDER form may be derived from a table. If a change is made to the price found in the table it is neither necessary nor desirable to propagate this change to the form.

The generality of box definition permits the modelling of a variety of structures and operations. For example, to model electronic mail one could use a PERSON box. The mail operation then corresponds to sending an object to a particular instance of PERSON. As another example, a FILE box can be defined; sending an object to such a box models the filing operation.

An SBA application consists of a number of type definitions and instances of these types. Users may control the degree of automation by choosing to perform operations explicitly or by adding the necessary logic to the type specifications. Applications thus evolve as the more structured operations are identified and automated.

3. Design of an Office Data Model

We will now attempt to synthesize the ideas from the previous sections by designing a data model for office objects. Here we will be concerned with choosing the basic constructs of the model and will disregard problems of their syntactic expression. (A more fully specified model, based on the following design, is described in [GiTs83,

Gibb84]. Models with similar objectives are presented in [BrPe83, ABBH84, LyMc84, Zdon84].) We will begin by formulating the requirements of an office data model. The actual design is then carried out by treating a data model in terms of its structures, operations, and constraints.

3.1. Model Requirements

If we look at the office information systems just described, it should be possible to generalize and isolate their common characteristics. It is then these characteristics that we expect to be supported by environments for implementing office information systems. The following is a list of similarities between Star, PLUME, and SBA.

- *object orientation*

    Both Star and SBA are clearly object-oriented systems. Icons in Star and boxes in SBA each represent independent and individual entities that may be created or destroyed. The hierarchical documents used by PLUME are objects in the sense that their structure is determined by type-like specifications. In fact object models provide a useful framework for describing modern document-handling systems such as syntax-directed editors and interactive editor/formatters [FuSS82].

- *abstraction mechanisms*

    In each of the three systems, classification is used to associate a type with an object and (Cartesian) aggregation to organize the properties of an object. None of the systems restrict objects to a flat structure, i.e., property aggregation can be repeated an arbitrary number of times. Specialization and generalization are used in both the Star and SBA; it is not clear whether PLUME supports this abstraction.

- *semantic integrity constraints*

    In both SBA and the Star it is possible to specify expressions for derived property values. In addition, SBA boxes, such as the MAPPING box, can be used to express a wide variety of constraints.

- *object movement*

    The Star and SBA make use of an operation which is not found in traditional data models. This operation is the MOVE command in Star and the TO operator in SBA. The object movement operation can be modelled by using cover aggregation. To move an object x from y to z, one models y and z as cover aggregates with x a member of y before the move and a member of z immediately after.

- *unformatted (multimedia) data*

    All three systems support text and various forms of graphic or image data. In addition the Buroviseur has some audio capabilities.

- *external and internal representations*

    The three systems distinguish between an external, user-oriented representation, and an internal, processing-oriented representation. In Star the external representation consists of windows and icons, in SBA a PICTURE box, and in PLUME a formatted document. The internal representations are hierarchically structured objects in all three cases.

The above list can be used to compare office information systems with data models. Of the six characteristics, the first four are also found in semantic data models and may be attributed to these models' concern with natural, or conceptual structure. Regarding the fifth characteristic, the addition of unformatted data to database management systems is a current research area. For example, there have been various proposals for handling text in a relational database [Falo82, KoLo82, KoMi83, SSLK83], and an image data model has been designed [Econ82, EcLo83]. However, these proposals consider only one data type when what is needed is a general treatment allowing for audio, image, and text data in addition to complex data structures such as forms. The final characteristic is the most neglected, particularly by data models. (External representations should not be confused with views or external schemas; an external representation determines the actual format in which data is displayed to the user, whereas views and external schemas specify the logical structure of data made available to the user.) Examples of where a differentiation between internal and external representations has been found useful are programming languages with abstract data types [Wall80] and text formatting systems [FuSS82]. (Text formatters, and graphics systems in general, tend to be overly concerned with external representation and may conceal useful logical structure from the user.) Forms data models [LSTC81, LuYa81, Tsic82] introduce external representations through the use of form blanks.

Some data models make a general distinction between an internal data-oriented representation and an external information-oriented representation. For example, in the work of Langefors [Lang77,

Lang80], there is reference to the *datalogical* and *infological* realms. Chen [Chen76] describes various levels of views of information. Yet, in practice, data models and database systems make little or no provision for specifying the external representation of complex data structures. Ad hoc components such as report-generators or other pieces of software are frequently used. Unfortunately this software is often designed for use by programmers rather than by general office personnel. Office data models should distinquish between an internal representation suitable for processing and an external representation which is more appropriate for the user. The realization of an object using an external representation in a particular medium is known as *presentation.*

In summary, with respect to data models, there is no single model possessing all the above characteristics. Semantic data models come closest to satisfying the requirements but are in need of extension in the areas of data types and user interaction (presentation). The remainder of this paper explores the design of an office data model, indicating, wherever possible, how the model requirements influence design choices.

3.2. Structures

This section develops the three structuring facilities of the office data model: object types, data types, and template types. These facilities correspond directly to the requirements for an object-orientation, multimedia data, and presentation.

3.2.1. Object Types

The following example will be used throughout this section to introduce new terms and concepts. Consider the head office of a large manufacturer where order requests are received from clients and regional sales offices. Suppose these requests are entered on standardized order forms either by sales agents or directly by clients. In general such order forms contain a large number of fields, each accompanied by various headings and instructions. Rather than burden the example with unnecessary detail, consider a simplified form consisting of an order number, an account name, and a list of part names and quantities. The problem is to define a representation of the order form that is amenable to computer processing but retains the conceptual structure perceived by the user.

In the relational model we could have the following relations:

ORDER(*ORDER − NO*, *ACC*)
ITEM(*ORDER − NO*, *NAME*, *QTY*)

Here, two problems are apparent: first, we have lost the object nature of forms since the order form involves two relations. So, for example, operations for creating or removing a form are not atomic but divided into two parts. Queries and updates must also contend with this division. Secondly, the fact that ITEM is subordinate to ORDER is not apparent from the relational schema. However, this is indeed the case as deletions from ORDER should trigger deletions from ITEM but not necessarily vice versa. A view, such as the derived relation

ORDER-ITEM(*ORDER − NO*, *NAME*, *ACC*, *QTY*)

is inadequate since a single order form may now correspond to more than one tuple; this leads to complications in removing or modifying a form. The above problems could be concealed from the user by a program that translates the user's form-oriented operations to operations on ORDER and ITEM. Such a program, though, is obviously application specific and would be inconvenient if the structure of the order form were to change or additional forms were to be introduced. Furthermore this approach has the disadvantage of locating structural information in two places − the application program and the relational schema.

What is required is a data model whose structural elements can represent the object nature of things such as forms. We are free to give a name to the model's structural elements and, in light of their function, can choose to call them *objects*. That is, the term object, when referring to the data model, is a structural or organizational unit used by the model. The decision as to which entities in the real world are to be represented by objects within the model is application dependent and left to the system designer.

After having hypothesized structures called objects we must now determine just what these structures are. Clearly a means for describing objects is needed. For this purpose we introduce *properties* and *values* as additional structural elements of the model. A property is a named relationship between an object and a value. The structure of an object is determined by the properties it possesses, its description by the value of these properties. The introduction of properties allows us to apply the classification abstraction to objects. An *object type* is defined as a set of objects with a specified structure; a member of the set is referred to as an *instance* of the object type. (To relate the terminology of this section to that of the first, one can say that object types are classes of concrete objects. We shall soon introduce data types which, as it turns out, are classes of abstract objects.)

At this point the model's structures resemble those found in the relational model; there seems to be a correspondence between object types, objects, and properties on the one hand and relations, tuples, and attributes on the other. The difference appears in the treatment of values. The relational model assumes that relations are in *First Normal Form* (1NF), i.e., the values of attributes are not themselves relations but simple data values [Codd70]. The advantage of 1NF relations is their structural simplicity and the resulting simplicity of relational operations. (It is the higher-order normal forms that deal with modification anomalies and redundancy [Codd71].) By dropping the 1NF provision, more general structures are allowed but with increased operational complexity. The suggestion that 1NF be abandoned has been made a number of times, both in the context of office systems [LSTC81, LuYa81, Tsic82] and other application areas [GuSt82, HaLo82, ScPi82].

The office data model departs from 1NF by generalizing the notion of a value to allow both objects as values and sets as values. Properties whose values are data items such as numbers or strings are known as *simple properties*. In contrast, the values of *composite properties* are special objects known as *characteristic objects*. To distinguish characteristic objects from object type instances, the latter will be referred to as *independent objects*[1]. Composite properties derive their name from how they may be viewed as the aggregation of groups of properties; in this sense their structure is similar that of an object type. However, the value of a composite property, i.e., a characteristic object, is always dependent upon the existence of an independent object (this is the origin of the terms "independent" and "characteristic" [ScSw75]).

The result of introducing composite and simple properties is that objects no longer have a flat structure but instead a hierarchy of properties and values. We may visualize an object as a tree where the root corresponds to the object itself; characteristic objects occupy the intermediate nodes, and data items the leaves. A similar hierarchical organization is found in forms data models [LSTC81, LuYa81, Tsic82] as well as in many semantic data models described in the first section. The model most resembling the office data model at this stage of its development is the basic semantic model of Schmid and Swenson [ScSw75]. Many of the concepts used here, such as independent and characteristic objects, have been obtained from this model.

The second generalization of the value notion is related to sets. A *multivalued* property takes a (possibly empty) set as its value. A *single-valued* property takes a single value: either a data item, a

---

[1] *However, unless noted otherwise, "object" without any qualification should be taken as referring to an independent object.*

characteristic object, or the special value *NULL*. The inclusion of multivalued properties is a feature found in many semantic data models and, again, in office data models.

Returning to the order form example, we can now adequately represent the structure of this form. The specification would involve an object type corresponding to the order form. This object type would have two simple single-valued properties for the order number and account name, and a composite multivalued property for the list of items. The composite property would be described, in turn, by two simple single-valued properties for the part number and quantity. The following notation indicates this structure:

order form → order number, account name, item, ..., item;

item → part number, quantity;

The preceding discussion has dealt with the use of property, or Cartesian aggregation in the office data model. Next we will demonstrate that specialization is required. The argument is based on the frequent collection of related objects, for example, a report and its supporting documents, and their placement in a single container such as a binder or file. This should not be viewed as mere aimless paper shuffling, but rather as a dynamic method of organizing information and one that is central to the user's conception of the office.

An illustration of this organizational method can be provided by the order form example. Suppose that within the sales office related orders are grouped by the use of dossiers. The grouping of orders within dossiers clearly implies a relationship of some sort between the two. A model well-suited for representing relationships is the entity-relationship (ER) model. (Here we are interested solely in whether the ER model can capture the containment relationship between objects and will disregard its inadequacy for the representation of their internal structure.) Suppose we represent containment using a relationship set called SUBPART between the two entity sets[1] ORDER and DOSSIER. It is assumed that an order form can be in at most one dossier at any given time, hence SUBPART is 1:N. At first glance this appears satisfactory; however, problems arise when new types of forms are introduced. It is quite likely that, in addition to order forms, the manufacturer will use shipping forms to record product shipments. If we now want to group order and shipping forms within dossiers we have two choices. First we can add a second relationship set, SUBPART', to model separately the relationship between dossiers and shipping forms. Secondly we can modify the original SUBPART relationship set to allow for three entity sets. Neither of these representations is satisfactory. In

---

[1] *An entity set is the term used in the ER model for what we have been calling an object type.*

both cases the schema has been modified extensively, more so than the introduction of a new type of form would seem to merit. Furthermore, in a realistic situation with many types of forms, such representations would be excessively complex.

This problem may be solved by realizing that SUBPART is not intrinsically a relationship between order forms and dossiers, or, for that matter, between any application-specific objects. The solution relies on the use of specialization hierarchies of object types, in which case one can define SUBPART as a relationship between the two general object types AGGREGATE and OFFICE-OBJECT. The AGGREGATE object type is a generalization of all object types which have the potential to contain other objects. So, for example, DOSSIER would be a specialization of AGGREGATE, as would the object types for mail trays, envelopes, files, and so on. OFFICE-OBJECT is simply the most general type used in modelling the office environment. Its specializations would include ORDER and SHIPPING. (In addition AGGREGATE could be defined as a specialization of OFFICE-OBJECT. This would allow SUBPART to be used "recursively", i.e., a dossier could then contain a second dossier.) The SUBPART relationship is inherited by the specializations of AGGREGATE and OFFICE-OBJECT.

We have now looked at three semantic data modelling abstraction mechanisms as they appear in the office data model. These three, classification, Cartesian aggregation, and specialization, combined with an ER-like representation of relationships seem sufficient for modelling office objects. However, a well-known difficulty with ER-like relationships is that they are not objects themselves and so cannot participate in other relationships. Furthermore, additional constructs are needed if properties are to be attached to relationships. Consequently, we will reformulate our representation of relationships and make use of the fourth abstraction mechanism — cover aggregation.

An object type is specified by giving the property structure for instances of the type. Now consider some object that is an instance of an object type. Suppose we view this object as also being an instance of a relationship. If this is the case the object type must also specify which objects may appear in the relationship. Such objects are called *constituents* of the original object. Thus, for example, the object type MARRIAGE would have HUSBAND and WIFE constituents, both of which would be based on the object type PERSON.

As with properties, constituents may be single-valued or multivalued. The value of a single-valued constituent is a single independent object or the special value *NULL*; the value of a multivalued constituent is a set of independent objects. It is not necessary to decompose constituents as was the case with properties. The reason is that the internal structure of an object appearing as a constituent value is determined by the object type definition for that object.

Constituents can be used to represent many forms of inter-object relationships. A group of single-valued constituents corresponds to an ER-like relationship or an associative entity, while a multivalued constituent, in general, depicts cover aggregation. For example, an object type for representing convoys would be defined with a multivalued constituent taking a set of ships as its value. The containment relationship for office objects is represented by including a multivalued constituent called SUBPART within the specification of the AGGREGATE object type. Values of SUBPART are constrained to be instances of OFFICE-OBJECT.

In summary, the office data model represents real-world entities using objects classified into object types. Object types may be related by specialization and generalization. The specification of an object type identifies the property structure and constituent structure of its instances. Properties are hierarchically ordered and take as values data items or characteristic objects. Constituents take independent objects as values. Both properties and constituents may be single or multivalued.

This section began by describing the difficulties encountered when using the relational model as the basis for office modelling. We then demonstrated the need for several high-level abstraction mechanisms in an office data model. We now complete the circle and show that a relational schema can, in fact, capture these same abstractions so long as certain conventions on how objects map to relations are employed.

As a specific example we will consider the problem of order forms, shipping forms, and dossiers as expressed within a semantic data model. RM/T has been chosen since it provides an underlying relational schema. The relations used are shown in figure 1. (Here we have assumed that an order form has the structure mentioned previously and that a shipping form has fields for the order number of the shipment, the part name shipped, the quantity shipped, and the factory from which the shipment originated.) The situation depicted in figure 1 appears to be rather complex. However, the user would not operate directly upon these relations; instead a database management system based on RM/T would interpret user operations and maintain inter-relational consistency.

OFFICE-OBJECT

OFFICE-OBJECT%
o1
s1
s2
s3
d1

AGGREGATE

AGGREGATE%
d1

ORDER

ORDER%
o1

ITEM

ITEM%
i1
i2

SHIPPING

SHIPPING%
s1
s2
s3

DOSSIER

DOSSIER%
d1

ORDER-ITEM

ORDER%	ITEM%
o1	i1
o1	i2

ORDER-HD

ORDER%	ORDER-NO	ACC
o1	0073	Acme

ITEM-HD

ITEM%	NAME	QTY
i1	X63	40
i2	DZ1	20

SHIPPING-HD

SHIPPING%	ORDER-NO	FACTORY	NAME	QTY
s1	0073	Toronto	XL3	10
s2	0073	Oshawa	XL3	30
s3	0073	Toronto	DZ1	20

PG

SUP	SUB
ORDER	ORDER-HD
ITEM	ITEM-HD
SHIPPING	SHIPPING-HD

CG

SUP	SUB
ORDER	ITEM

EKG

SUP	SUB
d1	o1
d1	s1
d1	s2
d1	s3

KG

SUP	SUB
AGGREGATE	OFFICE-OBJECT

UGI

SUP	SUB
OFFICE-OBJECT	AGGREGATE
OFFICE-OBJECT	ORDER
OFFICE-OBJECT	SHIPPING
AGGREGATE	DOSSIER

Figure 1: RM/T relations

In RM/T, attributes whose names end with a special character (here we will use "%") take internal object identifiers as values. Relations with a single such attribute identify object types (entity types in RM/T terminology). Here there are six object types: OFFICE-OBJECT, AGGREGATE, ORDER, ITEM, SHIPPING, and DOSSIER. RM/T makes use of a number of special relations known as *graph relations*. In general graph relations have two attributes, named SUP and SUB, which play superior and subordinate roles. Figure 1 uses the property graph (PG) relation, characteristic graph (CG) relation, cover membership (KG) relation, entity cover membership (EKG) relation[1], and the unconditional generalization (UGI) relation[2]. The PG relation indicates that the properties associated with ORDER, ITEM, and SHIPPING are identified in the ORDER-HD, ITEM-HD and SHIPPING-HD relations. The CG relation here indicates that ITEM is a characteristic object type subordinate to ORDER. The associations between particular ITEM objects and ORDER objects are expressed in the ORDER-ITEM relation. The KG relation indicates that AGGREGATE is a cover aggregate type for which the allowable constituents are instances of OFFICE-OBJECT. The EKG relation shows that dossier instance d1 has as constituents o1, s1, s2 and s3. Finally, the UGI relation records the specialization relationships that occur in the example.

3.2.2. Data Types

The discussion of properties in the previous section stated that the value of a simple property may be a data item such as a number or a string. We now expand on this notion of data item by including unformatted or multimedia data values.

---

[1] *Actually Codd does not explicitly name this relation but mentions that a graph relation defined on object identifiers may be used to represent membership of individual objects in a cover member.*

[2] *This relation has a third attribute which need not concern us here.*

In data modelling a set of data values with similar structure or semantic reference is often referred to as a *data type*. Data types can be divided into two categories: predefined *primitive data types* and application-specific or *user-defined data types*. Primitive data types are the subject of this section, defined data types will be dealt with in the section on constraints.

The primitive data types found in conventional general-purpose programming languages usually include *integer* and *real*, for which there may be various choices related to range or precision, *boolean* and *char* for single-bit and byte values, and frequently *string* for variable-length character strings. (In fact, *string* literals often have a maximum length imposed by the compiler while string variables may be limited by main memory considerations.) Languages designed for particular application areas may have specialized data types. For example, MUMBLE [Guib82], a language used with raster graphics, has a built-in data type for bit-maps. Mallgren [Mall82] discusses the formal specification of graphic data types.

The primitive data types required by office applications include the traditional types and, in addition, four new types: *audio*, *image*, *text*, and *digital*. The *audio* and *image* types[1] would be used for digitized voice and image data, *text* for very long variable-length character strings. The *digital* type is a common representation for the previous three and would be used in modelling objects that handle uninterpreted digital data (such as a digital telephone). The four, *text*, *image*, *audio* and *digital*, are referred to as *unformatted* or *multimedia* data types.

Assuming that the office data model may use the unformatted data types it becomes possible to model a great many of the common office objects. For example, objects with text-valued properties correspond to documents and letters, audio-valued properties can represent recorded voice messages, and image-valued properties are used with pictures and graphs. However, allowing such varied objects complicates both their presentation to the user and the operations available to the user for their modification.

---

[1] *Here we will simplify matters and avoid choosing between such things as vector and raster graphics and encoded or nonencoded speech. A more detailed treatment would use many image and audio data types.*

3.2.3. Template Types

One of the requirements for the office data model concerned the presentation of information to the user. This appears to be a non-trivial problem for two reasons. First, the introduction of unformatted data types implies a multimedia environment for operation of the office system. This environment would include a two-dimensional graphic medium for image data (e.g. a raster display), a two-dimensional character-oriented medium for text data (e.g. a printed page or alphanumeric display), and for audio data a medium based on an audible time-varying signal. The disadvantage with a multimedia interface is that it is possible to disorient the user by presenting unrelated information simultaneously through two or more media. The result is that a method for coordinating the presentation of information is necessary. Secondly, office objects tend to carry a large amount of information. This is due both to complex property structure (e.g. forms) and to the use of large data values (e.g. documents). Thus a method is needed for presenting information which reconciles model objects with the physical characteristics of the various media and the perceptual limitations of users.

A *template type* is a model construct that specifies the presentation of a particular object type. The structure of the template type mirrors the structure of the object type and gives general rules for the external representation of the object type's properties. An instance of a template type, referred to as a *template*, determines the presentation of a specific object. In other words there is a correspondence between template types and object types, and templates and objects. It is useful to think of templates as a mechanism for mapping objects into physical media (sometimes called "realization" or "materialization" [KoLo82]). The external structure of an object, more readily perceived by the user, is the structure of the template type, while the internal structure is that of the object type.

The advantages of templates appear when one realizes that it is not necessary to restrict an object to the use of a single template [Tsic82]. So, for example, a single object type may use one template for the text medium and a second template, containing additional information, for the image medium. Similarly, templates allow the specification of different views or perspectives of an object. A common example is the need to withhold information from unauthorized users; here a template would be defined to filter out properties considered sensitive.

3.3. Operations

Data model operations are often divided into two groups: operations which are definitional in nature and operations for manipulating instances. (This division is not always present; for example, in TAXIS, defining a new class involves creating an instance of a metaclass.) The two sets of operations are referred to, by traditional database management systems, as the *data definition language* (DDL) and the *data manipulation language* (DML). Data definition operations take place primarily during the design stage of an application. The goal of the design process is to produce a schema, i.e., a specification of the structure of the database representing the application environment.

In the office data model, a schema identifies the model constructs which have been defined by the designer. Thus a schema is a list of object type definitions, template type definitions, and, possibly, explicitly defined constraints. The model must, then, provide operations for adding new definitions to the schema. These definitions can be related. For example, in the case of object types, a new object type could be defined independently of previous definitions, or, alternatively, as a specialization of one or more object types from the schema. The operation that adds new definitions to the schema will be referred to as **define**. This is the only schema-level operation used. Semantic data models often include more extensive operations such as schema modification and restructuring [McSm80], or view and context definitions [AlCO83]. For office systems, the ability to change the schema is very important because of the dynamic nature of the office. The office data model provides much flexibility by allowing schema extension through specialization.

It is convenient to discuss the manipulation operations of the office data model in terms of the structures within the model. Thus we will consider the operations for manipulating instances of object types, data types, and template types respectively.

The operations required for object instances include the generic operations used in data modelling. These operations have been identified as [TsLo82]:

insert - add data to the database,
delete - remove data from the database,
update - change data in the database,
set currency - identify a portion of the database of interest,
retrieve - obtain data from the database.

In the office data model, the insert and delete operations correspond to creating a new object instance or removing an existing object instance. We shall refer to these operations as **create** and **destroy**. The update operation corresponds to changing the values of an object's properties or constituents. Here, since properties and constituents may be multivalued, two operations are required. The **assert** operation will be used to assign a value to a property or constituent, **remove** to undo the assignment. (A set of operations very similar to **create**, **destroy**, **assert**, and **remove** is found in Abrial's data model [Abri74].)

The use of a specialization hierarchy introduces two operations not found in traditional data models. These operations are associated with the phenomenon of entity-migration [Codd79], i.e., a dynamic change in the type of an object. We will use the **admit** operation to add an object to a more specialized type and **prohibit** to delete it from such a type.

For queries a method is needed for specifying the set of objects satisfying a given condition and then retrieving members of the set. This faculty is provided by the two operations called **set** and **for**. The **set** operation is used to select a set of objects that have been previously created. The **for** operation allows iteration over a set.

The next group of operations are related to constraint enforcement. As we will see in the following section, many constraints are expressed by explicitly identifying those operations which lead to their violation. Merely forbidding such operations as they are encountered is not always sufficient. It may also be necessary to undo the effects of earlier operations in order to return to a consistent state. For this purpose we will use the transaction operations called **tbegin**, **tend**, and **abort** [Gray81].

Now consider operations on data values. Here the applicable operations should include those commonly found in programming languages. Thus, for *integer* we have the standard arithmetic operations, and for *string* such operations as string concatenation and comparison. In this sense the formatted data types do not add anything new or unusual to the data model. The unformatted data types, though, are uncommon and require more attention. It is necessary to identify the operations on text, image, and audio values that the user is likely to require in performing office work. Also some knowledge of signal processing and pattern recognition technology is needed to determine which operations are currently possible. A discussion of these operations is found in [Gibb84].

It is possible to identify four operations involving template instances. First one must be able to acquire an instance of a particular template type. We will refer to this operation as **template**; it is analogous to the **create** operation for objects. The most complex operation, in terms of processing required, is associating an object with a template. This operation is called **embed** and performs the mapping of an object's structure onto the template's structure. In addition an operation is needed to realize a template in the medium specified for the template's type. We shall refer to this operation as **present**. Finally, in the case of image and text media, it may be necessary to remove a presented template from view. This is accomplished with the **erase** operation.

3.4. Constraints

In designing a constraint specification mechanism, one consideration is to keep the data definition language as simple as possible. Yet, as more constraints are expressed declaratively, the number of state predicates in the data definition language, and hence its complexity, tends to increase. This problem is relevant to office data modelling since a great variety (not just number) of constraints is encountered [Ferr82, Geha82]. Consequently, we will use declarative specifications only for the most common constraints, the remainder will be expressed in a procedural manner.

In the office data model the constraints that can be specified declaratively are:

-    the data type of a simple property,

-    the object type of a constituent,

-    uniqueness of simple properties and constituents.

The first two constraints resemble type constraints as found in programming languages. Their effect is to restrict the type of the value assigned to a simple property or a constituent. The uniqueness constraint is essentially a generalized key; it may be used with multivalued properties or properties which are not the immediate sub-properties of an object type. Constraints other than the above are expressed using the constructs described in the following sections.

3.4.1. Data Types

Data type constraints restrict the values a property may take and prevent the occurrence of meaningless operations (such as the comparison of two properties based on different data types). Primitive data types are insufficient for representing many properties [McLe76]. For example, a property which depicts the ages of people should be constrained to take only a sub-range of integer values, say from 0 to 150. This is not possible, however, if only the *integer* type is available. A similar problem occurs during the data entry phase of many office applications. This typically involves a series of validation checks which ensure that the new value agrees with some predetermined format. In addition, to give the user greater flexibility, more than one format is often allowed. An example would be "month day, year" and "mm/dd/yy" for dates. Moreover, it may be necessary to define new operations for data type elements. For example, queries on date values need to compare the relative order of dates. This is not possible if the type for dates is simply the data type *string*.

What is needed is a method for specifying more refined or restricted data types than are provided by the primitive data types. Thus we suggest a data type definition language that will allow one to specify the data structure used to store elements of the type, referred to as the *internal representation* of the data type, and the allowable formats or *external representations* of the data type. Additionally the data type definition will specify the operations for the elements; these generally include a function that tests for membership in the data type and functions for transforming between internal and external representations. This description of a data type is close in concept to that of an abstract data type (ADT) [LiZi74, GeMS77, LSAS77, ShWu77] as used in programming languages. In fact the use of ADTs for specifying data type constraints has been suggested previously [McLe76], and data models based on ADTs have been designed [SmFL81, AlCO83, AlOr83].

Membership-testing functions have appeared previously in the data modelling literature. For example Abrial's model [Abri74] and TAXIS [MyBW80] use this technique. Defining a data type by means of a function is very flexible since one has access to a programming language. It is a simple matter to provide functions that support the equivalent of sub-ranges or enumerated types.

The motivation for distinguishing between internal and external representations is not to provide a protection mechanism as in programming languages but to allow for multiple external representations for data type elements and so gain flexibility in the presentation of data values.

3.4.2. Triggers

Many semantic integrity constraints impose further restrictions on objects and their properties than are expressed in object type definitions. For example, two properties of an object may be functionally related (derived properties) or a condition may be imposed on the constituents of an object. Data type definitions make no reference to the object types present in the schema; the only information available within the definition is related to the data elements themselves. There is a need then, for a constraint specification mechanism which operates at the level of object types.

There are two possible approaches for dealing with constraints on and among objects. The first would be to continue with an ADT-like formalism and replace the generic object operations (**create**, **assert**, etc.) with individualized operations for each object type. The second approach, and that followed here, makes use of *triggers*. A trigger is a group of operations performed when a change is made to the database (in which case the trigger is said to have been *activated*). The method by which triggers are activated resembles pattern-directed invocation [Hewi72] as used in artificial intelligence. Triggers have also had a long history within database research. They derive from the database procedures of the CODASYL proposal [CODA71] and have been used in commercial database management systems [Astr76]. More recently triggers have appeared in forms data models [SLTC82, Tsic82] and object-oriented office systems such as SBA [deBy80] and OBE [Zloo82].

There are a number of reasons for choosing triggers, as opposed to abstract data types, as a constraint specification mechanism for the office data model. First, since triggers are not explicitly called, they can be added or removed from the schema with little difficulty. This is the aspect of triggers which makes the SBA's gradual automation of procedures possible. Secondly, triggers are useful in modelling events. The office is largely event-driven, as Zisman notes [Zism77;17]:

> Oftentimes the difficulties in offices do not arise as much from task performance as from *recognizing* the need to perform a particular task. The difficulty is not in *doing*, but in knowing *when* something should be done.

Furthermore, office systems have many special conditions (such as timing requirements and authorization conditions) that are easily expressed by using triggers. Finally, data modelling in general places greater emphasis on structural representation than is found in programming languages [TsLo82]. Thus the structure of an object type is not hidden, as with ADTs, but instead used to represent visible aspects of the application.

In their simplest form, triggers consist of two components: a condition and a set of actions. The trigger is activated and the actions performed whenever the condition is satisfied. An alternative is to add, as a third component, a pattern identifying the operation which leads to satisfaction of the condition. In this case the trigger is activated when the pattern is matched. The actions are not performed, however, unless the condition is also satisfied. This method has the advantage of being easier to implement as the system has some warning of when a trigger may be activated. Also, since the pattern identifies a particular operation, one can now refer to *pre-conditions* (conditions which must be satisfied before the operation is performed) and *post-conditions* (conditions which must be satisfied after having performed the operation). A final addition to trigger structure, particularly useful in interactive environments, is to include an error message that is displayed when the trigger is activated but the condition fails.

4. Conclusion

One of the difficulties with modelling office data is the extremely general and versatile structuring constructs that are required. In this paper we have looked closely at three office information systems and shown how the data-structuring constructs implicit in these systems can be traced to conceptual data modelling. This led us to propose a data model for office systems based firmly on data modelling principals in the hope that it would produce a sounder understanding of office information systems.

It is too early to tell if data modelling offers the best approach to office information system design and implementation. However it is certain that many of the traditional problems facing data modellers — data structuring, persistent and shared data, data retrieval — occur in office information systems and also that the peculiarities of office information systems — multimedia data types, templates and presentation, triggered events — will enrich data modelling.

5. References

[ABBH84] [Abri74] [ACM80] [AlCO83] [AlOr83] [Astr76] [AtBS79] [BoWi77] [Brod78] [Brod80] [BrPe83] [BrPe84] [BySD82] [BYTE81] [Chen76] [Cheu79] [CODA71] [Codd70] [Codd71] [Codd79] [deBy80] [deJo80] [deZl77] [EcLo83] [Econ82] [ElBe82] [ElNu80] [Falo82] [Ferr82] [Fike81] [FuSS82] [Geha82] [GeMS77] [Gibb79] [Gibb84] [GiTs83] [GoBo80a] [GoBo80b] [GoRo77] [Gray81] [Guib82] [GuSt82] [HaLo82] [HaMc75] [HaMc78] [HaMc81] [HeBS73] [Hewi72] [Hewi77] [HHKW77] [Hogg81] [HoNT81] [Inga78] [KeKT76] [Kent79] [KoLo82] [KoMi83] [Lang77] [Lang80] [Lee81] [Lee82] [Lefk79] [LiZi74] [LSAS77] [LSTC81] [LuCS82] [LuYa81] [LyMc84] [Mall82] [McKi81] [McLe76] [McLe78] [McSm80] [MeBo76] [MyBW78] [MyBW80] [Naff81a] [Naff81b] [Nier81] [PuFK83] [Quin81] [RaGi82] [RoMy75] [Rous76] [Sche81] [ScPi82] [ScSw75] [Senk75] [Ship81] [ShWu77] [SIKH82] [SIKV82] [SIKV82] [SLTC82] [SmFL81] [SmSm77a] [SmSm77b] [SmSm79] [SSLK83] [SuLo79] [TaFr76] [TRGN82] [Tsic80] [Tsic82] [TsLo76] [TsLo82] [Wall80] [Will83] [WoMy77] [Wong83] [Zdon84] [Zism77] [Zism77] [Zloo77] [Zloo80] [Zloo82]

10
A Model for Multimedia Documents

F. Rabitti

ABSTRACT *The problem of a model for representing multimedia documents and supporting operations on documents is
addressed. Particular attention is given to the concept of type,
since multimedia documents do not fit the static schema
definition of database models. A syntax directed approach is
proposed for the model. Three levels of specification for a multimedia document are discussed. The layout level describes the
document presentation. The logical level describes the document internal structure. The conceptual level describes the
document semantic composition. The layout structure and the
logical structure are compatible with the Office Document
Architecture currently undergoing standardization (ISO,
ECMA, CCITT).*

1. Introduction

In the office environment a very large amount of information is
manipulated in terms of documents. This information can be either in
formatted form (i.e. attributes in office forms) or in free form (i.e.,
text, image, graphics and voice).

In this paper we will deal with models for representing a general
class of office *Multimedia Documents* (MDs). MDs are structurally more
complex than objects usually managed in document processing or
retrieval systems [Crof83], in message systems [TRGN82], or in form
systems [Geha82, Tsic82]. An MD is a collection of components which
contains the different types of multimedia information and may be
further structured in terms of other components (such as the body of a

paper that is composed of sections and paragraphs and contains images and attributes embedded in text). The task of formally representing all the possible documents occurring in an office environment is very difficult. MDs have complex structures which tend to differ from one document to another.

Let us compare the role of a document model to the role of a data model in a database management system. There are three concepts in the database field which are carefully distinguished: a *data model* (a formal language used to describe the real world in a manner that is useful for the computer), a *schema* (a specification describing the structure of the realm that is of interest to a particular application) and a *database* (an extension of a schema containing the set of values that describes the realm at some instant in time). These three notions also arise in office information systems. For example, in a form system such as OFS [Tsic80], the analogous concepts are *the form description language, form types and form instances*. The form description language is used to define the form types used by a particular application. Users can then create and modify form instances belonging to any of these types.

The type concept as it appears in data models is useful when dealing with structured documents like forms, but leads to difficulties when applied to the representation of general documents. We will use a specific example to illustrate some of the difficulties. Consider a hypothetical letter giving information about a new product (see figure 1, at the end of section 5). The internal structure can be considered as being comprised of:

> company logo,
> date of the letter,
> sender address,
> name of the product,
> introduction,
> product description,
> picture of the product,
> cost summary,
> table of component costs,
> histogram of cost comparison,
> sender signature.

Clearly, not all letters will contain the same eleven components; some letters may have no tables while others will have two or more, and so on. Hence, if a type for letters is defined, it may not have the above structure. It is easy to imagine realistic situations where the above structure is violated.

A document model should support types with a high degree of flexibility in their structure. (See the companion paper, "Conceptual

Modelling and Office Information Systems".) The document type will be viewed as the minimal specification of the corresponding instances. Instances cannot have a simpler structure than that indicated by their type definition. During document production the user can add or delete document components subject only to the type constraints, i.e., a required component cannot be deleted since it is included in the minimal structure for the type. This kind of modification is different from the updating of a form or record field. By adding components to the document, it is possible to alter the document structure. Using database terminology, we can say that some editing operations, such as adding a new figure or table, have a data definition aspect in addition to a data manipulation aspect. Similarly query formulation involves specifying the structure as well as the conditions on values of that structure. For example, a document query might ask for reports written on a specific date (a traditional selection condition) and with a graph having "profits" in the title. If graphs are not part of the minimal structure for reports, then the second condition implies an additional structural constraint as well as the obvious selection condition.

MDs are represented by different models. We can find an implicit MD model definition in the different proposals for document management systems. However, these models are often limited in scope. They reflect the special characteristics of the system with which they are associated. We find Multimedia Document Models in two areas. The first area deals with editing, formatting and interchanging of documents. The second area deals with filing and retrieval of documents.

In the area of editing/formatting MDs, the structure oriented and syntax directed modelling approaches [MeVa82] are particularly interesting. The philosophy of structure editors is to exploit knowledge about a document to simplify its editing. Many structure editors have been proposed, mainly for text documents [Fras80, Walk81, DKLM83]. These editors usually use tree structures for representing hierarchies of document elements. One category of structure editors, the syntax directed editors, aims at ensuring that the structure of the document satisfies syntactic integrity constraints [MeVa82]. This idea has been exploited by editors which have knowledge of a programming language's syntax (eg. PL/1, LISP, or PASCAL) [Teit77, Fras81]. The syntax directed document editors accept a grammar describing a hierarchical data structure for formatted documents and allow the user to enter and edit arbitrary trees having this structure. They do not require interleaved formatter commands in the text, yet can display the final formatted result [Coul76]. Besides checking the document for syntactic correctness as it is entered, these editors provide prompts guiding the user at each step.

In the area of document retrieval systems the more common approach is to extend a database management system, adding the capability to deal with text, images and voice (see the companion paper, "Office Filing"). The associated models are usually extensions of well-known database models. Particular attention has been given to the relational model [Sche84] and the entity-relationship model [AdNg84, CrCZ83, LoVe84]. For example, in the BIG project [CrCZ83] MDs can be described in a conceptual schema defined using a database model, derived from the entity-relationship model. The model is extended by the introduction of text units and picture units as attributes of entity classes. These units do not have the atomicity property of data attributes. In fact, the system allows complex operations on their content. For example, text operations such as searching for keywords and inserting and deleting strings of characters are defined in the system. Moreover, the system enforces properties such as data non-redundancy, integrity, etc. which are more typical of database systems than document retrieval systems.

In another example the TIGRE project [LoVe84] aims at the implementation of a DBMS with capabilities for handling generalized data. The TIGRE data model is defined as an extension of the entity relationship model that includes the document formalism as a type constructor. Two categories of abstractions are supported: generalization and aggregation. They are similar to those defined in other semantic data models [SmSm77b, Brod80]. Three main data structures are defined: basic type, constructed type and class type data structures. Type constructors are rename (for associating names to basic types), array, record (as in programming languages) and documents. Each document is represented by using a standard form that takes into account its logical structure and its presentation and semantic attributes. A parenthesized list representation of the standard form is used to transfer the document between different processes. Operators are defined on document types. These include access operators (i.e. browsing through the structure) and manipulation operators (i.e. edit, print, mail). Documents can contain hierarchical and non-hierarchical elements.

The type concept is the key factor characterizing different MD modelling approaches. A document type for editing/formatting models is a skeleton specified either by its syntax or by formatting commands. It can be useful for creating new document instances of that type without having to start every time from scratch [FuSS82]. The document type in models oriented to filing and retrieval is borrowed directly from the data type concept in database models. A document type is the specification of the structure and components common to all the document instances belonging to the same class. This enables the system to efficiently manage the objects (documents) in its scope, since they all belong to some already defined type. The system can interpret the contents of any component of a document in a class (according to the definition of the corresponding type).

MDs have complex structures which tend to differ from one document to another. As a consequence, a document model should satisfy two conflicting criteria.

1.   To provide as much knowledge as possible about the structure of a given MD, in order to assist in its creation, storage, and retrieval.

2.   To provide flexibility since the structure of the documents is very difficult to predetermine.

The first criterion leads to a strongly typed document model, such as we find in filing and retrieval systems. The second criterion leads to a model without types (in the database sense), letting each document instance have a structure defined separately (as in document editors and formatters). A multimedia document model should aim at a good compromise between the two criteria. It should try to obtain the advantages of database-oriented models (for filing and retrieval operation) and the advantages of editing/formatting models (for composition, editing and presentation operations). The major emphasis of such a document model should be a flexible type definition.

The organization of the paper is as follows. In section 2 the main issues arising in MD modelling are presented. In section 3 a syntax directed modelling approach is introduced. In section 4 the syntax directed modelling formalism is used to define the concepts of type and instance. Differences between our definition and types in data models are underscored. In section 5, a complete MD model is defined. It contains a conceptual level, a logical and layout level. The latter two levels reflect the specification of the international standards for Office Document Architecture. We also give an example, in which the conceptual, logical and layout structures are described, and their interrelations discussed. In section 6 the operations of the model are presented. Finally, in section 7, some conclusions and directions for future work are presented.

2.   Issues in the model definition

The following issues in MD model definition can be summarized.

1.   **Data types**
     The model should support a complete range of data types. Basic data types include the usual data types, such as *boolean, integer, real, string*, etc. Basic data types also include multimedia data types such as *text, image* (uncompressed or run-length encoded raster images), *graphic* (images encoded as graphic instructions)

and *audio* (uncompressed or LPC compressed audio values). Composed data types, including sets, lists, arrays, etc. should be defined. Derived data types should be included, such as date, address, etc. Finally, various application specific derived data types that depend on the particular environment may be needed. Derived data types should be defined using abstraction mechanisms, and starting from basic and/or composed data types [SmSm77b, Brod80, Brod81].

2. **Document types**

The concept of type and instance should be very carefully defined in the model. In data models the logical objects (entities) are classified according to structural similarity [TsLo82]. This classification helps in efficiently storing the corresponding system objects, such as records, forms, or tuples. The system can take advantage of the object regularity and generate storage structures on a per-type rather than per-instance basis. This approach is not always helpful when dealing with more general documents. Similar documents can have different structures. However, the type concept is still useful for formulating queries and creating and modifying documents. A document model, however, should support types with a high degree of flexibility in their structure.

3. **Document internal structure**

In many existing document models the internal structuring of MDs has been optimized according to different requirements. The requirements can be transmission speed for document interchange, or processing speed for editing and formatting, or access speed for filing and retrieval. In an office all these functions are successively applied to a document. If we have a different model for each function an MD may go through several conversions of its internal structure. A unified model allows us to define a unified MD internal structure. This internal structure should be complete, meaning that it should include all the structuring aspects necessary for the different operations. However, in order to be useful this model should be widely accepted. If an MD is generated in an office workstation, an internal structure is associated to the visible (and perceivable) data elements composing the MD. In a distributed office system, it is likely that this MD and its internal structure will be transmitted among different workstations and servers, for further editing, printing or archiving [Tayl83]. All of the workstations have to know about its model in order to understand the MDs internal structure.

4. **Document modification**

An MD may undergo successive editing operations after its creation. It is not enough to store an MD in its *final form* [HoKr84]. It is necessary to store the MD in a *revisable form* which can be further modified. A part of the MD internal structure should include the description of how the document has been composed (i.e. created and modified). This part should describe the MDs syntactic components. Without this description a document created in one site could not be modified in another site.

5. **Document presentation**
    MDs must be presented on physical output devices by mapping the internal structure into the external representation. This is called the *rendition process* [HoKr84]. The information necessary for this process should be included in the MDs internal structure. The structure necessary for document presentation should be defined in a formal manner (for example, see the template concept in the companion paper, "Conceptual Modelling and Office Information Systems" and in [GiTs83]). This part of the internal structure should also be widely accepted since MDs should be presented on different sites, having different capabilities.

6. **Document retrieval**
    Two modes of retrieval should be possible: retrieval by location (i.e. position within a classification hierarchy) and retrieval by content. In the first mode of retrieval documents are retrieved on the basis of the location in which they were stored. In the second mode of retrieval the user specifies a filter by creating a partial specification of the MDs internal structure and providing certain conditions on the MDs contents [TCEF83, TTRC84] (see companion paper by Christodoulakis). It is important to allow the retrieval of MDs both by location and by content. Some documents can be carefully classified and associated with precise positions in file cabinets and drawers (or their electronic equivalent [ElBe82]). Other documents cannot (or should not) be precisely classified. For retrieval by location, the model should support collections of MDs such as dossiers or files [BrPe83]. Dossiers are collections of MDs dealing with the same topic. Files are collections of MDs having similar internal structure.

7. **Document communication**
    The interchange of MDs is the operation where the need of standardization is apparent. When a MD and its internal structure are encoded in a certain format at one site, the same format should be known on the other side of the transmission in order to decode and reconstruct the MD and its internal structure. In fact, an Office Document Architecture is in the process of being standardized, in conjunction with the Office Document Interchange Formats, in TC-29 of the European Computer Manufacturers Association (ECMA) [ECMA83] and TC-97/SC-18/WG3 of the International Standards Organization (ISO) [ISO-83a, ISO-83b]. Their work is strongly connected to the work of the CCITT Commission

VIII, which is standardizing the Telex and Facsimile Group 4 Mixed Mode of Operation [CCIT83]. A document model should be compatible with the ideas present in the Office Document Architecture.

3. Proposed approach

We will follow the approach of syntax directed editors, for the problem of MD types. Syntax directed document editors are very flexible in defining document internal structures. They usually allow operations on the definition of each MD instance structure. We will explore this approach and describe a more complete definition of a document model, operating not only at the instance level but also at the type level.

We will define a *context free grammar* containing the rules for the generation of multimedia documents. The set of rules is applied step by step starting from the root to obtain a specific document. At the same time, we define the document's internal structure, called the *structure tree* of the document. A document is stored by keeping the structure tree together with all data items. In this way, the system has the advantage of always knowing exactly the *internal structure* of the document. Data items can appear only as terminal nodes in the structure tree. Nonterminal nodes correspond to higher-level structures that group elements into more complex components of the document.

We also allow nonterminal nodes to appear as leaves in the structure tree. This is the main conceptual difference between this document modelling approach and syntax directed editors. In this way, we are able to represent in the same manner document types of different generalization-specialization levels and document instances.

We will call a *live node* a node which corresponds to a nonterminal in the grammar, and to which grammar productions can be further applied. A live node in a document type can generate a new subtree in the document type structure tree, containing new live nodes. This document generation process allows us to derive a more specialized document type or instance from an existing document type or instance. A structure tree with no live nodes is a *pure document instance.* Pure document instances correspond to our intuitive notion of a document instance.

There exists a continuum of possible structure trees, going from the most general document type to the pure document instances. As a result, we can de-emphasize the distinction between types and instances. Structure trees correspond to general definitions of documents. If they have no live nodes they correspond to pure document instances.

The notation for the MD model definition will be based on a grammar G used to specify the MD structure:

$$G = (N, T, R, P)$$

where

N is the set of nonterminal symbols,

T is the set of terminal symbols,

R is the root symbol, and

P is the set of grammar productions.

We use a context-free grammar as a restricted grammar with the power necessary for describing document structures (regular grammars are too restrictive). Productions have the form:

$$A \rightarrow \alpha$$

where A is a nonterminal and α is a string of terminals and nonterminals.

A is the left hand side (LHS) of the production, α is the right hand side (RHS) of the production. We impose a further restriction on the format of the productions in P. The RHS is either a string of nonterminals *or* it is a single terminal. That is, we do not allow the mixing of terminal and nonterminal symbols in the RHS. The first is called a *nonterminal production* while the second is a *terminal production*. This restriction on the format of productions does not restrict the power of context-free grammars [AhUl72].

For the specification of the productions we use an extended BNF representation, where each production has the form:

$$<A> \rightarrow <B_1>[+]...<B_N>[+]$$

$<B_i>$ are nonterminal symbols which can be optionally tagged by a "+".

A $<B_i>+$ is called a *repeating symbol*. It means that a variable number of $<B_i>$ can be generated from $<B_i>+$. Formally, a repeating symbol $<B_i>+$ in the RHS of an extended BNF production is equivalent to a new nonterminal symbol $<Z>$ with the new following productions, in the usual BNF format, added to P:

1. $<Z> \rightarrow <Z><B_i>$
2. $<Z> \rightarrow <B_i>$

4. Structure representation

The internal structure of an MD is called a *Structure Tree (ST)*. It is conceptually equivalent to the parse-tree containing all the productions of *G* applied from the root symbol until the document itself is obtained.

We are now ready to give a formal definition of the structure tree of an MD.

A *statement S* is a triplet (PN, LHS, RHS) where:

- PN is a positive integer indicating a production in *P* of *G*. The statement *S* is called the *instantiation* of the production PN.

- LHS contains an identifier ID which is the instantiation of the nonterminal symbol in the LHS of the production PN.

- RHS contains a list of identifiers ID, which are the instantiations of the non-terminal symbols (in the same order) in the RHS of the production PN.

The identifier corresponding to a repeating symbol may or may not be repeating. If it is repeating it is tagged by a "+", i.e., ID+. Notice that for the statements instantiating a terminal production (called *terminal statements*), the RHS contains only one identifier that is the instantiation of a terminal symbol. We assume in this case that ID is the *actual value* (or pointer to) of the entity represented by the terminal symbol.

A *Structure Tree (ST)* is a set of statements *S* which obey the following conditions:

Condition 1

For any *S* in ST, an ID in the RHS of a statement cannot appear in the RHS of another statement, *and* an ID in the LHS of a statement cannot appear in the LHS of another statement, *and* an ID cannot appear in both the LHS and the RHS of the same statement.

As a consequence, if the same ID appears in two different statements of ST, then it must be in the LHS of one statement and in the RHS of the other statement.

Condition 2

In ST, for all statements except one, the ID in its LHS must also be in the RHS of another statement. The exception statement is called the *root statement* and the ID in its RHS is the instantiation of the root symbol *R* of the grammar *G*.

Condition 3

In ST, if the same ID is in the LHS of more than one statement, then there must be a statement with ID+ in its RHS.

The definition of ST as a set of statements allows one to formally check its properties and to formally define operations in the model. The structure tree can be visualized in graphic form. The correctness conditions ensure that a tree equivalent to the ST can be constructed, where each node corresponds to an ID (a node is a repeating node if it corresponds to a repeating identifier). The root of the tree is the ID instantiating the root symbol R of G. Then a subtree can be added to the structure tree for every statement in ST. For a node named ID in the structure tree, a subtree can be added with an *aggregation edge* (see figure 2a) connecting the ID node with as many new nodes as there are IDs in the RHS of S.

The aggregation edge reflects the aggregation concept found in semantic modelling [SmSm77b]. Starting from a repeating node, several aggregation edges can be generated since several statements in *ST* can have that ID in the LHS. This results in a new type of connection called *association of aggregation edges* (see figure 2b). This reflects the association concept found in the extended semantic hierarchical modelling [Brod81].

In the following, we will introduce further concepts about Structure Trees in terms of statements that can be easily translated into the equivalent graphic form for better visual comprehension.

We define a *leaf statement* as a statement with at least one ID in its RHS which is not in the LHS of any other statement in ST. A terminal statement is a leaf statement, but not all leaves are terminals.

We define a *live statement* as a statement whose RHS contains an ID that may appear in the LHS of a new statement not already in ST. A live statement is essentially a source for additional statements to an ST.

Restrictions are dynamic constraints (besides the static correctness conditions) for the introduction of additional statements to an ST. Restrictions are expressed in the form of special statements which are present in the ST. Two types of restrictions are introduced.

Quality restriction

If an ID in the RHS of a live statement does not appear in the LHS of any other statement, we can restrict the set of productions in P of G that can be used to instantiate a new statement with ID in LHS. A new special statement is introduced with the format:

$$(QL, ID, (PN_1, \ldots, PN_k))$$

Here QL is a number outside the range of production numbers in P used to flag a quality restriction statement and ID is the target of the restriction. This says that a new statement in ST having a LHS equal to ID must be the instantiation of one of the productions $PN_1, \cdots, PN_K$ listed in the RHS of this restriction statement.

Quantity restriction

If there is a repeating ID in the RHS of a live statement, we can restrict the number of statements which can be generated from ID. A new special statement is introduced with the format:

$$(QN, \ ID, \ MAX)$$

where QN is a number outside the range of production numbers in P used to flag a restriction statement and ID is the target of the restriction. This says that, at most, MAX statements (where this number is contained in RHS of this restriction statement) having LHS equal to ID can be present. Both quality and quantity restrictions can be applied on a repeating ID, while only quality restrictions can be applied on a non-repeating ID.

From these definitions, the relationships between the different types of statements can be derived. We can identify the following cases (see figure 3). A terminal statement is a leaf, but is not alive (Case A). A leaf statement which is not terminal is alive (Case B). There are live statements which are not leaves (Case C). For example, statements in which for each ID in their RHS there is a statement whose LHS equals ID and some ID is repeating belongs to case C. If a quantity restriction on ID forbids adding new statements with ID in the LHS, the statement is neither alive nor a leaf (Case D).

The previous definitions can also be translated into the equivalent graphic representation of the structure tree. For example, a leaf node is a node with no emanating edges. A terminal node is a leaf node instantiation of a terminal symbol of G. A live node is a node which can generate a new subtree according to the production of the grammar and the restrictions introduced. As a result, a leaf node which is non-terminal is alive, and any live node which is not a leaf must be repeating.

A quantity restriction on a live repeating node indicates the maximum number of emanating edges.

A quality restriction on a live node indicates the possible productions which can be applied for instantiating new subtrees. Having presented the modelling formalism, it is possible to define the concept of a document type and instance within this approach.

A Structure Tree, ST, corresponds to a *pure instance* iff there are no live statements in it. Since all leaf statements which are alive are nonterminal we can deduce that in a pure instance ST *all leaf statements are terminals.*

Intuitively, any instance document has a "complete" structure tree, that is, a structure tree where all the possible production sequences (top-to-bottom path in the equivalent graphic tree) are completed. The final multimedia entities are instantiations of the terminal symbols.

A Structure Tree, ST, corresponds to a *type* if and only if there is at least one live statement in it. This type concept is more general than the usual data modelling concept [TsLo82] of type for formatted data.

The *instantiation or specification* process on a type consists in adding new statements in ST which are consistent with the correctness conditions and with the restriction statements already in ST.

We define a *strong type* as a type which can only be instantiated by terminal statements. We define a *weak type* as a type which can be instantiated by any statement (including non-terminals).

The concept of strong type is equivalent to the type concept at the schema level of database models. In fact, instantiating a strong type can only consist in adding multimedia data values of specific data types, which is equivalent to adding terminal statements to ST. The data types allowed for terminal statements are specified in the non-terminal symbols corresponding to the IDs in the RHS of the live statements. This is the reason for the restriction to one terminal in the RHS.

The concept of weak type is more general. Since non-terminal statements can be added to ST, composed objects can be added during the instantiating process. These document components correspond in the graphic representation to subtrees of any complexity. Thus, the specification of a weak type may correspond to a phase of type definition, at the schema level, in database models. This is a DDL operation in the database terminology.

It is clear that by using the partial specification process on the structure trees we can obtain complex hierarchies among weak types. They may be, in the general case, non-tree-like hierarchies.

The flexibility resulting from the weak type definition is needed in multimedia documents for adding new complex components (i.e. a new section with tables and graphics). Moreover a system based on this model can exploit the complex hierarchies of weak types by keeping catalogs of system enforced types for user access. These system defined types are useful for document instantiation, for query definition, and for query processing.

It is also useful to define the *intersection* operation among structure trees. Intuitively, the intersection between two structure trees is the most specialized structure tree "equivalent" to both original structure trees. Formally, the intersection ST of ST1 and ST2 is obtained from ST1 and ST2 applying the following recursive procedure:

1. If the root statements of ST1 and ST2 have different PNs (production numbers), the intersection is empty; otherwise tag both statements as homomorphic.

2. For any couple of homomorphic statements in ST1 and ST2, do:
   - for any ID1 in RHS of the homomorphic statement in ST1, check if there is a statement S1 in ST1 (not already tagged) with ID1 in LHS. Let PN1 be its production number.
   - in this case, consider the ID2 in RHS of the homomorphic statement in ST2, and corresponding in the production to ID1.
   - check if there is a statement S2 in ST2 (not already tagged) with ID2 in LHS. Let PN2 be its production number.
   - If PN1=PN2, and PN1 shows a non-terminal statement, the two statements S1 and S2 are homomorphic, so tag them.
   - If PN1=PN2, and PN1 shows a terminal statement, tag the two statements S1 and S2 as homomorphic only if the values in RHS of both statements (instantiations of terminal symbols) are the same.

3. Stop when no more tagging is possible. The set of tagged statements in ST1 is the intersection ST inside ST1 (the same holds for ST2).

The system could apply the intersection operation of structure trees to all the combinations of the objects (types and instances) stored. In this way it would be possible to have an a posteriori definition of types. It would be possible to discover how appropriate are the a priori defined types. For example, the system could count the number of instances and subtypes for catalogued types, discover equivalent types and identify new types which could be useful to several user defined instances.

We expect that application environment experts will design the types, will name them, and then will instruct the users in their use. A suitable user interface should assist the expert designing the types. The flexibility of this typing approach will allow one to define types for the different classes of documents in an office environment. Strong types are suitable for all form-like documents, with very stable structure. Weak types are more suitable for less structured objects, such as memos, business letters, reports, brochures etc. Such documents may contain tables, graphics, images and voice comments. The possibility of establishing hierarchies of weak types is very useful. Moreover, since structure trees can represent the internal structures of both types and instances, it is possible to query types as well as instances. In fact, the query specification mainly consists of a partial structure specification including certain conditions on data values. Query resolution matches partial structures and example values in the correct order. The same process can be applied on structure trees of both instances and types (values are usually not present in this case). Querying types can be very useful in this environment since there is no well-defined schema as in database Systems. Naming is a crucial problem for a system adopting this approach. Different names can be defined for types and type components that are structurally very similar. A system should support catalogues of type and component names, for the system enforced types.

5. Levels of description

In a multimedia document we can distinguish different levels of structures. At a more general level, we see the document as composed of semantic components. They reflect the common user understanding of a class of similar documents. Referring to the example of a product announcement letter, the class of such letters is characterized by a header/introduction part, a product presentation part and a cost discussion part. These semantic components describe the *conceptual structure* of the particular document, which is also common to several documents with the same function in an office organization.

At another external level, the syntactic structure of the document is apparent. In fact, what is externally seen is the composition of multimedia data values in the document. These syntactic components constitute the *logical structure* of the document. This structure can sensibly vary even among documents with the same semantic structure.

In order to guide the presentation of the MD, a *layout structure* should be strictly associated to the logical structure. The layout structure shows how and where the logical elements should be displayed in the physical document. Logical structure and layout structure are the parts of the internal structure which should more strictly obey the standards.

The *conceptual structure* describes the semantic components of the MDs, giving *names* to them. Names are useful in defining the type-level part of the document structure and they correspond to names that are assigned in database Systems during schema definition. Name catalogues should be maintained by the system in order to facilitate the users in naming choices. The conceptual structure can be exploited in creating new MD instances starting from system enforced types, in controlling the editing of system enforced types, and in defining queries on MDs.

The form of MD conceptual structure depends on the semantics of the document. The syntax for defining it must be very flexible. A meta-grammar is introduced which allows any semantic component's hierarchical decomposition according to the MD type conceptual structure. The grammar gives internal names ("meta-names") to the hierarchical semantic categories. The productions defining the semantic components are:

PN1: <conceptual_document> → <semantic_component>

PN2: <semantic_component> → <component_name> <semantic_component> +

PN3: <component_name> → [meta_name]

PN4: <semantic_component> → <component_name> [logical_structure_component]

Notice that "meta-names" need not be distinct. This allows the definition of semantic interrelationships. In this case the semantic component associated with the meta-name will not have descendents since it is assumed to be identical to the already defined semantic component with the same name.

Starting from the grammar defining semantic components, we can use the formalism to describe the conceptual structure (CST) in the form of statements, or in graphical form. The same grammar shows how the conceptual structure is connected to the logical structure. Logical_structure_components are names found in the grammar defining the logical structure. In fact, after a certain level towards the bottom, the conceptual structure is merged with the logical structure. This transition from statements as instantiations of the conceptual grammar to statements as instantiations of the logical grammar happens on a specific boundary of the logical structure.

Logical and layout structures should be based on standards. From the guidelines available at this moment for the Office Document Architecture, we can outline a meta-format of the productions for both logical and layout grammars. The logical grammar will have the format:

a1.   <logical_document> → <composite_logical_object>

a2.   <composite_logical_object> →
      <property> + <constructor> <composite_logical_object> +
      | <property> + <constructor> <basic_logical_object>

a3.   <basic_logical_object> → <MD_content_portion>

The layout grammar format will be the same, where <logical_document>, <composite_logical_object> and <basic_logical_object> are to be substituted in a1, a2 and a3.

Properties define particular aspects of the logical and layout objects. Their type differs from object to object.

A *constructor* defines how a composite object is built by its constituents, and which selectors can be used to access the constituents. There are three types of constituents.

1. The *sequence* constructor specifies a sequential order for the con-
    stituents of an object. The constituents are of the same type and
    are sequentially accessible.

2. The *array(n)* constructor specifies an n-dimensional order for the
    constituents. They can be of the same type or different types and
    are directly accessible. In case of constituents of the same type,
    the selectors are n-tuples of indices.

3. The *aggregate* constructor specifies either no particular order or a
    sequential order of the constituents, which can be of the same
    type or of different types. They are directly accessible by the con-
    stituent names.

Once the logical grammar and the layout grammar are defined, we
can use the formalism in section 4 to describe the logical structure
(LGST) and the layout structure (LYST) of an MD. Logical and layout structures are correlated throughout the MD content portions,
which are common to the two structures. The boundary between the
two structures lies at their lowest level (leave level). In fact, there is a
link between any basic logical object and basic layout object. This link
relates to the MD content portion of which both basic objects are the
direct ascendants. This is called *correspondence relation* in the standard
document architecture terminology. All the other non-hierarchical relations in the Office Document Architecture are confined inside logical
and layout structures, but not between them.

Two document types, to which the example MD belongs, are
shown in figures 1 and 2. The type called "generalized letter" (figure 1)
is a weak type suitable for a large variety of office letters. The structure
tree for this type contains some rather general conceptual components,
such as "letter body" and "letter header", and also some lower-level logical components, such as "letter address". These conceptual components
are generated by using the grammar outlined in this section for the conceptual level of the model.

In figure 2, the type "product announcement letter" is described.
This is a specialization of the previous type, since some live nodes (i.e.
"letter header" and "letter body") are expanded into other nodes at the
conceptual and logical levels. This figure also illustrates how multimedia data types (in this case the graphic-valued "company logo") are
contained in the structure defining a document type. The "product
announcement letter" is a strong type at the conceptual level, since all
leaf nodes lead down to the logical level. The conceptual structure of
the MD in the example is contained in the structure of the type in
figure 2, considering only the nodes at the conceptual level.

The logical structure of the MD of the example is illustrated in
figure 3. The interconnection between conceptual and logical structures
is apparent from these figures, since the leaf nodes in figure 2 are

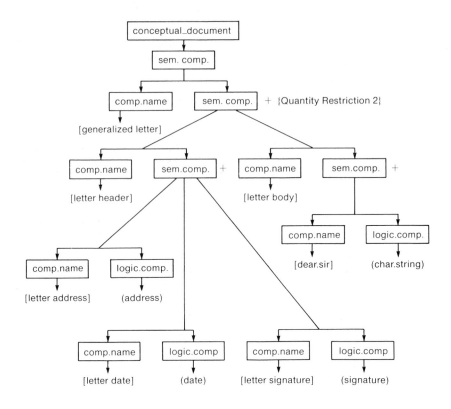

Figure 1: "Generalized letter" type

mapped to intermediate nodes in figure 3. The form of productions in the logical grammar should be:

<logical_document> → <composite_logical_object>

<composite_logical_object> → <property> + <constructor>
<composite_logical_object> + <basic_logical_object> +

<basic_logical_object> → [multimedia_data_item]

These productions express the recursive decomposition of the composite logical objects (for example, sections, tables, figures, etc.) into simpler composite logical objects. The decomposition halts when basic logical objects, which are mapped directly to multimedia data items, are reached. At any step of this hierarchical structure composition the constructor used is specified (i.e. aggregate, sequence, array) and the relevant properties are associated. The allowable types of composite and basic logical objects will be specified by the standards, as well as their properties and the value ranges. Property values can be

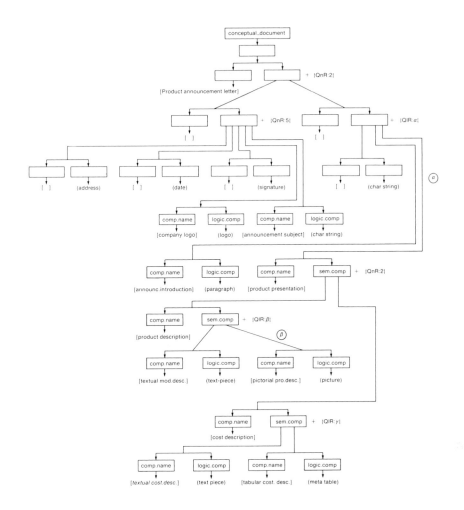

Figure 2: "Product announcement letter" type

explicitly assigned or computed by the system from the context (i.e. section number). In particular, the inheritance of properties in the hierarchy can be applied. In figure 3, the substructures resulting from instantiating property productions are not shown.

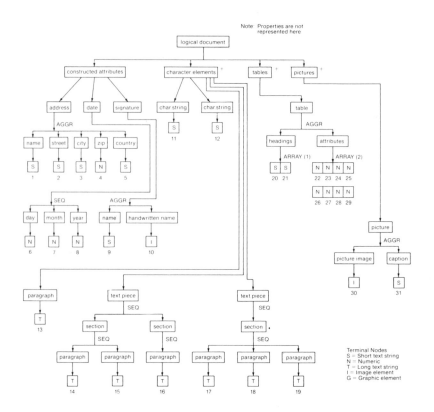

Figure 3: Logical structure

6. Model operations

In this section, the document model operations are outlined. Some issues regarding their implementation are also discussed.

Document creation

When a new MD is created, the associated internal structure should be generated according to the model. There are essentially two ways of entering a document into the system.

A.   Creation via an editor

The document is entered through an interactive document editor. The user can take advantage of the already defined document types. The structure tree is created step by step during the editing process. The system has information on the admissible steps and helps the user to issue the right operations.

B. **External input**

The document is presented in facsimile format for input to the system. Completely automatic scanning is difficult. Improvements are expected for character recognition [Free83]. However, it is difficult to recognize the logical components and associate a document to a weak type. Documents for which the structure representation is known are handled much more easily. It is necessary to scan and parse the facsimile as a compiler would parse a program. The user associates the document with an existing document type. The system recognizes the types of the external syntactic elements (parsing the logical structure) and applies the syntax rules in a bottom up fashion.

The previous input modes were concerned with entering a document. There is also the possibility of receiving a document from another system. In this case it is essential to adopt standardized protocols and formats [CCIT83] for the description of electronic documents (at least at logical and layout levels).

Document filing

Filing a MD implies storing the MD structure tree, with the three internal structures (i.e. conceptual, logical and layout) and the associated multimedia data elements. For storing the structure tree it is possible to consider either the direct statement form or a linear representation of the equivalent graphic form. It should be noted that the overhead for storing productions associated with actual data values is minimal. If an MD belongs to a system type, it is possible to store only the type names and the statements missing from the type specification. By exploiting the existence of system types in storing MDs, it is possible to facilitate the query processing. During retrieval, a type specification will facilitate the MD identification. Values can be stored separately from the structure tree. Special devices can be used providing improvement in access speed and storage cost [RaZi84].

Document retrieval

Interactive query formulation in the model does not need a new environment or language. A query filter can be defined using the same interface as for on-line document creation and modification. The user can usually recall only an approximate structure of some portions of the document as well as some content specifications within these portions. The user defines a structure tree with certain values as leaves and asks the system to match it with stored documents. The specified structure tree and the item values will act as a filter. The system matches the structure as well as the values (see the companion paper, "Office Filing").

The interactive query interface must allow some undefined areas in the filter structure tree specified by the user. These undefined areas can match with any structure portions of stored documents. The defined areas of the filter structure tree are only required to match with some of the structure portions of stored documents.

The query processing problem is similar, in principle, to the partial subtree matching problem found in semantic network interfaces to database systems. If data values are supported by indexes it is best to locate the data item values first and then compare the structures. If the system has some mechanism of partial classification, as in the case of system types, the process of subtree comparison can be performed efficiently. The system can sort the retrieved documents in order to facilitate their scanning. Thus, the user can decide to scan a retrieved document in detail, to dynamically change the filter or to choose a retrieved document type as a new filter. This provides flexible environment for dynamic filter definition by the user.

Collection retrieval and document retrieval through collections can be done in the same way. An initial query defined according to the collection grammar is used to find and select the required collection. A second query defined according to the grammar is used to find the desired documents within the scope of the collection.

Document modification

Modifying a stored document means changing its logical and layout structures and/or the linked multimedia data values. The statements should be changed and/or substituted according to the correctness conditions. If the document is the instantiation of a system defined type, the statements contained in the type structure tree could not be changed arbitrarily. The new instantiation and specialization statements should obey the eventual restriction statements of the type.

Document rendition

The MD rendition (presentation) process consists of obtaining the MD external representation by processing the document internal structure. Presenting an MD on an output device implies its composition according to its layout structure. The external representation of the document is obtained by:

- retrieving the physical elements of the document after having identified them via the internal structure;

- organizing the physical elements in higher-level objects logically connected (e.g., an image and its caption) using the logical structure;

- ordering and composing the obtained objects as specified in the layout structure.

Some degree of freedom should be allowed, in order to allow the rendition of an MD (display or print-out) at different levels of detail according to workstation capability.

Document type definition

The MD type definition is very similar to the MD creation since it involves essentially the creation of a structure tree. Particular care should be taken in the definition of system enforced types (either weak or strong). In this case the type editor will operate on the conceptual structure defining the semantic object internal names and their hierarchical structuring. Live statements and restriction statements should be defined. It should be possible to operate also at the logical and layout levels, when some logical and layout characteristics of the semantic objects are known. Some multimedia values can also be specified; for example, the company logo in business letters. MD type definition can start from scratch or from an already defined weak type, specializing it. In this case, a query facility for types can be very useful since the appropriate information may be distributed in several structure trees.

7. Conclusions

Documents containing data, text, image, graphic and audio components can have very complex structures. Moreover, these structures tend to differ from instance to instance making it difficult to obtain a strict type definition for a class of documents. Models for Multimedia Documents must be flexible in order to allow a suitable representation for their structure and contents, as well as for operations such as editing/formatting, filing/retrieval, interchanging and presentation.

A model for representing documents and supporting document operations on them has been proposed. It differs from data models used in databases. It allows dynamic schema changes which are not allowed by data models. A formalism based on a syntax directed approach has been presented, allowing the definition of types at different levels. It allows hierarchies of weak types as well as strong types. Type definition at the conceptual level is based on a meta-grammar. At the layout and logical levels type definition can be performed according to the document class definition rules. The model defined is compatible with the anticipated standards for document description at the presentation level (layout structure) and the internal structuring level (logical structure). In order to support content retrieval, a conceptual level of the document description has been added.

We plan to work on formal specification of operations on documents. An important topic is the investigation of fast access methods to document internal structures. Such access methods will provide an effective implementation of content retrieval. Efficient storage representations of document modelling structures should also be studied.

8. References

[AdNg84] [AhUl72] [Brod80] [Brod81] [BrPe83] [CCIT83] [Coul76]
[CrCZ83] [Crof83] [DKLM83] [ECMA83] [ElBe82] [Fras80] [Fras81]
[Free83] [FuSS82] [Geha82] [GiTs83] [HoKr84] [ISO-83a] [ISO-83b]
[LoVe84] [MeVa82] [RaZi84] [Sche84] [SmSm77b] [Tayl83] [TCEF83]
[Teit77] [TRGN82] [Tsic80] [Tsic82] [TsLo82] [TTRC84] [Walk81]

Part VI

Analysis

11
Properties of
Message Addressing Schemes

P. Martin

ABSTRACT *Message addressing schemes are an abstract framework for dealing with the naming and addressing problem in electronic mail systems. We use this model to analyze three important properties of a naming and addressing mechanism — completeness, serializability and time-independence. The importance of these properties is illustrated with examples.*

1. Introduction

The naming and addressing mechanism is one of the most important, and visible, components of an electronic mail system. Its role is to identify and locate all the intended recipients of a message. The correct and consistent functioning of the naming and addressing mechanism is crucial to user acceptance of a mail system. Rather than discovering problems with the naming and addressing while a system is running, we describe how the naming/addressing logic can be modelled and then analyzed. This analysis will become more important with the introduction of advanced mail systems which share the responsibility for identifying and locating recipients with the users [Mart84, MaLo83, HMGT83, Vitt81].

Current mail systems require the originator of a message to know all the recipients, and perhaps even paths to these recipients, at message creation time. The determination of the recipients is both static and centralized.

But very often a user has only partial knowledge of the recipients of a message. He may not know all the other users that should receive a message or may not have enough information about a recipient to totally identify him to the system. Future mail systems must be able to augment the user's knowledge. The systems should contain their own routing knowledge that will allow them to act with only partial information from the users. The systems will have to make decisions based on the contents of the messages and the state of the system. Further, with the communication and micro-computer technology available this knowledge will have to be distributed. Thus the determination of the recipients will be dynamic and distributed.

We make the distinction between logical and physical routing. In logical routing, a series of decisions is made that eventually results in the identification and location of the set of recipients of a message. The knowledge required to make these decisions may be distributed among a network of logical nodes. The actual physical distribution of the nodes is transparent. One step in the logical routing may involve several steps in the physical — over one or more local area networks and long-haul networks. Alternatively, two or more logical nodes may be in the same physical host.

We use the message addressing scheme model as a framework for representing and analyzing routing knowledge. An *addressing scheme* is a way of specifying and interpreting information on messages that eventually brings them to the attention of the proper recipients. We examine the properties of completeness, serializability and time-independence.

A *complete* addressing scheme is one that eventually delivers all possible messages. If all possible routings in a scheme are *serializable* then the addressing scheme is correct. That is, messages are treated consistently along all paths and routed as we would expect. An addressing scheme is *time-independent* if the length of time a message spends in circulation is guaranteed not to affect its final destinations.

2. Message Addressing Schemes

Message addressing schemes were proposed by Tsichritzis [Tsic84] as a framework for dealing with the problem of naming and addressing in electronic mail systems. Instead of dealing with the problem in a specific manner [Schi82, GaKu81, BLNS82, OpDa83], addressing schemes abstract naming and addressing from any considerations of the physical routing. They allow for a dynamic and distributed evaluation of the set of recipients for a message.

The main objects in the addressing scheme model are messages and addresses. Messages have a unique identifier and belong to a generator set of messages $\{m\}$. Addresses, belonging to a set $\{a\}$, are also uniquely identified and are nodes in a directed graph. The graph defines the connectivity of the addresses — if address a is connected to address b then a can send mail to b. The term address is a logical notion. Each address serves as a context for making routing decisions.

There are two types of addresses. Addresses which never originate or keep messages, but always forward them to other addresses, are called *routing addresses*. These provide flexibility in representing routing knowledge. The rest of the addresses, where messages can originate and be delivered, are called *mail addresses*.

The state of an addressing scheme associates a set of messages from $\{m\}$ with each address in $\{a\}$. Namely, those messages received by, but not yet sent by, the address. The mapping between states is described in terms of the operations at a single address with a single local message. There are four operations:

1. A message m is inserted in an address a (generation of a new message).

2. A message m present in an address a is moved to another address connected with a (message forwarding).

3. A message m present in an address a is accepted (message delivery).

4. A message m is kept in an address a and a copy is forwarded to another address connected with a (message delivery and forwarding).

There are two properties that have to do with the interdependence of messages. An addressing scheme is called *memoryless* if an address does not retain information from messages that have reached it in the past. An addressing scheme is called *coordination-free* if its mapping handles each message separately, without being affected by the presence of other messages. Both memory and coordination may be desirable properties but their presence complicates the operation and analysis of a scheme.

3. Complete Message Addressing Schemes

The routing logic of a message addressing scheme can be represented in a graph. Nodes correspond to addresses and directed edges correspond to the connections between addresses.

We associate a *routing procedure* P_a with each address a that embodies the routing logic at that address. When a message arrives at an address the routing procedure is executed to determine the next step(s) in the message's routing. We assume each procedure execution is *atomic*, that is, the arrival of one message cannot interrupt the processing of another. So using a "first-in-first-out" priority at an address will ensure that each message is processed.

The results of a routing procedure execution can be a change of state in the addressing scheme. One (the message being processed) or more (in the case of coordination) messages are moved along one or more connections from that address. The use of coordination in a message addressing scheme may mean that a procedure execution does not change the current state. The message being processed may have to wait for other messages to arrive before it is allowed to continue.

We represent routing procedures in the graph by labelling each edge (a,b) with a predicate p_{ab} such that if p_{ab} is true a message is moved along the connection from a to b. The results of a routing procedure execution for a message m at an address a are determined by the set of predicates on edges from a that are true for m.

As an example, consider the graph in figure 1. Messages that come into the address s are forwarded to the addresses $a_1, \cdots, a_n$ depending upon the name of the recipient specified in the contents.

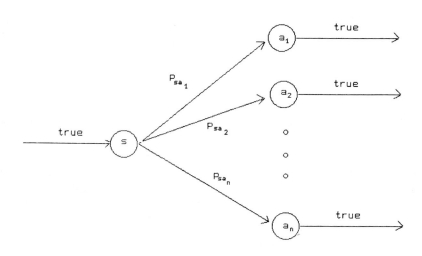

$$p_{sa_k} = \text{"name of recipient is k"}$$

Figure 1

We introduce three special addresses to simplify the analysis. The address o is a source address that is connected with all mail addresses in a scheme. When an insert operation is performed it is represented as the message moving from o to the originating address. So in figure 1, an insert operation corresponds to a message moving along the edge leading into address s. The *true* predicate on the edge means that a message can always follow the edge. The address θ is a sink address. It is also connected to all mail addresses. When a message is accepted at a mail address it is represented in the graph as the message moving to θ. So in figure 1, an accept operation moves the message along the edge from the particular a_i. A third special address is δ. It is connected to all addresses that can "drop" a message, that is a message leaves circulation without arriving at one of its destinations. This is represented as the message moving to δ.

We define a *path* in a message routing to be a set of at least two addresses $\{a_1, \ldots, a_n\}$ visited in succession by a message and a_i connected to a_{i+1} for all $1 \leqslant i \leqslant n-1$. We identify a path by the conjunction of the predicates labelling the connecting edges

$$p_{a_1 a_2 \cdots a_n} = p_{a_1 a_2} \wedge p_{a_2 a_3} \wedge \cdots \wedge p_{a_{n-1} a_n}$$

which must be true for a message to follow the path. A *cycle* is defined to be a path that begins and ends at the same address.

We now consider the requirements for completeness for three categories of addressing schemes: (1) memoryless and coordination-free schemes; (2) schemes with memory but coordination-free, and (3) schemes with memory and coordination.

3.1. Memoryless and Coordination-free Addressing Schemes

Memoryless and coordination-free addressing schemes are the simplest category. Each message is routed independently of all other messages in circulation. At each address the routing decisions are based solely on the information present in the contents of the message being processed.

A message will become stuck in circulation if it either becomes trapped at an address or follows a path of infinite length. A message would be trapped at an address if it was forced to wait forever to be processed. But we know this is impossible since, practically, there can be only a finite number of messages at an address and each address processes messages on a first-in-first-out basis. A message could also become trapped at an address if an execution of the associated routing procedure failed to halt. We can avoid this problem if we choose appropriate constructs for the routing language [Mart84].

So a message will only become stuck in circulation if it follows a path of infinite length. Practically, there can be only a finite number of addresses in any addressing scheme. Therefore a path of infinite length must contain a cycle.

It is possible to detect a cycle in a memoryless and coordination-free addressing scheme. We can catch all messages that would follow a cycle and eliminate them to obtain an equivalent and complete addressing scheme.

Observation:

Suppose A is a memoryless and coordination-free addressing scheme. Then it is possible to construct an equivalent scheme A' that is complete for the set of messages delivered by A.

Argument:

We say two addressing schemes are *equivalent* if they handle the same set of messages, have the same set of mail addresses and deliver messages to the corresponding mail addresses [Tsic84].

We construct a graph representation for A. Each possible path in the scheme is represented by some predicate p determined from the graph. The predicate p defines an equivalence class of messages (those that satisfy p) and each message in the class is routed in the same manner by each address in the path.

We obtain all the path defining predicates by performing the algorithm in figure 2 starting at o with an initial predicate of "true". The algorithm is a variation of a depth-first search [AhHU74]. The predicate is outputted when the end of the path is reached. The algorithm allows for backing up to consider all edges from a node.

```
define-path (o, true)
proc define-path (a,p)
a,b are addresses
p is a predicate
begin
if a = θ or a = δ or a already in path
        then output p
        else begin
                for each b connected with a
                        p←p∧p_ab
                        define-path (b,p)
                        p←p∧ p_ab
                end
        end
end
```

Figure 2

We need only deal with paths of finite length so that the process must halt. A path will either end with the message being delivered (i.e. forwarded to θ) or the message being dropped (i.e. forwarded to δ) or a cycle will appear. This is assured since there are a finite number of addresses in any scheme. We assume that the contents of a message cannot be changed. Changing the contents of a message means that a message may change equivalence classes. This makes path determination a very difficult problem. So the second appearance of any address in a path means that the message has entered a cycle. Suppose we are following a path and encounter a cycle. Say so far we have built up the predicate

$$p_{ab\,\cdots\,h} = p_{ab}\wedge p_{bc}\wedge\,\cdots\,\wedge p_{gh}$$

We create a new procedure P_a' by altering the procedure P_a to check for, and drop, any messages that match the predicate.

We must assume that no two paths with the same origin can have the same path predicate. Otherwise, if one of these paths has a cycle we remove the possibility of messages being delivered via the other path.

The scheme A' delivers all the messages that were delivered by A and drops any messages that got stuck in A. Therefore A' is complete for those messages delivered by A. A' handles the same messages as A, has the same mail addresses as A and routes those messages delivered by A to the same destinations. Therefore A' is equivalent to A.

3.2. Coordination-free Addressing Schemes with Memory

The inclusion of local memory at some addresses allows routing decisions to be made on the basis of information kept about previously processed messages. The memory can be used to store patterns from messages and counters. The patterns are used to represent properties such as the same origin, same subject, a particular attribute value or a particular string of text. All messages containing the pattern are assumed to have the associated property. If memory is used in this way then cycles in a path can be detected.

As with memoryless schemes, we must deal with the case where a message follows a cycle. But the presense of a cycle does not necessarily imply that the message will become stuck in circulation. An address with memory can keep track of the number of times a message loops in a path and stop the message after a finite number of times. So not only is the presence of a cycle important, but also how memory is used by addresses in the cycle.

We provide addresses with a finite amount of memory. We consider memory at each address to be in one of a finite set of states $\{s_1, s_2, \cdots, s_n\}$. We assume, without loss of generality, that addresses with memory route messages to a single address on the basis of the state. Further distribution can occur from that point. We also assume that routing decisions at an address are based solely on the state. Further decisions based on the contents of a message can be made at subsequent addresses. We are able to separate these decisions because addresses are logical entities. Tsichritzis [Tsic84] discusses reduction methods that can be used to merge the routing logic of several addresses after the analysis is performed.

When a message is processed at an address α with memory a state change in local memory may result. If the current state is s_i then a new state s_j will result if some predicate q_{ij} is satisfied by the message contents. After the state change, all messages held at α will be moved to an address a_j provided they satisfy the predicate $p_{\alpha a j}$ relating the state s_j to the address a_j. The edge (α, a_j) in the graph of the scheme is labelled $p_{\alpha a j}$. A held message is one that has been processed but could not be moved on. A message m is held at an address α until the address reaches a particular state from which m can proceed. So the execution of a routing procedure can now result in a change to the state of the local memory, or to the state of the addressing scheme or to both. This view of memory also represents coordination as seen in the next section.

Observation:

Suppose A is a coordination-free addressing scheme with memory. We can construct an addressing scheme A'that is equivalent to A and A'is complete for the set of messages that get delivered in A.

Argument:

We proceed as in the memoryless case. We perform a search of the graph representing A starting at o and obtain the path predicates. We look for cycles in the paths.

We handle cycles of only memoryless addresses as in the first observation. So we must deal with cycles containing one or more addresses with memory.

Suppose we have a cycle containing the addresses with memory α, β, $\cdots$, γ. We have to determine whether the loop in the path is finite or infinite. In effect, we examine each P_α to see how memory is used. We want a P_α to store information about previously processed messages, including the number of times each has visited α, and an upper bound on the number of visits. P_α should compare the number of visits by the current message with the upper bound and take the message out of the cycle if the bound is exceeded. With such a P_α the loop will be finite and no change is required.

In terms of the graph representation, we want at least one state s_j of α that forces a message out of the cycle. That is, there is an edge (α, a_j) labelled $p_{\alpha a j}$, where address a_j is not part of a cycle with α, and state s_j is reachable in a finite number of steps from some state s_i that occurs during the looping of the message.

If this is not the case we insert a new routing address τ' with memory into the graph such that for some pair of addresses β and γ that are part of the cycle and (β, γ) is an edge, the graph for addressing scheme A' replaces (β, γ) by (β, τ') and (τ', γ). The procedure P_β is altered to send message to τ' if they originally went to γ. The procedure $P_{\tau'}$ uses memory as described, and drops any messages (i.e. moves them to δ) that have previously passed by.

The new scheme A'handles the same messages and has the same mail addresses, and any messages that reached a destination in A reach the same destinations in A'. Those messages that got stuck in A are dropped in A'. Therefore A'is equivalent to A and is complete for those messages delivered by A.

We can see that a scheme will be complete if the connectivity is such that every cycle in the address network contains at least one address with memory and the address uses the memory appropriately.

3.3. Addressing Schemes with Memory and Coordination

The introduction of coordination into a scheme means it is now possible that a message may have to wait at an address until one or more other messages arrive before it can be routed. We represent coordination with addresses that can hold messages in their local memory. Coordination presents the possibility of *deadlock*. Two (or more) addresses may each hold messages that the other needs to continue the routing of those messages. The existence of deadlock cannot be detected with merely an initial inspection of the address network. It also depends upon the messages in circulation and the routings of those messages.

Deadlock occurs in a routing if the messages in a set all follow a path that contains two or more coordinating addresses but the messages do not visit these addresses all in the same order. This means there must be a cycle in the address network that contains the coordinating addresses in order for deadlock to be a possibility.

We use our definition of memory in the previous section to represent coordination also. Messages can be held at an address α until some state s_j of the local memory is reached. The arrival of all the messages in some coordination set causes the change to this state s_j. Without loss of generality, we assume that all messages go to the same address a_j where further distribution can be performed. The edge (α, a_j) is labelled with the predicate $p_{\alpha a j}$ that relates the state s_j to the address a_j.

Observation:

Suppose A is an addressing scheme with memory and coordination. We can construct an addressing scheme A' that is equivalent to A and complete for the set of messages delivered by A.

Argument:

We proceed as in the previous two arguments. We perform a search of the graph representing A starting at o and obtain the path predicates.

We look for cycles. From the previous two arguments we know how to modify A to handle cycles that contain only memoryless addresses or some addresses with memory. So we must only consider cycles with two or more coordinating addresses. By eliminating those messages that deadlock we ensure the completeness of A'.

We cannot tell if a particular message will deadlock at the time of its submission. Coordination involves several messages and the occurrence of deadlock depends upon their routings. We remove deadlock from A by installing a mechanism that can detect deadlock and eliminate the messages from circulation.

Suppose there is a cycle that contains coordinating addresses $\alpha_c, \ldots, \alpha_d$ which all coordinate the messages $m_c, \ldots, m_d$. We create two new routing addresses β_1' and β_2'. The address β_1' handles the coordination for all the α_i's and the address β_2' distributes the coordinated messages from β_1' back to the α_i's or to δ in the case of deadlock in the original scheme.

We also replace each α_i by the two addresses α_{i1}' and α_{i2}'. The address α_{i1}' is connected with all the addresses connected to α_i in A and receives all the messages that went to α_i. α_{i1}' is connected to α_{i2}' and to β_1' and forwards any messages in the coordination set to β_1'. All other messages are forwarded to α_{i2}'. The address α_{i2}' is connected to all the addresses α_i is connected with in A and distributes messages in exactly the same manner as α_i. By using two addresses we remove the need for a single α' to determine whether the messages are returning from β_2' or are coming from another address outside the cycle.

The address β_1' handles coordination for the cycle. Once the messages $m_c, \ldots, m_d$ have all arrived they are forwarded as a group to β_2'. The address β_2' must decide if deadlock would have occurred in A.

If any two of the messages come from different α_i's then deadlock would have occurred in A and the set of messages is dropped from circulation. If all the messages come from the same address then deadlock would not have occurred in A and the messages can be returned for processing.

In order for β_1' to be able to tell where each message comes from we assume that each path predicate is unique. Then for each coordinating address α_i in the cycle, we take the disjunction of all path predicates that define possible paths to α_i. If all messages satisfy one of the disjunctions for some α_i then deadlock would not have occurred in A. For example, if there are paths from the mail addresses $a_1, a_2, \ldots, a_k$ to α_i, then β_2' would test for messages satisfying

$$p_{a_1 \cdots \alpha_i} \vee p_{a_2 \cdots \alpha_i} \vee \cdots \vee p_{a_k \cdots \alpha_i}$$

to determine if they would have been held by α_i.

So A' will drop any messages that get deadlocked in A or that get stuck in a loop in A. Therefore A' is complete. Also A' is equivalent to A since the same messages are handled by both schemes, both have the same mail addresses and all messages delivered by A are processed in exactly the same way by A'.

Figure 3 shows a cycle in an addressing scheme A consisting of the addresses α_1, α_2 and α_3, all with coordination. Figure 4 shows how that cycle would be represented in the equivalent and complete addressing scheme A'.

The above proof assumes that if one of the m_js is submitted then all will eventually be submitted. We do not consider deadlock caused by users failing to submit all the required messages. This is beyond the control of the addressing scheme. For a scheme in which coordination is complete for all messages, we must construct the network so that there is at most one link (set of arcs in one direction) between any two coordinating addresses and that link is acyclic.

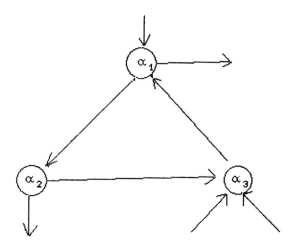

Figure 3

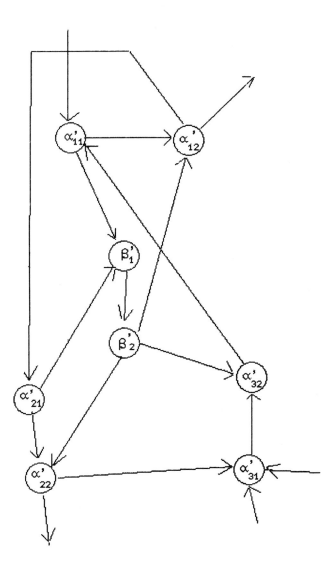

Figure 4

4. Serializability in Message Addressing Schemes

Serializability is one of the primary concurrency issues in database systems [Ullm82]. Serializability theory gives precise conditions under which transaction executions can be considered correct [BeGo82]. Concurrency in a database system means there are a number of possible ways the execution of a set of transactions can affect the state of the database. We assume the concurrent execution of several transactions is correct if and only if its effect is the same as that obtained by running the transactions serially in some order. This notion of correctness is intuitively appealing since we are able to comprehend the effect of a set of transactions if they happen one after the other.

Concurrency is also found in addressing schemes. More than one message may be in circulation and processing at several addresses may occur at any one time. This concurrency, combined with the properties of memory and coordination, can greatly complicate the message routings within an addressing scheme. There may be a number of possible routings for a set of messages. A notion of serializability allows us to determine when the routing of a set of messages is correct with respect to concurrency. An addressing scheme can be judged correct if all its routings are correct.

The use of local memory at an address means the prior arrival of one message can have an effect on the routing of a later message. For a routing to be intuitively "correct", these two messages should be processed in the same order at all addresses that both messages visit during the routing. Otherwise, the routing of the two messages may be inconsistent among different paths followed by the messages.

A routing where all the procedures for a message m_i are executed before the procedures for another message m_j satisfies this intuitive notion of correctness. Concurrency is limited to the processing of a single message and the paths followed by a message are independent. But, with coordination present in a scheme, a message may only go so far down a path and then have to wait until other messages arrive, messages that cannot be routed until the original message is completely routed. So we have deadlock in the routing.

To accommodate coordination, we say a routing is *serial* if the order of processing is the same at all addresses. We define a routing to be correct if it has the same effect as a serial routing.

We assume the addressing schemes to be complete. Thus we are guaranteed that every message routing will eventually halt and we will not face the problem of never finishing a serial execution.

4.1. Routing Logs

A *routing* $R[m_1, \ldots, m_n]$ for a set of messages $\{m_1, \ldots, m_n\}$ is the circulation of the messages through the address network of an addressing scheme. At each address visited by a message the procedure associated with the address is executed to determine the next step in the routing. This next step can be a transfer of the message to one or more connected addresses or the transfer of the message out of circulation, i.e. the message reaches one of its destinations. A message may concurrently travel several paths in the network. This corresponds to a message going to a set of destinations. A routing ends when all the messages leave the scheme from all paths in the routing.

We model message routings with a construct called a *log* (adapted from logs in serializability theory [BeGo82]). A log indicates the procedures executed during a routing and the order in which they were executed. Formally, a log over a routing $R[m_1, \ldots, m_n]$ is a partially ordered set $L = (\Sigma, <)$ where Σ is the set of routing procedures executed at the addresses visited by all the m_is $(1 \leqslant i \leqslant n)$ and $<$ is the partial ordering on these executions. The partial order $<$ indicates the order of the addresses visited or, equivalently, the paths followed by each m_i, and other constraints on the order of execution (which we discuss below). We note that the partial order $<$ is transitive.

We represent each element of Σ with the notation $P_{ij}[V_{ji}]$, i.e. message m_i visits address a_j and procedure P_j is executed. During the execution the set of variables V_{ji} in local memory (V_j) is accessed. We assume that $V_{ji} \subseteq V_j$ and that each variable $x \in V_{ji}$ is accessed and has its value altered. We require that every variable in V_{ji} have its value altered because otherwise there is no way to tell that message m_i has been processed by address a_j and that the variable was used to determine the routing of m_i. We let $P_{ij}[]$ represent a procedure execution where no local memory is accessed. We assume that the execution of a procedure at an address is *atomic*. An execution of the procedure for one message cannot be interrupted in order to execute for another message.

A log can be represented by a graph whose edges indicate the partial order $<$. The graph for the routing of a single message is simply a tree. Figure 5 shows the graph of a log over a routing $R[m_1]$ where m_1 originates at address a_1 and then follows two paths — $a_1 - a_2 - a_4$ and $a_1 - a_3$. These paths are indicated by the partial orderings $P11[] < P12[] < P14[]$ and $P11[] < P13[]$.

If an address is visited by a message m_i more than once in a routing then its associated procedure appears more than once in Σ. A loop in a path followed by m_i results in a partial order

$$\cdots \; P_{ij} < P_{ik} < \cdots < P_{ij} < P_{ik} < \cdots$$

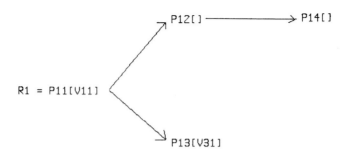

$$R1 = P11[V11]$$

$$P12[\ ] \longrightarrow P14[\ ]$$

$$P13[V31]$$

Figure 5

and the corresponding path in the graph is of infinite length. A procedure may also appear more than once if an address is on more than one of the paths followed by a message. These executions may not be related by the partial order $<$.

There are two further constraints on the form of logs. We say two procedure executions *conflict* if they are at the same address and their memory references overlap. That is, for messages m_1 and m_2, the executions $P_{1i}[V_{i1}]$ and $P_{2i}[V_{i2}]$ conflict when $V_{i1} \cap V_{i2} \neq \varnothing$. We assume that all variables in local memory that are referenced during an execution affect the routing of the message and have their values changed by the execution. So the prior execution of P_i for m_1 has an effect on the routing of m_2. We require that all conflicting pairs of executions in a log be ordered. Otherwise, there is no way to tell if the subsequent steps in a routing are valid, i.e. they follow from the processing done at the address. An example of a log L over $R[m_0, \ldots, m_4]$ with conflicting executions is shown in figure 6.

The second constraint deals with the coordination of messages. Coordination is represented by a set of procedure executions (not necessarily consecutive) at a particular address. The result of all but the last execution is to hold the current message and leave the state of the addressing scheme unchanged. The result of the last execution is to route the current message and all those messages stored by the previous executions. The order of arrival of the messages is not important. We assume that the same routing is performed when all the messages are present no matter what the order. If order does matter, then we can represent this by accesses to variables in local memory, eg. $P_{ij}[V_{ji}]$. Otherwise we will simply use the notation $P_{ij}[\ ]$ when referring to coordinated executions.

Formally, we say a set of procedure executions at the same address $(P_{1i}[\ ], \ldots, P_{ni}[\ ])$ *coordinate* if all procedure executions must

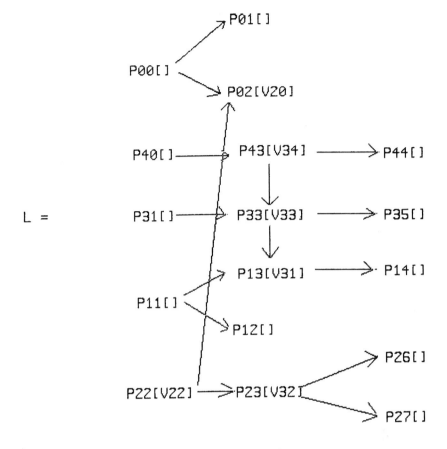

Figure 6

be performed before the routing of all the associated messages can continue. That is, if $P_{ji}[] < P_{jk}[]$ for some $1 \leqslant j \leqslant n$ and $i \neq k$ then $P_{li}[] < P_{lk}[]$ for all l such that $1 \leqslant l \leqslant n$. The presence of coordination in a log can be indicated as in figure 7. The messages m_0 and m_1 are coordinated at address a_2 and both executions $P_{02}[]$ and $P_{12}[]$ must occur before both messages can be transferred to a_4.

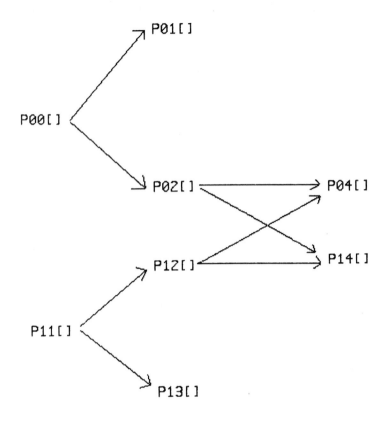

Figure 7

4.2. Log Equivalence

If L is a log over some routing $R\,[m_1, \ldots , m_n]$, we say $P_{hj}\,[V_{jh}]$ *is affected by* $P_{ij}\,[V_{ji}]$ if $P_{ij}\,[V_{ji}] < P_{hj}\,[V_{jh}]$ and $V_{ji} \cap V_{jh} \neq \varnothing$ and there does not exist $P_{kj}\,[V_{jk}]$ such that $P_{ij}\,[V_{ji}] < P_{kj}\,[V_{jk}] < P_{hj}\,[V_{jh}]$ and $V_{ji} \cap V_{jk} \cap V_{jh} \neq \varnothing$. In other words, the prior arrival of message m_i affects the routing of message m_h at address a_j and there is no message m_k that arrives in between which can override the effect.

Intuitively, two logs are equivalent if the same addresses are visited by the same messages in each of the logs (same state changes to the addressing scheme with respect to the individual messages) and they have the same effect (if any) on the local memory of each of the addresses. Formally, we say two logs are *equivalent* if they have the same Σ and

1.   each procedure execution is affected by the same procedure execution in both logs;

2.   they have the same set of *final accesses*;

3.   they have the same *coordination sets*.

A procedure execution $P_{ij}[V_{ji}]$ is a final access to some set of variables $V_{jf} \subseteq V_{ji} \subseteq V_j$ if there is no $P_{kj}[V_{jk}]$ such that $P_{ij}[V_{jk}] < P_{kj}[V_{jk}]$ and $V_{jf} \subseteq V_{jk}$. A coordination set is a set of procedure executions $\{P_{1i}[], \ldots, P_{ki}[]\}$ that all coordinate on some message set at address a_i.

4.3. Serializable Logs

A *serial* log over a routing $R[m_1, \ldots, m_n]$ is a partial ordering on Σ such that for each pair of messages $m_i, m_j \in \{m_1, \ldots, m_n\}$ and all addresses a_k visited by both m_i and m_j, either $P_{ik} < P_{jk}$, or vice versa. An example of a serial log is shown in figure 8.

A log is *serializable* if it is equivalent to a serial log. We consider the routing associated with the log to be correct. For example, the log L over $R[m_0, \ldots, m_4]$ shown in figure 6 is serializable. We can see that it is equivalent to the serial log S over R in figure 8.

Suppose L is a log over the routing $R[m_1, \ldots, m_n]$. The *serialization graph* for L, $SG(L)$, is a directed graph whose nodes are $R[m_1], \ldots, R[m_n]$ and whose edges are all $R[m_i] \rightarrow R[m_j]$ such that for some set of variables V_{kl} at address a_k visited by both messages m_i and m_j, $P_{ik}[V_{ki}] < P_{jk}[V_{kj}]$ and $V_{ki} \cap V_{kj} = V_{kl}$.

A cycle will occur in $SG(L)$ if the routing procedure executions for a set of messages are in a different order at two or more addresses. This is not correct since the routings of two or more messages affect each other in different ways on different paths. So L cannot be serializable. Figure 9 shows the serialization graph $SG(L)$ for the log L of figure 6. There are no cycles and we already know L is serializable. The independent subgraphs in a serialization graph mean that individual routings have no effect on each other, eg. $R[m_0]$ and $R[m_1]$, $R[m_0]$ and $R[m_3]$ in $SG(L)$. So in a memoryless scheme, there will be no edges at all in any of the serialization graphs since each routing is totally independent.

Observation:

For any addressing scheme A and log L over a routing $R[m_1, \ldots, m_n]$ if $SG(L)$ is acyclic then L is serializable.

Argument:

We will give a proof by contradiction. Assume that L is not serializable, so by definition we know L is not equivalent to some serial

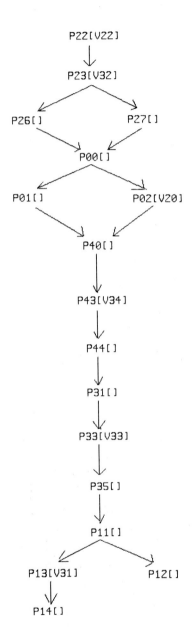

Figure 8

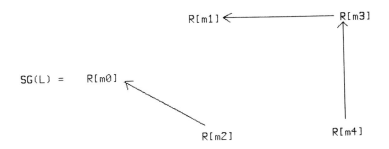

Figure 9

log S. That is one, or both, of the following statements is not true
1. every procedure execution is affected by the same procedure execution in both L and S;
2. L and S have the same set of final accesses.
We will consider the two cases where each of the above statements is false.

case (1): When compared with every serial log S over R there is some $P_{ij}[V_{ji}]$ affected by some $P_{kj}[V_{jk}]$ in L that is not in S. This implies that there is an edge $R[m_k] \rightarrow R[m_i]$ in $SG(L)$.

We know L is not serializable by assumption, so there must be some other address a_h visited by both m_i and m_k such that $P_{ih}[V_{hi}]$ conflicts with $P_{kh}[V_{hk}]$ and $P_{ih}[V_{hi}] < P_{kh}[V_{hk}]$. $P_{ih}[V_{hi}] < P_{kh}[V_{hk}]$ implies that there is an edge $R[m_i] \rightarrow R[m_k]$ in $SG(L)$ though this may be obtained by transitivity. Therefore $SG(L)$ has a cycle but this is a contradiction.

case (2): When compared with every serial log S over R there is at least one $P_{ij}[V_{ji}]$ in the set of final accesses of L that is not in S.

If $P_{ij}[V_{ji}]$ is the final access on V_{jf} in L, but $P_{kj}[V_{jk}]$ is the final access in S, then $P_{kj}[V_{jk}] < P_{ij}[V_{ji}]$ in L and there is an edge $R[m_k] \rightarrow R[m_i]$ in $SG(L)$, though perhaps by transitivity; i.e., there may be conflicting accesses between them.

We know by assumption that L is not serializable. There must also be some other address a_h with variable set $V_{hf} \subseteq V_h$ such that $P_{kh}[V_{hk}]$ and $P_{ih}[V_{hi}]$ conflict, $V_{hk} \cap V_{hi} = V_{hf}$ and $P_{ih}[V_{hi}] < P_{kh}[V_{hk}]$. So there must be an edge $R[m_i] \rightarrow R[m_k]$ in $SG(L)$, though perhaps by transitivity. Therefore $SG(L)$ has a cycle, but this is a contradiction.

Therefore L is serializable if $SG(L)$ is acyclic.

5. Time Independence in Message Addressing Schemes

An addressing scheme is called time independent if the time needed to process a message at each address does not affect where the message gets delivered [Tsic84], i.e. the final destination(s) for each message does not depend on the sequence of applying the next state mapping in the network.

Observation:

Any addressing scheme A is time independent if it is complete and there are no conflicts at any of the addresses in A.

Argument:

For A to be time independent we know that the amount of time spent by a message at any of the addresses must not affect the final destinations of the message.

For a given set of messages $\{m_0, \ldots, m_k\}$ in circulation, and two routings of the messages $R[m_1, \ldots, m_n]$ and $R'[m_1, \ldots, m_n]$, a message m_i spends more time at an address a_j in R' than in R if messages processed after m_i at a_j in R are processed ahead of it in R' (we assume the time a message spends at an address is directly proportional to the number of messages ahead of it to be processed).

If a_j is memoryless and coordination-free we know by definition that each message is processed independently. So the order of processing does not alter the destinations.

If a_j has memory, then order can matter, since the prior arrival of a message can alter memory and affect the routing of succeeding messages. But we assume there are no conflicts; so for any two executions $P_{ij}[V_{ji}]$ and $P_{kj}[V_{jk}]$ we know $V_{ji} \cap V_{jk} = \emptyset$. The memory used by the executions does not overlap so they can have no affect on each other. Therefore the order of processing does not alter the destinations.

If a_j has coordination then again order does not matter. The messages will be kept until all the messages to be coordinated have arrived and then the set of messages will be routed. The order does not affect the routing.

Therefore A is time independent.

6. Examples

We illustrate the properties of message addressing schemes in this section with a pair of examples. The first example deals with completeness. The second example deals with serializability and time independence.

6.1. Mail Handling

Figure 10 contains a message addressing scheme for a set of typical mail handling instructions that a pair of managers, *M1* and *M2*, might give to their secretaries. There is no global design. The instructions are based on reasonable local procedures. Both managers give identical instructions to their secretaries.

Incoming mail is first divided into personal and business mail (mail addresses *a* and *d*). This division could be determined by how the mail is addressed, who the originator is, or by special markings. The personal mail is forwarded directly to the manager's office (mail addresses *b* and *e*) where it leaves circulation.

The business mail is routed according to whether or not the manager is on vacation. The routing addresses α and β (for *M1* and *M2* respectively) have memory that can be in one of two states. If the state is s_1 then the manager is at work and mail can be forwarded to his office. Otherwise the state is s_2 and the manager is on vacation. A manager inserts a special message *p*, just before he goes on vacation and upon return from vacation, to change the state of his corresponding address.

If the manager is on vacation then it must be determined whether or not the mail is urgent. Before leaving for vacation, the manager would identify properties (e.g., certain subjects, originators) which indicate that mail is urgent. Mail with these properties is forwarded to the substitute manager. We assume that *M1* and *M2* cover for each other. If the mail is not urgent then it can be forwarded to the manager's office to be dealt with later.

Using the methods we have outlined, we produce predicates for all paths in the addressing scheme graph starting at address *a*. The paths starting at *d* are of the same form as those starting at *a* and are not discussed here. We assume o is connected to *a* and *d* with edges labelled *true* and *b* and *e* are connected to θ with edges labelled *true*. The predicates corresponding to these edges can be left out of the path predicates since they will play no role in determining the resulting value.

The path predicates for the paths starting at *a* are

$$Personal_{ab} \tag{1}$$

$$Business_{a\alpha} \wedge M1 - Here_{\alpha b1} \tag{2}$$

$$Business_{a\alpha} \wedge M1 - Vacation_{\alpha c2} \wedge NotUrgent_{cb} \tag{3}$$

$$Business_{a\alpha} \wedge M1 - Vacation_{\alpha c2} \wedge Urgent_{cd} \wedge Personal_{de} \tag{4}$$

$$Business_{a\alpha} \wedge M1 - Vacation_{\alpha c2} \wedge Urgent_{cd} \wedge Business_{d\beta}$$
$$\wedge M2 - Here_{\beta e1} \tag{5}$$

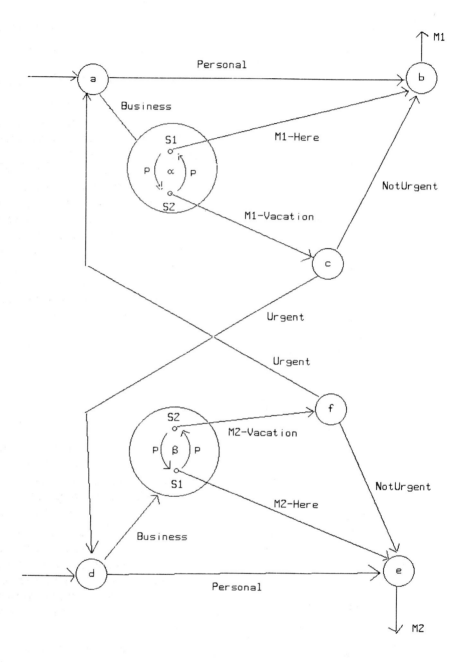

Figure 10

$$Business_{a\alpha} \wedge M1 - Vacation_{\alpha c2} \wedge Urgent_{cd} \wedge Business_{d\beta}$$

$$\wedge M2 - Vacation_{\beta f2} \wedge Not\, Urgent_{fe} \tag{6}$$

$$Business_{a\alpha} \wedge M1 - Vacation_{\alpha c2} \wedge Urgent_{cd} \wedge Business_{d\beta}$$

$$\wedge M2 - Vacation_{\beta f2} \wedge Urgent_{fa} \tag{7}$$

The exercise of determining the path predicates points out several flaws in the routing logic when viewed globally. Path predicate (4) indicates a possible path in which *M1* considers the mail to be business while *M2* considers it to be personal mail. If the latter were the case, the mail should not have gone to *M1* in the first place. Also, there is no action for incorrectly addressed mail in this scheme. Path predicate (6) indicates a possible path in which *M1* considers mail to be urgent while *M2* does not. There is an inconsistency between the local procedures that should be resolved. Finally, we see that path predicate (7) defines a cycle. So, if both *M1* and *M2* are on vacation, urgent business mail will just cycle around until one of the managers returns from vacation. We only notice the incompleteness when procedures at all the addresses are analyzed in combination. As more complex addressing schemes are designed it will become more difficult to comprehend all the possible paths in a scheme; therefore this type of analysis will be vital to ensuring completeness.

6.2. Calendar Manager

Figure 11 shows an addressing scheme for a very simple calendar manager. Each user has a routing address with memory (the α_is) that is used to keep track of booked time slots (figure 11 shows two users). Each address has a set of states $\{s_1, \ldots, s_k\}$. The current state indicates which time slots are free and which are booked.

When a message is received at an α_i, if the requested time slot is free, there is a state change $s_i \rightarrow s_j$, where s_j is the same as s_i except that the requested time slot is booked, and the message is forwarded to a mail address that delivers it to the user. If a message is received by an α_i and the requested time slot is booked, then there is no state change and the message is forwarded to mail address a_7 where it is delivered to a user designated to handle the problem.

A message routing in this scheme will be incorrect if there is more than one message in circulation that wants to book the same free time slot and these messages are processed in different orders at the α_is. Different users will book different meetings for the same time slot. Figure 12 contains a log L_1 over a routing $R[m_1, m_2]$ and the serialization graph $SG(L_1)$. The two messages try to book the same time slot for a meeting with both users. So the memory references overlap in both α_3 and α_4. The serialization graph contains a cycle so the routing is not serializable and different meetings get booked at the same time. Figure 13 shows a log L_2 over a routing $S[m_1,m_2]$ for the same messages and its serialization graph $SG(L_2)$. We can see that L_2 is serializable and that both users get booked for the same meeting.

Also, this addressing scheme is obviously not time independent. Any messages that request the same time slot conflict over the same part of local memory in an α_i. So the time spent in circulation, i.e. the order of processing, by conflicting messages has a definite effect on the final destination of the messages.

7. Concluding Remarks

We can view the study of message addressing schemes as analogous to the study of data models in database management systems. Message addressing schemes provide a general way of representing the "data" of a mail system, that is the naming and addressing information.

We need to understand the properties of mail systems before we can effectively build advanced mail systems. We have described how message addressing schemes are used as a framework for this analysis. We dealt with the properties of completeness, serializability and time independence, and discussed the conditions necessary for their existence.

The naming and addressing mechanisms of both existing and proposed mail systems can be represented as message addressing schemes and then analyzed to uncover problems. By assuring the existence of such properties as completeness, serializability and time independence we can increase user confidence in a system.

8. References

[AhHU74]   [BeGo82]   [BLNS82]   [GaKu81]   [HMGT83]   [MaLo83]
[Mart84] [OpDa83] [Schi82] [Tsic84] [Ullm82] [Vitt81]

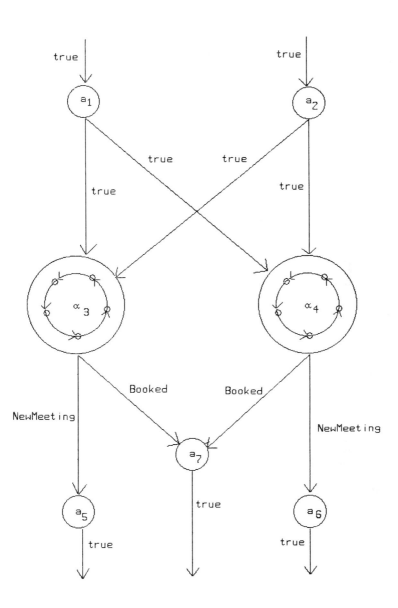

Figure 11

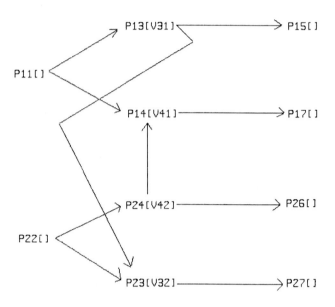

$$R[m1] \xleftarrow{\hspace{3cm}} R[m2]$$

Figure 12

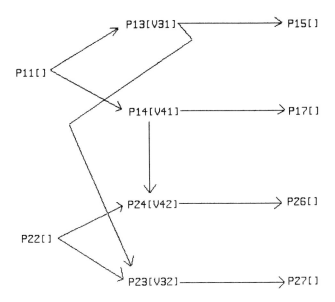

Figure 13

12
Message Flow Analysis

O.M. Nierstrasz

ABSTRACT *Message management systems with facilities for the automatic processing of messages can exhibit anomalous behaviour such as infinite loops and deadlock. In this paper we present some methods for analyzing the behaviour of these systems by generating expressions of message flow from the procedure specifications. Message domains are partitioned into state spaces, and procedures can be interpreted as automata effecting state changes. Bloeking of procedures and procedure loops can then be detected by studying the resulting finite automaton and Petri net representations of message flow.*

1. Overview

Automatic processing and routing of electronic documents yields some interesting problems when the work that is done with them is sufficiently complicated. In this paper we consider the task of determining what global behaviour is exhibited by messages in a message management system when there exist a number of automatic procedures running at user workstations, examining, processing and routing incoming messages.

If the logic built into these procedures is anything but entirely routine, then we may see messages being routed through the system in various ways. If the automatic procedures are adapted from existing manual procedures, there is always a possibility that the translation will be faulty: that messages may get improperly routed, or that procedures will wait indefinitely for messages that do not arrive. We therefore propose some techniques for studying and analyzing the behaviour that can be expected to result from such automatic procedures. The intended behaviour can thus be verified to some degree, and anomalous behaviour can be detected in advance.

In the following section we describe informally the systems that we are interested in modelling and analyzing. Collections of workstations connected by a network are used to pass electronic documents, or "messages". These messages are typically highly-structured, and often resemble forms. Similar messages are classified into "message types". High-level automatic procedures may in fact be implemented by the workers using the workstations. Complex activities can be broken down into simple steps that collect a set of messages satisfying "trigger conditions", perform transformations on those messages, possibly creating or destroying some, and then route or file them.

In the third section we introduce a formal model for discussing these systems. The model is then used to develop a characterization of global behaviour in terms of message flow. The message domains (the sets of values that messages may assume) are partitioned into state spaces. Procedures can then be viewed as effecting state transition on messages, and the entire system can be viewed as a collection of finite state automata, one per message type. We then show how to recover the coordination of messages performed by the automatic procedures by "welding" the finite state automata into a Petri net (a popular modelling tool).

Sections six and seven are concerned with detecting anomalous behaviour. In section six we discuss the problem of blocking, in which a procedure may wait indefinitely for a missing message to arrive. This is especially troublesome if there are other messages waiting to be processed by that procedure. There are various scenarios in which blocking may occur, including *deadlock*, where two procedures are each waiting for messages that are stuck at the other procedure.

In section seven we discuss "procedure loops". Here we may see procedures firing indefinitely, passing messages back and forth between them. A special case is the "message loop", in which some messages visit the same sequence of procedures indefinitely. These problems may also cause blocking, if a procedure is waiting for a message in a loop. If messages are created in the loop, the file system will eventually get saturated, and the network may even get overloaded with message traffic. We show how it is possible to use the Petri net model of message flow to detect possible procedure loops.

2. Message Management

We are interested in office information systems that are superficially very similar to real offices. We have a collection of *workstations* ("stations", for short) that are the logical equivalent of desks. Users communicate with each other by using electronic documents or *messages* instead of paper documents. Other familiar objects may also have their counterparts in a computerized office system (bulletin boards, calculators, calendars and so on). By "simulating" a real office with the computerized system, the task of computerization is simplified and the likelihood of acceptance by office workers is increased [AtBS79, ElNu80, HaSi80]. If naive-user programming is to work, then electronic objects should have immediately recognizable counterparts to familiar physical objects, and the operations we normally perform on the real objects should translate naturally into operations on the electronic ones.

The static objects in these systems are electronic documents containing the information that we would normally find on paper documents. They resemble our intuitive notion of a message in that they can be sent from workstation to workstation, but in this setting they may have other constraints. Messages in an office information system may be required to continue to exist after they have been received — documents in offices often change many hands, possibly residing at a location for a long period of time before being passed on. Furthermore, many messages fall into well-defined groups or "types". Forms and records are highly structured — a collection of them resembles a relational database. Questions about forms can resemble database queries ("tell me what customers owe us more than a thousand dollars").

Operations on messages include creation, destruction, display, modification and mailing. In addition, since messages in this context may be a permanent record of information, we may wish to query a database of messages. Such operations as selections and joins over several messages by matching comparable fields, for example, can be very useful. Similarly, when modifying messages, it should be possible to easily transfer data from one message to another, or to use information in one field of a message to compute or generate new information for another field.

In order to automate office activities, one must be able to recognize conditions that cause events to be triggered. Events may, in turn, cause other events to be triggered. Visible events include the arrival of messages and the creation and modification of messages. One must be able to select precisely those messages that are of interest. A trigger condition thus resembles a query ("get me a message satisfying this condition") that applies to the future rather than just the present. Since a collection of messages may be required in order to complete some activity, these conditions may potentially include joins, or matching between messages.

A simple example is mail-forwarding. All messages satisfying a simple constraint can be automatically forwarded to a particular location. Order forms for large amounts could be forwarded to a manager for approval.

It is instructive to decompose activities into steps: in each step we must gather a set of resources (messages), possibly transform them in some way, and release them. New messages may be created in the process. Although an activity may consist of several steps chained together, we will concentrate on the steps themselves. The advantage of this is that we can consider the steps to be atomic — they either succeed or fail in entirety. Multi-step activities naturally do not necessarily have this property. It is the steps that we shall speak of as "procedures", though one should keep in mind that more complex activities exist in general.

We also assume that these procedures are local to workstations. This view is very natural and consistent with the principle that computerized office systems resemble real offices: users of the system and their automated procedures only have *direct* control over the documents "belonging" to them. (We may extend this, however, by allowing the presence of local procedures at other sites that "belong" to someone else. A manager may, for example, be able to install a procedure at a worker's station that selects and forwards certain messages back to him.) Another advantage of local procedures is that we do not have to address the problem of activities that are triggered by events that take place at several *physically* different locations. If all the "workstations" are timeshared on a single mainframe then we do not have serious problems implementing such behaviour, but it is another matter when each workstation is a separate machine on a network.

3. Message Flow Modelling

Before we can begin to address questions of global behaviour in message management systems, we need a formal framework for discussing automatic procedures. This framework must be powerful enough to capture quite general procedures but should be divorced from any particular implementation of them. It is immaterial, for example, whether procedures are written in some high-level programming language or in some intermediate code generated by a programming-by-example interface.

We will first present a model for describing messages and the procedures that manipulate them. Although we make some simplifying assumptions about procedures, we will show that quite general behaviour can be captured within the confines of our model.

3.1. Locations

The logical configuration of an office information system is similar to that of a physical office. There are a number of workstations ("stations", for short), each of which is capable of communicating with any of the others. Whether or not the system runs as a collection of physically independent communicating machines or not is immaterial. Similarly the nature of the communication medium does not concern us here.

The collection of workstations is represented by:

$$S = \{s_1, \cdots s_N\}$$

In addition we have two *pseudo-stations*, α and ω, that represent creation and destruction of objects. Creation and destruction are thus explicitly modelled. In some situations such stations will exist in truth: destruction of documents may in fact be implemented by permanently archiving them; also, creation of documents may be the responsibility of a privileged authorizing agent that assigns, say, unique identifiers. We require only that no messages be sent to α and that none be received from ω. That is, they must behave as *source* and *sink*, respectively. The set of stations and pseudo-stations is:

$$S^+ = S \bigcup \{\alpha, \omega\}$$

Mailboxes are intermediate locations between stations. Messages passed between stations must be put into a mailbox just as physical documents are placed in an "in-tray". Although there may not be any "real" mailboxes in the system we are modelling, this allows us to distinguish between new mail and previously-seen messages. Furthermore, our model has one mailbox for every ordered pair of stations. This allows us to readily identify the sender of a message without having to resort to modelling a *sender* field for messages in transit. The latter approach would be entirely equivalent, however. The set of all mailboxes is thus:

$$M = \{m_{ij} \mid 1 \leqslant i \leqslant N, 1 \leqslant j \leqslant N\}$$

where m_{ij} is the mailbox for messages sent from s_i to s_j. Note that α and ω do not have mailboxes. A message "from" α appears at the station creating the message. A message that is destroyed goes directly to

ω. A station is allowed to mail messages to itself.

The set of all locations is

$$L = S \bigcup M$$

and, with the pseudo-stations:

$$L^+ = S \bigcup M \bigcup \{\alpha, \omega\}$$

The set of locations from which s_i may receive messages is:

$$L(s_i) = \{\alpha, s_i\} \bigcup \{m_{ki} \mid 1 \leqslant k \leqslant N\}$$

This is the *local scope* of s_i — the locations that are accessible to the procedures at s_i. Messages may be created at α, they may already reside locally at s_i, or they may arrive by mail from any of the N stations (including s_i itself, if desired).

Similarly s_i may route messages to anything in the set:

$$R(s_i) = \{\omega, s_i\} \bigcup \{m_{ik} \mid 1 \leqslant k \leqslant N\}$$

(Note the reversal of subscripts on the mailboxes.)

3.2. Messages

Messages are assumed to be structured, and belong to one of several *message types* that encode this structure. The set of message types is:

$$X = \{X_1, \cdots X_K\}$$

The *domain* of a message type is assumed to be the Cartesian product of the attribute domains. (The attributes are the "fields" of a structured message.) We have, therefore:

$$dom(X_i) = \prod_{j=0}^{n_i} dom(X_{ij})$$

where n_i is the number of attributes of message type X_i.

We reserve two attributes, X_{i0} and X_{i1} for the *identity* and the *location* of a message, respectively. The identity of a message instance is the only attribute that is never allowed to change. Since message instances may change value, we need some convention that allows us to keep track of their identity. We thereby also distinguish between a *message instance* and a *message value*: a message instance may assume different message values at different points in time. $dom(X_{i0})$ may be any enumerable set; for simplicity's sake we may assume it to be the set of positive integers. Of course, $dom(X_{i1}) = L$ (a message whose "location" is α or ω is not explicitly represented). A message value is represented by

$$x \in dom(X_i)$$

The kth attribute of x is denoted by either x_k or $x[k]$. The latter notation is generally used when x is the jth message in a tuple of messages, $\tau = (...,x,...)$, so $x = \tau[j]$, and $x_k = \tau[j][k]$. Message tuples are discussed below, in the section on procedures. The identity of x is x_0, and its location is x_1.

The *system state* is the collection of all the values of existing message instances. There is a set of message values D_i for each message type X_i. The system state is:

$$D = <D_1, \cdots D_K>$$

where $D_i \subseteq dom(X_i)$. We do not represent messages whose "location" is α or ω. Such messages have not yet entered, or they have already left, the system. We also insist that each D_i contain at most one message with a given identifier, i.e.

$$\forall x \in D_i,\ y \in D_i,\ y_0 = x_0 \Rightarrow y = x$$

In addition, we adopt the convention that

$$D(I) = D_i \text{ where } I = X_i$$

(i.e. if I is an arbitrary message type then $D(I)$ represents the set of instances of that type).

3.3. Procedures

At each station $s_i \in S$ there may be a set of procedures that automatically process messages:

$$P(s_i) = \{p_{ij} \mid 1 \leqslant j \leqslant k_i\}$$

where k_i is the number of procedures at s_i. The set of all procedures is:

$$P = \{p_{ij} \mid 1 \leqslant i \leqslant N, 1 \leqslant j \leqslant k_i\}$$
$$= \bigcup_{i=1}^{N} P(s_i)$$

Every $p \in P$ has a set of *input types*, *trigger conditions* and *actions*. A procedure (within our model) is a single-step activity. A collection of messages (inputs) matches the trigger condition and the actions are performed, causing messages to be modified (possibly created or des-troyed) and routed. The input types are the types of the messages p needs in order to evaluate its trigger conditions:

$$I(p) = \langle I_{p1}, \cdots I_{pl_p} \rangle$$

where $I_{pi} \in X$. l_p is the number of inputs to p.

The inputs to a procedure p form a set, or rather a tuple, of mes-sages that we call an *input tuple*. We usually represent such a tuple by the symbol τ, where $x = \tau[j]$ is the jth input message and $x_k = \tau[j][k]$ is the kth attribute value of the jth message. Such a tuple τ may trigger procedure $p \in P(s_i)$ if $\tau \in \prod_{j=1}^{l_p} dom(I_{pj})$ and it satisfies the trigger conditions of p. In addition, the messages in τ must be available to p, that is, $\tau[j][1] \in L(s_i)$, and each of the messages in τ must be unique (a message cannot play two roles for a single pro-cedure). We formalize this in the set $T(p)$ of message instances that may trigger $p \in s_i$, where:

1. $T(p) \subseteq \prod_{j=1}^{l_p} dom(I_{pj})$

2. $(\tau \in T(p)) \wedge (I_{pj} = I_{pk}) \wedge (\tau[j][0] = \tau[k][0]) \Rightarrow j = k$

3. $\tau \in T(p) \Rightarrow \forall j \; \tau[j][1] \in L(s_i)$

Tuple τ can thus *trigger* p if $\tau \in T(p)$ and for all $I_{pj} \in I(p)$ we have $\tau[j] \in D(I_{pj})$ or the jth message is to be created by p (i.e. $\tau[j]$ does not exist yet). We then say that p is *enabled*.

In order to disambiguate conflicts between procedures, we allow for a partial ordering ">>" of procedures. If both p and p' are enabled and $p \gg p'$, then procedure p must be fired. We say that p *has priority over p'. p' may only be fired if it is enabled and p is not. This is useful if p is triggered when message x matches some coordinating message y and p' is triggered when there is no coordinating y. Without partial ordering of procedures it would be impossible to express the condition: "fire p' with message x only if there is no matching message y". For example, if procedure p matches inventory forms to order forms and p' looks for order forms for non-existent items, then the only way to cap-ture the trigger condition of p' is to have it accept all order forms not accepted by p.

Actions map input tuples to output tuples. In our model, there is a one-to-one correspondence between input messages and output mes-sages *even if the procedure creates or destroys some messages*. This is why we need the pseudo-stations α and ω. They allow us to (somewhat artificially) model messages that have not been created as arriving from α, and those that are destroyed as being sent to ω.

The action of procedure p is a mapping:

$$A(p):T(p)\rightarrow \prod_{j=1}^{l_p} dom\,(I_{pj})$$

such that the identities of input messages are never changed, and they are routed only to valid locations. We use the notation a_{jk} to refer to the individual attribute mappings of $A(p)$. If $\tau'=A(p)(\tau)$, then

$$a_{jk}:\tau\,|\longrightarrow\tau'[j][k]$$

For each j, therefore, a_{j0} is the identity map (can't alter identity of $\tau[j]$). Also, the a_{j1}s are the *routing functions*, since they are responsible for updating the location attributes. Clearly, the domain of a_{j1} is $R(s_i)$, where $p \in P(s_i)$.

Within our model, user input, external databases and other outside sources of information are not explicitly represented. When procedures make use of external information, we consider the mappings of the procedures to map to a *set* of possible values (modulo the outside information sources). Consequently, when we perform our analysis with traditional machine models such as finite automata and Petri nets, a certain amount of non-determinism appears that may not necessarily be evident in the system under analysis. A function that sets a field of a message to anything a user wishes to enter is therefore modelled as a mapping from the input message to the entire domain of that message field. We should therefore keep in mind that this "non-determinism" is often an artifact of our attempt to exclude arbitrary information sources from the outside world.

If τ triggers p then the system state D is updated to reflect the firing of p. Input message instances are replaced by their new values. If $\tau'=A(p)(\tau)$, then the new system state $D'=<D'_1,\cdots D'_K>$ is defined by:

$$D'_i = (D_i - \{\tau[j]\,|\,I_{pj}=X_i\}) \bigcup \{\tau'[j]\,|\,(I_{pj}=X_i)\wedge(\tau'[j][1]\neq\omega)\}$$

Messages that are destroyed are simply deleted from D'_i.

4. Message Paths and States

Our model of message management views procedures and locations as basically static entities. Although procedures are altered and workstations may be added to a system, we expect these events to occur infrequently compared to the rate at which messages are processed and modified by the procedures. Also, we do not expect to be able to formalize the changes in procedures and in system configuration in the same way that we can formalize the changes in messages (through the procedures). We may try to measure the large-scale changes in procedures, however, through how they effect the behaviour of messages. Since it is the behaviour of the messages that best characterizes what is actually happening on a *regular* basis, it is here that we are to concentrate our efforts in analyzing global behaviour.

What is immediately visible is that messages are created, are modified and routed by sequences of procedures at different workstations, and are eventually destroyed. We can think of messages as tracing a *path* through the network of stations as they encounter different procedures. In between the procedures they acquire different *values* (including their *location*) which they hold until the next procedure changes their value. We may thus think of a *message path* as being not merely a sequence of procedures encountered by the messages, but as an alternating sequence of values and procedures. This message path is an expression of "message flow" since it encapsulates all the locations a message visits during its lifetime, especially if we allow ourselves to think of procedures as extremely brief, temporary "locations".

Unfortunately this expression of message flow is impractical. In [Nier84] it is shown that there is no effective way of comparing the message paths of two different messages. Briefly, it is shown how two messages can "simulate" two different Petri nets in such a way that the message paths are equivalent to the Petri net languages. Since there is no effective way of determining whether two Petri net languages are equivalent [Pete83], we cannot compare message paths.

We must therefore seek some less demanding way of describing message flow. By partitioning message domains into finite state spaces we limit the possible combinations of messages and procedures to be considered. Furthermore, since procedures can be thought of as effecting transitions of messages from state to state, we can derive a finite state machine representation of message flow. We can thus extend the notion of message paths to be alternating sequences of message *states* and procedures. As finite state machines are a well-understood formalism, this leads to a classical interpretation of system behaviour.

We need not necessarily consider all message attributes when we partition our message domains into a state space. Some attributes may not affect the path of messages at all. Attributes that do affect the path do so by affecting either the triggering of procedures or the routing of the message.

To begin with, although the domain of a procedure's actions and triggers is all of $T(p)$, it is in fact likely that only some of the attributes of the input messages are examined or modified. We would like to identify the *true* arguments of a function as the ones that are actually used in the computation of the value returned. We are assuming, of course, that all the functions we will be dealing with are effectively computable, and describable by algorithms. A procedure that increments a field of a message clearly does not need any of the information contained in the other fields of the message in order to compute the result. The only true argument to the incrementing function is therefore the field that is modified.

The true arguments to a function can generally be determined by inspection. (There are situations where this may not be so, but we shall not discuss them here.) For example, the true arguments to $f(x,y,z)=x^2+y$ are clearly x and y, provided the domains of x and y have more than one element.

We will now define *selection attributes, routing attributes* and *control attributes*:

Selection attributes are defined to be those attributes that are true arguments to the trigger conditions.

X_{ij} is a *selection attribute* if $X_{ij} \in arg(T(p))$ for some p

Routing attributes are those that are true arguments to some routing function (recall that routing functions are the components of an action $A(p)$ that modify the locations of the input messages).

X_{ij} is a *routing attribute* if $X_{ij} \in arg(a_{k1})$ for some routing function a_{k1}.

Control attributes are attributes that are true arguments to any action that modifies some selection attribute, some routing attribute, or (recursively) some other control attribute:

X_{ij} is a *control attribute* if:

(i) X_{ij} is a selection attribute or

(ii) X_{ij} is a routing attribute or

(iii) $X_{ij} \in arg(a_{kl})$ for some a_{kl} and attribute l of input I_{pk} is a control attribute

Routing attributes are those that directly affect routing decisions. *Selection* attributes indirectly affect routing by determining which procedure is likely to "grab" the message (and consequently route it). *Control* attributes affect routing even more indirectly by influencing the value of routing or selection attributes. Note that the definition of *control attribute* is recursive, and so includes attributes that affect routing even indirectly.

Non-control attributes (the ones left over) do not influence routing or message flow in any way. Consequently we may ignore these when we decide how to partition our message state space. The non-control attributes are only of interest to us if we have specific questions about their value. We might, for example, like to know the range of values of a particular message field when it arrives at our station, even though that field in no way affects its flow through the network.

Control attributes can be determined by a recursive application of the definition given above. Once the routing and selection attributes are determined, it is a relatively straightforward operation to detect the control attributes. An algorithm for doing this is described in [Nier84].

4.1. Obtaining message states

We will now consider the matter of how best to partition message domains into state spaces. Simple trigger conditions provide us with excellent partitions, but complex conditions yield unusual message subdomains whose images under actions can be hard to follow. Since we are interested especially in the effect of actions on message states, it is important to have states that are as simple as possible to trace. We may therefore try to "box" complex subdomains, or reduce a complex condition to a collection of simple conditions that cover it. We may also try to refine our partition by discovering new message states that result from applying actions to existing message states. This "fine-tuning" may be continued indefinitely, however, and so it is generally not practical to carry it too far.

Generally speaking, the best message state space would identify one message state per message value. Since we require a finite number of message states to begin to analyze message flow, we must consider carefully how we choose our partition.

Since control attributes are the only attributes that affect routing, our message states should correspond to predicates over the control attributes. We can gather this information at the same time that we collect the control attributes.

Selection attributes are those that are arguments to trigger conditions. The trigger conditions thus automatically yield conditions that may be usable for generating message states. If a trigger condition can be expressed as $\vee(\wedge C_j)$ where each C_j is a predicate involving one or more control attributes, then we can use the C_j to generate message states. The conditions collected in this way at all stations yield a state space by considering messages that may or may not satisfy each of these conditions. If, for example, there are c conditions in total that involve messages of type X_i, then a message $x \in dom(X_i)$ may potentially fall in one of 2^c message states, corresponding to success or failure in matching each of these conditions.

Of course, not all combinations of conditions necessarily yield a usable message state: some combinations may be contradictory. Conditions $x_i > 5$ and $x_i < 3$ clearly cannot both be true at the same time. There may therefore be considerably less than 2^c non-empty message states.

Message states that are expressible as a Cartesian product of attribute subdomains allow us to consider each attribute independently. We would thus have

$$\sigma = \prod_{j=0}^{n_i} R_j$$

or

$$\sigma = \{x \in dom\,(X_i) \mid \bigwedge_j C_j\}$$

where each C_j represents R_j. C_j is therefore a simple condition involving only attribute X_{ij}, for example: $4 \leqslant x_j \leqslant 10$.

If the trigger conditions $\vee(\wedge C_j)$ have the property that each C_j is a simple condition of this form, then we automatically are able to derive our desired message states. Furthermore, when the attributes are numeric and the conditions are of the form $x_i \theta u$ where u is a constant and $\theta \in \{=, \neq, <, \leqslant, >, \geqslant\}$ then the conditions yield attribute ranges bounded by the constants. In this case, if we have c_j conditions involving attribute X_{ij}, we have at most c_j constants and at most $c_j + 1$ ranges. Consequently we would have $\prod_j (c_j + 1)$ message states (where $c_j = 0$ for non-control attributes). This is considerably less than the potential 2^c states resulting from non-simple conditions (where c is the total number of conditions involving all X_{ij}, i.e. $c = \sum c_j$).

Unfortunately we cannot reasonably expect all trigger conditions to be this well-behaved. There are two options available. The first is to ignore all C_j that are not of the form $x_i \theta u$, and the other alternative is to try to convert them to simpler conditions that are more useful. The idea is to "box" the messages satisfying the condition by discovering the attribute ranges that correspond to solutions of the predicate. This can be done, for example, with a condition like:

$$x_i^2 + x_j^2 \leqslant 25$$

Here we can deduce that $-5 \leqslant x_i \leqslant 5$ and $-5 \leqslant x_j \leqslant 5$. With the condition:

$$x_i = x_j$$

however, we can deduce nothing since both attributes potentially range over their entire domains. Note that we may use combinations of conditions to extract more information. If, for example, the condition above were combined with $x_j > 0$, then we may deduce that $x_i > 0$ is also of interest. In a trigger condition of the form $\vee(\wedge C_j)$, one should use the conjunctions $\wedge C_j$ to deduce the simple conditions.

In the cases of both selection attributes and routing attributes, the problem is greatly simplified if triggers and routing actions are expressed by users in terms of fairly simple conditions on attributes. Furthermore, the user may be asked to supply any additional information implied by conditions that involve comparisons of several attributes. Of course, depending on the complexity of the triggers and actions expressible within the system, it would be desirable if the system itself could do all the analysis of attribute ranges.

Other control attributes are slightly more complicated to handle since they appear in actions that may not map to finite sets. We have, however, already obtained ranges for the control attributes found thus far (the routing and selection attributes), so we may feel free to use this information at this point.

Consider a control attribute X_{ij} that is modified by a_{kj} of procedure p (where $X_i = I_{pk}$). By the definition of "control attribute", we know that all attributes in $arg(a_{kj})$ must also be control attributes. Also, since X_{ij} is a control attribute already discovered, we presumably have some range information about it. If R_l is a range for X_{ij}, then:

$$a_{kj}(\tau) \in R_l$$

is a predicate over the inputs τ to procedure p. We may therefore attempt to "box" the set of inputs that satisfy this condition, and thereby obtain ranges for the control attributes in $arg(a_{kj})$. The new ranges can be used to further subdivide, or "fine-tune" the message states.

Note again that "boxing" may be impossible in some cases, yet trivial in others. Specifically, if a_{kj} is a function of a single argument, then the condition $a_{kj}(\tau) \in R_l$ is a predicate over a single attribute. For example, if a_{kj} returns something like $x_h + 1$, and R_l is the range $[a,b]$, then the resulting predicate is $x_h + 1 \in [a,b]$, and the resulting range for this attribute will (trivially) be $[a-1, b-1]$.

If, on the other hand, a_{kj} is a complicated function of several arguments (for example, a high-order polynomial), then the task of obtaining attribute ranges is a problem in numerical analysis with only approximate solutions available.

4.2. State transitions

At this point in our analysis we expect each station to know what message states are currently of interest. What is left is to determine what state transitions are effected by the procedures. For a message in a given input state σ we would like to know the possible next state, σ', that may result if the message triggers some procedure p.

To tell what happens when p fires, it is not, in general, sufficient to know the state of a single input message. Attributes of all coordinating messages are potentially available to the actions that modify the message we are interested in. Although we cannot predict what states the other inputs will be in, we know that they must satisfy the trigger condition. We therefore introduce the following notation to represent the possible inputs given one message in state σ:

$$\tau_p(\sigma) = \{\tau \mid \tau \in T(p),\ \tau[k] \in \sigma\}$$

$$(\text{where } \sigma \subseteq dom(X_i) \text{ and } X_i = I_{pk})$$

(For simplicity, X_i and k are understood.) Note that $\tau_p(\sigma)[k]$ is the set of message values in σ that may trigger p (possibly empty). This is equal to $\sigma \cap T(p)[k]$.

We also introduce $\hat{p}(\sigma)$ as the set of procedures that σ might trigger, and $\hat{a}_p(\sigma)$ as the set of values that σ might be mapped to after triggering p:

$$\hat{p}(\sigma) = \{p \in P \mid \tau_p(\sigma) \neq \varnothing\}$$

$$\hat{a}_p(\sigma) = \{A(p)(\tau)[k] \mid p \in \hat{p}(\sigma),\ \tau \in \tau_p(\sigma),\ X_i = I_{pk}\}$$

Procedure p then effects a state transition from σ to σ' if $p \in \hat{p}(\sigma)$ and $\hat{a}_p(\sigma) \cap \sigma' \neq \varnothing$. That is $p : \sigma \to \sigma'$ if p is capable of mapping some message in state σ to some message in state σ', given the right coordinating messages. We also introduce $\hat{l}(\sigma)$ as the set alternating strings of message states and procedures encountered by messages starting in state σ:

$$\hat{l}(\sigma) = \begin{cases} \{p\hat{l}(\sigma') \mid p \in \hat{p}(\sigma),\ \hat{a}_p(\sigma) \cap \sigma' \neq \varnothing\} & \text{if } \sigma \neq \omega \text{ and } \hat{p}(\sigma) \neq \varnothing \\ \lambda \ \text{(the empty string)} & \text{otherwise} \end{cases}$$

$\hat{l}(\sigma)$ therefore is the message flow language for message state σ. It represents all sequences of procedures that messages in state σ may possibly encounter. $\hat{l}(\sigma)$ may be "computed" by recursively applying its definition. Sequences of procedures are generated as $\hat{l}(\sigma)$ is expanded. (Of course, a straightforward expansion is impractical since infinite strings may be generated.)

Since messages in different states may still be able to trigger the same procedures, it is useful to keep track of the message states together with the sequences of procedures encountered. We spoke earlier of a message path as an alternating sequence of message values and procedures. We may easily extend this idea to message states in the following definition:

$$\phi(\sigma) = \begin{cases} \{\sigma p\phi(\sigma') \mid p \in \hat{p}(\sigma),\ \hat{a}_p(\sigma) \cap \sigma' \neq \varnothing\} & \text{if } \sigma \neq \omega \text{ and } \hat{p}(\sigma) \neq \varnothing \\ \sigma & \text{otherwise} \end{cases}$$

Note the similarity to the definition of $\hat{l}$. In fact, we may obtain $\hat{l}(\sigma)$ by mapping the states in $\phi(\sigma)$ to the empty string. $\phi(\alpha)$ represents paths starting from message creation. Paths terminate when messages are destroyed, so $\phi(\omega)=\omega$.

At this point we can easily see that message behaviour can be compared to that of a finite state automaton. Let Σ_i be the set of message states for message type X_i, i.e. Σ_i is a partition of $dom(X_i)$ obtained by the approach described in the previous section. Then the finite automaton of X_i is:

$$<\Sigma_i, P\times\Sigma_i, \delta_i, \alpha, \omega>$$

The states of the automaton are the message states. Inputs are strings over $P\times\Sigma_i$, i.e. pairs of procedures and next-states. The initial state is α, the final state ω, and the next-state function is:

$$\delta_i(\sigma, (p, \sigma')) \mid\rightarrow \sigma'$$

where $X_i=I_{pk}$, $p\in\hat{p}(\sigma)$ and $\hat{a}_p(\sigma)\bigcap\sigma'\neq\varnothing$. Note that we have K automata, one for each message type. We shall discuss how these automata can been seen to interact in the next section.

The set of all state transitions can be found by having each station determine what transitions may occur there. Not all message states may be reachable, however. (Similarly, not all state transitions are "reachable".) An alternative way of finding the state transitions is to start with the procedures that are capable of creating new messages, and to trace message state transitions starting from there. The reachable state transitions are thus collected by following the paths in $\phi(\alpha)$. Since there are only a finite number of transitions, an algorithm to compute $\phi(\alpha)$ should terminate after encountering each transition at most once. Such an algorithm is described in [Nier84].

Briefly, "symbolic messages" gather all the reachable state transitions by simply traversing a "spanning tree", starting at α, and visiting each station where the information about the transitions resides. A symbolic message represents a choice of possible current message states and keeps track of the transitions that have been traversed up to that point. Since different messages are often routed in different directions by procedures, we need the ability to *split* a symbolic message whenever this happens. A symbolic message may thus split into many parts going in different directions before all reachable states and all state transitions are found.

When there are no new states and state transitions to visit, the symbolic message returns to the station initiating it. Since the symbolic message may have split into separate parts, the work is not finished until each of the parts returns. When the transitions have all been gathered, we may then generate a regular expression capturing the message flow automaton by using a standard algorithm such as in [AhHU74].

5. Petri Net Representation

Although message behaviour can be compared to the behaviour of a finite automaton, this does not tell the whole story since coordination is not explicitly represented. What we in fact have is a *collection* of finite automata, one for each message type, interacting with each other. For procedures to fire, several of these automata must be in the right state at the same time. In fact, it is possible to "weld" these automata together in such a way as to produce a Petri net that captures the procedure interactions. The resulting Petri net not only models the message flow and control flow apparent in the automata, but also captures the coordination of messages by procedures. We thus explicitly represent the flow of messages of all types at once, and the necessary trigger conditions (in terms of message states) of all procedures.

Consider, to begin with, a Petri net with one transition for each procedure, and places for the inputs and outputs of the procedures. Each input and each output may correspond to several message states, however. Let us then add one place for each message state of each message type. Now add transitions from the places representing message states to the places representing inputs whenever messages in those states match the trigger conditions for the procedure. Similarly add transitions from outputs to message states when actions may map messages to those states. In figure 1 we represent procedure p with inputs i_1 and i_2 and outputs o_1 and o_2 as a single transition. Message states σ_1 through σ_4 and σ'_1 through σ'_5 are represented by places. Petri net transitions are also present to represent the fact that input i_1 corresponds to message states σ_1 and σ_2, and that p generates outputs in state σ_4. An entire Petri net may be built in this way with transitions mapping message states of various types to other message states.

There is a serious problem here, however. In figure 1 it appears that messages in states σ'_1 or σ'_2 may map to messages in states σ'_3 or σ'_4. Suppose that in fact we only have state transitions $p:\sigma'_1|\rightarrow\sigma'_3$ and $p:\sigma'_2|\rightarrow\sigma'_4$. In this case that information would be lost by our Petri net interpretation. It is possible to remedy this situation by adding extra Petri net states to "remember" what the previous message states were. In figure 2 we have added states t_1, t_2, t'_1 and t'_2 to accomplish precisely that.

We may formalize this construction as follows:

Let P be the set of procedures in the system. $I(p) = <\cdots, I_{pj}, \cdots>$ is the list of input types to p.

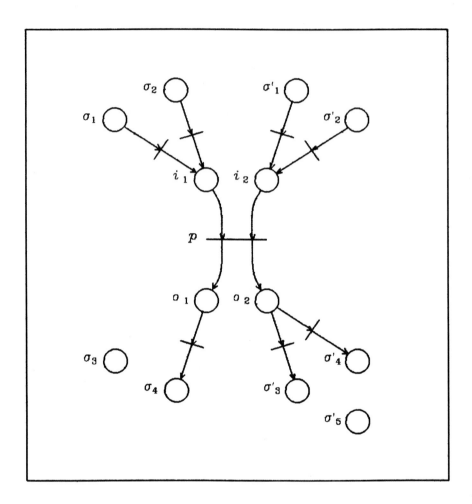

Figure 1: A Petri net interpretation of message flow

$O(p) = < \cdots, O_{pj}, \cdots >$ is a "copy" of $I(p)$ representing the out-puts. Σ_i is the set of message states of type X_i. $T_i \subseteq \{(p, \sigma_j, \sigma_k) \,|\, \sigma_j, \sigma_k \in \Sigma_i, p \in \hat{p}(\sigma_j), \hat{a}_p(\sigma_j) \cap \sigma_k \neq \varnothing\}$ is the set of state transitions for messages of type X_i. There are at most $|P| \times |\Sigma_i|^2$ of these (and, in general, far fewer). Also, let $r_i = \{(p, \sigma_j) \,|\, \exists \sigma_k \text{ such that } (p, \sigma_j, \sigma_k) \in T_i\}$. The r_is represent the σ_js that trigger some procedure p. We shall use the elements of these sets as labels for the places and transitions of our Petri net.

Let our Petri net have places with labels in:

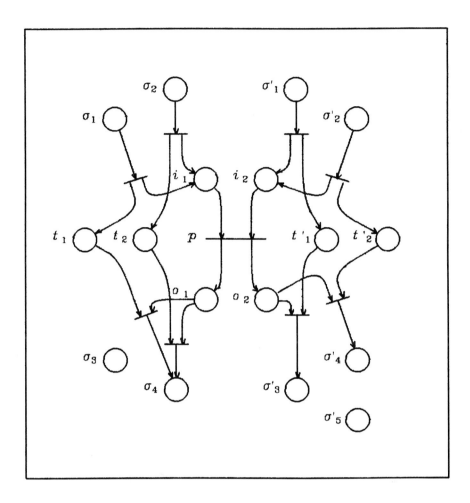

Figure 2: An "improved" Petri net interpretation

$$\{I_{pj} \mid p \in P, \ I_{pj} \ in \ I(p)\} \bigcup$$
$$\{O_{pj} \mid p \in P, \ O_{pj} \ in \ O(p)\} \bigcup$$
$$(\bigcup_{X_i \in X} \Sigma_i) \bigcup (\bigcup_{X_i \in X} r_i)$$

and transitions with labels in:

$$P \bigcup (\bigcup_{X_i \in X} r_i) \bigcup (\bigcup_{X_i \in X} T_i)$$

Note that we have both places and transitions labeled $(p, \ \sigma_j) \in r_i$, but they are in fact to be considered disjoint. We therefore have places representing message states, procedure inputs and outputs, and "state reminders" to remember previous states. The transitions represent procedures and the acts of "grabbing" and "releasing" messages. The "grabbing" and "releasing" allows us to capture the idea that procedure inputs and outputs may correspond to several states.

The transitions have the following inputs and outputs:

1.   a transition labeled $p \in P$ has inputs $I(p)$ and outputs $O(p)$,

2.   a transition labeled $(p, \sigma_j) \in r_i$ has input σ_j, and has outputs (p, σ_j) and I_{pk} where $I_{pk} = X_i$.

3.   a transition labeled $(p, \sigma_j, \sigma_k) \in T_i$ has inputs (p, σ_j) and O_{pk} where $O_{pk} = X_i$, and has output σ_k.

It is now clear from the construction that tokens may "travel" from message state σ_j to state σ_k via procedure p only if there is a state transition labeled $(p, \sigma_j, \sigma_k) \in T_i$. This is the problem that we set out to correct after our first attempt at a Petri net representation. In addition, procedure p may only fire if it has at least one message available for each of its inputs. We have therefore succeeded in "welding" together the finite automata of message flow by reclaiming the coordination that we "sacrificed" in the previous section.

Note that the Petri net we have obtained is "conservative". (A Petri net is *conservative* if we can assign weights to tokens according to their places so that the net weight of the entire net never changes.) Since tokens represent message instances in certain states, this means that messages are "honestly" represented. We neither gain nor lose messages. To prove this, let us assign double the weight to tokens in the places representing message states. Consider the transition firings in 1, 2 & 3 above. Transitions representing procedures are trivially conservative since they all have the same number of inputs as outputs. The "grabbing" and "releasing" transitions are also conservative since the former "splits" a message state token into a procedure input token and a "reminder" token, and the latter "joins" a "reminder" token and a procedure output token. In either case, the total weight of the tokens is the same before and after.

The net is no longer conservative if we add extra transitions to represent the creation and destruction of messages. This may be done by adding one transition for each place representing an α state or an ω state. Tokens could then be added at will to the α states, and removed from the ω states. Equivalently, we may simply delete procedure input and output places corresponding to the creation or destruction of messages. Message states α and ω need not be explicitly represented in this case.

6. Blocking and Deadlock

A procedure is *blocked* if it waits indefinitely for one of its inputs to arrive. If the procedure has only one input, that simply means the procedure does not fire, but there may not necessarily be any far-reaching effects. If, on the other hand, the procedure does have other inputs, then inputs that arrive to be processed by that procedure may wait forever because of the blocking.

There may be several reasons for an input not to arrive:

1. The input is never created.

   This causes blocking when a coordinating message is uniquely determined, but does not, in fact, exist. If, for example, an order is placed for some "feeblevetzers", and no such items exist, then a procedure that attempts to match such an order with a corresponding inventory record will be blocked.

2. The message states corresponding to the trigger conditions of the procedure are unreachable.

   This may happen because the message reaches a dead end, or because it enters an infinite loop, or it may simply be that all possible paths avoid the procedure in question.

3. The message states corresponding to the trigger conditions of the procedure are avoidable.

   Messages of the input type in question may be able to reach the procedure to trigger it, but alternative paths may avoid it entirely. Blocking may occur here if the message is uniquely determined by the other inputs. An order form that is to be matched against an inventory record for "veeblefetzers" will be unable to proceed if the inventory record happens to be routed along a path that avoids it. (We assume that there is a unique inventory record for any given item.) If, on the other hand, an inventory record is waiting to be matched against an order form, then it may not matter that the order form can be routed along alternative paths — there will be other orders for that item, so the procedure will not necessarily be blocked.

4. There is a "blocking loop".

   Two procedures are each waiting for a message that is stuck at the other. This is what is most commonly thought of when we speak of "deadlock" in systems where there is contention for resources. The resources in our case are the messages.

5. The missing input is itself stuck at another procedure that is blocked.

   The other procedure may be blocked for any of the first four reasons.

Note that in cases 1, 3, 4 and 5 we only have blocking if the awaited message is uniquely determined by the other inputs. If it is not, then another message in the same state may eventually arrive, so we would not have blocking. For example, since order forms would not be uniquely determined by any procedure matching them against inventory forms, they could never be the cause of blocking in such a situation. In case 2, we have blocking even if the awaited message is not uniquely determined since *no* message may ever reach the desired state.

Let us consider each of the cases in turn.

6.1. Message creation

The first case seems a degenerate one, and not so much a candidate for analysis. At any rate, one may easily identify all the procedures that are responsible for creating messages of the awaited type. Possibly this information can be useful in determining whether the awaited message has been created. If we can determine that procedure p may not be supplied with some inputs for this reason, we say that p is *1-blocked*, or *1-BL*, for short.

Of course, if the procedure creating the messages is blocked, then no messages will be created. This may be considered an instance of case 5, however.

6.2. Unreachable states

Cases 2 and 3 are quite similar in that we are interested specifically in the message paths. In case 2 it is simply a matter of determining whether the message states corresponding to the trigger condition of a procedure are reachable or not. This information is readily available as we collect the state transition information, since only reachable states are encountered. Lists of reachable and unreachable states can thus be compiled.

Exactly *why* a particular message state is not reachable is another matter. A characterization of message flow may be useful in tracking down what is wrong, but it is well-nigh impossible to tell this without a deeper understanding of what the procedures are supposed to do. There are, however, two readily identifiable situations that suggest that something is amiss:

i.   A message may hit a *dead end*.

A message that ends up at a location where no procedure is prepared to handle it at all is at a "dead end". Without user intervention the message will stay there forever. A dead end may be the consequence of incorrect routing. Naturally this will prevent a message from reaching waiting procedures. Again, we may discover dead ends as we collect the state transitions.

ii.   A message may enter an infinite loop.

This happens if a message reaches a set of mutually reachable states from which there is no escape. States *outside* that set would not be reachable. In particular, ω could never be reached. This too may be the result of incorrect routing. In a directed graph, a set of mutually reachable nodes is called a *dicomponent* [BoMu76], or a *strongly connected component* [AhHU74]. Once a message leaves a dicomponent it may (by definition) never return. If the dicomponent cannot be left, then the message is in an infinite loop. A depth-first search algorithm can partition a directed graph into its dicomponents in order $O(max(n,e))$, where n is the number of nodes and e is the number of edges [AhHU74]. To identify infinite loops, one need only determine whether there are any dicomponents with no arcs leaving them for another dicomponent.

A procedure for which a certain input cannot arrive because the input message states are not reachable is *2-blocked*, or *2-BL*.

6.3. Avoidable states

In case 3 we are concerned with messages that may or may not arrive. A state may be reachable, but not necessarily by all messages of the specified type. Blocking is possible if any given message is not guaranteed to reach at least one of the message states corresponding to the trigger condition, *and* that message is uniquely determined by one of the other inputs. To determine the latter, one needs to know something more about constraints on the messages. If, for example, we know that a certain field of a message is a key field, and we have a procedure that matches that message against another via that key field, then we know that for any matching input it is uniquely determined. An inventory record, for example, is uniquely determined by any order form.

As to the matter of reachability, we may rephrase it as follows: Is it possible for messages of a given type to avoid *all* of the message states corresponding to the trigger condition for a given procedure? In figure 2, message states σ_1 *and* σ_2 must be simultaneously avoidable for input i_1 to be avoidable. In this light it is clear that we may easily

answer this question. One need simply traverse the directed graph of
the message state automata, starting at α, and avoiding all nodes that
are input message states to that procedure. If we can construct a path
to ω that avoids all these nodes, then it is possible for a message never
to trigger the procedure in question. Clearly we need only traverse
each edge of the graph at most once, so the problem is solvable in
order $O(t)$, where t is the number of state transitions (i.e. the number
of edges in the graph). If all paths encounter at least one of the input
states, then they are unavoidable (as a set), and this cannot be a source
of blocking.

If the reachable message states corresponding to some input of
procedure p are all avoidable, then p is *3-blocked*, or *3-BL.*

6.4. Deadlock

There is the possibility of deadlock, wherein two procedures are
each waiting for a message held by the other.

Suppose that procedure p has some input x that uniquely determines some other input y. Suppose also that y may come to p from p',
and it uniquely determines some input z at p'. Finally suppose that z
comes to p' from p'', where z uniquely determines the same x of procedure p. We then have a potential deadlock in which x waits at p for
y, y waits for z at p', and z waits for x at p''.

Let us suppose that we know for all procedures p when some
input $X_i \in I(p)$ uniquely determines some other input $X_j \in I(p)$, *and*
there is no other procedure p' accepting messages of type X_i in the
same states as those accepted by p. Messages of type X_i must therefore
wait at p for the arrival of some *specific* message of type X_j. A message
of type X_i would uniquely determine one of type X_j whenever we have
some trigger condition of the form $x_n = y_m$ where $x \in dom(X_i)$,
$y \in dom(X_j)$ and X_{jm} is a key field of messages of type X_j. We
represent this information as a set of tuples:

$$AWAITS \subseteq \{(p, X_i, X_j) \mid p \in P, X_i, X_j \in X\}$$

For $(p, X_i, X_j) \in AWAITS$, we say that $p:X_i \rightarrow X_j$, or simply $X_i \rightarrow X_j$.
Furthermore, we say that:

$$X_i \overset{*}{\rightarrow} X_k$$

if we have a sequence:

$$X_i \rightarrow X_j \rightarrow \cdots \rightarrow X_k$$

If $p:X_i \rightarrow X_j$, then messages of type X_i must *await* uniquely determined messages of type X_j. Similarly, if $X_i \overset{*}{\rightarrow} X_k$, then messages of type X_i must await messages of type X_k, since the latter are uniquely determined by the former.

If $X_i \overset{*}{\rightarrow} X_j$, and $X_j \overset{*}{\rightarrow} X_i$, (i.e. $X_i \overset{*}{\rightarrow} X_i$) then a message of type X_i awaits a message of type X_j and vice versa. If the "two" messages of type X_i are in fact one and the same, then we have the distinct possibility of deadlock. We need only find ourselves in the situation where messages of type X_i and X_j are awaiting each other at precisely the same time. Since there is no other procedure that these messages can trigger, then they will both wait forever, neither able to reach the other.

The set *AWAITS* of dependencies defines a directed graph with nodes in X and arcs in *AWAITS*. $X_i \overset{*}{\rightarrow} X_i$ occurs precisely when there is a cycle in the directed graph. Cycles, of course, occur within the dicomponents of the graph. As we mentioned earlier in this section, dicomponents can easily be determined by a standard algorithm such as in [AhHU74]. Any dicomponent with more than one node in it would yield an instance of $X_i \overset{*}{\rightarrow} X_j$, and would therefore provide us with a potential deadlock.

If a procedure p can be blocked due to deadlock, then we say that p is *4-blocked* or *4-BL*.

6.5. Recursive blocking

Finally, blocking in one procedure may cause blocking in other procedures. If the first procedure is preventing messages from moving on, then other procedures waiting for those messages will also be blocked.

To detect recursive blocking we must find out not only which states are unreachable or avoidable, but also which states are "blocking states". We call a message state a *blocking state* (*BL-state*) if every procedure effecting a transition to that state is blocked, that is:

for each $(p, \sigma, \sigma) \in T_i$, p is blocked $\Leftrightarrow$ σ' is a blocking state

Conversely, if every state leading to an input of some procedure p is a blocking state or is unreachable, then that procedure is *5-blocked*, or *5-BL*. This is a consequence of the fact that blocking states are a variation on unreachable states — they are unreachable only as a result of other blocking.

Similarly, if an input is uniquely determined, and the reachable, non-blocking states are all avoidable, then the procedure is *6-blocked, or*

6-BL. We therefore end up with a recursive form of blocking.

We may summarize potential blocking detection in the following algorithm to be run at all stations ("new" BL-states mentioned in step 8 come from steps 7 or 13, whichever is appropriate):

1.   **for each** procedure p **do** {
2.   **for each** input $X_j \in I(p)$ **do** {
3.   **if** $p:X_i \rightarrow X_j$ **then**
4.   check if p is 3-BL
5.   **else** check if p is 2-BL }
            }
6.   determine which p are 4-BL
7.   identify all BL-states arising from the above
8.   **for each** p not BL, such that $(p, \sigma, \sigma') \in T_i$ where σ is a new BL-state **do** {
9.   **for each** input $X_j \in I(p)$ **do** {
10.   **if** $p:X_i \rightarrow X_j$ **then**
11.   check if p is 6-BL
12.   **else** check if p is 5-BL
            }
    }
13.   identify all new BL-states arising from the new 5-BL or 6-BL procedures, if any
14.   **if** there are no new BL states **then** STOP
15.   **else** continue from step 8

Steps 4, 5, 6 and 7 are as described earlier in this section. Steps 11 and 12 are similar to 4 and 5.

The algorithm must terminate since there are only a finite number of procedures and a finite number of states. As long as the algorithm continues to run, at least one new BL-state must be found at step 13. Eventually we must run out of candidates for BL-states. Similarly, we eventually run out of candidates for 5-BL or 6-BL procedures.

The blocking that we uncover can be of interest in several ways. If a procedure p is 2-BL, then we know that it cannot fire under normal circumstances. This means that (according to our analysis) there is at least one input to the procedure for which there is no known path to the procedure. This may mean that p is incorrect, in the sense that it has been created under the delusion that its inputs *will* arrive, or it may mean that some incorrect procedure elsewhere is improperly routing messages, possibly to dead ends, or into message loops. An examination of the message flow automaton will reveal how it is being routed, and possibly provide some insight into what the problem is.

If procedure p is 3-BL, then that means that a uniquely-determined input is (theoretically) capable of avoiding p. An examination of the path that does (appear to) avoid p can provide insight into whether there is truly a problem or not. Note that our analysis may have generated spurious paths, if there are state transitions present in our model that for some reason never take place in the running system.

Procedure p and p' are 4-BL if there is some theoretically possible configuration in which p and p' are each preventing the progress of messages required by the other procedure. It remains for someone to look more closely at that configuration to tell whether it is in fact reachable in the running system. If it is, then we can either modify the procedures to avoid the blocking, or we can monitor the flow of these messages to detect blocking if it ever occurs.

Procedures that are 5-BL or 6-BL are only blocked if message inputs are stuck at a blocked procedure. Naturally, if we solve the blocking at the other procedure, or if that blocking is not reflected in the running system, then the 5-BL or 6-BL problem goes away.

7. Procedure Loops

Infinite loops may be thought of as the opposite extreme to blocking and deadlock. In the case of blocking we had problems with messages being "stuck" and nothing happening as a consequence. Here we have problems with too much happening. Messages either loop endlessly, visiting the same stations and procedures, or procedures are fired repeatedly, creating an unending stream of messages. We shall discuss here the kind of infinite loops that may arise, and how we may go about detecting them. The different kinds of loops all turn out to be variations on what we call "procedure loops". Our Petri net model provides us with an analytical approach to detecting when procedure loops may occur.

Our earlier discussion of message loops revealed that there may be situations in which messages encounter the same states infinitely often. This may happen naturally with certain messages that are in fact records expected to be handled repeatedly and indefinitely in more-or-less the same way. The inventory records of a previous example are repeatedly processed by the same procedures whenever new order forms arrive. This sort of message loop does not cause any problems since the inventory records must wait before they are processed again. If, on the other hand, they do not have to wait, then we may have a message loop that is unmoderated. Procedures will fire repeatedly, as fast as they possibly can until someone notices the problem and repairs it.

Unmoderated message loops can be thought of as a special case of *procedure loops*. A procedure loop exists when a given configuration of procedures and message instances provides the opportunity for some procedures to fire infinitely often without human intervention. Every unmoderated message loop, then, is clearly part of a procedure loop. Some procedure loops, however, may not contain any message loop. Consider figure 3. Procedure p generates message x, which is consumed by procedure p'. p' in turn generates y, which triggers p. We have a procedure loop, but no message loop exists since all messages handled by p and p' have finite paths.

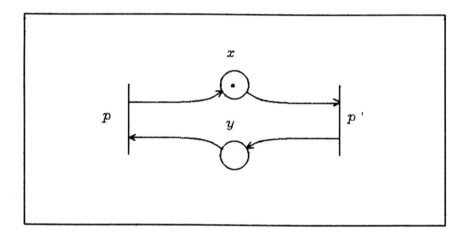

Figure 3: A procedure loop

Procedure loops depend not only on the presence of an unusual configuration of procedures, but also on a corresponding configuration of messages to start the "chain-reaction". Our Petri net interpretation of message flow can help us now. A Petri net can represent the interaction of procedures (up to the accuracy of the message state-space partition), and a marking of that net can represent the current message states of all the messages in the system. We limit our Petri net to those procedures that do not require any user input. A procedure loop exists if the Petri net can be fired forever. This may happen if and only if there is some transition firing sequence that may be repeated infinitely often [KaMi69]. Such a sequence must yield a new marking that is "at least as big as" the initial marking, that is, the sequence must at least restore all of the tokens used. If μ is a marking of the Petri net, and $t_1 \cdots t_n$ is a transition firing sequence yielding new marking μ', then $t_1 \cdots t_n$ can be repeated infinitely often if $\mu_i \leqslant \mu'_i$ for each i.

We approach the problem of detecting procedure loops by translating it into an equivalent problem expressible in matrix equations. Petri nets are equivalent to *vector addition systems* [KaMi69]. This alternative representation encodes the transitions of a Petri net by using two matrices, A^- and A^+. Each matrix has n rows and m columns, where n and m are the number of places and transitions, respectively. The (i,j) entry of A^- is -1 if place i is an input to transition t_j and the (i,j) entry of A^+ is $+1$ if place i is an output to transition t_j. For the net in figure 3, we have:

$$A^- = \begin{bmatrix} 0 & -1 \\ -1 & 0 \end{bmatrix} \text{ and } A^+ = \begin{bmatrix} 1 & 0 \\ 0 & 1 \end{bmatrix}$$

with p and p' represented by the first and second columns of each matrix, respectively.

Transition t_j is enabled in marking μ if $\mu + A^-_j \geq 0$ (where A^-_j is the jth column of A^-). Suppose $A = A^- + A^+$. In our example:

$$A = \begin{bmatrix} 1 & -1 \\ -1 & 1 \end{bmatrix}$$

If t_j is enabled in μ, then the result of firing t_j is $\mu' = \mu + A_j$. Furthermore, if we have a sequence of transitions that can be fired from μ, and we represent that sequence by a column vector x where x_j is the number of times t_j is fired, then $\mu' = \mu + Ax$ is the marking that results after firing the sequence.

If we can find some non-negative integer column vector $x \neq 0$ such that $Ax \geq 0$, then $\mu' = \mu + Ax > \mu$, so that any transition sequence represented by x can be fired indefinitely, starting from some appropriate initial marking μ. Furthermore, we can always find a marking μ "big enough" that the transition sequence represented by x can be fired at least once. The marking $\mu = -A^- x$, for example, guarantees this. Consequently, we have a procedure loop if and only if there is some x such that $Ax \geq 0$. The question that remains is whether or not we can easily solve $Ax \geq 0$. To this end we present the following theorem:

Theorem : The problem, "Does a Petri net have a marking in which some transition sequence can be fired infinitely often?" can be solved in polynomial time.

Proof : By reduction to linear programming. Let A be the matrix encoding the transitions of the Petri net, as described above. Then the problem is solved if we can answer whether there exists a non-negative integer column vector $x \neq 0$ such that $Ax \geq 0$. Let A' be the matrix obtained by adding a column of zeroes at the left side of A, followed by a row of ones at the top of A. A' is therefore an $(n+1) \times (m+1)$ matrix such that:

$$A'_{ij} = \begin{cases} A_{ij} & \text{if } i \geq 1, \, j \geq 1 \\ 0 & \text{if } i \geq 1, \, j = 1 \\ 1 & \text{if } i = 0 \end{cases}$$

Intuitively this corresponds to adding one place, p_0, which is an output of every transition, and adding one transition, t_0, whose only output is p_0. Consequently, p_0 serves to *count* the total number of transition firings.

Consider the linear programming problem $A'x \geqslant (1, 0, \ldots, 0)^T$ where we seek to minimize the cost function cx', $c = (1, 0, \ldots, 0)$. (If v is a row-vector, then v^T is the column-vector, v *transpose*.) The cost is therefore x'_0, the number of times that we need to fire t_0.

The constraint $A'x \geqslant (1, 0, \ldots, 0)^T$ guarantees that at least one transition fires, since each transition places a token in p_0. Furthermore, $x' = (1, 0, \ldots, 0)^T$ is a basic feasible solution, since transition t_0 places a token in p_0. The cost of this solution is 1, since t_0 fires once. This is therefore an upper bound on the cost. The lower bound is 0, corresponding to a solution x' that does not use t_0. Such a solution would also be a solution to our original problem, since it guarantees that we fire only transitions represented by A.

Furthermore, the solution is always either zero or one. Suppose that we have a solution such that $cx' = x'_0$ lies between 0 and 1. (Such a solution would correspond to a "fractional" number of firings of t_0.) Consider $x' = x'' + x'''$ where:

$$x''_i = \begin{cases} 0 & \text{if } i = 0 \\ x'_i & \text{if } i \neq 0 \end{cases} \quad \text{and} \quad x'''_i = \begin{cases} x'_0 & \text{if } i = 0 \\ 0 & \text{if } i \neq 0 \end{cases}$$

Now

$$A'x'' + A'x''' \geqslant (1, 0, \ldots, 0)^T$$
$$A'x'' \geqslant (1, 0, \ldots, 0)^T - A'x'''$$
$$A'x'' \geqslant (1 - x'_0, 0, \ldots, 0)^T$$

Since $(1 - x'_0) > 0$, there exists some k such that $k(1 - x'_0) > 1$, so

$$A'k\,x'' \geqslant (1, 0, \ldots, 0)$$

but then $c\,kx'' = 0$, a contradiction to our assumption that the minimum lay between 0 and 1.

The linear programming problem has a solution with cost 0 if and only if $Ax \geqslant 0$ has a solution $x \neq 0$. This is easily seen by letting $x_i = x'_i$ for all $i > 0$. Furthermore, x' cannot be all zero else $A'x' = 0$, violating our constraint, $A'x \geqslant (1, 0, \ldots, 0)^T$. Hence x is a non-zero solution. Finally, x' may be non-integral, but linear programming always yields rational solutions. Since x' is a rational solution, there exists a positive integer k such that kx' is an integer. Furthermore, if x' is a solution, then clearly so is kx'. This then yields an integer solution for x, if one exists.

Since linear programming is solvable in polynomial time in the size of the input (by the ellipsoid method [PaSt82]), so is infinite fireability of Petri nets. □

8. Conclusions

We have presented a formalism for modelling message systems with automatic processing of messages, and we have introduced some concepts that are useful in characterizing the global behaviour of these systems. We have shown how to generate finite state automaton and Petri net interpretations of message flow by using our model. Finally, we have shown how these derived interpretations can be useful in analyzing message behaviour. In particular, procedure loops and various kinds of blocking (including deadlock) can be detected.

A number of extensions to the model would be desirable. Messages are currently very simple. There is no explicit way of representing repeating groups within messages, nor do we explicitly handle "specializations" of message types. Similar and related (but non-identical) message types must therefore be treated as being distinct. We also do not currently allow procedures to handle inputs with a choice of input types. (One way to handle specializations, however, is to model them with a single "master" type combining the attributes of all the specializations, and simply assign null values to the inapplicable fields of particular message instances.)

A more radical extension is to allow for "intelligent messages" that carry procedures around with them. Procedures are currently associated with workstations, and not messages. An alternative is to consider the behaviour of a system that manages "objects", where an object combines the data-storing of messages and the functionality of procedures. It is not at all clear, however, how one would begin to analyze object-flow, once the distinction between data and procedure is lost.

Other interesting issues are the evaluation of incremental changes to systems, and the evaluation of transformations. In the first case we only make small, occasional changes such as adding or altering procedures, and in the latter case we may coalesce or split workstations, or move procedures from one workstation to another. What questions are appropriate to ask about the effect of such changes, and can we make cheap evaluations based on the analysis of the unchanged system?

9. References

[AhHU74] [AtBS79] [BoMu76] [ElNu80] [HaSi80] [KaMi69] [Nier84] [PaSt82] [Pete83]

Part VII

Performance

13
Access Methods for Documents

C. Faloutsos
S. Christodoulakis

ABSTRACT *We describe and compare access methods for documents in an office environment. We discuss the operational requirements of an office, and we survey methods for formatted data and for text retrieval, in an attempt to find an integrated method for both. Comparison of these methods indicates that the signature file method is suitable for the office environment. We examine this method in more detail, and we compare several signature extraction techniques.*

1. Introduction

In this paper we describe and compare access methods for documents in an office environment. A document is composed of attribute values and text. The user retrieves the documents on the basis of contents. Traditionally, retrieval of formatted data has been examined mainly in the context of file structures and Data Base Management Systems (DBMS), while the retrieval of unformatted data has been examined in the context of library science and information retrieval. Before we proceed, we shall mention the operational characteristics of the office environment and its differences from the DBMS and library environments:

1. Insertions are frequent in an office system. New documents arrive and have to be filed. In a library system, the new documents are usually batched, and the insertions are performed by the System Administrator. In contrast, in an office environment, not only may the system administrator not exist, but it has been

observed that data is more "private" (more decentralized users). In addition, the users want to spend as little time as possible organizing their data.

2.   Deletions and updates are rare in both an office and a library system. DBMSs usually operate in more dynamic environments.

3.   In office and library systems, the results of a query are returned to a human being rather than to a program. A human user is willing to tolerate a few "false hits" (e.g., some documents that do not qualify in a query are returned by the system). In a library system, he or she may also be willing to tolerate a few "false dismissals" (e.g., some documents that qualify in a query, that are not returned by the system). In an office system false dismissals may be unwelcome.

4.   Most documents are never accessed.

False hits and false dismissals are captured by the terms *recall* and *precision*, respectively. *Recall* is the proportion of relevant, retrieved documents over the total number of relevant documents in the data base. Small recall implies many false dismissals. *Precision* is the proportion of relevant, retrieved documents over the total number of retrieved documents. Small precision implies many false hits. Table 1.1 summarizes the characteristics of the three environments.

	DBMS	*office*	*library*
frequency of			
retrievals	*any*	*medium*	*large*
insertions	*any*	*large*	*small*
deletions	*any*	*small*	*small*
updates	*any*	*small*	*small*
administration	*large*	*small*	*large*
recall	*1*	*1*	*<1*
precision	*1*	*<1*	*<1*

Table 1.1.
Description of the environments.

2. Access Methods for Formatted Data

Many access methods for formatted data have appeared in the literature and are used in commercial DBMSs. The most important access methods form the following sub-classes:

1.   Methods based on trees.

2.   Methods based on hashing.

3.   Methods using "signature" files.

In the following sections we shall examine each of these classes in more detail.

2.1. Methods based on trees

The idea here is to create a file structure that will give the addresses of the qualifying records. The simplest representative of this sub-class is the inverted file method (e.g., [TeFr82, p. 344]). For each attribute, an index is created and maintained. Given an attribute value, this index provides a list of the addresses of the qualifying records. When an attribute takes many distinct values, inverted files are usually organized as B-trees [BaMc72] and variations (B*-trees, prefix B*-trees, etc. — see, e.g., [Knut73, pp. 471-479], [Come79], or [TeFr82]).

The advantage of the methods based on inversion is the fast response. The disadvantages are the space overhead and the increased amount of work required to maintain the indices in the presence of insertions.

Multiattribute tree access methods can also be used. Probably the most prominent representative of this class is the k-d tree [Bent75]. K-d trees show reasonable behaviour for updating and searching for exact match queries. Bentley showed that the search effort for partial match queries decreases exponentially with the number of attributes specified in the query. k-d trees were originally designed for core-resident files. [Robi81] proposed the k-d B-trees, which are more suitable than k-d trees for files on secondary storage.

The disadvantages of this method are the low storage utilization (50-70% according to experiments by Robinson) and the (possibly) expensive reorganization of the tree structure in environments with many insertions.

2.2. Methods based on hashing

Several methods using hashing have been proposed in the literature [SeDu76, Lars78, FNPS79, Litw80, Mart79, Knut73, TeFr82]. In this method the address where a record is stored is determined by a value of an attribute. A *hashing function* transforms this value to an address. Methods based on hashing usually provide fast access to qualifying records. A serious problem of these methods is the deterioration of response time when the file grows. [Lars78] uses a "forest" of binary trees whose leaf nodes keep pointers to blocks with records. The "signature" of a record determines the tree and the path that should be followed within the tree, upon insertion or searching. If a block fills up, another block is allocated and a hashing function utilized, which will divide the records (hopefully) evenly between the old and the new blocks. The tree structure will change appropriately, to reflect the new situation. In [FNPS79] it is proposed to store pointers to blocks in a hash table which doubles in size whenever an expansion is necessary. Again, the signature of the record determines an entry of the hash table. This entry points to the block that the record should be stored in. [Mart79] suggested the "spiral hashing", which is based on an exponential (non-uniform!) hashing function, and allows smooth growing of the file, without using pointers.

In *multiattribute hashing*, the address that a record is stored in, is determined by the values of (some or all of) the attributes of this record. [RoLo74] suggested a hybrid scheme that uses inversion for some attributes and multiattribute hashing for the rest of them. [Rive76] proposed hashing each attribute value into a bit pattern, concatenating all these patterns, and using the resulting binary number as the address of the record. He provided detailed analysis for the average and worst case performances of the method. [AhUl79] extended this method to in the case in which the attributes do not appear uniformly in the users' queries.

Lloyd [LlRa82] suggested a multiattribute hashing method for a growing file. He combined the method of [AhUl79] and the method of [FNPS79]. The main advantage of multiattribute hashing methods is the fast response. The main disadvantage is the difficulty of handling a growing file efficiently.

2.3. Signature files

The idea here is to create a signature of each record, and store all the record signatures sequentially in a "signature" file. A record signature is created by transforming the attribute values of the record, usually via a hashing function. In order to process a query, the attribute values specified in the query are transformed by using the same transformation. Then, the signature file is scanned sequentially, and the records whose signature qualifies are retrieved.

The problem with this method is the "false hits" (or "false drops"), which are records that do not actually qualify, although their signature shows the opposite. The average number of false drops can usually be controlled by careful design of the signature-extraction method, and by allowing large enough signature size.

Vallarino [Vall76] applied this idea in order to compress a bit-map. Roberts [Robe79] used superimposed coding to create signatures for records of a telephone directory. Pfaltz, Berman, and Cagley [PfBC80] suggested using more than one level of signature files. Christodoulakis [Chri83] examines the use of signature files when the queries are batched. His performance analysis takes into account the frequency of queries on each attribute.

The advantages of these methods are the simple handling of insertions, the small storage overhead, the ability to handle records with a large number of attributes, and the ability to exploit the advantage of sequential scan.

The disadvantage is that the response may be slow for large databases, because the signature file has to be scanned sequentially. However, careful architecture (e.g., a variation of Roberts's bit sliced method [Robe79]) and a large blocking factor can speed up the sequential searching. Special purpose hardware is another effective solution [AhRo80], although it is expensive.

3. Access Methods for Text Retrieval

Many access methods for text retrieval have been proposed in the literature. They form four classes. The first three of them have been studied in the computer-science literature, while the fourth class is based on clustering, the dominating approach in the library science literature. We shall describe each class and comment on its advantages and disadvantages.

3.1. Full text scanning

The most straightforward way of locating the documents that contain a certain search string (*term*) is to search all the documents for the specified string (*substring test*). *String* is defined as a sequence of characters without "Don't Care" characters. If the query is a complicated Boolean expression involving many terms, then we need an additional step, namely to determine whether the term matches found by the sub-string tests satisfy the Boolean expression (*query resolution*).

The forthcoming discussion will not examine searching methods for general regular expressions. This subject is discussed in more detail in the context of Automata Theory [HoU179, pp. 29-35]. However, if the search patterns are restricted to strings, some more efficient methods can be applied. We shall discuss these methods.

The obvious algorithm for the substring test is as follows:

- Compare the characters of the search string against the corresponding characters of the document.

- If a mismatch occurs, shift the search string by one position to the right and continue until either the string is found or the end of the document is reached.

Although simple to implement, this algorithm is too slow: if m is the length of the search string and n is the length of the document (in characters), then it needs $O(m*n)$ comparisons.

Knuth, Morris, and Pratt [KnMP77] proposed an algorithm which needs $O(m+n)$ comparisons. Their main idea was to shift the search string by more than one character to the right whenever a mismatch is predictable. The method needs some preprocessing of the search string, to detect recurring sequences of letters. The time required for preprocessing is $O(m)$.

The fastest known algorithm was proposed by [BoMo77]. The idea here is to perform the character comparisons from right to left. Thus, if a mismatch occurs, the search string may be shifted up to m positions to the right. The number of comparisons is n+m in the worst case, and usually is much less (especially if the size of the alphabet is large). Again, it requires $O(m)$ preprocessing of the search string.

Another approach to this problem is based on automata theory. [AhCo75] proposed a method that is based on a finite automaton, and allows searching for several strings simultaneously. The search time is $O(n)$, and the construction time of the automaton is linear on the sum of characters in the strings.

In general, the advantage of every full text scanning method is that it requires no space overhead and minimal effort on insertions and updates (no indices have to be changed). The disadvantage is the bad response time. This might be severe in the case of large data bases. Therefore, full text scanning is usually carried out by special purpose hardware [HSCE83], or is used in cooperation with another access method (e.g., inversion) that restricts the scope of searching.

3.2. Inversion of terms

Each document can be represented by a list of (key)words, which are supposed to describe the contents of the document for retrieval purposes. Fast retrieval can be achieved if an index on those keywords is created. All the well-known methods can be used to build this index: sorted file (of keywords), B-tree, TRIE, hashing, or variations and combinations of the above (e.g., see [Knut73, pp. 471-542]). The MEDLARS system uses a sorted file (according to [SaMc83]). STAIRS [IBM79] uses a two-level index for the dictionary of (key)words: Words that start with the same pair of letters are stored together in the second level, while the first level contains pointers, one for each letter pair. [Lesk79] uses an overloaded hash table with separate chaining, in order to achieve fast retrieval in a database of bibliographic entries.

The disadvantages of the method are:

- The storage overhead (50-300% of the original file size, if word-level indexing is used [Hask81]).

- The cost of updating and reorganizing the index, if the environment is dynamic.

- The difficulty in handling search terms with initial "Don't Care" characters.

The advantages are that it is relatively easy to implement, it is fast, and it supports synonyms easily: for example, the synonyms can be organized as a threaded list within the dictionary. For these reasons, the inversion method has been adopted in a significant number of library systems [SaMc83, ch. 2].

3.3. Superimposed coding and signatures

Methods based on superimposed coding appear to be suitable for text retrieval. An introduction to superimposed coding can be found in [Bour63, pp. 57-59] or [Knut73, pp. 559-563]. In this method, each word of a given document is hashed to give a bit pattern of fixed length. In this pattern, a prespecified number of bits have been set to "1". These patterns are superimposed (OR-ed together), and the resulting bit pattern is the *signature* of the document (see figure 1). There are two approaches from this point on: either this *signature* is used to determine the location of the document (as in primary-key hashing), or the signatures of all the documents are stored in a separate file (signature file) which provides a filtering facility.

The first approach was proposed by [Gust71]. He considers documents with a constant number of terms (records). For each record, he creates a signature with a constant number of "1"s. Then he uses a

Word	Signature
free	*001 000 110 010*
text	*000 010 101 001*
document signature	*001 010 111 011*

Figure 1

Illustration of the superimposed coding method. It is assumed that the document consists of 2 words only. The signature size is 12 bits. Each word sets 4 bits to "1".

sophisticated one-to-one function that maps the above bit pattern to an address. Given a term, a list of addresses that contain records having this term can be derived. The interesting point of the method is that the amount of search decreases very fast with the number of terms in the (conjunctive) query. Variations of Gustafson's idea have been studied by [RoLo74], [Rive76], [AhUl79], and [Lloy80]. However, as mentioned before, they deal with formatted records and propose that the signature of the record be created by *concatenating* the signatures of the attributes instead of superimposing them. This detail creates problems if one tries to apply their methods directly to text retrieval: even a simple, single-word query has to be expanded to a disjunctive query, which requires much time. For example, assume that we have six keywords per document, and we are looking for documents that contain the word "information". This single-word query corresponds to the query:

keyword1 = "information" or
keyword2 = "information" or

...

keyword6 = "information".

The main advantage of Gustafson's method is the retrieval speed. An obvious disadvantage is that the performance deteriorates as the file grows.

The signature file approach has attracted more interest in different application environments. [FiHu69] applied this method on a database of bibliographic entries. They used a stop list to discard the common words and an automatic procedure to reduce each non-common word to its stem. They also used a numeric procedure as a hashing function, instead of a look-up table. [Harr71] used the signature file approach in order to speed up the substring testing. He suggested using consecutive letters as input to the hashing function. In [TCEF83], superimposed coding is used for both attributes and text in a prototype multimedia office filing system. The method proposed in [TsCh83] and followed by [Lars83] tries to use signature files without superimposed coding. There, the signature of the document consists of the concatenation of each word signature (see figure 2). This way, the positioning information is preserved.

Document	free	text	retrieval	methods
	|	|	|	|
	v	v	v	v
Word signature	0000	0100	0111	1011
Doc. signature		0000 0100 0111 1011		

Figure 2

Illustration of the word signature method. The document consists of four words. Each word yields a 4-bit word-signature

[Gonn82] discusses a number of text retrieval methods. Most of them use superimposed coding, either as an abstraction technique to create the signature file or as a "Bloom filter" [Bloo70] to speed up the membership testing during full text scanning. Signature files with superimposed coding are used in [ChFa84]. The main ideas discussed are:

- The hashing function is based on triplets of consecutive letters, to allow searching for parts of words.

- Each document is divided into "logical blocks", and a separate signature is derived for each block. A logical block is a piece of text that contains a fixed number (say 40) of distinct non-common words.

- The need to adapt the signature file to the users' access patterns is considered, and an efficient scheme to condense the signatures is proposed.

Some other signature extraction methods are based on compression [Falo85] and will be discussed later.

Research on the design and performance of superimposed coding methods started long ago. The first person who applied superimposed coding for retrieval was C.N. Mooers, in 1947, according to [Knut73, p. 559]. He invented an ingenious *mechanical* device based on edge-notched cards and needles. The device was able to handle conjunctive queries on a database of bibliographic entries very quickly. The keyword extraction was performed manually while the hashing function utilized a look-up table.

This method of edge-notched cards attracted a great deal of interest: [Stia60] suggested using pairs of letters to create each word signature. He also proved that, for a given signature size, the false drop probability is minimized if the number of "1"s is equal to the number of "0"s in the document signatures. [OrTa56], using Jordan's theorem, gave a closed form formula for the probability distribution of the number of "1"s in a document signature. [KaSi64] discussed the problem of designing a system of signatures that would not have false drops. They attacked the problem from the point of view of coding and information theory. Although theoretically interesting, their method has practical drawbacks: it needs a look-up table, it cannot handle a growing vocabulary easily, and it needs much overhead to design the set of signatures.

In closing the discussion on the signature file approach, we should mention that the main disadvantage of the method is the response time, if the file is too large. The advantages are the simplicity of the implementation, the efficiency in handling insertions, and the ability to handle queries on parts of words, to tolerate typing and spelling errors and to support a growing file.

3.4. Clustering

This approach suggests that similar documents are grouped together to form clusters. The underlying reason is the so-called cluster hypothesis (e.g., [Rijs79, p. 37]): closely associated documents tend to be relevant to the same requests. Clustering has attracted much interest by researchers in information retrieval and library science [SaMc83, Rijs79]. A great deal of work has also been done on clustering in the area of pattern recognition [DuHa73].

Document clustering involves two procedures: the cluster generation and the cluster search.

The typical cluster generation procedure works as follows: First, each document is processed, and the important terms are extracted automatically. This procedure utilizes the following dictionaries [Salt71]:

- A negative dictionary that is used to remove the common words ("and", "the", etc.).

- A suffix and prefix list that help to reduce each word to its stem.

- A dictionary of synonyms that helps to assign each word-stem to a concept class.

Thus, each document is represented by a t-dimensional vector, where "t" is the number of permissible index terms (concepts). Absence of a term is indicated by a 0 (or by -1 [Coop70]). Presence of a term is indicated by 1 (binary document vectors) or by a positive number (term weight), which reflects the importance of the term for the document [Spar72, YuLS82].

After we have decided how to represent the documents as t-dimensional points, the next step is to partition them. There are two classes of methods:

- theoretically "sound" methods, which are based on the document-document similarity matrix (e.g., [Rijs71], [Zahn71], [DuHa73, p. 238], [Rijs79, p. 46]). These methods are stable under growth, robust, and independent of the initial ordering of the items. However, they are slow: $O(n^2)$, where n is the number of items (documents) of the collection.

- Efficient methods, which proceed directly from the document descriptions (e.g., [SaWo78], [SaMc83, p. 137, 222]). They are fast, on the average, $(O(n\,logn))$, but they do not meet all of the soundness criteria.

Searching in a clustered file is much simpler than cluster generation. The input query is represented as a t-dimensional vector and compared with the cluster-centroids. The searching continues in the most similar clusters, e.g., those whose similarity with the query vector exceeds a threshold.

The vector representation of queries and documents allows the so-called *relevance feedback,* which increases the effectiveness of the search [Rocc71]: the user pinpoints the relevant documents among the retrieved ones, and the system reformulates the query vector and starts the searching from the beginning. The usual way to carry out the query reformulation is by adding to the query vector the (weighted) vectors of the relevant documents, and by subtracting the non-relevant ones.

The main advantages of clustering are the following:

- The output documents can be ranked in decreasing similarity value.

- The volume of the output can be controlled (e.g., the ten most relevant items are returned to the user every time).

- It is possible to allow relevance feedback, which is an effective and user-friendly method of searching.

The main disadvantage is that clustering is not well-suited to a dynamic environment. Insertions of new documents create problems: if an $O(n^2)$ clustering method is used, an insertion will require $O(n)$ time. If an $O(n \log n)$ method is used, reorganization will soon be necessary [Rijs79 pp. 58-59].

The storage requirements and response time of cluster-based methods do not appear to constitute great disadvantages.

4. Considerations in Integrated Access Methods

In the office environment, an interesting approach is to integrate text retrieval systems with database management systems (DBMS). [HaLo82] is extending the relational system R to handle "long" fields (text, digitized images), but is not concerned with content addressibility. In [TsCh83], superimposed coding and signature files are used for both attributes and text. In [Fox84], clustering is used: a document vector contains attribute values, in addition to terms. There are also efforts to apply the network schema [Datt79] or the relational [McLe81] on bibliographic data bases. [SSLK83] extends the language of INGRES in an attempt to provide text-editing facilities through a DBMS.

In this context, the design of an access method for both attributes and text is an interesting problem. We have to consider primary-key, secondary-key, and text retrieval methods. A qualitative comparison of access methods will be presented next.

4.1. Comparison of primary-key access methods

There are two dominating methods here: B-trees [BaMc72] and hashing (e.g., [Seve74]). Some important points for performance comparison are the following:

- Space utilization (disk and main memory requirements).
- Response time for search.
- Handling of modifications (insertions, deletions, and updates).
- Handling of growing file.
- Preservation of key order.
- Ability to integrate with text retrieval methods.

Table 4.1 illustrates the advantages and disadvantages of each method. The strong points are indicated by a "v" and the weak points by an "x". Blank entries indicate that the specific method shows acceptable, but not exceptional, performance as far as the specific requirement is concerned.

	B-trees		hashing
space	[1]		[2]
response	[3]	v	[2]
modifications			
growth	v		[4]
key order	v		[5]
integration			

Table 4.1.
Primary-key access methods.

Notes on Table 4.1:

1. B-trees guarantee at least 50% utilization. B*-trees [Knut73, p. 478] guarantee 67% utilization.

2. Knuth [Knut73, p. 535] estimates 1.45 probes in a hash table with load factor 90% (separate chaining, successful search, bucket size = 1).

3. Tree structures exhibit logarithmic behavior upon search. However, hashing methods are faster in general.

4. The extendible variations of hashing seem less elegant than B-trees. Moreover, B-trees have been heavily used in practice.

5. There exist order-preserving hashing functions (e.g., [Knot71, p. 189]). However, they require knowledge of the distribution of keys in advance. Moreover, the above distribution should not be changed with the insertion of new records.

4.2. Comparison of secondary-key access methods

The classes of methods that we shall examine are:

- Inversion with B-trees.
- Multiattribute hashing (e.g., [RoLo74]).
- Signature files with superimposed coding (e.g., [Robe79]).
- k-d trees (e.g., [Bent75]).

The points for comparison are the same as in the previous section. Table 4.2 indicates the strong and weak points of each method.

Notes on table 4.2:

	invers.	mult. hash.	sign.	trees
space			V	[1]
resp.	V	V		V [2]
insert.	X	V	V	[2]
del.-upd.	X			
growth	V	[3]	V	V
key ord.	V	X	X	V
integr.	V [4]		V	

Table 4.2.
Secondary key access methods.

1. [Robi81] reports a space utilization of 50-70% for the k-d B-trees. Pure B-trees have a space utilization of about 70%.

2. According to [Bent75], the search time in k-d trees is an exponentially decreasing function of the number of specified attributes.

3. [LlRa82] has proposed an extendible multiattribute hashing method.

4. E.g., the STAIRS system [IBM79] is based on inversion, and offers facilities for accessing both formatted data and text.

We should also note that special purpose hardware has been proposed.

● [Stel77] and [Holl78] have proposed list-merging hardware that improves the response time of the inversion method.

● [AhRo80] suggested storing the signature file in associative memory. They report average response time of 50 msec, but they do not give estimates of the cost.

4.3. Comparison of text retrieval methods

The methods that will be examined here are: full text scanning, inversion of terms, signature files and clustering. The points of comparison include those of the previous section, except for the preservation of key order. In addition, we have to consider here:

● Retirement of old (useless) documents.

- Approximate string matching (i.e., handling of typing and spelling errors).
- Ability to answer queries on parts of words.
- Ability to handle synonyms.
- Ability to integrate with formatted-data access methods.

Table 4.3 summarizes the performance of each class of text retrieval methods.

	full text. sc.	invers.	sign.	clust.
space	v	x [1]	v [2]	v
response	x	v	x	v
inser.	v	[3]	v	
del.-upd.	v	x		
growth	v		v	[9]
retir.			v [4]	
appr. match.	[5]	[5]	[6]	x
word parts	v	x	v	x
synonyms		v	[7]	v
integr.		v	v	[8]

Table 4.3.
Performance of text retrieval methods.

Notes on Table 4.3.

1. The overhead can be 50-300% of the initial file size [Hask81]. The STAIRS requires 55-97% overhead, depending on the size of the stop-word list [RaZi84].

2. The size of the signature file is usually 10% of the size of the text file [ChFa84].

3. There is a trade-off between retrieval and insertion efficiency in the inversion-based methods: if the index is compacted (sorted sequential file of word occurrences), then retrieval is fast, but the index has to be rewritten upon every insertion (or batch of insertions). If there is a more flexible structure for the index, such as a B-tree for the dictionary and lists for word occurrences, then performance degrades considerably.

4. In [ChFa84], an efficient method for handling old documents is described.

5.   [JoTo84] describe a way to build a fault-tolerant FSA for full text scanning.

6.   [AnFW83] suggest using overlapping triplets to measure the distance between two strings. This seems to match well with the triplet-based signature extraction method that is proposed in [ChFa84].

7.   Superimposed coding can handle synonyms, if synonyms yield the same signature. However, the only way this can be achieved is through a lookup in a dictionary of synonyms. The dictionary search will slow down the document-signature extraction operation. Moreover, the construction and maintenance of the dictionary is not trivial.

8.   A recent attempt to use clustering for both text and attributes has been reported in [Fox84].

9.   Clustering methods will not perform well in rapidly changing environments, where new clusters are frequently created.

5. Signature Methods

The previous section indicated that the method of signatures seems suitable for data and text access. We shall examine signature methods in more detail.

The first two methods have been described already in section 3.3. The word signature method [TsCh83] suggests that we concatenate the individual word signatures to form the document signature (see figure 2, for example). It will be referred to as WS. The second method [ChFa84] suggests that we split the document into logical blocks and superimpose (OR) the word signatures to create the block signature (see figure 1, for example). It will be referred to as SC (for Superimposed Coding).

The next method [Falo85] is based on compression. Again, we split the document into logical blocks, as in SC. The idea is that we use a (large) bit vector of B bits and hash each word into one (or perhaps more, say n) bit position(s), which are set to "1" (see figure 3). The resulting bit vector will be sparse and therefore can be compressed.

The compression method proposed in [Falo85] is based on bit-blocks. For the rest of the paper, it will be referred to as BC (for bit-Block Compression). In this method, the sparse vector is divided into groups of consecutive bits (bit-blocks). The size of the bit-blocks is chosen in such a way that the performance is optimized. For each bit-block, we create a signature, by recording (a) whether there are any "1"s in the bit-block, (b) how many "1"s there are, and (c) which are

free	0000 0000 0000 0010 0000
text	0000 0001 0000 0000 0000
retrieval	0000 1000 0000 0000 0000
methods	0000 0000 0000 0000 1000
block	
signature	0000 1001 0000 0010 1000

Figure 3

Illustration of the compression-based methods.
With $B=20$ and $n=1$ bit per word,
the resulting bit vector is sparse and can be compressed.

the offsets of these "1"s from the beginning of the bit-block.

An important consideration is that the BC method can be slightly modified to become insensitive to changes in the number of words D per block. This is desirable because the need to split documents into logical blocks is eliminated, thus making the resolution of complex Boolean queries much easier. The modification is as follows: we treat a whole document as a logical block and calculate the appropriate bit-block size, according to the vocabulary D of the document. Then we store this value along with the rest of the document signature. This method will be referred to as VBC (Variable bit-Block Compression) for the rest of the paper.

Another method that uses compression was suggested by McIlroy [McIl82] for a different environment. His goal was to compress a dictionary of 30,000 words for a spelling-error detector program. Using a coding technique proposed by Golomb [Golo66] and Gallager and Van Voorhis [GaVa75], he achieved very good compression of the sparse vector.

This compression technique can also be used for signature file construction in a text data base as proposed in [Falo85]. There the method is generalized by allowing $n \geqslant 1$ (i.e., each word may hash to one or more positions in the sparse bit vector). The motivation behind this generalization is to investigate whether we can achieve better performance with $n > 1$. In the rest of the paper we shall refer to this generalized method as RL (Run-Length encoding).

5.1. Performance comparison

Next we shall present the results of a comparison of the five signature methods with respect to their screening capacity for single word queries. All signature methods introduce "false drops", that is, a signature may seem to qualify in a query, although the corresponding text does not qualify. The probability of this event happening is called *false drop probability* F_d. Mathematically,

$$F_d = \text{Prob}\{\text{the sign. of a block seems to qualify /}$$

$$\text{the block does not }\}$$

The reasons we have chosen F_d as a measure for comparison are:

- Unlike the other measures, F_d depends solely on the method and not on other factors, such as hardware configuration, buffering algorithms, etc.

- Discovering the dependency of F_d on the signature size F seems to be a mathematically complicated problem. If this was solved, one could calculate the other measures for a specific setting (hardware, operating system etc.).

In addition to the five methods above, we present formulas that give the theoretical bound on the performance of the compression based methods. These formulas are based on the entropy of a bit in the sparse vector. The quantities in these formulas will have a subscript EN (for entropy).

WS	Word Signatures
SC	Superimposed Coding
RL	compression with Run Length encoding
BC	bit-Block Compression
EN	ENtropy based bounds
VBC	Variable bit-Block Compression

Table I
List of signature extraction methods.

In [FaCh84] we studied the cases of WS and SC. For the case of word signatures it can be shown that the false drop probability is

$$F_{d,WS} = 1 - \left[1 - \frac{1}{S_{max}} \right]^D \tag{1}$$

Symbol	method (s)	definition
$F_{d,XX}$	all	False drop probability for the "XX" method
F_{XX}	all	(expected) size of a block signature for the "XX" method
D	all	number of distinct non-common words per block
S_{max}	WS	maximum number of distinct word signatures
m	SC	number of bits that a word sets to "1"
m_{opt}	SC	the optimal value of m
B	RL, BC, EN	size of the sparse vector
n	RL, BC, EN	number of bits that a word sets to "1".
b	BC	size of a bit-block
b_{opt}	BC	optimal value of b

Table II.
Definitions of the symbols.

where the symbols are defined in table II. Equation (1) can be justified in an intuitive way. It gives the answer to the question: "Given the signature of a (non-qualifying) block, what is the probability that at least one of its D word signatures will (accidentally) match the search signature σ ?"

The implications of Equation (1) are interesting. It states that the false drop probability is independent of the vocabulary size, the size of the data base, and the occurrence or query frequencies of words. It is not affected by word inter-dependencies and is the same for successful and unsuccessful search.

The conclusions that hold for SC are similar to those for the WS method. It can be shown that

$$F_{d,SC} = \left[\frac{1}{2}\right]^{m_{opt}} \qquad (2)$$

$$m_{opt} = \frac{F \ln 2}{D} \qquad (3)$$

both for successful and unsuccessful search, regardless of the occurrence and query frequencies, regardless of the vocabulary size V, and regardless of the size of the data base. Experiments that we performed on a 3.3 Mb data base of bibliographic entries indicate that

Equation (2) and (3) hold (see [ChFa84] figures 7-9).

In [Falo85] we derived the exact formulas for the compression-based methods and plotted graphs of the logarithm of the false drop probability F_d versus the signature size F. The conclusions are the following:

1.   All the compression-based methods (RL, BC, and EN) give better results than both WS and SC for $n=1$.

2.   The RL method gives excellent results, very close to the EN curves.

3.   For methods based on compression, the optimal value of number of bits per word n is $n=1$.

4.   All curves (log_2 F_d versus F) become almost straight lines for large signature sizes.

5.   The graphs of all the compression-based methods have the same slope, which is the same as the slope of the WS method. As observed in [FaCh84], SC has a smoother slope because it does not make full use of all the available $2**F$ bit patterns, since it requires that half of the bits be "1".

The fourth observation provided the motivation to look for approximate asymptotic formulas, as the signature size F increases. These formulas are:

$$log_2 F_{d,WS} = log_2 D - \frac{F_{WS}}{D} \tag{4}$$

$$log_2 F_{d,SC} = -\frac{F_{SC}}{D \, log_2 e} = -\frac{F_{SC}}{D} 0.693 \tag{5}$$

$$log_2 F_{d,RL} = n \, (1 + log_2 log_2 e) - \frac{F_{RL}}{D} = 1.528n - \frac{F_{RL}}{D} \tag{6}$$

$$log_2 F_{d,BC} = n \, (1 + log_2 e - log_2 log_2 e) - \frac{F_{BC}}{D} = 1.913n - \frac{F_{BC}}{D} \tag{7}$$

$$log_2 F_{d,EN} = n \, log_2 e - \frac{F_{EN}}{D} = 1.442n - \frac{F_{EN}}{D} \tag{8}$$

It should be noted that the above formulas are very accurate. The maximum observed error was $<6\%$.

In addition to the false drop probabilities for a given signature size (which are given by these formulas), several other factors may affect the choice of the most desirable method. We discuss some of these factors in the next section.

6. Concluding remarks.

The signature file method seems to be suitable for an integrated data and text environment, mainly for the following reasons:

1.   It requires small storage overhead.

2.   It is efficient on insertions.

3.   If carefully designed, it can handle errors and queries on parts of words.

4.   The method may be applicable to optical disks [Fuji84]. The reason is that signature files do not require updates and rewrites, like the inversion-based methods. Thus the "write-once" restriction of the optical disks does not create problems.

Pinpointing the best signature extraction method is not easy. In the last section we described and compared a number of methods. In our discussion we focused our attention on the false drop probability of each method for single word queries. The result of the study is that, from the chosen point of view, the best method is RL, followed by BC, WS, and SC (in that order). From a practical point of view, there are additional considerations. To name the most important of them:

1.   Speed of searching a block signature.

2.   Performance on more complicated queries.

3.   Ability to answer queries on parts of words.

4.   Preservation of the sequencing information.

We shall briefly discuss these points:

1.   The fastest method for searching a signature (given that it has been brought into main memory) seems to be SC: it requires only m (typically ≈ 10) bit comparisons to accept or reject a signature in a single word query. The BC method requires additional bit comparisons, as well as calculations, in order to determine the length of Parts II and III of the block signature. The RL method needs approximately half of the encoded zero-intervals to be decoded and added, thus giving slow search time. The WS method requires the whole block signature to be examined, but it does not need decoding or any additions.

2.   All the signature methods do well on conjunctive (AND) queries. Methods that split documents in logical blocks (that is, SC, BC, and RL) require more bookkeeping than the rest of the methods (such as the WS method without logical blocks and the VBC method).

3.   For the present time, only SC [ChFa84] can handle queries on parts of words.

4.   Only the WS method preserves the sequencing information.

As a final conclusion, it is still difficult to pinpoint the most preferable method. However, we believe that the most promising candidates are:

- Superimposed coding (SC), because it is the fastest (at least for single word queries), it is simple (does not need any decoding), and it can handle errors in the data base as well as queries on parts of words.

- Variable bit-Block Compression (VBC), because it is fast (second only to SC), economical in space (second only to RL), and does not need to split documents in logical blocks.

7. References

[AhCo75] [AhRo80] [AhUl79] [AnFW83] [BaMc72] [Bent75] [Bloo70] [BoMo77] [Bour63] [ChFa84] [Chri83] [Come79] [Coop70] [Datt79] [DuHa73] [FaCh84] [Falo85] [FiHu69] [FNPS79] [Fox84] [Fuji84] [GaVa75] [Golo66] [Gonn82] [Gust71] [HaLo82] [Harr71] [Hask81] [Holl78] [HoUl79] [HSCE83] [IBM79] [JoTo84] [KaSi64] [KnMP77] [Knot71] [Knut73] [Lars78] [Lars83] [Lesk79] [Litw80] [Lloy80] [LlRa82] [Mart79] [McIl82] [McLe81] [OrTa56] [PfBC80] [RaZi84] [Rijs71] [Rijs79] [Rive76] [Robe79] [Robi81] [Rocc71] [RoLo74] [Salt71] [SaMc83] [SaWo78] [SeDu76] [Seve74] [Spar72] [SSLK83] [Stel77] [Stia60] [TCEF83] [TeFr82] [TsCh83] [Vall76] [YuLS82] [Zahn71]

14
Text Retrieval Machines

D.L. Lee
F.H. Lochovsky

ABSTRACT *Various approaches to text retrieval machines for large text database are surveyed. Signature processors for supporting superimposed coding are first described. Text processors for pattern matching are then categorized and discussed. Finally, various designs for multiple response resolution, an important but often ignored issue in associative memory and processors, are reviewed.*

1. Introduction

Information management and, in particular, information retrieval have been major applications of computer systems for a long time. This is evident from the rapid development and widespread use of database management systems (DBMSs) and text retrieval systems (TRSs). Recent developments in office information systems place an even higher demand on such capabilities of computer systems.

Traditionally, research in information retrieval and management has been divided into two areas. The first area is database management systems. In these systems, information is usually extracted manually from the real world and stored in a structured way, e.g., as relations and trees, in the system. For instance, information in an office may be embedded in business forms, memos, letters, reports, etc. It is the responsibility of human users to extract information from these media and enter it into the data base.

In DBMSs, the data represented must have a well-defined logical organization which is known to the user. The data must have unique meaning and should be interpreted in a consistent way by different users. This structured organization enables the system, as well as users, to process the data efficiently. Unfortunately, it also restricts the system to handling formatted data only and leaves the burden of data capture to the users. These limitations have hindered the use of DBMSs in many office applications in which a large amount of data are unformatted [Loch81].

Another area of research is concerned with text retrieval systems such as library automation systems. Materials handled by TRSs usually involve memoranda, papers, reports, and books which are *unformatted*. It is impossible so far, and indeed undesirable, to represent these documents in a formatted way in computers. For instance, the full text of legal documents is often required, or we may be more interested in reading a book than in reading its surrogate (e.g., keywords and abstract).

Retrieving textual data is more difficult than retrieving formatted data because of the large search space involved, and the lack of organization and style in texts. Furthermore, more complex query expressions than those for formatted databases are required for satisfactory retrieval [Holl83], since the same information may be expressed in different written forms. To improve the response time, indexing methods are used to reduce the search space, and special purpose processors have been designed to speed up the search process [Holl79]. For query formulation, many aids are also available. These include the use of thesaurus and relevance feedback to increase the precision and recall of a query [Salt71]. However, formulating queries with high precision and recall remains a difficult process.

On the other hand, the usage patterns of TRSs have made the design of some aspects of the systems easy. In TRSs, retrieval is the dominant activity; insertion is rare; and update and deletion are in general unavailable to general users. Therefore, re-organization of the text database is seldom, if ever, required. Little concurrency control is necessary, since insertion, deletion, and update are infrequent so that coarse locking granularity will not affect system performance significantly.

Due to the traditional separation of research into DBMSs and TRSs, their hardware support, namely database machines (DBMs) and text retrieval machines (TRMs), also exhibit different emphases on their functionality and architectural design. DBMs emphasize arithmetic comparison and relational operations, such as projection and join, while the major function of TRMs is pattern matching.

DBMs have been an active research area for more than a decade; many designs have been proposed and some of them implemented. A number of commercial products are also available, notably Britten Lee's IDBM [EpHa80], Intel's iDBP[Lowe82], and ICL's CAFS [Mall80]. On the other hand, the number of TRMs designed thus far is significantly less. This may be due in part to the problems associated with TRSs, and hence TRMs, which hindered their wider use. However, TRSs and TRMs are becoming more and more important as office information systems proliferate. In this paper, we focus on the design of TRMs for supporting large text databases (e.g., a file server of size greater than 10^{12} bits on a local network). DBMSs and DBMs are not discussed further in this paper, although some design issues and design approaches are applicable to DBMs as well. As such, the term "database" hereafter refers to a text database when no ambiguity arises. Section 2 discusses the technological advances which have impact on hardware designs. Section 3 surveys approaches to the design of TRSs. Previous work on text retrieval machines is examined in section 4, with emphasis on the hardware support for superimposed coding. Three components, namely signature processor, text processor, and multiple response resolver (MRR), are discussed.

2. Technological Implications

The most important characteristics of TRSs are the vast amount of storage required and the large number of users simultaneously accessing the data. These characteristics impose severe constraints on the choice of storage technology in providing satisfactory response time with affordable costs.

The rapid advancement of processor and memory technology has released many constraints previously imposed on hardware designs. On the other hand, it has also prompted the design of many "future" (and in some cases "unrealistic") machines, which are based on technology that will probably be unavailable for a decade. Most of these designs, as exemplified by MPC[ArGi81] and Bentley's and Song's tree machines [BeKu79, Song80] are based on the assumptions that the whole database can reside in fast memory and that a processor is associated with a small segment of the database. These assumptions are unrealistic when the database size is large and growing rapidly. In this paper, we only consider designs which are based on available or emerging technologies.

Due to the size of the database, processor-per-track, fixed-head disks and semiconductor memories such as CCDs are too expensive for storing the whole database. The trend of mass storage technology indicates that moving-head magnetic disks remain (and will continue to remain for some time to come) the prime candidate for inexpensive, on-line bulk storage. Optical disks which are suitable for image and archival data storage are appearing [Chi82]. However, in both technologies, the access time and transfer rate are slow; as such, they must be augmented with semiconductor memory to avoid bottlenecks.

There are basically two different ways to exploit fast semiconductor memory in reducing disk access time. First, cache memory can be used to reduce the effective disk access time. The application of cache memories is well-known and has been proven effective in conventional computer systems. DBMs with disk cache memory have also been proposed [ScOS76, Shaw80]. However, locality of reference for formatted databases is not well supported by empirical results [KeDe83], and little work has been done on the reference behavior in TRSs. Nevertheless, this does not indicate that disk cache cannot improve access time. However, design parameters such as cache size may differ substantially from those of a programming environment. For instance, it is known that the access frequency of a given document decreases exponentially with the age of the document on the system [Grav78]. Therefore, recently created documents can be "paged" into fast memories to improve their access time. However, a large cache may be required to give any significant improvement in access time. The application and evaluation of a large disk cache in TRSs remain important research areas.

Another way of exploiting fast memory is to use it as the storage for indexing information, so that the location of the desired information can be obtained rapidly without searching the database exhaustively. Furthermore, indexing information is more amenable to parallel processing, since it is more structured than the text database itself.

The performance of cache memory is excellent if the data required reside in the cache. However, if they are not in the cache and no (or very coarse) indexing information is available, a long access time is incurred. Indexing, on the other hand, provides performance somewhere in between these two extremes, since access to the index information and a small portion (seldom the whole) of the database is required for every retrieval. In general, both techniques can be applied within the same system.

3. Some Approaches to Text Retrieval Systems

3.1. Full text approach

In the full text approach, the text is searched directly against users' queries: no access method is employed. As a result, no storage and processing overhead are required for the access structures. Furthermore, since the text is searched directly, all information inherent in the text can be used as search criteria, allowing complex search expressions to be formulated (e.g., word proximity, word fragments, etc.). The obvious drawback of this approach is the large amount of processing and disk I/O required when the database is large.

With the advent of semiconductor technology, TRMs employing multiprocessing techniques are often exploited to improve the response time. Although TRMs based on full text scanning eliminate the need for maintaining access structures, they are too expensive for large databases. For instance, scanning a database of 10^{12} bits with 1,000 processors which operate in parallel at a speed of 1 Mbits/sec* will require 17 minutes. In addition, since only a small portion of the database usually contains the desired data (known as the 90-10 rule) [Hsia80] , most of the processors do not retrieve any relevant data. Therefore, a more efficient way of exploiting hardware resources is desirable.

3.2. Inverted file approach

The inverted file approach takes the other extreme. It attempts to reduce the amount of data to be searched, by eliminating the need to search the (primary) database. This is accomplished by keeping an index of keywords extracted from the text. Each keyword is associated with a list of pointers pointing to the locations at which the keyword appears. Thus, when searching for a keyword(s), only the index has to be examined. This greatly reduces the processing time required.

There are, however, a number of disadvantages. First, depending on the size of the vocabulary and the granularity of the index, the storage overhead can be very large, ranging from 50% to 300% of the primary database [BiNT78]. Second, the processing time rises rapidly as the search expression becomes complex, since intersection of lists of pointers is required when the expression contains logical AND operations. Finally, queries are limited by the vocabulary used in the index; complex queries such as word fragments and word proximity cannot be handled directly. These drawbacks seriously limit the applications of inverted files to text retrieval systems.

This figure is limited by the memory transfer rate. Magnetic bubble memories typically have a transfer rate less than 300 Kbits/sec. Magnetic disks can operate at a transfer rate of about 10 Mbits/sec.

3.3. Signature file approach

The signature file approach can be considered as a compromise between the first two approaches. To facilitate subsequent discussions, we first define the following notation:

B_i : the ith block of the text database;

S_i : the signature generated from B_i, represented as a bit vector $S_i^1 S_i^2 \cdots S_i^m$;

p_i : the pointer associated with S_i, pointing to B_i;

m : the number of bits per signature;

n : the number of signatures in the signature file (i.e., the number of blocks in the text file);

Q : user queries expressed as patterns;

S_Q : the signature generated from Q, represented as a bit vector $S_Q^1 S_Q^2 \cdots S_Q^m$;

w_{S_Q} : the number of one's (weight) in S_Q.

w_{S_i} : the number of one's in S_i;

The database is divided into a number of fixed-length blocks. Each block B_i is associated with a signature S_i. Algorithm 1 depicts a typical way for generating S_i from B_i [Harr71].

> 1) **for** $1 \leqslant j \leqslant m$ **do**
> $S_i^j := 0$;
> 2) **for all** substring t of length k of B_i **do**
>   **begin**
>   hash t into an integer j where $1 \leqslant j \leqslant m$;
> $S_i^j := 1$;
>   **end**

Algorithm 1. Algorithm for generating the signature of
a text block.

In practice, common words in B_i are ignored when S_i is generated, and trigrams ($k = 3$ in algorithm 1) or digrams ($k = 2$) are used. The signatures, together with the block numbers (or physical pointers) are stored separately in a signature file.

When a pattern Q is searched for, a signature S_Q is first generated from Q, with the same algorithm used for generating S_i's. Then, algorithm 2 can be used to search for the patterns. The signatures act as a filtering mechanism to eliminate from the database blocks which are guaranteed not to contain the required data. The condition in the algorithm is referred to as *inclusion*. That is, a signature satisfies the condition (i.e., it *qualifies*) if it *includes* the query signature. The inclusion condition is a necessary but not sufficient condition for a block to satisfy the query, since bits in a signature set by one or more words in a text may overlap with the bits set by another, different, word. Blocks whose signatures satisfy the inclusion condition, but do not satisfy the query, are called *false drops*. Therefore, after a signature is qualified, the corresponding block must be compared to the query to check if it really matches the query. Figure 1 depicts the block diagram of a TRS based on this approach.

for all S_i **do**
    if $(S_i^j = 1$ **for all** j **where** $S_Q^j = 1)$ **then**
        begin
            retrieve B_i and compare with Q,
            if match return B_i;
        end

Algorithm 2. Search algorithm for superimposed coding.

The query processor generates S_Q from Q and passes S_Q and Q, respectively, to the signature processor and the text processor. The signature processor searches the signature file and obtains a (possible null) set of pointers for the text processor, which compares the corresponding blocks with Q. Matched blocks (or documents containing the matched blocks) are returned to the user. Note that these three processors can be implemented as three hardware processors or as three software modules running on a conventional computer.

It is clear that only the signature file and a small portion of the database need to be searched. In some applications, only 2-50% of the database has to be searched [ThTa82]. Since the size of the signature is usually 10-20% the size of the database, the overall processing time is significantly reduced. Furthermore, complex queries can be handled, since the pattern is also compared to the text directly. This approach effectively combines the advantages of the first two approaches and has been shown to be very effective for text retrieval [ChFa84].

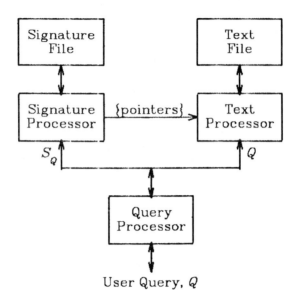

*Figure 1: Block diagram for a TRS based on
signature files*

4. Previous Work on Text Retrieval Machines

4.1. Signature file processor

In this section, we consider several designs for the signature processor, and evaluate their performance. To simplify the analysis,
storage for pointers in the signature file is ignored, since they occupy
approximately the same space in the designs under consideration and
have minimal effect on the performance; or they can be omitted completely if the signatures are retrieved according to their logical order, in
which case, the ith signature retrieved corresponds to the ith text block.

4.1.1. Sequential file

The simplest approach is to store the signature file sequentially on
disks and scan it bit-serially. Obviously, this takes $n \cdot m$ time units.
There is no special hardware required other than a simple controller
and a comparator.

4.1.2. Transposed file

The signature file can be organized as a transposed file on disk. The first bit from every signature is stored consecutively, starting from an addressable block. Similarly, the second bit from every signature is stored in the same manner, starting from another addressable block, and so on [Robe79]. To search for a pattern, the bit slices corresponding to bit positions of S_Q which contain one's are ANDed together. A one in the ith bit position of the result vector indicates that S_i qualifies. The operations can be described formally with algorithm 3. A simple processor implementing the algorithm is shown in figure 2.

1) **for any** i **where** $S_Q^i = 1$, **do**
   load i^{th} bit slice into register R;

2) **for all** j **where** $j \neq i$ **and** $S_Q^j = 1$, **do**
   begin
      AND the jth bit slice with R bit-serially;
      circulate the result back to R;
   end

3) return p_i if the ith bit of R is one.

Algorithm 3. Search operations of a signature processor based on transposed file organization.

In this approach, only $n \cdot w_{S_Q}$ bits are examined in the signature file. Thus, the total time required is
$$n \cdot w_{S_Q} + n = n \cdot (w_{S_Q} + 1)$$
The last term represents the time for scanning the register R to obtain the pointers to qualified text blocks (step 3 in the algorithm). This approach is *optimal* in the sense that it examines the smallest possible number of bits from every signature.

4.1.3. Word-serial, bit-parallel organization

The premise of the word-serial, bit-parallel (WSBP) approach is that the signature file is small compared to the size of the database. Therefore, with the decreasing cost of memory, the whole signature file can be stored in faster memory, such as CCDs, magnetic bubbles or

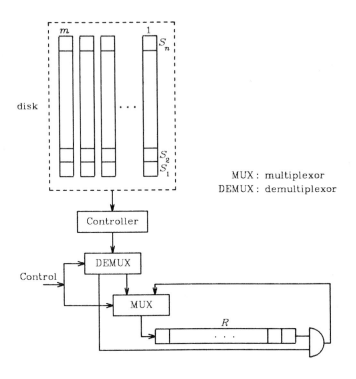

MUX : multiplexor
DEMUX : demultiplexor

Figure 2: Signature processor
based on transposed file organization

even RAM, which allows a word (bit vector) to be read in parallel (as opposed to disks which transfer data bit- or byte-serially).

A signature processor was proposed by Ahuja and Roberts at Bell Laboratories in 1980, based on this approach [AhRo80]. The whole signature file was stored in CCD modules connected to a common bus and searched in a word-serial, bit-parallel fashion.* The organization of a module with a capacity of n_i signatures is depicted in figure 3. Signatures are read from the signature file sequentially and masked by S_Q. The bits of the masked signature are ANDed together to produce a hit signal. If the hit signal is set, the signature is qualified and the corresponding pointer is output.

---

* In [AhRo80], the search method was referred to as "word-parallel". However, we use the term "word-serial, bit-parallel" to conform with the common terminology in computer architecture.

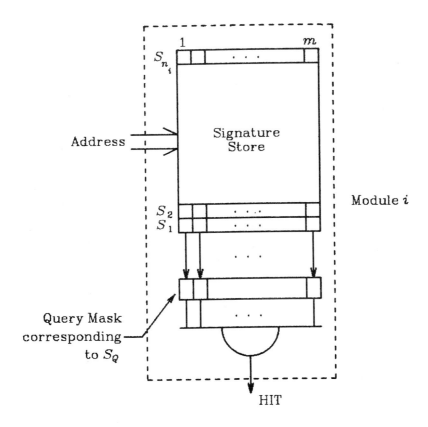

*Figure 3: Signature processor
based on WSBP organization*

A number of identical modules connected to a bus with a central controller can operate in parallel. The time for searching the signature file is ideally the time to search one module if bus contention is ignored. Obviously, a module with n_i signatures can be searched in n_i steps.

This method is a straightforward application of parallelism. However, it is not optimal in the sense that the whole signature file (i.e., $n \cdot m$ bits), rather than $n \cdot w_{S_Q}$ bits, is read. Consequently, only w_{S_Q}/m of the total I/O bandwidth and the associated hardware (e.g., the query mask) of the signature store are utilized. When w_{S_Q} is much less than m, this approach is inefficient in the use of hardware and, more importantly, I/O bandwidth, resulting in a longer processing time than is otherwise achievable if the full bandwidth were utilized.

4.1.4. Word-parallel, bit-serial organization

A natural way to make full use of the I/O bandwidth of the signature store is to base the design on a transposed file organization. In this section, we present a design based on a word-parallel, bit serial (WPBS) organization and demonstrate that it is better than a WSBP design [Lee84].

The signature file is transposed and stored in a module, as shown in figure 4 (i.e., word i of the signature store holds the ith bit slice of the signatures). S_Q is sent to the controller, which then addresses the signature store according to the bits set in S_Q. That is, if the ith bit of S_Q is set, the ith word which contains the ith bit from every signature is read. The output words are ANDed together by the comparator C. At the end of the operation, the ith bit of C will be set to one if and only if S_i includes S_Q. The operations of the processor are detailed in algorithm 4. As in the transposed file approach, only w_{S_Q} bits from every signature are examined. Thus, the search takes only w_{S_Q} steps and is independent of the number of signatures in the module (i.e., n_i).

In the last step of algorithm 4, if more than one pointer has to be sent to the controller, the output of pointers must be serialized by the *multiple response resolver* (MRR) (see section 4.3). The MRR sends the pointers (responders) to the controller in sorted order. Sorting the pointers is not an essential requirement of the algorithm, but it can minimize disk arm movements when the blocks are retrieved from the database. It is sufficient to note at this point that the MRR consumes only a small amount of time (e.g., $< 10 \mu sec$). Furthermore, the output of pointers can be overlapped with the search of the signature store and, as such, will not degrade the performance significantly.

The size of a module can be expanded both horizontally and vertically, as shown by the arrows in figure 4. A *row* of signatures is a block of n_i signatures stored together, side by side. *Horizontal* expansion increases the word width of the store so that more signatures can be stored. This approach does not affect the time for searching a module, but consumes a larger amount of hardware for the comparators and MRR. *Vertical* expansion increases the number of words ("height") of a module. It serves two purposes. First, the number of signatures per module can be increased. For instance, if the number of words is doubled, two rows of signatures can be accommodated, one at the lower address portion and the other at the higher address portion. This method requires little extra hardware, but it becomes slower, since the module must now be searched row by row. Second, and more importantly, it enables the number of bits per signature to change after initial installation. For instance, the number of bits per signature can be

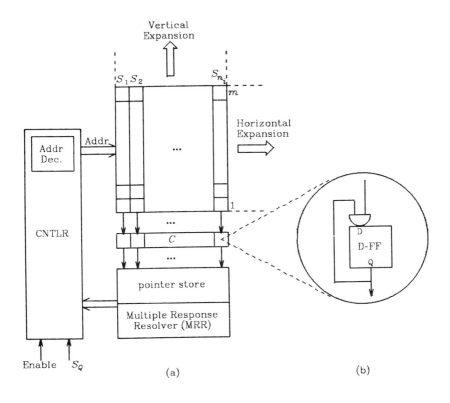

Figure 4: (a) Signature processor based on WPBS search;
(b) its serial comparator

1) **for** $1 \leqslant i \leqslant n_i$ **do** $C_i := 1$ /* initialize C */

2) **for** $1 \leqslant j \leqslant m$ **where** $S_Q^j = 1$ **do**
   for $1 \leqslant i \leqslant n_i$ **do** $C_j := C_j$ **AND** S_i^j

3) output p_j's in sorted order if $C_j = 1$

Algorithm 4 Search operations of a WPBS module.

increased to reduce the number of false drops, or decreased to take into account the decreasing access frequency for old documents [ChFa84]. In general, a module may initially contain more than one row. The choice is determined by the available size, configuration, and technology of the memory employed.

Table 1 summarizes the performance of a module based on **WPBS** and **WSBP** search. In both cases, the module contains n signatures and uses m comparators (i.e., m signatures per row in the WPBS approach). In the WPBS approach, when n is greater than m, $\left\lceil \dfrac{n}{m} \right\rceil$ rows are required. It can be observed that when w_{S_Q} is much less than m, a substantial gain in speed is achieved in the WPBS approach.

	word-parallel bit-serial	word-serial bit-parallel
number of signatures	n	n
number of comparators	m	m
number of comparators utilized	m	w_{S_Q}
time to search a module	$\left\lceil \dfrac{n}{m} \right\rceil \cdot w_{S_Q}$ (+ MRR time)	n
additional hardware	controller + MRR	controller

Table 1.   A comparison of word-parallel, bit-serial search and word-serial, bit-parallel search.

It is assumed in the above design that conventional memory which can address only one word at a time is used. However, superimposed coding only requires the result of the conjunction of the bits from a signature, which correspond to the one's in S_Q, not the values of the individual bits. Thus, the one's of S_Q can be used as enable signals to the signature store to select bits from a signature simultaneously. The selected bits are then wired-ANDed together. Figure 5 illustrates the design of the signature store based on this approach, and its implementation using nMOS technology.

$B_{i,j}$ is the bit cell holding the jth bit of the ith signature (i.e., S_i^j). $B_{i,j}$ is enabled if and only if S_Q^j is active. The outputs of the enabled bit cells of a column are then wired-AND together. It is easy to show that the result, C_i, equals 1 if and only if S_i includes S_Q. This approach allows the search of one row to be performed in one step. Furthermore, it does not require the address decoder in figure 4(a) and the comparator, C, in figure 4(b). The disadvantage is that custom-

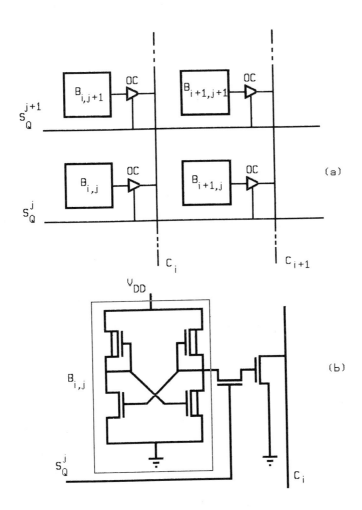

Figure 5: (a) Signature store based on simultaneous enable and wired-AND, (b) nMOS implementation of a bit cell

design memory is used; the design and development costs are high.

4.2. Text processor

The text processor receives from the signature processor a (possibly null) list of pointers which point to all text blocks containing the patterns specified by the user query, with the addition of a small number of false drops. The main purpose of the text processor is to compare the user query directly with the text blocks, to eliminate false drops. User queries are usually represented as regular expressions, and the comparison, of course, can be done by software. However, when the patterns are complex, or a large number of signatures are qualified, the comparison still consumes a substantial amount of time. In this section, we are only concerned with hardware alternatives for performing pattern matching operations. Therefore, pattern matching refers to *hardware* pattern matching, unless indicated explicitly to the contrary. We also use t to denote the length of a text string and p to denote the length of a pattern.

In essence, pattern matchers proposed in the literature for full-text scanning (e.g., [Robe78], [HaHo83] and [Mukh79]) can be used as a text processor. However, when used with superimposed coding, the search space for the text file is reduced dramatically and consists of fixed length blocks. These two properties strongly influence the design of the text processor.

Pattern matchers can be classified into two categories: *logic-with-pattern* and *logic-with-text*. In the logic-with-pattern category, processing power is associated with patterns. That is, patterns are stored directly or in an encoded form in one or more processors or logic cells. Text strings are retrieved from secondary storage and sent to the patterns for comparison. Since every pattern character can be compared to a text character concurrently*, this hardware approach is faster than software approaches which compare one text character with one pattern character at a time. Neglecting other overhead, the speed is upper-bounded by the time required to read the whole text string from secondary storage. When comparison can be overlapped with the reading of a character from disk, this approach requires t steps to process a text string.

In the logic-with-text category, processing power is associated with the text strings; pattern characters are sent to the text sequentially for comparison. In general, every text character is compared to a pattern character in parallel. Assuming the text is already loaded into logic cells, the speed of this approach is upper-bounded by p (i.e., the time to broadcast the pattern). Since p is much less than t, this approach is potentially much faster than the first approach. The obvious disadvantage of this approach is the large amount of hardware required to

---

* *Note that the pattern characters can be compared to the same text character broadcast to them, or to different text characters.*

accommodate the text. Furthermore, the variation of t is very large. Thus, it is difficult to determine beforehand how long the text could be and, therefore, the size of the pattern matcher to be used (e.g., the size of the memory and/or the number of logic cells).

4.2.1. Logic-with-pattern category

In this section, we will discuss three different approaches within the logic-with-pattern category. They all share the common characteristics that t steps are required to match a pattern with a text string, and a relatively small amount of hardware is required.

4.2.1.1. Associative memory

Associative memory is perhaps the simplest way of performing pattern matching in hardware. As depicted in figure 6, patterns are stored in an associative memory. Each memory word is, in effect, a parallel comparator with storage capability. If a pattern is shorter than the word size of the memory, the pattern must be padded with don't care characters, which are represented by dots in the figure, to fill the whole word.

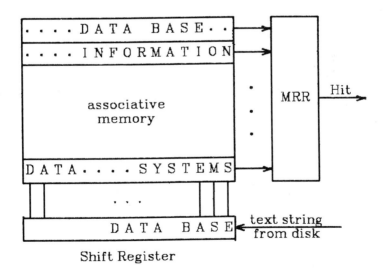

Figure 6: Pattern matching with associative memory

The text string is shifted into the register from secondary storage. The text segment in the register is compared simultaneously with every pattern. Patterns which match the string segment in the register will respond with a signal to the controller through the multiple response resolver (MRR). The text is shifted by one character, and the comparison is repeated until the end of the text is reached.

This approach is simple, both conceptually and in hardware design. Since the number of patterns is usually small and their lengths short, the size of the memory is reasonably small. Furthermore, designs employing conventional RAM and hashing techniques in place of truly associative memory have been proposed, to lower the costs further while retaining most of the properties of truly associative memory [Burk82]. However, associative memory is not flexible. It allows exact match with FLDCs (fixed-length don't cares) but does not allow VLDCs (variable-length don't cares). Alternations within a pattern can only be handled indirectly, by replacing the pattern with a number of patterns each of which represents one alternation in the original pattern. Patterns with closures are not allowed at all. Furthermore, the length of a pattern and the number of patterns are respectively limited by the word length and the number of words in the memory.

4.2.1.2. Cellular logic array

In an associative memory, a pattern matches with a text segment in parallel and reports immediately (usually within one clock cycle) whether the comparison is successful. In a cellular logic array, an array of logic cells is used to hold a pattern. (When there is more than one pattern, a two-dimensional array is required.) Each cell compares the pattern character it is currently holding with a character from the text, and passes a partial match result to its neighbouring cell, which will act according to the received partial match result and in turn produce another partial match result to its neighbour. Although a pattern is compared to a text segment in parallel, the result is not known immediately, as in an associative memory; rather, a partial match signal is established at the beginning of the pattern and propagates down the pattern as the comparison continues. A match of the full pattern is eventually established, when the signal is able to propagate to the end of the pattern.

There are many designs based on cellular logic arrays. Foster and Kung proposed a systolic array for pattern matching [FoKu80]. A *systolic array* is composed of a (large) number of simple logic cells. A cell is connected only to its neighbours (e.g., as a linear array or matrix). Thus, data and control signals are exchanged only between neighbour cells, and the signal flow between cells is simple and regular. This structure allows easier VLSI implementation. Figure 7 is a pattern matcher based on the concept of systolic array.

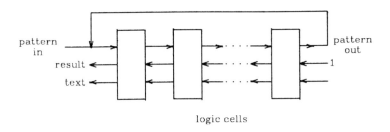

Figure 7: Architecture of a systolic pattern matcher

The pattern is shifted into the array from the left and cycled through the array, while the text is shifted at the same time from the right. Each cell compares the corresponding characters from the pattern and the text and sets its output line to one if and only if the two characters match and its input result line has been set to one (thus establishing a partial match signal). When the result line of the leftmost cell is set to one, the pattern is found in the text. The design has the same pattern matching capability and limitations of associative memories.

A more powerful design was given in [Mukh79] and [Mukh80]. Its basic structure is the same as the systolic pattern matcher above. However, more logic has been put into the cells and more control lines are used. The pattern remains stationary after it is loaded into the array. Among other capabilities, it can handle VLDCs.

A disadvantage of cellular logic arrays as well as associative memories is that when a number of patterns have to be matched simultaneously, a two-dimensional array of logic cells must be used. However, since the array is connected in a fixed way, both the length and the number of patterns that can be matched at the same time are fixed. This inflexibility leads to an inefficient use of hardware. For instance, an array of 20x20 cells cannot be used to match 21 patterns simultaneously, no matter how short each pattern is. Similarly, it cannot accommodate a pattern longer than 21 characters, even though the pattern is the only one to accommodate.

4.2.1.3. Finite state automaton

Another method for implementing a pattern matcher is based on a finite state automaton (FSA) [HoU179]. The patterns to be matched are first translated into a state transition table, which is then loaded into a finite state machine (FSM). Starting from its initial state, the FSM accepts characters from the input text and makes corresponding transitions according to the state transition table. If the FSM reaches one of its final states (accepting states), the pattern associated with the final state is found in the text. Pattern matchers based on deterministic FSA (DFSA)[Robe78] and non-deterministic FSA (NFSA)[HaHo83] have been proposed.

A DFSA can be implemented with a two-dimensional array containing the "next state" information. The next state of a transition can be obtained by addressing the array with two indexes representing the current input character and the current state. However, this simple approach requires a memory of size $|\Sigma| \cdot |Q| \cdot log_2 |Q|$ bits (where $|\Sigma|$ is the size of the alphabet and $|Q|$ is the number of states). A more sophisticated encoding technique called Bird's indexing can reduce the memory size dramatically. Since a state with only one outgoing arc, called a *sequential* state, matches only one character, it can be represented by a pair containing the character and a number representing the next state. In practice, 90% of the states are sequential states. Thus, the memory required is reduced substantially. States with more than one outgoing transition are called *index* states. The next states of an index state are numbered in order according to the collating sequence of the characters causing the transitions, and are stored in adjacent memory locations. An index state can be represented by a base (its lowest-numbered next-state) and a bit vector of $|\Sigma|$ bits. The ith bit of the vector corresponds to the ith character in the alphabet (ordered with the same collating sequence). A bit is set to one if its corresponding character causes a valid transition, and to zero otherwise. Therefore, when a character is read, the corresponding bit is checked. If it is a zero, the default transition is taken; otherwise, the next state is obtained by adding to the base the number of 1's to the right of the bit. Thus, an index state can be represented by $log_2 |Q| + |\Sigma|$ bits, rather than $log_2 |Q| \cdot |\Sigma|$ bits in a direct array implementation. To make Bird indexing effective, the DFSA is separated into three smaller DFSAs. The first DFSA detects single-word patterns without VLDCs; the second one detects single-word patterns with VLDCs (initial or embedded); the third one, taking input from the first two, detects multiple-word patterns. If the DFSAs are combined, every state will be an index state when the pattern contains VLDCs, and thus more storage is required.

This technique requires more setup time and sophisticated hardware than a direct array implementation. Furthermore, sequential states and index states, as well as different index states, demand different amounts of processing time. As such, buffering between the DFSA and disk is required.

The advantage of NFSA is that it can occupy several states simultaneously. This allows several search paths to be followed at the same time. When a search path finds a mismatch (reaches a dead end), it simply stops, without the need of backtracking. Thus, the state transition diagram can be simpler and, as a result, requires much less storage.

A NFSA can be implemented by a replication of DFSAs. When a "fork" to multiple states occurs, one or more DFSAs are activated in such a way that each of the activated DFSAs, including the activating DFSA, assumes one of the next states. Haskin and Hollaar proposed an implementation of NFSA called partitioned FSA, or PFSA [HaHo83]. Instead of replicating complete copies of the state transition table in each DFSA (called character matcher, or CM), each DFSA is assigned only a specific subset of the original table. The partition of the state table must ensure that no CM will be forced to occupy more than one state. This partitioning is not trivial, and requires a larger amount of setup time than the deterministic approach.

Pattern matchers based on FSA have the advantage that the number and lengths of patterns are limited only by the total size of the memory in the FSM. Thus, it is more flexible in that, with a fixed memory size, the matcher can match a large number of short patterns or a small number of long patterns.

This method has the full pattern matching capability of regular expressions and, as such, possesses a higher query capability than the other designs discussed so far. However, it requires extra set-up time for the translation and loading of the transition tables, and the hardware is more complicated. Even with special coding techniques, the state transition tables require a large amount of storage. For example, when the query interarrival time is 4 seconds, and each query has 23 patterns containing a total of around 165 characters, the storage required is 800 Kbits for the deterministic FSA approach, and 50 Kbits (10 CMs with 5 Kbits storage each) for the non-deterministic approach [Hask80, HaHo83].

4.2.2. Logic-with-text category

A straightforward approach in the logic-with-text category is to store the text in an associative memory. Each word of the memory holds a text segment such that a pattern can be compared with every segment in parallel. However, this approach can only locate patterns within a segment but not between segments, since memory words usually do not have any communication among themselves. This problem can be alleviated by using a large word length, but at the expense of a slower speed, since the pattern, if shorter than the word size, has to shift down the word, so that it can compare to every successive p substring of the segment. A more serious disadvantage of this approach is that, for a reasonably large database, the associative memory is too large to be economical, if ever implementable. Even with the VLSI technology available in the near future, it will be impossible to associate a sufficient amount of logic with *every* text character, for performing comparison (and, of course, for storing the character), given that the size of the database may exceed 10^{10} characters. In order to reduce the amount of hardware, pseudo-parallelism is usually employed instead of full parallelism. One approach, discussed in the following section, is to divide the text into segments, and to compare the pattern to every segment in parallel, but sequentially within a segment. Thus, the speed is much slower than the upper bound p.

4.2.2.1. Associative Linear Array Processor (ALAP)

The Associative Linear Array Processor (ALAP) was originally proposed for performing fast arithmetic operations, and later extended to perform pattern matching operations as well [FiLo77, Love77]. As depicted in figure 8(a), ALAP consists of a linear array of logic cells connected to three busses. Two of these busses are for input and output. The third bus allows both arithmetic and pattern matching operations to be performed between the data stored in selected cells and an external operand. (For pattern matching, the external operand is a pattern character.) In addition, a channel, called the *chaining channel*, connects the cells in series; it allows each cell to transfer data and status bits to its immediate right neighbour.

A cell consists of an arithmetic logic unit for performing arithmetic and comparison operations, and a shift register (e.g., CCD) of length 64-Kbit, called the *data register*, for storing text segments. The chaining logic of each cell permits all cells to shift their contents simultaneously on the chaining channel. As such, the entire ALAP can be regarded as a very long shift register, and cell boundaries can usually be ignored.

ALAP can perform a number of arithmetic operations, such as addition and multiplication, in an elegant way. Unfortunately, the facility for pattern matching is very primitive. Comparison within a cell is carried out sequentially. The ALU acts as a serial comparator, which compares one pattern character with one character from its data register and accumulates the partial results. Since the data register is much

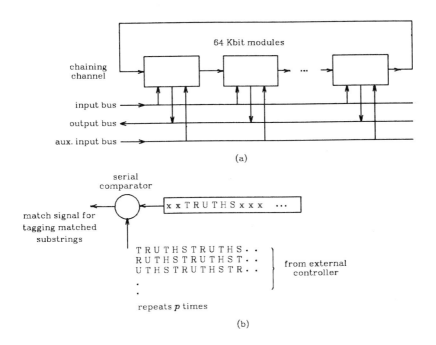

Figure 8: (a) Organization of ALAP,
(b) comparison operations of an ALAP cell

longer than the pattern, the pattern has to be broadcast repeatedly until the last character in the data register is compared. Furthermore, in order to locate all occurrences of the pattern in the data register, regardless of their orientation, the pattern has to be broadcast p times, such that each time it starts with a different pattern character. An example is shown in figure 8(b), in which the pattern is "TRUTHS". It is clear that this design only allows exact match with FLDCs, and requires a number of steps equal to p times the length of the data register for pattern matching.

Since processing and control logic are associated with every 64-Kbit text segment, the cost per bit is lower than that of truly associative memories. However, when the database is very large, the data register still requires an appreciable amount of logic.

4.2.2.2. Associative Linear Text Processor (ALTEP)

The Associative Linear Text Processor (ALTEP) is similar to ALAP in that the text string resides in a linear array of logic cells. However, ALTEP is designed specifically for pattern matching; it has the full pattern matching capability of a regular expression and is much faster than ALAP. With signature file as an access method, the database consists of fixed-length blocks, and only a small portion of them are examined. Therefore, an array of pre-determined length can be used in ALTEP, and a text block can be loaded into the cells on demand. Once the block is in the cells, the array functions as a truly associative processor which, in most cases, requires only p steps to match a pattern with a text [Lee84].

ALTEP is a linear array of identical logic cells connected to two common busses (see figure 9). The *instruction* bus is used to broadcast instructions to the cells. Every cell executes concurrently the instruction it receives, and acknowledges to the controller through the *acknowledgement* bus if the operation is successful. The controller may take different actions, depending on whether or not an acknowledgement is received. A uni-directional chaining channel connects all cells serially, to allow inter-cell communication.

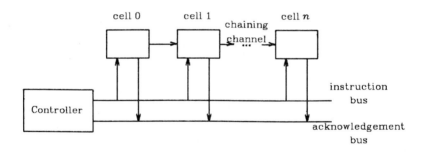

Figure 9: Organization of ALTEP

The text string is stored in cells 1 to n, one character in each cell. The operation of a cell is to compare the text character it is holding with the pattern character broadcast to it, and, according to the result, acknowledge the controller and change its internal state. Cell 0 is a pseudo cell. Its *only* purpose is to provide an initial signal to the input chaining channel of cell 1 at the beginning of an operation, and reset the signal afterwards. As such, the cell can be much simpler than the other cells. However, it is conceptually simpler to regard it as identical to the other cells, except that it does not match with *any* pattern character. Thus, every cell in ALTEP is identical and responds to an instruction in the same way.

ALTEP accepts patterns in the form of regular expressions [HoUl79]. Patterns without alternations and Kleene closures are called *simple* patterns. In principle, a regular expression allows any level of nesting, but a hardware implementation must impose a limit on the number of levels allowed (e.g., four levels) because of the restriction of hardware resources. This limitation, however, is not a serious one, since a pattern with many levels of nesting will be very complex (i.e., it matches a large number of different strings). It is unlikely that a user is able or willing to specify such complex patterns.

Simple patterns can be handled in an obvious manner. Initially, the chaining channel input to every cell is set. Each cell compares its text character to the pattern character it receives. Upon a match, it sets the chaining channel of its right neighbour and acknowledges the controller; otherwise, the channel is reset. After a text character is broadcast, the controller can abort the process if no acknowledgement is received. It is not difficult to observe that, after the last pattern character is processed, a cell with its output chaining channel set indicates that a substring which ends at this cell has matched the pattern.

Alternations and closures of simple patterns can be handled if the intermediate match results are properly saved in temporary storage within each cell. Let us consider the pattern $P_1(P_2 | P_3 | P_4)$; it is equivalent to the disjunction of three simple patterns P_1P_2, P_1P_3, and P_1P_4. Thus, they can be matched individually, as described above, and the results accumulated. However, this is not efficient, because P_1 is matched three times. To avoid this inefficiency, after P_1 is matched, the state of the cells is saved. After P_2 is finished, the state is restored, so that P_3 and P_4 can be processed as if P_1 has already been matched. The result for matching each of the alternations is accumulated, and restored after all alternations are finished.

The closure of a simple pattern P can be considered as the alternation of an infinite number of simple patterns, P^1, P^2, P^3, and so on (P^i means P is repeated i times). Therefore, a naive way of matching $P*$ is to successively match these patterns, starting from P^1, until a pattern P^i which does not occur in the text is reached. However, this simple method is not efficient. An important observation is that, after P^i is finished, the result of matching P^{i+1} can be obtained by repeating P just one more time, since the result of matching P^i is already available. Therefore, it is only necessary to save the state of the cells after P^i is processed, and broadcast P once more to get the result of P^{i+1}. The process is continued until a mismatch is encountered, and the accumulated match results are then restored. Alternations and closures can be nested to a depth determined by the size of the temporary storage.

For patterns without any closure, $O(p)$ steps are required. The closure of a simple pattern requires a number of steps equal to the length of the longest substring which matches the closure in the text string. These figures indicate tremendous improvements over ALAP, as well as other approaches in the logic-with-pattern category.

4.3. Multiple response resolution

Inherent to any multiprocessing system, there is some multiple response resolution scheme. For instance, a search of an associative memory or associative processor may yield more than one responder. Since there is usually only one common bus connecting the memory cells or processors, the output of the responders must be serialized (or prioritized) by a multiple response resolver (MRR). Multiple response resolution schemes can be based on a bus-contention protocol such as CSMA in Ethernet [MeBo76]. However, these protocols have poor performance when the system load is high (i.e., has many responders). Therefore, we only consider schemes which are collision free.

Collision-free multiple response resolution methods can be divided into two classes. In the first class, responders are output according to their physical locations in memory. That is, the responder with the lowest (or highest) address is output first, then the responder with the second lowest (or highest) address is output, and so on. We call this retrieval scheme *address-ordered* retrieval. In the second class, responders are output in sorted order according to their values rather than their addresses. We call this approach *value-ordered* retrieval.*

4.3.1. Address-ordered retrieval

The method depicted in figure 10(a) is perhaps the simplest way of finding the responder which is closest to one "end" of the memory. The tag bits of the cells are set according to their corresponding status bits which identify the responders. The leftmost cell with the tag bit set to one passes a reset signal along the priority line to all other cells to its right, resetting the tag bits to zero along its way. Thus, after the reset signal reaches the end of the array, only one (the leftmost) word with tag bit set to one remains. This word can be output and subsequently removed from the responder set by clearing its status bit. To retrieve the second responder, the tag bits are again set to their

---

* *In the literature, the second class is simply called ordered retrieval.* We use *address-ordered* and *value-ordered* to distinguish the two classes explicitly.

corresponding status bits, and the same process is repeated. The advantage of this method is the simple and identical logic structure of each cell. However, in the worst case, the reset signal has to propagate through n-1 OR gates, where n is the size of the memory. Given a delay of 5 nsec per gate, a memory with 1000 words will generate a delay of 5 μsec, and one mega-word will require 5 msec to settle down. This long settling time defeats the purpose of using high-speed associative memories when retrieval is frequent.

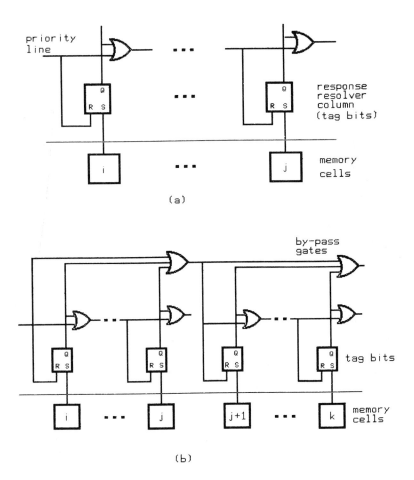

Figure 10: MRR with (a) a priority line,
(b) a priority tree

A faster method, employing by-pass gates, has been proposed (see figure 10(b)) [Land77]. The reset signal from cell i propagates to the

right as before. However, at the same time, the signal passes through
the by-pass gate *directly* to cell $j+1$. Hence, cell i to cell j and cell $j+1$
to cell k are reset in parallel. More than one level of by-pass gates,
organized as a tree, can be used. In general, the settling time is proportional to $log_m n$, where n is the number of cells and m is the fan-in of
the by-pass gates (i.e., the degree of the tree). The disadvantage of
this method is that the tree not only requires more hardware but also
destroys the regular, one-dimensional structure of the cells. Thus, the
memory is more expensive to implement and difficult to expand.

In summary, address-ordered MRRs retrieve responders according
to their locations in memory, but independent of their values. The
time to select a responder depends on the size of the memory. As
such, care must be taken to ensure that the settling time is within a certain limit (e.g., the time out period or the clock cycle of the system)
when the memory size is increased.

4.3.2. Value-ordered retrieval

One characteristic of the first class of MRRs is its asynchronous
and distributed decision process. After the controller has initiated the
retrieval operation, it is not involved in the process of selecting the first
responder. Instead, the cells decide among themselves which one is the
winner, by the use of priority circuits associated with them. When the
winner is selected, the memory controller is informed and the winner is
retrieved.

On the other hand, the decision process of value-ordered retrieval
can be centralized as well as distributed. In a centralized design, the
decision process is carried out solely by the memory controller.
Memory words have no communication with one another but respond
directly to the controller. The controller selects the first responder with
successive memory probes in which an increasingly restrictive search
criterion is used, and decides when the selection process is finished.
Therefore, the retrieval speed is measured in terms of the number of
memory probes. In a distributed design, the decision logic is distributed in each memory word. However, unlike address-ordered
retrieval, it does not make use of priority circuitry.

4.3.2.1. Centralized approach

Frei and Goldberg proposed a method which was based on a
binary search tree [FrGo61]. In principle, the responders are examined
by bit slice from left to right. If the slice being examined contains all

zero's, all responders are retained in the responder set. Otherwise, only those responders with one's in the slice are preserved.

In Frei and Goldberg's design, the tree search is carried out by probing the memory with binary patterns augmented with don't care symbols (X's). As illustrated in figure 11(a), the first digit in the initial pattern is set to one, and all other digits are set to X's (e.g., 1XXXXX in step 1). If there is at least one responder, the one in the pattern is preserved, and the next X is set to one (i.e., 11XXXX). Otherwise, the one in the pattern is reset to zero, and the next X is set to one (i.e., 01XXXX). The memory is searched again with the modified pattern, and the same procedure is repeated until all digits are set to either one or zero. The resulting pattern represents the value of the largest responder. Note that the smallest responder can be retrieved in a similar way by replacing zero's in the pattern with one's and vice versa. It is clear that w memory probes are required, where w is the word length of the memory.

step 1	step 2	step 3	step 4	step 5	step 6	
1XXXXX	11XXXX	111XXX	1101XX	11001X	110011	←patterns
110011	110011	110011	110011	110011	110011	110011
110010	110010	110010	110010	110010	110010	
110000	110000	110000	110000	110000		
000011						
000010						
000000						

(a)

step 1	step 2	step 3	step 4	
1X00XX	11001X	110011	←patterns	
110011	110011	110011	110011	
110010	110010	110010		
110000	110000			
000011				
000010				
000000				
00	1100**	11001*	←column readouts	

(b)

Figure 11: Examples illustrating the operations of
(a) Frei and Goldberg's method, and
(b) Lewin's method

An improvement based on this method was proposed by Lewin [Lewi62]. As is evident from the above example, when a column containing all one's or all zero's is processed, the set of responders is not reduced at all (steps 2, 3, and 4). In Lewin's method, special logic and encoding techniques allow the controller to recognize the state of each column. In each column, there are three possible outcomes: it contains all zero's, all one's or both zero's and one's, denoted by 0, 1 and $*$, respectively. Based on the column readout, the controller can skip over columns which contain the same digits and only concern itself with columns indicated by $*$'s. A pattern is obtained from the column readout by setting the most significant $*$ to 1 and all other $*$'s to X's, leaving the 0's and 1's unchanged. For example, in step 1 of figure 11(b), 1X00XX is obtained from $**$00$**$. The pattern obtained is used to search the memory, reducing the size of the responder set as a consequence, and producing a new column readout (1100$**$). This procedure is repeated until a column readout containing no $*$'s is found, which then represents the largest responder in the responder set. The best case performance of this method is one memory probe, when there is only one distinct responder. The worst case is w probes, when the active responders have both zero's and one's in every slice being examined.

4.3.2.2. Distributed approach

Ramamoorthy, Turner, and Wah proposed a design which combined many desirable features of the designs previously discussed [RaTW78]. In their design, responders are retrieved in order of their values and at a speed proportional to the word length. However, like address-ordered retrieval, the decision process is asynchronous and distributed.

The organization of the memory cells is depicted in figure 12(a), and the logic diagram of a bit cell is shown in figure 12(b). We consider the general case in which the responder set includes all n memory words. A bit cell $B_{i,j}$ is said to be *enabled* if its input enable signal $E_{i,j}$ is one. All enable signals of the first bit slice, $E_{i,1}$, are initialized to one and then propagate across the bit slices. As the enable signals pass through the bit slices, some enable signals are reset to zero, while others are allowed to retain their original values (i.e., one's), according to the algorithm described below. When they reach the last bit slice, exactly one enable signal, $E_{i,w+1}$, remains set; all others are reset to zero. This signal indicates that word i is the largest word in the responder set and can be subsequently retrieved and disabled.

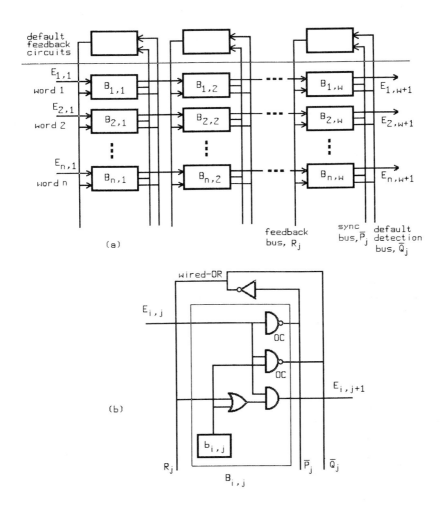

*Figure 12: (a) The organization of memory cells; and
(b) the logic diagram of a bit cell of Ramamoorthy et al.'s MRR*

The operations of a bit cell depend on the states of its residing bit slice. A bit slice can have either one of two states: (1) at least one enabled bit cell contains a one (called the *compete* state); (2) all enabled bit cells contain zero's (called the *default* state). In the compete state, every enabled bit cell containing a one passes its enable signal to the next cell on the right, while cells containing zero's pass zero's to their right neighbour and thus exclude themselves from the responder set. In the default state, all enabled bit cells pass their enable signals to the next bit cells on the right. The retrieval process is detailed in algorithm 5. The loop in step (2) is executed w times. The operations of the jth

bit slice are represented by the jth loop, called the jth *minor cycle*, in which the appropriate enable signals are passed to the $(j+1)^{th}$ bit slice.

1) /* initialize enable signals to 1 */
   for all i **do** $E_{i,1} := 1$;

2) /* for every bit slice do the following */
   for $j = 1$ **to** w **do**
        if $b_{i,j} = 1$ **for some** $1 \leqslant i \leqslant n$ **and** $E_{i,j} = 1$ **then**
             /* compete state */
             for all $1 \leqslant i \leqslant n$ **and** $E_{i,j} = 1$ **do**
                  if $b_{i,j} = 1$ **then**
                       $E_{i,j+1} := E_{i,j}$
                  else
                       $E_{i,j+1} := 0$
   else
             /* default state; all enabled cells are 0's */
             for all $1 \leqslant i \leqslant n$ **do** $E_{i,j+1} := E_{i,j}$;

Algorithm 5. Retrieval operations of Ramamoorthy's method.

When enabled, a bit cell detects the state of its own bit slice by means of the default detection bus Q_j, which is pulled down to zero in a compete state but remains at one in a default state (see figure 12(b)). This signal is fed back to the inputs of the cells through the default feedback circuitry and feedback bus, R_j. The output enable signal, $E_{i,j+1}$, is obtained from the disjunction of R_j and $b_{i,j}$. That is, $E_{i,j+1}$ is set only when the slice is in a default state $(R_j = 1)$, or in a compete state and $b_{i,j}$ is one. The default feedback circuitry of a slice is initially disabled by its *sync* bus signal, P_j. It is released after one of the cells is enabled and Q_j is stabilized.

We can observe that Ramamoorthy et al.'s method and Frei and Goldberg's method are both based on the same principle of binary search in which the responders are represented as a tree and the largest (smallest) responder is obtained by following the rightmost (leftmost) branches of the tree. The responder set (or the subtree at the node being visited) is indicated by the enable signals in Ramamoorthy's design and by the pattern in Frei and Goldberg's design.

There is, however, one major difference between them. In Ramamoorthy et al.'s method, the state of a bit slice is detected by its constituent bit cells. According to the state detected, each bit cell determines *locally*, by setting its output enable signal appropriately, whether the word it constitutes should remain in the responder set. In

Frei and Goldberg's method, the selection process is carried out by the memory controller. When a bit slice contains at least a one, the controller eliminates the words with zero's in that bit slice by putting a one at the corresponding position in the pattern. When a bit slice contains only zero's, the controller replaces the one with zero, thus retaining all responders in the responder set.

Since Ramamoorthy et al.'s design is asynchronous, signals can propagate across bit slices at the highest speed of the underlying logic. Each retrieval requires w minor cycles, or one major cycle.* In terms of gate delays, a minimum of w gate delays and a maximum of $4w$ gate delays are required.

Note also that a pitfall of asynchronous designs is that the propagation delay of even the same type of logic gates is not constant. If the enable signals, $E_{i,j}$'s, do not reach a bit slice at the same time, erroneous results may be produced. The situation becomes worse if the word length is large, since the difference in propagation delays in each cell accumulate. An example is given below to show that Ramamoorthy et al.'s design may function incorrectly under such circumstances. Suppose word 1 = 1110 and word 2 = 1111. If the enable signal of word 1 travels much faster than that of word 2, $B_{1,4}$ is enabled before $B_{2,4}$. Then $B_{1,4}$ will gate to the feedback bus an erroneous value of Q_j, which is one, but would have been zero if $B_{2,4}$ had been enabled on time. As a result, $E_{1,5}$ is set to one, indicating that word 1 is the largest responder. This problem can be avoided by adopting a synchronous design. However, both the best-case and worst-case performance will be $4w$ gate delays, since the clock cycle has to accommodate the worst propagation delay across a cell, namely, 4 gate delays.*

Ramamoorthy et al. had compared their design to other designs. It was concluded that their design was equal to or better than all other designs considered in terms of speed and the number of cycles needed to retrieve a word from memory.** Furthermore, the design was suitable for VLSI implementation, due to the regularity of its bit cells.

Value-ordered retrieval has a number of advantages. First, the speed only depends on the word length of the memory, which is rarely changed. Therefore, increasing the memory size will not affect the

---

* In Ramamoorthy et al.'s design, additional logic was provided to retrieve the largest and smallest responders at the same time, thus reducing the average retrieval time to half a major cycle per retrieval. However, we feel that this technique can be generally applied to other designs as well. For fairness, we still consider its speed as one major cycle per retrieval.

* A synchronous design usually has a longer delay per cell, since additional flip flops or latches must be introduced to synchronize the signals.

** An absolute comparison is not possible since the speed of some designs depends on the memory size.

speed of retrieval. Second, responders can be retrieved in ascending or descending order of their values. Thus, this class of MRRs provides a very attractive way for fast sorting. Third, if the address of each word is stored explicitly as part of the word, or in a separate register associated with each word, address-ordered retrieval is also possible. Finally, the regularity of each cell is preserved. Thus, VLSI implementation of the memory is easier.

In the rest of this section, we describe a MRR which has a number of improvements over Ramamoorthy et al.'s design. In Ramamoorthy et al.'s design, the speed can be further increased by terminating the selection process as soon as the largest responder is identified. There are two situations in which the largest responder can be identified before the enable signal reaches the last bit slice. First, the responder set contains only one responder. On the average, the number of words remaining in the responder set drops exponentially to one as the enable signal propagates through the first few bit slices. Second, if the largest responder includes all the other responders, then the disjunction of the responders will have the same value as the largest responder. This situation can be detected as follows. All memory words output their values onto the default detection bus, and the values are superimposed (wired-OR). After the bus has settled down, the memory words read the bus value and compare it with their own values and, upon a match, identify themselves as the largest responder by interrupting the memory controller. Note that the first situation is just a special case of the second, and thus can be detected in the same way. As soon as one of these situations is recognized, the controller reads the responder's value from the default detection bus. Unfortunately, there is virtually no communication between the bit cells of a word in Ramamoorthy et al.'s design to allow the detection of these situations.

There is yet another possible improvement. In Ramamoorthy et al.'s design, if n responders are to be retrieved, the same retrieval process has to repeat n times, since after a word is eliminated from the selection process, it forgets all history of the selection process it has gone through. Therefore, every retrieval has to start from the same initial state. However, it can be observed that responders dropped out in an early stage of the selection process have a smaller value than those dropped out in a later stage. Specifically, the responders dropped out in the jth minor cycle are larger than those dropped out in the $(j-1)^{th}$ cycle. Therefore, after the largest responder is retrieved in the jth $(1 < j \leqslant w)$ minor cycle, only those dropped out in the $(j-1)^{th}$ minor cycle are re-activated, with their states at which they were dropped out re-installed. The selection process then continues with this smaller set of responders, from a state at which these responders were dropped out (rather than starting from the initial state). In this case, every responder is required to retain its state when it is dropped out until it is re-activated.

Figure 13 shows the organization of memory cells in the improved design. For clarity, the clock signal connected to each cell is not shown.

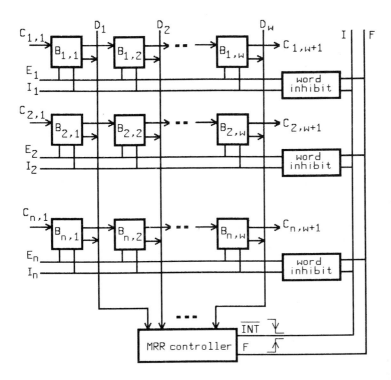

Figure 13: Organization of the memory cells

Every cell is connected to three busses, namely, an *enable* bus, E_i, a *default detection* bus, D_j, and an *interrupt* bus, I_i. One enable bus and one interrupt bus are dedicated to each word, and each bit slice has its own default detection bus. Therefore, there are a total of n enable busses, n interrupt busses, and w default detection busses.

A bus signal is the result of the wired-AND of the corresponding signals of the bit cells connecting to the bus. The enable bus signal indicates that the words with E_i set to one are in the responder set, and thus can continue in the selection process. The default-detection bus has the same functions as that of Ramamoorthy et al.'s design, except that it also serves as the data bus for the memory controller to read a responder from the memory. A memory word interrupts the memory controller, through the interrupt bus, when it knows it is the largest responder in the active responder set. When an interrupt occurs, the (negated) value of the responder is already on the default-detection bus, and thus can be read by the memory controller.

The cells of a word are connected by a serial *control* line, C_i. Initially, all $C_{i,j}$'s are set to one. When the retrieval operation starts, the first column of the control signals, $C_{i,1}$'s, is reset to zero by the controller (details not shown in the diagrams), and then propagates through the bit slices. When the control signal reaches a cell, the cell compares its stored bit value with the value on the default detection bus. A match in a bit cell indicates that the slice is either in a default state or in a compete state, but the cell contains a one. Thus, the cell can pass the control signal to the right. A mismatch in a cell indicates that the slice is in a compete state and that the cell has failed in the competition. The cell then enters an *inactive* state, in which it disables its residing word by pulling down the *enable* bus, but continues monitoring the default detection bus until a match is found. As more and more responders are disabled and removed from the default detection bus, eventually one of the responders will find a match in all its constituent cells. This responder will then interrupt the controller, and subsequently disable itself permanently after being read.

After the largest responder is retrieved, the default detection bus values may change, so that a slice previously in a default state transits to a default state. Thus, the responders disabled when that slice was processed may now be re-activated. The selection process then continues with these reactivated responders (rather than *all* disabled responders) to determine the second largest responder.

To retrieve the first largest responder, the MRR has a speed of 1 clock cycle in the best case, w cycles in the worst case, and $O(log_2 n)$ cycles on the average, where n is the total number of responders.

5. Conclusion

In this paper, we discussed various aspects of the design of a text retrieval machine based on superimposed coding. We emphasized superimposed coding as an indexing technique, because a considerable amount of research has been devoted to it [Robe79, ThTa82, ChFa84] and it has shown that it is very suitable for text retrieval.

After briefly surveying various software approaches to text retrieval, three major components, namely, the signature processor, the text processor, and the multiple response resolver of a TRM were discussed. We first surveyed existing designs for signature processors, then described a new design based on a WPBS organization and compared it with a WSBP design proposed by Ahuja and Roberts 1980. Text processors, originally proposed for full text scanning, were categorized and discussed. Then, ALTEP, a new design with significant improvement on speed as well as pattern matching capability, was outlined. Finally, designs of a multiple response resolver (MRR), an important but often ignored component of associative memories and processors, were discussed. An improved design over existing ones was also presented.

6. References

[AhRo80] [ArGi81] [BeKu79] [BiNT78] [Burk82] [ChFa84] [Chi82] [EpHa80] [FiLo77] [FoKu80] [FrGo61] [Grav78] [HaHo83] [Harr71] [Hask80] [Holl79] [Holl83] [HoUl79] [Hsia80] [KeDe83] [Land77] [Lee84] [Lewi62] [Loch81] [Love77] [Lowe82] [Mall80] [MeBo76] [Mukh79] [Mukh80] [RaTW78] [Robe78] [Robe79] [Salt71] [ScOS76] [Shaw80] [Song80] [ThTa82]

Epilogue

15
Objectworld

D. Tsichritzis

ABSTRACT *An environment is outlined in which programming objects collect and disseminate information, using analogies from the animal world. Objects have their own rules of behaviour. They coordinate their activities by participating in events. Objects get born, move around, communicate and receive information and, finally, die.*

1. Introduction

The purpose of Office Information Systems is hard to define. Offices usually deal with everything which has any significance in an organization. It is easier to define what offices are not. They are not plants producing goods. Any other centre of activity can potentially be called an office. We can also generally accept that offices deal with information. Information is a resource for the organization like money, personnel, etc. It is critical for decision support within the organization. Like other resources, information has to be mobilized in order to achieve certain results, e.g., arriving at a proper decision. We can, therefore, assume that one of the primary goals of offices is the mobilization of information. That is, to concentrate the "right" information at the "right" time at the "right" place, in order to help office workers in their functions. There are two aspects of mobilization, give and take. It follows that, in order to mobilize information, offices should be able to collect and disseminate information effectively. Office Information Systems should therefore provide the appropriate tools for collecting and disseminating information. In this paper we mainly discuss the concepts which, in our opinion, are needed for the implementation of such tools.

One way of viewing the information present in an organization is as part of a global Knowledge Base from which office workers draw the proper subset when they need it. It is implied that when office workers have relevant information they voluntarily introduce it into the Knowledge Base. In this way the Knowledge Base is kept current and it accurately reflects the cummulative knowledge of all the people using it. Such a model of the world is very appropriate when we deal with a relatively closed domain of discourse. It is also helpful if people accessing the Knowledge Base usually draw rather than add information. For example, an expert can create a Knowledge Base by distilling his expertise into facts, data and rules, and encoding it into a Knowledge Base. From then on other experts can draw on this knowledge, occasionally adding to it. We claim that this situation is far removed from what happens in most offices.

There are several difficulties to viewing information in an office environment as being part of one logically integrated Knowledge Base. First, the domain of discourse is not adequately focused, hence it will be difficult to view all knowledge in an Office System within a general and consistent framework. Second, Office Systems are distributed. It will be too much to expect that all persons will voluntarily place their knowledge in one system. Third, the knowledge in the office is continuously updated in a distributed fashion. There is a significant danger that the centralized, integrated Knowledge Base is not kept current of the latest activities and its usefulness will greatly diminish. It is a common practice, for instance, for people to keep their own databases on their personal machines without voluntarily notifying a central database about all their latest changes. Fourth, knowledge in the office is not monolithic. There are many inconsistencies among the Knowledge Bases of different persons, departments, etc. These inconsistencies are not unwelcome since they represent different opinions on common subjects. To integrate all these opinions in one Knowledge Base will be rather difficult. Many contexts will have to be defined which will create problems for inference. It is better to leave them in independent Knowledge Bases and collect them only when there is a need for concensus. If, however, we view the Knowledge Base as consisting of a set of independent yet cooperating Knowledge Bases then there is a need for tools for such cooperation. Probably the most important tool is a *knowledge collector and disseminator*, that is, an object that goes into different Knowledge Bases and obtains and leaves information on a specific topic. This knowledge carrier is fairly independent and able to have an existence of its own. We need, therefore, to view it as an *object* in an object-oriented environment with its own data, rules and behaviour.

We will define a KNOwledge collection and dissemination object (in short *kno*, pronounced *no*) as an object whose main purpose is to carry information around.

As an object, a *kno* consists of:

id: an identifier identifying it uniquely systemwide

r_i: rules, each rule consisting of preconditions and actions

v_i: variables providing storage and data structures for the object.

We do not elaborate on the exact definition of kno's as objects. We can assume without loss of generality that it follows the *Oz* definitions given in the companion paper by O.M. Nierstrasz, or any other reasonable definition of objects [ABBH84]. Kno's as objects have *acquaintances*, i.e., other objects with which they are supposed to coordinate their behaviour. They participate in *events*. When an event occurs all participating objects execute their corresponding rules and change state.

We will now elaborate on how such objects can help achieve the primary goal of Office Information Systems, i.e., the mobilization of information through collection and dissemination. In the scenario we will use analogies from the animal world. We hope to illustrate the points better and more easily in this manner. The reader is, therefore, advised to visualize kno's as funny animals (figure 1) in a funny imaginary world (for example, the world of *OZ*). Worms as in [Brun75, ShHu82] are such animals and we will see that there are others.

2. Kno Environment

Like animals, kno's have to live in a certain environment created by computers, telecommunications and their software systems. To begin, we need a notion of *god*. In conventional systems *god* corresponds to the end user. All actions emanate from him and he absolutely controls his environment. This is not the case in the world of kno's. In order to achieve any degree of automation we prefer that kno's are freed from the bondage of the users. In this way, users are not bothered with detailed control of kno's (being god creates overhead). As far as kno's are concerned the *object manager* is god (figure 2). It controls their actions according to their scripts. In a distributed environment there are many object managers. As in Olympian times having many gods creates trouble. We will assume that a kno is within only one god's jurisdiction at any point in time. Problems between gods are handled by a superior god, i.e., we propose a hierarchy of object managers.

Figure 1: A Kno

The reader may argue that object managers are not gods because people (system programmers) can go around changing them. We have to accept that situation. System programmers are high priests who define god and interpret its actions. However, as far as the kno's are concerned there is only one god, the object manager to which they currently belong.

We will assume that for each user there is a special anthropomorphic kno. It is not god, but it has special capabilities. This user kno (see example in O.M. Nierstrasz's paper) is capable of independent and unpredictable behaviour. It is capable of inspiration. Users interact with other kno's by changing their own special kno using I/O rules.

Kno's interact with other kno's which happen to be their acquaintances and are within the same object manager. In addition, kno's pass

Figure 2: A kno environment and its object manager

from one object manager to another at their own request. Such a request is triggered by events and can be initiated by users through their special kno's.

Kno's, like animals can be *alive* or *dead*. An alive kno is one which can potentially participate in events. A dead kno cannot participate in events and the object manager does not worry about it. Alive kno's are *active* when they participate in an event. Most of the time they are *asleep* waiting for an event. During that time the object manager worries about the event's preconditions and wakes up all the appropriate kno's when the event occurs.

Kno's are born by having the object manager blow life into them. They have to have a proper body which can be created from data structures copied from other kno's. More than one kno can be involved in creating a new kno through a coordination event. We depart here slightly from the animal world by allowing one, two, or more parents for the newborn kno (figure 3). The usual case is for kno's to die and be resurrected intact, or to clone themselves by producing another similar kno.

Kno's die by committing suicide. They participate in an event which makes them go to their terminating condition. They immediately

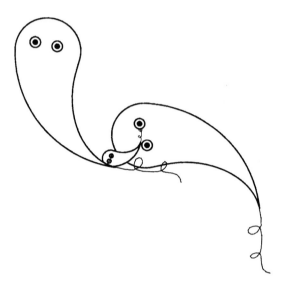

Figure 3: Kno's mating to give life to a new kno

become permanently inactive. Since the killing event can be triggered by another kno we can say that kno's can get killed, or more accurately they can be induced to commit suicide. However, it is important to note that a kno gets killed only because it has an a priori weakness, a tendency to die. It is also killed by an acquaintance which triggers the event, not by any old kno. Kno's can also die from malnutrition, age and natural disasters. Malnutrition corresponds to the absence of events. Kno's can be programmed to become totally inactive (dead) if there are no events in which they participate over a long time. Age corresponds to timer intervals after which the object becomes inactive. Finally, a natural disaster implies that the system and the object manager go beserk and wipe out a kno population. All kno's die because god (the object manager) declares them dead and takes their souls. Any kno can ask to die, but the object manager is the one who decides when.

It is tempting in an object world to avoid the distinction between alive and dead objects. We could treat all objects as sleeping or active but never dead. The implication is that a memory manager underneath deals with their needs. We claim that the issue is more than addressing space. If all objects are alive the object managers will have to worry about them. This will create overhead which may limit the number of objects which we can effectively have. We believe that, especially in office systems, many objects, e.g., letters and memos have a definite lifespan. After a certain time they are literally dead and we should not be bothered with them. Their information content may still be needed but they are inactive until further notice.

Dead kno's are very important because they include the facts which they had when they were alive. We will assume that there are cemeteries of dead kno's, which are called *databases*. If we assume that any input into the system involves a transaction which creates an object, this is a reasonable analogy. Cemeteries of dead kno's, very much like databases, are nicely arranged so that we can stack dead kno's very effectively. For instance, kno's of the same kno class are stripped of their rules when they get buried. The class stores the rules only once. After all, we only need to find dead kno's; we do not need to keep all their acquaintance relationships for firing events. Since everything in the system is an alive or dead kno we can stretch things a little and look at databases not only as cemeteries but as *mother earth*. All kno's end up as part of mother earth and most of them emanate from mother earth.

3. Kno Behaviour

Kno's like animals move, eat, produce and mate. Before we can explain such behaviour, we need to elaborate more on the nature of kno's. We have already indicated that a kno at any point in time is under the juristiction of one object manager. This does not necessarily imply that a kno cannot span more than one object manager. The limitation is that all its parts are ultimately controlled by one object manager. We can think of kno's as having a brain (the master object) and legs (copies of the object). The legs can be with separate object managers, possibly different from the brain's object manager. However, the brain is only in one object manager at any point in time. This type of kno resembles the *i*messages as they appear in J. Hogg's companion paper. A distributed imessage can have many copies but only one master copy. The coordination among the copies is achieved through metamessages between the object managers. A kno can generate legs at will. It can also lose some of its legs without any serious problem. It only becomes inactive if the brain is killed. We also make the restriction that legs cannot generate other legs. Only the brain can generate legs. We can visualize such a kno as an octopus with an unlimited number of legs (figure 4). The legs can be generated or cut off dynamically. We do not allow animals whose legs can be cloned to generate many more legs (the metamessage overhead would probably get very large).

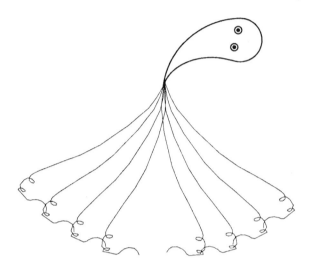

Figure 4: A complex kno

We are ready now to discuss how kno's move. The simplest way they move is by hopping around (figure 5). Consider, for example, a simple kno with one copy (brain, legs and all). The kno can move from object manager to object manager at its request by doing a hop. No trace is left in the previous object manager and the kno is taken over by the next object manager. The kno's complete body moves as a message between them. Such hopping can be *predefined, dynamic*, or *random*. In the predefined case the kno's script has the exact series of locations that a kno has to pass through. In the dynamic case the environment of the object manager in each hop determines the subsequent destination(s). For example, imessages in J. Hogg's paper could be routed dynamically. Finally, in the random case the kno's follow-up destination(s) is determined at random or according to a probability distribution. This case is not as funny as it seems. It can be useful for sampling information in an office environment. A randomly moving kno can also do other useful things like cleaning, reducing populations, etc. This may remind the reader of a commercial swimming pool cleaning device, which is thrown into a pool and moves around randomly eating up dirt. The result is that the swimming pool is continuously being cleaned.

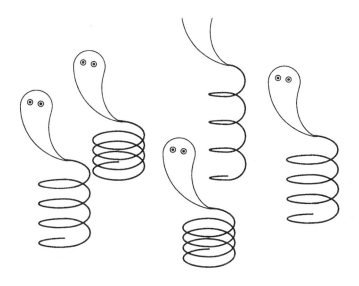

Figure 5: Kno's hopping around

Hopping around can also be visualized for complex kno's. In their case, the legs and/or brain can hop around independently. This type of movement can get very confusing (and it will probably generate much overhead since the brain has to know where the legs are). It is, therefore, better to move the legs and the brain in a much more organized way. A simple solution is to keep the brain static and to move only the legs. This is again the case of the centralized *i*messages in J. Hogg's companion paper. However, when "distances" between the legs and brain become large there is difficulty in providing the necessary coordination between them. We need, therefore, to move the brain. The safest operation is to move the brain to where a leg has already been. In this case the kno has already tried the environment by venturing a leg (which is, after all, dispensable and can grow back). When the leg becomes secure, control can pass over to the leg object, making it the brain. In this way, the kno can crawl all over by venturing out with legs then moving its brain then again venturing out, etc. The order and the rhythm with which the legs and brain move give us many kinds of kno's. For instance, a *worm* type kno has a sequence of legs with the brain somewhere in the middle (figure 6). It moves forward by moving a leg up front, then moving the rest of its legs and its brain, in sequence. The size (number of legs) of the worm and the position of the brain give us many types of worms.

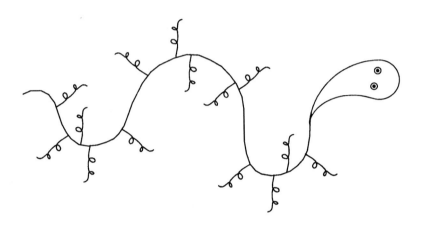

Figure 6: A worm-like kno

A *spider* type of kno has many legs moving independently. The decision about when to move the brain can become complicated, depending on where the legs are and how securely they are fastened (figure 7). We hope that the reader is persuaded that kno's can move around in many complicated ways. One important aspect, therefore, of their definition is their way of moving. Like animals, kno's can be categorized by the way they move.

Another important aspect of kno behaviour is the way in which they eat and produce. We visualize information as the food that kno's eat and also as what they can produce. This information can be both data and rules. Kno's can obtain (eat) information from mother earth (databases) and from other kno's. Since information can be copied, food is not strictly consumable (here is a case of eating your cake and having it too!). Kno's can also produce information which they have assembled during their lifespan while visiting places. Like animals kno's do not eat indiscriminately nor do they produce indiscriminately. They have rules which regulate what they eat, how they will digest it and how they will combine the information they eat in their product. We will call these rules *eating, digestion* and *producing* rules. Eating rules are filters, like database queries, which specify what kind of

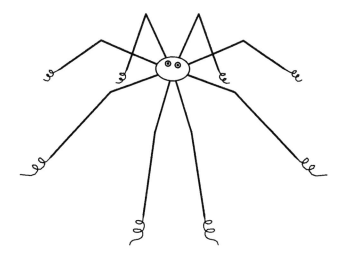

Figure 7: A spider-like kno

information a kno wants to get. Digestion rules take account of what the kno knows in its own variables to break down the information into what it keeps and what it discards. Producing rules indicate how a kno transforms the information into a form ready to be given out. For example, a kno (like an imessage) can ask questions and obtain answers (it eats answers). It then can discard some answers (digestion rules). It keeps and produces only statistics about the answers (producing rules). Such a kno can be sent out on a random walk to poll people's opinions on a subject. Like a cow, what a kno eats (grass) can be very different in format from what it produces (milk). The digestion rules can be arbitrarily complicated (data translation and text manipulation techniques apply here).

Finally, kno's mate (figure 8). Mating corresponds to coordination among objects as acquaintances to fire events and execute their rules together. Mating is under the strict supervision and initiation of the object manager. The case of complex kno's with many legs is interesting. In this case, the coordination can be among legs and/or among brains. It is reasonable to expect that complex objects will first coordinate among their legs and then move to coordinate among their brains. In this way, they can withdraw from the courtship by cutting a leg (no big loss) while preserving the purity of their brains. Complex objects can participate in many coordination activities through their legs (even concurrently), before they decide on the proper coordination for their brain.

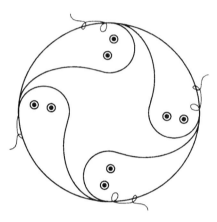

Figure 8: Kno's mating through a coordination event

As a result of coordination, two kno's can start moving together. This mating-turned-into-marriage allows kno's to coordinate moves and actions over the long term. We hope that the reader is persuaded that there are many ways for kno's to mate depending on courtship patterns, mating behaviour and after-the-fact behaviour. It should also be apparent that some very weird kno's can be defined. In the next section, however, we will concentrate on some well behaved species.

4. Kno Species

It will take a very long time to sort out useful from useless or even harmful kno's. We do not expect end users to be able to create nice kno's easily. We would expect that kno's are predefined by experts, and are mainly taken over and used by end-users. Giving people in the office object-oriented programming environments may create more problems than it solves. What people in offices need is useful objects. In the rest of this section we will outline some examples of what we consider to be useful objects. Most of these objects can be readily defined within an object-oriented programming environment.

A useful type of kno is a *carrier* kno (horse, camel). A carrier kno moves around on a prespecified, or dynamic path. It has storage in its variables to store one or more records, documents, etc. It takes information and moves it around intact, without complex digestion and producing rules. Carrier kno's can be used not only to transmit information, e.g., messages, but also to request information. A request is indicated by sending out an empty carrier kno which waits patiently, obtains its load and brings it back to the sender.

Figure 9: A herbivore kno feeding from Mother Earth

Another type of useful kno is a *herbivore* kno (figure 9). Its purpose is to peruse databases and obtain and reduce information from them. It can have arbitrarily complex eating, digestion and producing rules. It can either be static or it can move around. We can keep a herbivore static and feed it data continuously. Alternatively, we can have a free roaming herbivore that is sent out to feed on data and reduce information from it. A kno can also copy information from another kno which it meets through a coordination event. An interesting case is a *parasite kno* which continuously follows another kno, drawing information from it (Figure 10).

Another useful type of kno is a *hunter* kno (figure 11). A hunter kno moves around and assembles other kno's that may have gone astray, e.g., randomly-moving kno's. The hunter kno coordinates with each hunted kno, taking over their path specification and bringing it back to a particular place. In this way we can send out kno's not caring where they go and later on we can collect them. The hunter kno can move on a prespecified path, dynamically, or randomly. It can collect all or a fixed number of hunted kno's.

Figure 10: A parasite kno

Another useful kno is the *killer* kno. Its purpose is population control. It kills certain types of kno's by inducing their suicide when it coordinates with them within a particular object manager. Killer kno's only kill certain types of kno's, and only when they catch them. Killer kno's allow us to issue kno's which never die from old age. At some later time we may decide to kill all or some of these kno's, or thin them out by sending out killer kno's. The killer kno's can themselves be killed or can die. For instance, they can be programmed to die after a certain time (old age), or if they cannot find kno's to kill (malnutrition). Killer kno's can be simple *killers* or *predators.* In the first case they kill and move on. In the second case they feed on the victims by retaining certain information (figure 12). For example, a predator may retain how many, or the id's of the kno's it has killed, for future reference.

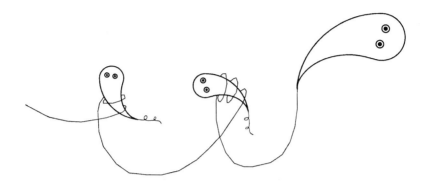

Figure 11: A hunter kno collecting other kno's

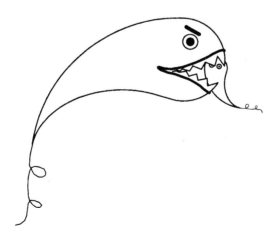

Figure 12: A predator kno eating up another kno

This description may sound like a jungle book. It certainly resembles it. It is a tough world out there for the kno's. It has to be, or they will overburden the systems. We also expect that user's workstations will be farms where only nice, well behaved, kno's are allowed to exist. Crazy kno's may be defined and turned loose on the networks but users can strictly control the kno's coming into their farms. They can keep out harmful kno's. This can be done by issuing guardian kno's which kill all unwelcome kno's on sight. The object manager can also change an incoming kno's behaviour by altering its rules before it takes over the kno. In this way even a weird or ferocious kno can be killed or made docile just before it enters a nice farm of friendly kno's.

Kno farms will be either like family farms or like big commercial farms. The first case is a user workstation where the user has many different useful kno's for local use. A commercial farm corresponds to a large application system where a large population of kno's are bred, fed and sold. A user can get a newborn kno for his farm (predefined object) from a commercial place. He can also get a ready-to-consume kno (database query or other transaction) from a commercial place.

5. Kno Intelligence

In our discussion so far, we have had objects being born, dying, mating, killing, etc. All of these actions were according to the fixed predefined rules of the objects. Objects could change behaviour, but they always had to conform to their scripts. This brings out an important issue, i.e., can objects change their scripts? A kno whose rules can change dynamically is a superior kno capable of "learning". We will discuss in this section such a notion of "learning" and its different manifestations.

A simple way for a kno to change behaviour is through its offspring. The kno gives birth to a new kno with new rules. The parent kno may instantly die which means that the new kno takes its place. This situation is not exactly self "learning". However, it can be fairly powerful. The limitation is that the new kno will have a different id, hence it will not inherit all its parents history and actions. We can anticipate, however, a kno gathering rules in its history, and encoding them as data. It then gives rise to a new "smarter" kno by using the rules (experience) it has accumulated.

A second way for kno's to change behaviour is through their acquaintances. We do not allow a kno to change its own rules, but we allow a kno to export some rules to an acquaintance kno. Since users are represented by special kno's this capability allows users to indirectly change rules in kno's. It allows transfer of "intelligence" between kno's. The users can also inspire kno's to actions different from those with which they have been programmed. Notice, however, that apart from this user inspiration there are no new rules, no new form of "intelligence", no originality.

A third way for kno's to change behaviour is by godly command, i.e., by the intervention of the object manager. So far, the object manager has only coordinated kno events. We could, however, visualize a more sophisticated object manager which fixes kno's, especially when they are overstepping their boundaries. This may sound arbitrary but it is less arbitrary than allowing an object manager, or a user to kill a difficult-to-deal-with kno. The object manager can enforce global constraints in a kno population by arbitrarily refusing to allow their events and actions. It is probably better to tame them by introducing special temporary rules while the objects are within its juristiction. The object manager's intervention is not restricted to negative actions. It can also introduce rules which are helpful to a kno. For example, it can provide local structures of data, endow kno's with access privileges, etc. Finally, the object manager can introduce rules to kno's uniformly or selectively. These additional rules may form the precondition for an object manager to take over an incoming kno.

The fourth way and probably the most intriguing is to allow for kno's to change behaviour by changing their own rules. Since rules are encoded as programs, there is no magic in that; it is simply programs changing other programs. This capability is very powerful, but it is also extremely dangerous. A self-changing kno can do many tricky things. It can masquerade as a benevolent kno while being a malicious kno. It can go absolutely crazy, so that we need to burn the forest and bring the system down to get it under control. It provides, however, the most intriguing examples of kno species. For instance, we can visualize a kno with no fixed rules a priori. It goes around borrowing rules from all over the place. It can grow up into almost anything, including a kno which nobody has ever thought of before. As much as we are intrigued by such potential, we will probably be better off without this capability. Not only because it will be hard to implement, but because it will probably be too dangerous to have around.

Finally, a philosophical note on kno intelligence. Most work on Knowledge Bases and Expert Systems concentrates on inference from a large set of facts, data and rules. This is similar to a guru in the Himalayan Mountains providing deep reasoning on a large but fixed amount of knowledge. Kno's do not provide exactly such intelligence. They do not know too much. Neither do they have complicated inference; but they can travel. They can travel far and wide collecting and giving information. Their intelligence is like Sinbad the sailor's. It comes not from reasoning and inference but from experience through travels. We feel that such intelligence is very useful, especially in an office environment. We leave the deep reasoning to humans, so long as kno's can gather the appropriate knowledge. To end with a pun: kno intelligence is a form of intelligence.

6. Concluding Remarks

A kno environment is not very difficult to prototype but it will be hard to implement well. Some of the issues have already been discussed in the companion papers, "Object Oriented Systems" (O.M. Nierstrasz) and "Intelligent Mail Systems" (J. Hogg).

Simple kno's within one object manager are straightforward objects, e.g., *OZ* objects. We need, however, to expand their capabilities in many significant ways. First, they should be able to issue queries on a database and deal with the replies. Some of the problems of tying programming variables to databases have already been dealt with in other systems, e.g., PASCAL R [Schm77]. The same approach can be followed. Second, we need to expand their rules to manipulate the data they receive (digestion and producing rules). We will inevitably have to deal with data translation and text manipulation issues for reformatting the information [Klug78, AhKW78]. Third, we need to have a birth capability. Most object-oriented systems deal with new objects as instances of a well-known class from which they inherit their rules. To define an arbitrary object or a new class, the user reverts to a complex programming language. We need to provide tools for the definition of new objects. We also need to allow objects to issue a request to the object manager for the creation of a new object. This problem is similar to spawning processes in an Operating System. The main difference is that the new object does not inherit resources from its parent, nor is it tied up for life to its parent. Processes in Operating Systems are strictly structured. Objects float around in the system in an independent fashion. They certainly do not obey their parents, nor do their parents care about them. Objects only inherit properties from their parents.

Killer and hunter objects do not present many problems. Killing is easily done through a coordinating event that fires the victim's rule leading it to termination. For hunter objects we need to develop the notion of a leader object in a group. The implication is that the group moves together to the place where the leader object points. The leader object has the precondition in its rule of deciding where to move. The rest of the group has rules without preconditions which coordinate with the leader object. All this can be done easily if we allow the splicing of a rule in an object by a "superior" object. Such capability is also needed for exporting rules as was discussed in the kno intelligence section. Care should be taken, however, in exporting rules so that we do not end up with conflicting rules. We will have to assume that in the case of a discrepancy either the new or the old rules take precedence.

Complex objects present many more problems. We need to establish communication between object managers. Since the object managers are fairly independent and sometimes live incommunicado, we may have problems. We need to accept that the legs of the complex kno's can live for quite some time without proper direction from the brain. If they are fairly independent and start moving around we may end up with the brain losing track of its own legs! One solution is to restrict the legs to be fairly unsophisticated, e.g., they stay put unless they are told by the brain to move. Another solution is to allow complex kno's to disintegrate and lose their limbs. Finally, we can force object managers to cooperate by supervising their actions through other object managers. There is a complex trade-off here which is influenced by the properties of the communication network connecting the object managers. Clearly, in an environment of many personal computers occasionally talking to each other we can not expect their object managers to cooperate fully and continuously. On the other hand, perhaps this is not the proper environment for the survival of complex kno's.

When complex kno's move around we may need to pass control from the brain to one of the legs. This is different from doing a hopping operation of the brain. We feel that such change of control is smoother and more useful. It brings us back to the notion of a pack of objects with a clear leader. In this case the pack is distributed in different object managers and the leadership may change. We can encode leadership by placing a token among the set of grouped objects which can move around. Notice that a group of objects is different than a set of coordinating objects. Coordination is only temporary, while grouping is longer-range. We still have the problem of cooperation between different object managers. This problem looks similar to cooperation for firing events in a distributed fashion, which we do not allow. It has, however, the important difference that coordination allows interference and competition between objects for firing events. Grouping does not allow objects to be in different and conflicting groups. The cooperation between object managers to keep the group together is therefore minimal.

Finally, if people are going to use kno's we need a nice user model. Our discussion can hopefully point to such a user model. We can illustrate kno behaviour with animation to explain their properties to users. Figures 1 to 12 are sketches which can be useful for visualizing kno's. The reader is asked to use his imagination to fantasize how all this kno behaviour will look in animation. Computers are used for animation. Kno animation can be useful for documentation of object-oriented systems for user interfaces and for tracing kno movements.

In conclusion, we should ask ourselves what the difference is between kno's and known concepts in Computer Science, such as objects, abstract data types, processes, actors, etc. Theoretically there is not much difference. In practice there are two important differences in emphasis. First, kno's are great in number, relatively stupid, and travel around. Second, kno's are not supposed to be a programming language. They are a user's tool, like spreadsheets or Query-By-Example. Everything we can do with kno's can be done in a programming environment. This is immaterial. Everything we can do with spreadsheets can be done within a programming language. Try, though, to substitute for a user MULTIPLAN or Lotus 1-2-3 with FORTRAN.

7. References

[ABBH84] [AhKW78] [Brun75] [Klug78] [Schm77] [ShHu82]

References

[ABBH84]   M. Ahlsen, A. Bjornerstedt, S. Britts, C. Hulten and L. Soderlund, "An Architecture for Object Management in OIS", *ACM Transactions on Office Information Systems*, 2(3), pp. 173-196, July 1984.

[Abri74]   J.R. Abrial, "Data Semantics", in *Data Base Management*, ed. J.W. Klimbi and K.L. Koffeman, North-Holland, Amsterdam, 1974.

[ACM80]   ACM, *Proceedings of the Workshop on Data Abstraction, Databases and Conceptual Modelling*, ed. M. Brodie and S. Zilles, June 1980.

[AdNg84]   M. Adiba and G. Nguyen, "Information Processing for CAD/VLSI on a Generalized Data Management System", *Proceedings of the Tenth International Conference on Very Large Data Bases*, Singapore, August 1984.

[AhCo75]   A.V. Aho and M.J. Corasick, "Fast Pattern Matching: An Aid to Bibliographic Search", *Communications of the ACM*, 18(6), pp. 333-340, June 1975.

[AhHU74]   A.V. Aho, J.E. Hopcroft and J.D. Ullman, *The Design and Analysis of Computer Algorithms*, Addison Wesley, 1974.

[AhKW78]   A.V. Aho, B. Kernighan and P. Weinberger, "Awk - A Pattern Scanning and Processing Language", *Report, Bell Telephone Laboratories*, September 1978.

[AhRo80]   S.R. Ahuja and C.S. Roberts, "An Associative/Parallel Processor for Partial Match Retrieval Using Superimposed Codes", *Proceedings of the Seventh Annual Symposium on Computer Architecture*, pp. 218-227, May 1980.

[AhUl72]   A.V. Aho and J.D. Ullman, *The Theory of Parsing, Translation and Compiling*, Prentice Hall, 1972.

[AhUl79]   A.V. Aho and J.D. Ullman, "Optimal Partial Match Retrieval when Fields are Independently Specified", *ACM TODS*, 4(2), pp. 168-179, June 1979.

[AlCO83]   A. Albano, L. Cardelli and R. Orsini, *Galileo: A Strongly Typed, Interactive, Conceptual Language*, CSRG Technical

Note #30, University of Toronto, 1983.

[AlOr83]   A. Albano and R. Orsini, "Dialogo: An Interactive Environment for Conceptual Design in Galileo", in *Methodology and Tools for Database Design*, ed. S. Ceri, North-Holland, 1983. To appear.

[Andr84]   H.L. Andrews, "Speech Processing", *IEEE Computer*, pp. 315-324, October 1984.

[AnFW83]   R.C. Angell, G.E. Freund and P. Willet, "Automatic Spelling Correction Using a Trigram Similarity Measure", *Information Processing and Management*, 19(4), pp. 255-261, 1983.

[ArGi81]   B.W. Arden and R. Ginosar, "A Single-Relation Module for a Database Machine", *Proceedings of the Eighth Annual Symposium on Computer Architecture*, pp. 227-237, May 1981.

[Astr76]   M.M. Astrahan, *et al.*, "System R: Relational Approach to Database Management", *ACM TODS*, 1(2), pp. 97-137, June 1976.

[AtBS79]   G. Attardi, G. Barber and M. Simi, "Towards an Integrated Office Work Station", AI Laboratory, MIT, Cambridge, 1979.

[BaBr82]   D. Ballard and C. Brown, *Computer Vision*, Prentice Hall, 1982.

[BaMc72]   R. Bayer and E. McCreight, "Organization and Maintenance of Large Ordered Indexes", *Acta Informatica*, 1(3), pp. 173-189, 1972.

[BAMT84]   J.F. Bucy, W.W. Anderson, M.L. McMahan, R.T. Tarrant and H.R. Tennant, "Ease of Use Features in the Texas Instruments Professional Computer", *Proceedings of the IEEE*, Special Issue on Personal Computers, 72(3), March 1984.

[BeGo82]   P.A. Bernstein and N. Goodman, "A Sophisticate's Introduction to Distributed Concurrency Control", *Proceedings of the Eighth International Conference on Very Large Data Bases*, pp. 62-76, 1982.

[BeKu79]   J.L. Bentley and H.T. Kung, "A Tree Machine for Searching Problem", *Proceedings of the International Conference on Parallel Processing*, pp. 257-266, 1979.

[Bent75]   J.L. Bentley, "Multidimensional Binary Search Trees Used for Associative Searching", *Communications of the ACM*, 18(9), pp. 509-517, September 1975.

[BFHL83]   W.A.S. Buxton, E. Fiume, R. Hill, A. Lee and C. Woo, "Continuous Hand-Gesture Driven Input", *Proceedings of Graphics Interface '83*, Edmonton, Alberta, May 1983.

[BiNT78]   R.M. Bird, J.B. Newsbaum and J.L. Trefftzs, "Text File Inversion: An Evaluation", *Proceedings of the Fourth Workshop on Computer Architecture for Non-Numeric Processing*, pp. 42-50, August 1978.

[BLNS82]   A.D. Birrell, R. Levin, R.M. Needham and M.D. Schroeder, "Grapevine: An Exercise in Distributed Computing", *Communications of the ACM*, 25(4), pp. 260-274, April 1982.

[Bloo70]   B.H. Bloom, "Space/Time Trade-offs in Hash Coding with Allowable Errors", *Communications of the ACM*, 13(7), pp. 422-426, July 1970.

[Bolt80]   R.A. Bolt, "'Put-that-there': Voice and Gestures at the Graphics Interface", *Proceedings Sigraph '80*, 14(3), pp. 262-270, July 1980.

[BoMo77]   R.S. Boyer and J.S. Moore, "A Fast String Searching Algorithm", *Communications of the ACM*, 20(10), pp. 762-772, October 1977.

[BoMu76]   J.A. Bondy and U.S.R. Murty, *Graph Theory with Applications*, North Holland, New York, 1976.

[Bour63]   C.P. Bourne, *Methods of Information Handling*, Wiley, New York 1963.

[BoWi77]   D.G. Bobrow and T. Winograd, "An Overview of KRL, a Knowledge Representation Language", *Cognitive Science*, 1(1), pp. 3-46, 1977.

[Brod78]   M.L. Brodie, *Specification and Verification of Data Base Semantic Integrity*, Ph.D. dissertation, Department of Computer Science, University of Toronto, 1978.

[Brod80]   M.L. Brodie, "Data Abstraction, Databases and Conceptual Modelling", *Proceedings of the Sixth International Conference on Very Large Data Bases*, pp. 105-108, 1980.

[Brod81]   M.L. Brodie, "On Modelling Behavioural Semantics of Databases", *Proceedings of the Seventh International Conference on Very Large Data Bases*, pp. 32-42, 1981.

[Brot83]   D.K. Brotz, "Message System Mores: Etiquette in Laurel", *ACM Transactions on Office Information Systems*, 1(2), pp. 179-192, 1983.

[BrPe83]   G. Bracchi and B. Pernici, "SOS: A Conceptual Model for Office Information Systems", *Proceedings of the ACM SIGMOD Conference*, pp. 108-116, 1983.

[BrPe84]   G. Bracchi and B. Pernici, "Design Requirements of Office Systems", *ACM Transactions on Office Information Systems*, 2(2), pp. 151-170, 1984.

[Brun75]   J. Brunner, *The Shockwave rider*, Ballantine, New York, 1975.

[BSdJ82]   R.J. Byrd, S.E. Smith and P. deJong, "An Actor-Based Programming System", *SIGOA Conference on Office Information Systems, SIGOA Newsletter*, 3(1,2), 1982.

[BuHR84]   W.A.S. Buxton, R. Hill and P. Rowley, "Issues and Techniques in Touch-Sensitive Tablet Input", 1984. Working paper.

[Burk82]   F.J. Burkowski, "A Hardware Hashing Scheme in the Design of a Multiterm String Comparator", *IEEE Transactions on Computers*, C-31(9), pp. 825-834, September 1982.

[BuSn80]   W.A.S. Buxton and R. Sniderman, "Iteration in the Design of the Human-Computer Interface", *Proceedings of the Thirteenth Annual Meeting of the Human Factors Association of Canada*, pp. 72-81, 1980.

[Buxt83]   W.A.S. Buxton, "Lexical and Pragmatic Considerations of Input Structures", *Computer Graphics*, 17(1), January 1983.

[BySD82]   R. Byrd, S. Smith and P. de Jong, "An Actor-Based Programming System", *Proceedings of the First ACM SIGOA Conference*, pp. 67-78, 1982.

[BYTE81]   Special issue on "Smalltalk", *Byte*, 6(8), August 1981.

[Cann83]   R.G. Canning, "Is VOICE in Your Future Systems?", EDP Analyzer, Canning Publications Inc., 21(8), August 1983.

[CCIT83]   CCITT/SG/VIII Working Party 4, "Document Interchange Protocol for Telematic Services", Third draft, October 1983.

[Chen76]   P.P.S. Chen, "The Entity-Relationship Model: Toward a Unified View of Data", *ACM TODS*, 1(1), pp. 9-36, March 1976.

[Cheu79]   C. Cheung, *OFS: A Distributed Office Form System with a Micro Relational System*, M.Sc. thesis, Department of Computer Science, University of Toronto, 1979.

[ChFa84]   S. Christodoulakis and C. Faloutsos, "Design Considerations for a Message File Server", *IEEE Transactions on Software Engineering*, SE-10(2), pp. 201-210, March 1984.

[Chi82]   C.S. Chi, "Advances in Computer Mass Storage Technology", *IEEE Computer*, 15(5), pp. 60-74, May 1982.

[Chri83]   S. Christodoulakis, "Access Files for Batching Queries in Large Information Systems", *Proceedings ICOD II*, August 1983.

[Chri84a]   S. Christodoulakis, "Implications of Certain Assumptions in Data Base Performance Evaluation", *ACM TODS*, June 1984.

[Chri84b]   S. Christodoulakis, "Framework for the Development of a Mixed-Mode Message System", *Proceedings of the ACM-BCS Symposium on Research and Development in Information Retrieval*, Cambridge, England, 1984.

[CODA71]   CODASYL, CODASYL Data Base Task Group Report, *Conference on Data Systems Languages*, 1971.

[Codd70]   E.F. Codd, "A Relational Model for Large Shared Data Banks", *Communications of the ACM*, 13(6), pp. 377-387, June 1970.

[Codd71]   E.F. Codd, "Further Normalization of the Database Relational Model", in *Database Systems, Courant Computer Science Symposia 6*, ed. R. Rustin, Prentice-Hall, Englewood Cliffs, N.J., pp. 33-64, 1971.

[Codd79]   E.F. Codd, "Extending the Database Relational Model", *ACM TODS*, 4(4), pp. 397-434, December 1979.

[Come79]   D. Comer, "The Ubiquitous B-Tree", *ACM Computing Surveys*, 11(2), pp. 121-137, June 1979.

[Coop70]   W.S. Cooper, "On Deriving Design Equations for Information Retrieval Systems", *JASIS*, November-December 1970.

[Coul76]   G. Coulouris *et al.*, "The Design and Implementation of an Interactive Document Editor", *Software Practice and Experience*, 6(2), April 1976.

[CrCZ83]   J.B. Crampes, C. Chrisment and Y. Zurfluh, "The BIG Project", *Proceedings of the Second International Conference on Databases*, Cambridge, England, September 1983.

[Crof83]   W.B. Croft, "Applications of Information Retrieval Techniques for the Office", *Proceedings of the Sixth ACM SIGIR Conference on Research and Development in Information Retrieval*, pp. 18-23, 1983.

[CVLL84]   S. Christodoulakis, J. Vandenbroek, J. Li, T. Li, S. Wan, Y. Wang, M. Papa and E. Bertino, "Development of a Multimedia Information System for an Office Environment", *Proceedings of the Tenth International Conference on*

Very Large Data Bases, Singapore, August 1984.

[Datt79]   R. Dattola, "FIRST: Flexible Information Retrieval System for Text", *JASIS*, 30, pp. 9-14, January 1979.

[deBy80]   P. de Jong and R.J. Byrd, "Intelligent Forms Creation in the System for Business Automation", *IBM Research Report*, RC #8529, 1980.

[deJo80]   P. de Jong, "The System for Business Automation: A Unified Application Development System", *Proceedings of IFIP Congress 80*, pp. 469-474, Tokyo, 1980.

[deZl77]   P. de Jong and M. Zloof, "The System for Business Automation (SBA): Programming Language", *Communications of the ACM*, 20(6), pp. 385-396, June 1977.

[DKLM83]   V. Domzeau-Gouge, G. Kahn, B. Lang, B. Melese and E. Marcos, "Outline of a Tool for Document Manipulation", *Proceedings IFIP-83*, General Conference, Paris, 1983.

[DuHa73]   R.O. Duda and P.E. Hart, *Pattern Classification and Scene Analysis*, Wiley, 1973.

[EcLo83]   P. Economopoulos and F.H. Lochovsky, "A System for Managing Image Data", *Proceedings of the Ninth IFIP Congress*, pp. 89-94, 1983.

[ECMA83]   ECMA, "Office Document Architecture", Fourth Working Draft, TC 29/83/56.

[Econ82]   P. Economopoulos, *An Image Database Management System*, M.Sc. Thesis, Department of Computer Science, University of Toronto, 1982.

[EGLT76]   K.P. Eswaran, J.N. Gray, R.A. Lorie and I.L. Traiger, "The Notions of Consistency and Predicate Locks in a Database System", *Communications of the ACM*, 19(11), November 1976.

[EHLR80]   L.D. Erman, F. Hays-Roth, V.R. Lesser and D.R. Reddy, "The Hearsay II Speech-Understanding System: Integrating Knowledge to Resolve Uncertainty", *ACM Computing Surveys*, 12(2), June 1980.

[ElBe82]   C. Ellis and M. Bernal, "OfficeTalk-D: An Experimental Office Information System", *Proceedings First ACM SIGOA Conference*, Philadelphia, pp. 131-140, June 1982.

[Elec83]   "Special Report on Voice Systems", Electronics, pp. 126-143, April 1983.

[ElNu80]   C. Ellis and G. Nutt, "Computer Science and Office Information Systems", *ACM Computing Surveys*, 12(1), pp. 27-60, March 1980.

[EpHa80]   R. Epstein and P. Hawthorn, "Design Decisions for the Intelligent Database Machine", *Proceedings of the National Computer Conference*, 49, pp. 237-241, 1980.

[FaCh84]   C. Faloutsos and S. Christodoulakis, "Signature Files: An Access Method for Documents and its Analytical Performance Evaluation", *ACM Transactions on Office Information Systems*, 1984. To appear.

[Falo82]   C. Faloutsos, *Extending a DBMS to Handle Text*, M.Sc. Thesis, Department of Computer Science, University of Toronto, 1982.

[Falo85]   C. Faloutsos, "Signature Files: Design and Performance Comparison of some Signature Extraction Methods", *ACM-SIGMOD*, 1985. submitted for publication.

[FeND81]   S. Feiner, S. Nagy and A. van Dam, "An Integrated System for Creating and Presenting Complex Computer-Based Documents", *Computer Graphics*, 15(3), August 1981.

[Ferr82]   J.C. Ferrans, "SEDL - A Language for Specifying Integrity Constraints on Office Forms", *Proceedings of the First ACM SIGOA Conference*, pp. 123-130, 1982.

[FiHu69]   J.R. Files and H.D. Huskey, "An Information Retrieval System Based on Superimposed Coding", *Proceedings AFIPS FJCC*, 35, pp. 423-432, 1969.

[Fike81]   R.E. Fikes, "Odyssey: A Knowledge-Based Personal Assistant", *Artificial Intelligence*, 16(3), pp. 331-361, July 1981.

[FiLo77]   C.A. Finnila and H.H. Love, "The Associative Linear Array Processor", *IEEE Transactions on Computers*, C-26(2), pp. 112-125, February 1977.

[FlUl80]   Floyd and Ullman, "The Compilation of Regular Expressions into Integrated Circuits", *Proceedings of the Twenty-first Symposium on Foundations of Computer Science*, October 1980.

[FNPS79]   R. Fagin, J. Nievergelt, N. Pippenger and H.R. Strong, "Extendible Hashing - A Fast Access Method for Dynamic Files", *ACM TODS*, 4(3), pp. 315-344, September 1979.

[FoKu80]   M.J. Foster and H.T. Kung, "The Design of Special-Purpose VLSI Chips", *IEEE Computer*, 13(1), pp. 26-40, January 1980.

[Fong83]   A.C. Fong, "A Model for Automatic Form-Processing Procedures", *Proceedings of the Sixteenth Annual Hawaii International Conference on System Sciences*, pp. 558-565, 1983.

[FoVa82]   J.D. Foley and A. Van Dam, *Fundamentals of Interactive Computer Graphics*, The Systems Programming Series, Addison Wesley Publishing Company, 1982.

[FoWC81]   J.D. Foley, V.L. Wallace and P. Chan, "The Human Factors of Graphic Interaction - Task and Techniques", *The George Washington University Report GWU-IIST-81-3*, January 1981.

[Fox84]   E.A. Fox, "Extended Information Retrieval with Data and Text", *PODS*, 1984. submitted for publication

[Fras80]   C.W. Fraser, "A Generalized Text Editor", *Communications of the ACM*, 23(3), pp. 154-158, March 1980.

[Fras81]   C.W. Fraser, "Syntax-Directed Editing of General Data Structures", *Proceedings of the ACM Symposium on Text Manipulation*, pp. 17-21, June 1981.

[Free83]   D.H. Freedman, "OCR Moves Into Office Automation", *Mini-Micro Systems*, pp. 211-219, May 1983.

[FrGo61]   E.H. Frei and J. Goldberg, "A Method for Resolving Multiple Responses in a Parallel Search File", *IEEE Transactions on Computers*, EC-10(4), pp. 718-722, December 1961.

[Fuji84]   L. Fujitani, "Laser Optical Disk: The Coming Revolution in On-Line Storage", *Communications of the ACM*, 27(6), pp. 546-554, June 1984.

[FuSS79]   A.L. Furtado, K.C. Sevcik and C.S. Dos Santos, "Permitting Updates Through Views of Data Bases", *Information Systems*, 4, Pergamon Press Ltd., pp. 269-283, 1979.

✓ [FuSS82]   Richard Furuta, Jeffrey Scofield and Alan Shaw, "Document Formatting Systems: Survey, Concepts and Issues", *ACM Computing Surveys*, 14(3), pp. 417-472, September 1982.

[GaKu81]   J.J. Garcia-Luna-Aceves and F.F. Kuo, "Addressing and Directory Systems for Large Computer Mail Systems", *Computer Message Systems, Proceedings of International Symposium on Computer Message Systems*, IFIP TC-6, Ottawa, April 1981, ed. R.P. Uhlig, North Holland Publishing Co, pp. 297-313, 1982.

[GaVa75]   R.G. Gallager and D.C. Van Voorhis, "Optimal Source Codes for Geometrically Distributed Integer Alphabets", *IEEE Transactions on Information Theory*, IT-21, pp. 228-230, March 1975.

[Geha82]   N. Gehani, "The Potential of Forms in Office Automation", *IEEE Transactions on Communications*, Com-30(1), pp. 120-125, January 1982.

[GeMS77]   C.M. Geschke, J.H. Morris Jr. and E.H. Satterthwaite, "Early Experience with Mesa", *Communications of the ACM*, 20(8), pp. 540-553, August 1977.

[Gibb79]   S.J. Gibbs, *OFS: An Office Form System for a Network Architecture*, M.Sc. Thesis, Department of Computer Science, University of Toronto, 1979.

√ [Gibb84]   S.J. Gibbs, "An Object-Oriented Office Data Model", CSRG Technical Report 154, University of Toronto, 1984.

[GIIT83]   Graphical Input Interaction Technique Workshop Summary, *Computer Graphics*, 17(1), January 1983.

[GiTs83]   S.J. Gibbs and D.C. Tsichritzis, "A Data Modelling Approach for Office Information Systems", *ACM Transactions on Office Information Systems*, 1(3), pp. 299-319, 1983.

[GoBo80a]   I.P. Goldstein and D.G. Bobrow, "Descriptions for a Programming Environment", *Proceedings of the First Annual Conference of the National Association for Artificial Intelligence*, August 1980.

[GoBo80b]   I.P. Goldstein and D.G. Bobrow, "Extending Object-Oriented Programming in Smalltalk", *Proceedings of the Lisp Conference*, August 1980.

[Gold84]   A. Goldberg, *Smalltalk 80: the Interactive Programming Environment*, Addison-Wesley, 1984.

[Golo66]   S.W. Golomb, "Run Length Encodings", *IEEE Transactions on Information Theory*, IT-12, pp. 399-401, July 1966.

[Gonn82]   G.H. Gonnet, "Unstructured Data Bases", Technical Report CS-82-09, University of Waterloo, 1982.

[Good81a]   M. Good, "Etude and the Folklore of User Interface Design", *Proceedings of the ACM SIGPLAN SIGOA Symposium on Text Manipulation*, Portland, Oregon, June 8-10, 1981.

[Good81b]   M. Good, *An Ease of Use Evaluation of an Integrated Editor and Formatter*, M.Sc. thesis, Technical Report TR-266, MIT Laboratory for Computer Science, November 1981.

[GoRo77]   I.P. Goldstein and R.B. Roberts, "NUDGE, a Knowledge-Based Scheduling Program", *Proceedings Fifth International Joint Conference on Artificial Intelligence*, pp. 257-263, 1977.

[GoRo83]   A. Goldberg and D. Robson, *Smalltalk 80: the Language and its Implementation*, Addison-Wesley, May 1983.

[GoWi77]   R. Gonzalez and P. Wintz, *Digital Image Processing*, Addison-Wesley, 1977.

[Grav78]   C.M. Gravina, "National Westminster Bank Mass Storage Archiving", *IBM System Journal*, 17(4), pp. 344-358, 1978.

[Gray81]   J. Gray, "The Transaction Concept: Virtues and Limitations", *Proceedings of the Seventh International Conference on Very Large Data Bases*, pp. 144-154, 1981.

[GrMy83]   S.J. Greenspan and J. Mylopoulos, "A Knowledge Representation Approach to Software Engineering: The Taxis Project", *Proceedings of the Conference of the Canadian Information Processing Society*, pp. 163-174, May 1983.

[Guib82]   L.J. Guibas and J. Stolfi, "A Language for Bitmap Manipulation", *ACM Transactions Graphics*, 1(3), pp. 191-214, July 1982.

[Gust71]   R.A. Gustafson, "Elements of the Randomized Combinatorial File Structure", *ACM SIGIR, Proceedings of the Symposium on Information Storage and Retrieval*, pp. 163-174, April 1971.

[GuSt82]   A. Guttman and M.. Stonebraker, "Using a Relational Database Management System for Computer Aided Design Data", *Bulletin of the IEEE Computing Society, Technology of Communications and Database Engineering*, 5(2), pp. 21-28, June 1982.

[Gutt77]   J. Guttag, "Abstract Data Types and the Development of Data Structures", *Communications of the ACM*, 20(6), pp. 396-404, June 1977.

[HaHo83]   R.L. Haskin and L.A. Hollaar, "Operational Characteristics of a Hardware-Based Pattern Matcher", *ACM TODS*, 8(1), pp. 15-40, March 1983.

[HaKS83]   M. Hammer, J.S. Kunin and S. Schoichet, "What Makes a Good User Interface?", *Proceedings AFIPS Office Automation Conference*, Philadelphia, Pennsylvania, February 21-23, 1983.

[HaKu80]   M. Hammer and J.S. Kunin, "Design Principles of an Office Specification Language", *Proceedings of the NCC*, pp. 541-547, 1980.

[HaLo82]   R.L. Haskin and R.A. Lorie, "On Extending the Functions of a Relational Database System", *Proceedings of the ACM SIGMOD Conference*, pp. 207-212, 1982.

[HaMc75]   M. Hammer and D. McLeod, "Semantic Integrity in a Relational Database System", *Proceedings of the First International Conference on Very Large Data Bases*, pp. 25-47,

1975.

[HaMc78]   M. Hammer and D. McLeod, "The Semantic Data Model: A Modelling Mechanism for Database Applications", *Proceedings of the ACM SIGMOD Conference*, pp. 26-36, 1978.

[HaMc81]   M. Hammer and D. McLeod, "Database Description with SDM: A Semantic Database Model", *ACM TODS*, 6(3), pp. 351-386, September 1981.

[HaMo82]   F. Halasz and P. Moran, "Analogy Considered Harmful", *Proceedings, Human Factors in Computer Systems*, Gaithersburg, Maryland, March 15-17, 1982.

[Harr71]   M.C. Harrison, "Implementation of the Substring Test by Hashing", *Communications of the ACM*, 14(12), pp. 777-779, December 1971.

[HaSi80]   M. Hammer and M. Sirbu, "What is Office Automation?", *Office Automation Conference*, Georgia, pp. 37-49, 1980.

[Hask80]   R.L. Haskin, "Hardware for Searching Very Large Text Databases", *Proceedings of the Fifth Workshop on Computer Architecture for Non-numeric Processing*, pp. 49-56, March 1980.

[Hask81]   R.L. Haskin, "Special Purpose Processors for Text Retrieval", *Database Engineering*, 4(1), pp. 16-29, September 1981.

[HeBS73]   C. Hewitt, P. Bishop and R. Steiger, "A Universal Modular ACTOR Formalism for Artificial Intelligence", *Proceedings of the Third International Joint Conference on Artificial Intelligence*, pp. 235-245, August 1973.

[HePa79]   Hewlett-Packard, "HP 3000 Computer System VIEW/3000 Reference Manual", 32209-90001, Hewlett-Packard, 1979.

[Hewi72]   C. Hewitt, "Description and Theoretical Analysis (Using Schemata), of PLANNER: A Language for Proving Theorems and Manipulating Models in a Robot", *MIT AI Laboratory*, AI-TR-258, 1972.

[Hewi77]   C. Hewitt, "Viewing Control Structures as Patterns of Passing Messages", *Artificial Intelligence*, 8(3), pp. 323-364, June 1977.

[HGLS78]   R. Holt, G. Graham, E. Lazowska and M. Scott, *Structured Concurrent Programming with Operating Systems Applications*, Addison-Wesley, Reading, U.S.A., 1978.

[HHKW77]   M. Hammer, W.G. Howe, V.J. Kruskal and I. Wladawsky, "A Very High Level Programming Language for Data Processing Applications", *Communications of the ACM*,

20(11), pp. 832-840, November 1977.

[HIAG81]   M. Hammer, R. Ilson, T. Anderson, E. Gilbert, M. Good, B. Niamir, L. Rosenstein and S. Schoichet, "The Implementation of Etude, an Integrated and Interactive Document Production System", *Proceedings of the ACM SIGPLAN SIGOA Symposium on Text Manipulation*, Portland, Oregon, June 8-10, 1981.

[Hill85]   R. Hill, "Using Production Systems to Specify Multi-Threaded Dialogues in User Interface Development Systems", Research Proposal, 1985.

[HMGT83]   J. Hogg, M. Mazer, S. Gamvroulas and D.C. Tsichritzis, "Imail - An Intelligent Mail System", *IEEE Database Engineering*, 6(3), September 1983.

[HoGa84]   J. Hogg and S. Gamvroulas, "An Active Mail System", *SIGMOD '84 Proceedings, SIGMOD Record*, 14(2), June 1984.

[Hogg81]   J. Hogg, *TLA: A System for Automating Form Procedures*, M.Sc. thesis, Department of Computer Science, University of Toronto, 1981.

[HoKr84]   W. Horak and G. Kroenert, "An Object-Oriented Office Document Architecture Model for Processing and Interchange of Documents", *Proceedings of the Second ACM-SIGOA Conference*, Toronto, June 1984.

[Holl78]   L.A. Hollaar, "Specialized Merge Processor Networks for Combining Sorted Lists", *ACM TODS*, 3(3), pp. 272-284, September 1978.

[Holl79]   L.A. Hollaar, "Text Retrieval Computers", *IEEE Computer*, 12(3), pp. 40-50, March 1979.

[Holl83]   L.A. Hollaar, "Architecture and Operation of a Large, Full-Text Information-Retrieval System", in *Advanced Database Machine Architecture*, ed. D.K. Hsiao, Prentice-Hall, Englewood Cliffs, New Jersey, pp. 256-299, 1983.

[HoNT81]   J. Hogg, O.M. Nierstrasz and D.C. Tsichritzis, "Form Procedures", in *Omega Alpha*, ed. D.C. Tsichritzis, CSRG Technical Report 127, University of Toronto, pp. 101-133, March 1981.

[HoPa74]   S. Horowitz and T. Pavlidis, "Picture Segmentation by a Directed Split-and-Merge Procedure", *Proceedings of the Second International Joint Conference on Pattern Recognition*, pp. 424-433, August 1974.

[Hort81]   M. Horton, "How to Read the Network News", Bell Labs, Columbus, Ohio 1981.

[HoSa76]   E. Horowitz and S. Sahni, *Fundamentals of Data Structures*, Computer Science Press, 1976.

[HoUl79]   J.E. Hopcroft and J.D. Ullman, *Introduction to Automata Theory, Languages, and Computation*, Addison Wesley, 1979.

[HSCE83]   L.A. Hollaar, K.F. Smith, W.H. Chow, P.A. Emrath and R.L. Haskin, "Architecture and Operation of a Large, Full-Text Information-Retrieval System", in *Advanced Database Machine Architecture*, ed. D.K. Hsiao, Prentice-Hall, Englewood Cliffs, New Jersey, pp. 256-299, 1983.

[Hsia80]   D.K. Hsiao, "Data Base Computers", in *Advances in Computers*, Volume 19, ed. C.Y. Marshall, Academic Press, New York, pp. 1-64, 1980.

[Hudy78]   R. Hudyma, *Architecture of Microcomputer Distributed Database Systems*, M.Sc. thesis, Department of Computer Science, University of Toronto, 1978.

[IBM79]   *STAIRS/VS: Reference Manual*, IBM System Manual, 1979.

[Inga78]   D. Ingalls, "The Smalltalk-76 Programming System: Design and Implementation", *Conference Proceedings of the Fifth Annual ACM Symposium on Principles of Programming Languages*, pp. 9-16, January 1978.

[Inst82]   Education and Information Systems Inc., *Operating Manual for the Instavox RA-12 Rapid Access Audio Unit*, Education and Information Systems Inc., Champaign, Illinois, 1982.

[ISO-83a]   ISO TC 97/SC 18/WG 3N 292, "General Introduction".

[ISO-83b]   ISO TC 97/SC 18/WG 3N283, "Office Document Architecture", Fifth working draft.

[John75]   S.C. Johnson, *Yacc: Yet Another Compiler Compiler*, Computer Science Technical Report No. 32, Bell Laboratories, Murray Hill, NJ, USA, 1975.

[JoTo84]   J.H. Johnson and F.W. Tompa, "Approximate String Matching in Query Languages", *PODS*, 1984. submitted for publication.

[Joy80]   W. Joy, "An Introduction to the C Shell", *UNIX Programmer's Manual*, Volume 2c, Department of Electrical Engineering and Computer Science, University of California, Berkeley, USA, 1980.

[KaMi69]   R.M. Karp and R. Miller, "Parallel Program Schemata", *Journal of Computer and Systems Science 3*, pp. 167-195, May 1969.

[KaSi64]   W.H. Kautz and R.C. Singleton, "Nonrandom Binary Superimposed Codes", *IEEE Transactions on Information Theory*, IT-10, pp. 363-377, October 1964.

[KCBC75]   J. Kulick, T. Challis, C. Brace, S. Christodoulakis, I. Merrit and P. Neelands, "An Image Processing Laboratory for Automated Screening of Chest X-rays", *Proceedings of the Third IEEE International Conference on Pattern Recognition*, November 1975.

[KeDe83]   J.P. Kearns and S. DeFazio, "Locality of Reference in Hierarchical Database Systems", *IEEE Transactions on Software Engineering*, SE-9(2), pp. 128-134, March 1983.

[KeKT76]   L. Kershberg, A. Klug and D.C. Tsichritzis, "A Taxonomy of Data Models", *Proceedings of the Second International Conference on Very Large Data Bases*, pp. 43-64, 1976.

[Kent79]   W. Kent, "Limitations of Record-Based Information Models", *ACM TODS*, 4(1), pp. 107-131, March 1979.

[KeRi78]   B.W. Kernighan and D.M. Ritchie, "The C Programming Language", Prentice-Hall Software Series, 1978.

[Klug78]   A. Klug, *Theory of Database Mappings*, Ph.D. Thesis, Department of Computer Science, University of Toronto, 1978.

[KnMP77]   D.E. Knuth, J.H. Morris and V.R. Pratt, "Fast Pattern Matching in Strings", *SIAM Journal of Computing*, 6(2), pp. 323-350, June 1977.

[Knot71]   G.D. Knott, "Expandable Open Addressing Hash Table Storage and Retrieval", *Proceedings SIGFIDET*, pp. 187-206, 1971.

[Knut73]   D.E. Knuth, *The Art of Computer Programming, Volume 3: Sorting and Searching*, Addison-Wesley, Reading, Mass, 1973.

[Knut79]   D.E. Knuth, *TEX and METAFONT: New Directions in Typesetting*, American Mathematical Society and Digital Press, 1979.

[KoLo82]   I. Kowarski and M. Lopez, "The Document Concept in a Data Base", *Proceedings of the ACM SIGMOD Conference*, pp. 276-283, 1982.

[KoMi83]   I. Kowarski and C. Michaux, "A Microcomputer System for the Management of Structured Documents", *Proceedings IFIP Congress*, 1983.

[Korn79]   J.Z. Kornatowsky, *The MRS User's Manual*, Computer Systems Research Group, University of Toronto, 1979.

[KuRo81]   H.T. Kung and J.T. Robinson, "On Optimistic Methods for Concurrency Control", *ACM TODS*, 6(2), June 1981.

[Ladd79]   I. Ladd, *A Distributed Database Management System Based on Microcomputers*, M.Sc. thesis, Department of Computer Science, University of Toronto, 1979.

[Lamp78]   B.W. Lampson, "Bravo Manual", in *Alto User's Handbook*, Xerox Palo Alto Research Center, Palo Alto, California, November 1978.

[Land77]   D. Landis, "Multiple-Response Resolution in Associative Systems", *IEEE Transactions on Computers*, C-26(3), pp. 230-235, March 1977.

[Land83]   J. Landau, "How is a Computer Like an Onion?", *BYTE*, 8(12), December 1983.

[Lang77]   B. Langefors, "Informations Systems Theory", *Information Systems*, 2(4), pp. 207-219, 1977.

[Lang80]   B. Langefors, "Infological Models and Information User Views", *Information Systems*, 5(1), pp. 17-32, 1980.

[Lars78]   P. Larson, "Dynamic Hashing", *BIT*, 18, pp. 184-201, 1978.

[Lars83]   P.A. Larson, "A Method for Speeding up Text Retrieval", *Proceedings of ACM SIGMOD Conference*, May 1983.

[Lee72]   E.T. Lee, "Proximity Measures for the Classification of Geometric Figures", *Journal of Cybernetics*, 2(4), pp. 43-59, 1972.

[Lee81]   D.L. Lee, *A Voice Response System for an Office Information System*, M.Sc. Thesis, Department of Computer Science, University of Toronto, 1981.

[Lee82]   D.L. Lee, "A Voice Response System for an Office Information System", *Proceedings of the First ACM SIGOA Conference*, pp. 113-121, 1982.

[Lee84]   D.L. Lee, *A Text Retrieval Machine*, Thesis proposal, Department of Computer Science, University of Toronto, 1984.

[Lefk79]   H.C. Lefkovits, *et al.*, "A Status Report on the Activities of the CODASYL End User Facilities Committee (EUFC)", *ACM SIGMOD Proceedings*, 10(2 & 3), pp. 1-26, August 1979.

[LeLo83]   D L. Lee and F.H. Lochovsky, "Voice Response Systems", *ACM Computing Surveys*, 15(4), December 1983.

[LeSc75]   M.E. Lesk and E. Schmidt, *Lex - A Lexical Analyzer Generator*, Computer Science Technical Report No. 39, Bell

Laboratories, Murray Hill, NJ, USA, 1975.

[Lesk79]   M.E. Lesk, "Some Applications of Inverted Indexes on the UNIX System", UNIX manual, Bell Laboratories, Murray Hill, New Jersey, 1979.

[Lewi62]   M.H. Lewin, "Retrieval of Ordered Lists from a Content-Addressed Memory", *RCA Review*, 23(2), pp. 215-229, June 1962.

[LeWL84]   A. Lee, C.C. Woo and F.H. Lochovsky, "Officeaid: An Integrated Document Management System", Proceedings of ACM SIGOA Conference, pp. 170-180, June 1984.

[Litw80]   W. Litwin, "Linear Hashing: A New Tool for File and Table Addressing", *Proceedings of the Sixth International Conference on Very Large Data Bases*, pp. 212-223, October 1980.

[LiZi74]   B. Liskov and S. Zilles, "Programming with Abstract Data Types", *Proceedings of the ACM Symposium on Very High Level Languages, SIGPLAN Notices*, 9(4), pp. 50-59, 1974.

[Lloy80]   J.W. Lloyd, "Optimal Partial-Match Retrieval", *BIT*, 20, pp. 406-413, 1980.

[LlRa82]   J.W. Lloyd and K. Ramamohanarao, "Partial-Match Retrieval for Dynamic Files", *BIT*, 22, pp. 150-168, 1982.

[Loch81]   F.H. Lochovsky, "Human Factors Issues in Office Information Systems", *Proceedings of the International Congress on Applied Systems Research and Cybernetics 5*, pp. 2497-2501, 1981.

[Lodd83]   K.N. Lodding, "Iconic Interfacing", *IEEE Computer Graphics and Applications*, March/April, 1983.

[Love77]   H.H. Love, "A Modified ALAP Cell for Parallel Text Searching", *Proceedings of the International Conference on Parallel Processing*, pp. 23-16, August 1977.

[LoVe84]   M. Lopez and F. Velez, "Modelling and Handling Generalized Data in the TIGRE Project", Report, Centre de Recherche CII Honeywell Bull, c/o IMAG, St. Martin d'Heres, France, 1984.

[Lowe82]   E. Lowenthal, "Multiuser Microprocessor Systems Get a Data-base Manager", *Electronics*, 55(13), pp. 113-117, June 1982,

[LSAS77]   B. Liskov, A. Snyder, R. Atkinson and C. Schaffert, "Abstraction Mechanisms in CLU", *Communications of the ACM*, 20(8), pp. 564-576, August 1977.

[LSTC81]   V.Y. Lum, N.C. Shu, F. Tung and C.L. Chang, "Automating Business Procedures with Form Processing", *IBM Research Report*, RJ3050, March 1981.

✓[LuCS82]   V.Y. Lum, D.M. Choy and N.C. Shu, "OPAS: An Office Procedure Automation System", *IBM System Journal*, 21(3), pp. 327-350, 1982.

[LuYa81]   D. Luo and S.B. Yao, "Form Operation By Example: A Language for Office Information Processing", *Proceedings of the ACM SIGMOD Conference*, pp. 212-223, 1981.

[LyMc84]   P. Lyngback and D. McLeod, "Object Management in Distributed Information Systems", *ACM Transactions on Office Information Systems*, 2(2), pp. 96-122, 1984.

[MaCa83]   R.E.A. Mason and T.T. Carey, "Prototyping Interactive Information Systems", *Communications of the ACM*, 26, pp. 347-354, 1983.

[Mall80]   V.A.J. Maller, "Information Retrieval Using the Content Addressable File Store", *IFIP 80*, pp. 187-192, 1980.

[Mall82]   W.R. Mallgren, "Formal Specifications of Graphic Data Types", *ACM Transactions on Programming Languages and Systems*, 4(4), pp. 687-710, October 1982.

[MaLo83]   M.S. Mazer and F.H. Lochovsky, "Routing Specification in a Message Management System", *Proceedings of the Sixteenth Hawaii International Conference on System Science*, 1, pp. 566-575, January 1983.

[MaLo84]   M.S. Mazer and F.H. Lochovsky, "Logical Routing Specification in Office Information Systems", *ACM Transactions on Office Information Systems*, 2(4), October 1984.

[Mart79]   G.N.N. Martin, "Spiral Storage: Incrementally Augmentable Hash Addressed Storage", *Theory of Computation*, Report No. 27, University of Warwick, Coventry, England, March 1979.

[Mart84]   T.P. Martin, *A Communication Model for Message Management Systems*, Ph.D. Thesis, Department of Computer Science, University of Toronto, 1984.

[Maxe80]   N.F. Maxemchuk, "An Experimental Speech Storage and Editing Facility", *Bell Systems Technical Journal*, 59, pp. 1383-1395, 1980.

[Maye81]   R.E. Mayer, "The Psychology of How Novices Learn Computer Programming", *ACM Computing Surveys*, 13(1), March 1981.

[Maze83]   M.S. Mazer, *The Specification of Routings in a Message Management System*, M.Sc. Thesis, Department of

Computer Science, U. of Toronto, 1983.

[McIl82]   M.D. McIlroy, "Development of a Spelling List", *IEEE Transactions on Communications*, COM-30(1), pp. 91-99, January 1982.

[McKi81]   D. McLeod and R. King, "Semantic Database Models", in *Principles of Database Design*, ed. S.B. Yao, Prentice-Hall, 1981.

[McLe76]   D. McLeod, "High Level Domain Definition in a Relational Database System", *Proceedings of the ACM SIGPLAN/SIGMOD Conference on Data: Abstraction, Definition, and Structure*, pp. 47-57, 1976.

[McLe78]   D. McLeod, *A Semantic Database Model and Its Associated Structured User Interface*, Ph.D. dissertation, Laboratory for Computer Science, MIT, 1978.

[McLe81]   I.A. McLeod, "A Data Base Management System for Document Retrieval Applications", *Information Systems*, 6(2), pp. 131-137, 1981.

[McLe83]   R. McLeod, *Management Information Systems*, SRA, Second Edition, 1983.

[McSm80]   D. McLeod and J.M. Smith, "Abstraction in Databases", *Proceedings of the Workshop on Data Abstraction, Databases, and Conceptual Modelling*, ed. M. Brodie and S. Zilles, June 1980.

[MeBo76]   R.M. Metcalfe and D.R. Boggs, "Ethernet: Distributed Packet Switching for Local Computer Networks", *Communications of the ACM*, 19(7), pp. 395-404, July 1976.

[MeVa82]   N. Meyrowitz and A. Van Dam, "Interactive Editing Systems", *ACM Computing Surveys*, 14(3), September 1982.

[Mill82]   M.I. Mills, "'Visual Thinking' Reconsidered: Some Implications for Computer Graphics", *Proceedings of Graphics Interface '82*, Toronto, Ontario, May 1982.

✕ [Moon84]   J. Mooney, *Oz: An Object-based System for Implementing Office Information Systems*, M.Sc. thesis, Department of Computer Science, University of Toronto, 1984.

[Mora81]   T.P. Moran, "Guest Editor's Introduction: An Applied Psychology of the User", *ACM Computing Surveys*, 13(1), March 1981.

[Morg80]   Howard L. Morgan, "Research and Practice in Office Automation", *Proceedings 1980 IFIP Congress*, pp. 783-789.

[MoRo79]   H.L. Morgan and D. Root, "A Concept of Corporate Memory", *Proceedings of the NYU Symposium on Office Automation*, May 1979.

[Mukh79]   Mukhopadhyay, A., "Hardware Algorithms for Nonnumeric Computation", *IEEE Transactions on Computers*, C-28(6), pp. 384-394, June 1979.

[Mukh80]   Mukhopadhyay, A., "Hardware Algorithms for String Processing", *Proceedings of the International Conference on Circuits and Computers*, pp. 508-511, October 1980.

[MyBW78]   J. Mylopoulos, P.A. Bernstein and H.K.T. Wong, "A Preliminary Specification of TAXIS: A Language for Interactive Systems Design", Technical Report CCA-78-02, Computer Corporation of America, 1978.

[MyBW80]   J. Mylopoulos, P.A. Bernstein and H.K.T. Wong, "TAXIS: A Language Facility for Designing Database-Intensive Applications", *ACM TODS*, 5(2), pp. 185-207, June 1980.

[Myer85]   B. Myers, "The Importance of Percent-Done Progress Indicators for Computer-Human Interfaces", *Proceedings of the ACM SIGCHI '85 Conference*, April 1985.

[Naff81a]   N. Naffah, "Distributed Office Systems in Practice", *ONLINE Conference*, May 1981.

[Naff81b]   N. Naffah, "Editing Multitype Documents", *Proceedings of the International Workshop on Office Information Systems*, October 1981.

[NeSp79]   W.M. Newman and R.F. Sproull, *Principles of Interactive Computer Graphics*, (Second ed.), Computer Science Series, McGraw-Hill Book Company, 1979.

[Nier81]   O.M. Nierstrasz, *Automatic Coordination and Processing of Electronic Forms in TLA*, M.Sc. thesis, Department of Computer Science, University of Toronto, 1981.

[Nier84]   O.M. Nierstrasz, *Message Flow Analysis*, Ph.D. thesis, Department of Computer Science, University of Toronto, CSRI Technical Report #165, 1984.

[NiMT83]   O.M. Nierstrasz, J. Mooney and K.J. Twaites, "Using Objects to Implement Office Procedures", *Proceedings of the Canadian Information Processing Society Conference*, Ottawa, pp. 65-73, May 1983.

[OpDa83]   D.C. Oppen and Y.K. Dalal, "The Clearinghouse: A Decentralized Agent for Locating Named Objects in a Distributed Environment", *ACM Transactions on Office Information Systems*, 1(3), pp. 230-253, July 1983.

[OrTa56]   G. Orosz and L. Tackacs, "Some Probability Problems Concerning the Marking of Codes into the Superimposed Field", *Journal of Documentation*, 12(4), pp. 231-234, December 1956.

[PaSt82]   Christos H. Papadimitriou and Kenneth Steiglitz, *Combinatorial Optimization*, Prentice-Hall, 1982.

[Pavl77]   T. Pavlidis, *Structural Pattern Recognition*, Springer-Verlag, 1977.

[Pete83]   J.L. Peterson, *Petri Nets Theory and the Modeling of Systems*, Prentice-Hall, 1983.

[PfBC80]   J.L. Pfaltz, W.H. Berman and E.M. Cagley, "Partial Match Retrieval Using Indexed Descriptor Files", *Communications of the ACM*, 23(9), pp. 522-528, September 1980.

[Prop83]   D.L. Propp, *A Forms Programming By Example System for Non-programmers*, M.Sc. thesis, Department of Computer Science, University of Toronto, January 1983.

[PuFK83]   R. Purvy, J. Farrel and P. Klose, "The Design of Star's Records Processing: Data Processing for the Noncomputer Professional", *ACM Transactions on Office Information Systems*, 1(1), pp. 3-24, 1983.

[Quin81]   V. Quint, "Editing Mathematics on the Buroviseur", *Proceedings of the International Workshop on Office Information Systems*, October 1981.

[RaGi82]   F. Rabitti and S.J. Gibbs, "A Distributed Form Management System with Global Query Facilities", in *Office Information Systems*, ed. N. Naffah, North-Holland, 1982.

[RaTW78]   C.V. Ramamoorthy, J.C. Turner and B.W. Wah, "A Design of a Cellular Associative Memory for Ordered Retrieval", *IEEE Transactions on Computers*, C-27(9), pp. 800-815, September 1978.

[RaZi84]   F. Rabitti and J. Zizka, "Evaluation of Access Methods to Text Documents in Office Systems", *Proceedings of the Third Joint ACM-BCS Symposium on Research and Development in Information Retrieval*, 1984.

[Redd75]   D.R. Reddy, *Speech Recognition*, Academic Press, 1975.

[Redd76]   D.R. Reddy, "Speech Recognition by Machine: A Review", *Proceedings of the IEEE*, 64(4), pp. 501-531, April 1976.

[Reis81]   P. Reisner, "Formal Grammar and Human Factors Design of an Interactive Graphics System", *IEEE Transactions on Software Engineering*, SE-7(2), March 1981.

[Rhod81]   Rhodnius Inc., "MISTRESS: The Query Language", 1981.

[Rijs71]   C.J. Van-Rijsbergen, "An Algorithm for Information Structuring and Retrieval", *Computer Journal*, 14(4), pp. 407-412, 1971.

[Rijs79]   C.J. Van-Rijsbergen, *Information Retrieval*, Butterworths, London, England, 1979. Second edition.

[Rive76]   R.L. Rivest, Partial Match Retrieval Algorithms, *SIAM Journal of Computing*, 5(1), pp. 19-50, March 1976.

[Robe78]   D.C. Roberts, "A Specialized Computer Architecture for Text Retrieval", *Proceedings of the Fourth Workshop on Computer Architecture for Non-Numeric Processing*, pp. 51-59, August 1978.

[Robe79]   C.S. Roberts, "Partial-Match Retrieval via the Method of Superimposed Codes", *Proceedings of the IEEE*, 67(12), pp. 1624-1642, December 1979.

[Robi81]   J.T. Robinson, "The k-D-B-Tree: A Search Structure for Large Multidimensional Dynamic Indexes", *Proceedings of the ACM SIGMOD Conference*, pp. 10-18, 1981.

[Robs81]   D. Robson, "Object-Oriented Software Systems", *Byte*, 6(8), August 1981.

[Rocc71]   J.J. Rocchio, "Relevance Feedback in Information Retrieval", in *The SMART Retrieval System -- Experiments in Automatic Document Processing*, ed. G. Salton, Prentice-Hall Inc., Englewood Cliffs, New Jersey, 1971. Chapter 14.

[RoLo74]   J.B. Rothnie and T. Lozano, "Attribute Based File Organization in a Paged Memory Environment", *Communications of the ACM*, 17(2), pp. 63-69, February 1974.

[RoMy75]   N. Roussopoulos and J. Mylopoulos, "Using Semantic Networks for Data Base Management", *Proceedings of the First International Conference on Very Large Data Bases*, pp. 144-172, 1975.

[RoSh82]   L.A. Rowe and K.A. Shoens, "A Form Application Development System", *Proceedings of the ACM SIGMOD Conference*, pp. 28-38, June 1982.

[Rous76]   N. Roussopoulos, *A Semantic Network Data Base Model*, Ph.D. dissertation, Department of Computer Science, University of Toronto, 1976.

[RoYe82]   D. Rosenthal and A. Yen, "User Interface Models Summary", Graphical Input Interaction Technique (GIIT) Workshop Summary, pp. 27-36, 1982.

[Salt71]   G. Salton (ed.), *The SMART Retrieval Systems*, Prentice-Hall, Englewood Cliffs, New Jersey, 1971.

[Salt80]   G. Salton, "Automatic Information Retrieval", *IEEE Computer*, 13(9), pp. 41-56. September 1980.

[SaMc83]   G. Salton and M.J. McGill, *Introduction to Modern Information Retrieval*, McGraw-Hill, 1983.

[SaWo78]   G. Salton and A. Wong, "Generation and Search of Clustered Files", *ACM TODS*, 3(4), pp. 321-346, December 1978.

[Sche81]   B. Scheurer, "Office Workstation Design", *Proceedings of the International Workshop on Office Information Systems*, October 1981.

√ [Sche84]   H.J. Schek, "Nested Transactions in a Combined IRS-DBMS Architecture", *Proceedings of the Third joint BCS and ACM Symposium on Research and Development in Information Retrieval*, Cambridge, England, July 1984.

[Schi82]   P. Schicker, "Naming and Addressing in a Computer-Based Mail Environment", *IEEE Trans on Communications*, COM-30(1), pp. 46-62, January 1982.

[Schi84]   D.E. Schiferl, *Pragmatics of Interaction and User Interface Management Systems*, M.Sc. thesis, University of Toronto, Department Computer Science, January 1984.

[Schm77]   J.W. Schmidt, "Some High-Level Language Constructs for Data of Type Relation", *ACM TODS*, 2(3), pp. 247-261, 1977.

[Schw83]   J. Schwarz, "Emily Post for Usenet", *net.announce.newusers*, 1983.

[ScOS76]   S.A. Schuster, E.A. Ozkarahan and K.C. Smith, "A Virtual Memory System for a Relational Associative Processor", *Proceedings of the National Computer Conference*, 45, pp. 855-862, 1976.

[ScPi82]   H.J. Schek and P. Pistor, "Data Structures for an Integrated Data Base Management and Information Retrieval System", *Proceedings of the Eighth International Conference on Very Large Data Bases*, pp. 197-207, 1982.

[ScSw75]   H.A. Schmid and J.R. Swenson, "On the Semantics of the Relational Data Model", *Proceedings of the ACM SIGMOD Conference*, pp. 211-223, 1975.

[SeDu76]   D.G. Severance and R.A. Duhne, "A Practitioner's Guide to Addressing Algorithms", *Communications of the ACM*, 19(6), pp. 314-326, 1976.

[Senk75]   M.E. Senko, "Information Systems: Records, Relations, Sets, Entities, and Things", *Information Systems*, 1(1), pp. 3-13, 1975.

[Seve74]   D.G. Severance, "Identifier Search Mechanisms: A Survey and Generalized Model", *ACM Computing Surveys*, 6(3), pp. 175-194, September 1974.

[Seyb81]   J. Seybold, "Xerox's 'Star'", *The Seybold Report*, 10(16), April 1981.

[Shaw80]   D.E. Shaw, "A Relational Database Machine Architecture", *Proceedings of the Fifth Workshop on Computer Architecture for Non-Numeric Processing*, pp. 84-95, March 1980.

[ShHu82]   J. Shoch and J. Hupp, "The Worm Programs - Early Experience with a Distributed Computation", *Communications of the ACM*, 25(3), pp. 172-180, March 1982.

[Ship81]   D.W. Shipman, "The Functional Data Model and the Data Language DAPLEX", *ACM TODS*, 6(1), pp. 140-173, March 1981.

[Shne83]   B. Shneiderman, "Direct Manipulation: A Step Beyond Programming Languages", *IEEE Computer*, 16(8), pp. 57-69, 1983.

[Shoe79]   K. Shoens, "Mail Reference Manual, Version 1.3", *UNIX Manuals*, 1979.

[ShWu77]   M. Shaw and W. Wulf, "Abstraction and Verification in Alphard: Defining and Specifying Iteration and Generators", *Communications of the ACM*, 20(8), pp. 553-564, August 1977.

[SIKH82]   D.C. Smith, C. Irby, R. Kimball and E. Harslam, "The Star User Interface: An Overview", *Proceedings AFIPS National Computer Conference*, 51, pp. 515-528, June 1982.

[SIKV82]   D.C.S. Smith, C. Irby, R. Kimball, B. Verplank and E. Harlem, "Designing the Star User Interface", *Byte*, 7(4), pp. 242-282, April 1982.

[SLTC82]   N.C. Shu, V.Y. Lum, F.C. Tung and C.L. Chang, "Specification of Forms Processing and Business Procedures for Office Automation", *IEEE Transactions Software Engineering*, SE-8(5), pp. 499-512, September 1982.

[SmFL81]   J.M. Smith, S. Fox and T. Lancers, *Reference Manual for ADAPLEX*, Technical Report CCA-81-02, Computer Corporation of America, 1981.

[SmSm77a]   J.M. Smith and D.C.P. Smith, "Database Abstractions: Aggregation", *Communications of the ACM*, 20(6), pp.

405-413, June 1977.

[SmSm77b] J.M. Smith and D.C.P. Smith, "Database abstractions: Aggregation and Generalization", *ACM TODS*, 2(2), pp. 105-133, June 1977.

[SmSm79] J.M. Smith and D.C.P. Smith, "A Database Approach to Software Specification", Technical Report CCA-79-17, Computer Corporation of America, 1979.

[Song80] S.W. Song, "A Highly Concurrent Tree Machine for Database Applications", *Proceedings of the International Conference on Parallel Processing*, pp. 259-268, August 1980.

[Spar72] K. Sparck-Jones, "A Statistical Interpretation of Term Specificity and its Application in Retrieval", *Journal of Documentation*, 28(1), pp. 11-20, March 1972.

[SSKH82] M. Sirbu, S. Schoichet, J. Kunin and M. Hammer, "OAM: An Office Analysis Methodology", in *Office Automation Conference 1982 Digest*, pp. 317-330, AFIPS, 1982.

√ [SSLK83] M. Stonebraker, H. Stettner, N. Lynn, J. Kalash and A. Guttman, "Document Processing in a Relational Database System", *ACM Transactions on Office Information Systems*, 1(2), pp. 143-158, April 1983.

[Stel77] W.H. Stellhorn, "An Inverted File Processor for Information Retrieval", *IEEE Transactions on Computers*, C-26(12), pp. 1258-1267, December 1977.

[Stia60] S. Stiassny, "Mathematical Analysis of Various Superimposed Coding Methods", *American Documentation*, 11(2), pp. 155-169, February 1960.

[SuLo79] S.Y.W. Su and D.H. Lo, "A Semantic Association Model for Conceptual Database Design", *Proceedings International Conference on the Entity-Relationship Approach to Systems Analysis and Design*, 1979.

[Sun82] ----, "The SUN Workstation Architecture", SUN Microsystems Inc., April 1982.

[SwBa82] W. Swartout and R. Balzer, "On the Inevitable Intertwining of Specification and Implementation", *Communications of the ACM*, 25, pp. 438-440, 1982.

[TaBu83] P.P. Tanner and W.A.S. Buxton, "Some Issues in Future Interface Management System Development", Invited paper presented at IFIP WG 5.2, Workshop on User Interface Management, Seeheim, Federal Republic of Germany, November 1-3, 1983.

[TaFr76] R.W. Taylor and R.L. Frank, "CODASYL Database Management Systems", *ACM Computing Surveys*, 8(1), pp.

67-104, March 1976.

[Tayl83]   R. Taylor R., "Databases for Office Workstations", Report RJ 4091 (45989), IBM Research Laboratory, San Jose, CA, 11/9/83.

[TCEF83]   D.C. Tsichritzis, S. Christodoulakis, P. Economopoulos, C. Faloutsos, A. Lee, D. Lee, J. Vandenbroek and C. Woo, "A Multimedia Office Filing System", *Proceedings of the Ninth International Conference on Very Large Data Bases*, Florence, Italy, pp. 2-7, 1983.

[TeFr82]   T.J. Teorey and J.P. Fry, *Design of Database Structures*, Prentice-Hall, Englewood Cliffs, New Jersey, 1982.

[Teit77]   W. Teitelman, "A Display-Oriented Programmer's Assistant", Report CSL-77-3 Xerox PARC, March 1977.

[Tesl81]   L. Tesler, "The Smalltalk Environment", *BYTE*, 6(8), August 1981.

[ThRi78]   K. Thomson and D. Ritchie, "The UNIX Time-Sharing System", *Bell System Technical Journal*, 57(6), pp. 1905-1929, 1978.

[ThTa82]   A.L. Tharp and K. Tai, "The Practicality of Text Signatures for Accelerating String Searching", *Software Practice and Experience*, 12(1), pp. 35-44, January 1982.

[ToGo74]   J.T. Tou and R.C. Gonzalez, "Pattern Recognition Principles", Addison Wesley, 1974.

[TRGN82]   D.C. Tsichritzis, F. Rabitti, S.J. Gibbs, O.M. Nierstrasz and J. Hogg, "A System for Managing Structured Messages", *IEEE Transactions on Communications*, Com-30(1), pp. 66-73, January 1982.

[TsCh83]   D.C. Tsichritzis and S. Christodoulakis, "Message Files", *ACM Transactions on Office Information Systems*, 1(1), pp. 88-98, January 1983.

[Tsic80]   D.C. Tsichritzis, "OFS: An Integrated Form Management System", *Proceedings of the Sixth International Conference on Very Large Data Bases*, pp. 161-166, 1980.

[Tsic82]   D.C. Tsichritzis, "Form Management", *Communications of the ACM*, 25(7), pp. 453-478, July 1982.

[Tsic84]   D.C. Tsichritzis, "Message Addressing Schemes", *ACM Transactions on Office Information Systems*, 2(1), pp. 58-87., January 1984.

[TsLo76]   D.C. Tsichritzis and F.H. Lochovsky, "Hierarchical Database Management: A Survey", *ACM Computing Surveys*, 8(1), pp. 105-124, March 1976.

[TsLo82]   D.C. Tsichritzis and F.H. Lochovsky, *Data Models*, Prentice-Hall, Englewood Cliffs, N.J., 1982.

[TTRC84]   D.C. Tsichritzis, C. Thanos, F. Rabitti, S. Christodoulakis, S.J. Gibbs, E. Bertino, A. Fedeli, C. Faloutsos and P. Economopoulos, "Design Issues of a File Server for Multimedia Documents", First ESPRIT Technical Week, Brussels, September 1984.

[Tuck82]   J. Tucker, "Implementing Office Automation: Principles and an Electronic Mail Example", *Proceedings of the Second SIGOA Conference on Office Information Systems*, SIGOA Newsletter, 3(1) and 3(2), June 1982.

√ [Twai84]   K.J. Twaites, *An Object-based Programming Environment for Office Information Systems*, M.Sc. thesis, Department of Computer Science, University of Toronto, 1984.

[Ullm82]   J.D. Ullman, *Principles of Database Systems*, Second edition, Computer Science Press, Rockville Maryland, 1982.

[Vall76]   O. Vallarino, "On the Use of Bit Maps for Multiple Key Retrieval", *Conference Proceedings on Data Abstraction, Definition and Structure*, in ACM SIGPLAN Notices (Special issue), 11, pp. 108-114, March 1976.

[Vitt81]   J. Vittal, "Active Message Processing: Messages as Messengers", *Proceedings of the International Symposium on Computer Message Systems*, IFIP TC-6, Ottawa, April 1981, ed. R.P. Uhlig, North Holland Publishing Co, pp. 175-195, 1982.

[VLDB83a]   "Panel on Complex Data Objects: Text, Voice, Images: Can DBMS Manage Them?", *The Ninth International Conference on Very Large Data Bases*, 1983.

[VLDB83b]   "Panel on Office Information Systems: What is Our Role?", *The Ninth International Conference on Very Large Data Bases*, 1983.

[VLDB84]   "Panel on Multimedia Management Systems", *The Tenth International Conference on Very Large Data Bases*, 1984.

[Walk81]   J.H. Walker, "The Document Editor: A Support Environment for Preparing Technical Documents", *Proceedings of the ACM Symposium on Text Manipulation*, June 1981.

[Wall80]   P.J.L. Wallis, "External Representations of Objects of User-Defined Type", *ACM Transactions Programming Languages and Systems*, 2(2), pp. 137-152, April 1980.

[WEFS84]   F.A. Wang, A.H.M. El-Sherbini, S. Fry, M. Smutek and N. Webb, "The Wang Professional Image Computer: A New Dimension to Personal and Office Computing",

Proceedings of the IEEE, 72(3), Special Issue on Personal Computers, March 1984.

[Wied83]   G. Wiederhold, "Database Design", McGraw Hill, 1983.

[Will83]   G. Williams, "The Lisa Computer System", *Byte*, 8(2), pp. 33-50, February 1983.

[Will84]   G. Williams, "The Apple Macintosh Computer", *BYTE*, 9(2), pp. 30-54, 1984.

[WoCW82]   K.Y. Wong, R.G. Casey and F.M. Wahl, "Document Analysis System", *IBM Journal Research Development*, 26(6), November 1982.

[WoLo83]   C.C. Woo and F.H. Lochovsky, "A System for Interactively Designing Message Templates", *Proceedings of the IEEE COMPCON Conference*, pp. 27-34, September 1983.

[WoLo84]   C.C. Woo and F.H. Lochovsky, "Authorizations in a Computer-based Office Information System", *Proceedings of the First IEEE OA Conference*, December 1984.

[WoMy77]   H.K.T. Wong and J. Mylopoulos, "Two Views of Data Semantics: Data Models in Artificial Intelligence and Database Management", *INFOR*, 15(3), pp. 344-383, October 1977.

√[Wong83]   H.K.T. Wong, *Design and Verification of Information Systems*, Ph.D. dissertation, Department of Computer Science, University of Toronto, 1983.

[Woo83]   C.C. Woo, *A Communication Base Design System for a Message Management System*, M.Sc. thesis, Department of Computer Science, University of Toronto, January 1983.

√ [YHSL84]   S. Bing Yao, Alan R. Hevner, Zhongzhi Shi and Dawel Luo, "FORMANAGER: An Office Forms Management System", *ACM Transactions on Office Information Systems*, 2(3), pp. 235-262, July 1984.

[YuLS82]   C.T. Yu, K. Lam and G. Salton, "Term Weighting in Information Retrieval Using the Term Precision Model", *Journal of the ACM*, 29(1), pp. 152-170, January 1982.

[Zahn71]   C.T. Zahn, "Graph-Theoretical Methods for Detecting and Describing Gestalt Clusters", *IEEE Transactions on Computers*, C-20(1), pp. 68-86, January 1971.

√ [Zdon84]   S. Zdonik, "Object Management System Concepts", *Proceedings of the Second ACM SIGOA Conference, pp. 13-19, 1984.*

√ [Zism77]   M. Zisman, *Representation, Specification and Automation of Office Procedures*, Ph.D. dissertation, Wharton School,

University of Pennsylvania, 1977.

[Zism78]   M. Zisman, "Use of Production Systems for Modelling Asynchronous Concurrent Processes", *Pattern-Directed Inference Systems,* Academic Press, pp. 53-68, 1978.

[Zloo75]   M.M. Zloof, "Query-by-Example", *Proceedings NCC,* 44, May 1975.

[Zloo77]   M.M. Zloof, "Query-by-Example: A Database Language", *IBM System Journal,* 16(4), pp. 324-343, 1977.

[Zloo80]   M.M. Zloof, "A Language for Office and Business Automation", *1980 AFIPS Office Automation Conference Digest,* Atlanta, USA, March 1980.

[Zloo81]   M.M. Zloof, "QBE/OBE: A Language for Office and Business Automation", *IEEE Computer 14,* pp. 13-22, May 1981.

[Zloo82]   M.M. Zloof, "Office-by-Example: A Business Language that Unifies Data and Word Processing and Electronic Mail", *IBM System Journal,* 21(3), pp. 272-304, 1982.

Subject Index

On Conceptual Modelling:

Perspectives from Artificial Intelligence, Databases, and Programming Languages

Editors: **M.L.Brodie, J.Mylopoulos, J.W.Schmidt**

1984. 25 figures. XI, 510 pages
(Topics in Information Systems)
ISBN 3-540-90842-0

Conceptual modelling relates to all areas of computer science, but especially to articificial intelligence, databases, and programming languages. Here is the first published collection of state-of-the-art research papers in these domains. Its purpose is to consider conceptual modelling as a topic in its own right, rather than as an aspect of data modelling, and to present and compare research on knowledge representation, semantic data models, and data abstraction in this context.

The contributions consist of overviews and reports, each chapter having been written and edited for readers in all three areas. Also included are transcripts of symposium discussions which took place among the contributors during a workshop on conceptual modelling at Intervale; these interdisciplinary discussions of each paper clarify many aspects which might otherwise remain obscure to nonspecialists. Key features of the book include introductions to pertinent concepts, and the integration of recent results; focus in twelve research projects, involving specific applications such as database design; and challenging suggestions for further research, especially in the concluding comments by leading experts in the three main fields of inquiry.

Springer-Verlag
Berlin
Heidelberg
New York
Tokyo

Query Processing in Database Systems

Editors: **W. Kim, D. S. Reiner, D. S. Batory**

1984. Approx. 127 figures.
Approx. 352 pages
(Topics in Information Systems)
ISBN 3-540-13831-5

Contents: Introduction to Query Processing. – Query Processing in Distributed Database Manegement Systems. – Query Processing for Multiple Data Models. – Database Updates through Views. – Database Access for Special Applications. – Techniques for Optimizing the Processing of Multiple Queries. – Query Processing in Database Machines. – Physical Database Design. – References. – List of Authors.

This book is an anthology of research and development results in data-based query processing during the past decade. The book guides the reader through most of the important topics in query processing, organised around 7 sections. These sections each include one to three articles that summarize different views and emphasize different aspects of research.

Springer-Verlag
Berlin
Heidelberg
New York
Tokyo